NYIKA 1960

ETHIOPIA

SOMALI

NYA

OLONY

MOUNT
KENYA

SHIFTA

NAIROBI

LAMU

MALINDI

MOMBASA

NT
ANJARO

PEMBA ISLAND

RUSHA

SULTANATE OF
ZANZIBAR

DAR-ES-SALAAM

INDIAN OCEAN

MAFIA
ISLAND

KILWA

RA

MCHINJA

HATARI!

LESE

A

SPEAK SWAHILI, DAMMIT!

Speak Swahili, Dammit!

James Penhaligon

UNITED WRITERS
Cornwall

UNITED WRITERS PUBLICATIONS LTD
Ailsa, Castle Gate, Penzance, Cornwall.

British Library Cataloguing in Publication Data:
A catalogue record for this book is
available from the British Library.

ISBN 9781852001483

Originally published in 2010 by AuthorHouse.
This is a new and revised edition
copyright © 2011 James Penhaligon

Printed in Great Britain by
United Writers Publications Ltd
Cornwall.

This book is dedicated to friends and relatives,
past and living, still in Africa, or everywhere
they have flown.

Foreword

Memory is a strange thing. They say that there is no history – only biography, the way a particular person recalls an event. Others may remember the same thing differently. Fifty-odd years is a long time. Enough to forget a lot, and to warp and alter other recollections.

This book is based on my recall of events. Big things, like my father's death, the leopard which hitched a ride on the constabulary motorbike, my failure to conquer Mount Meru, or the events surrounding *Uhuru* or independence for Tanganyika territory, are accurate enough. Smaller, day to day, happenings draw on memory with a varying level of accuracy, glued together by some necessary invention.

People's names, and some of their details, have been altered to protect their privacy.

One

It's 1966. I'm fifteen and a half years old, and in just a few minutes we're leaving Geita forever. It's five in the morning. The sun won't come up till half past six. I'm sitting on my suitcase in the lounge of our wooden bungalow. I'm heartbroken. The Land Rover will be here soon, Fritz the old driver keen to get on the road. Gretchen is coming too, to see us off. I'm so much in love with her, I don't know how I'm going to say goodbye at the railway station in Mwanza. I'm sure I'll never see her again. I ache deep inside. Maybe I'll die of heartbreak. I rather hope so. It's pitch-dark outside, and the only sound is crickets creaking.

Mum and Becky are still packing, finding space to force last minute things into their luggage. I'm thinking how our lives were changed by this place, how we came to this point. Outside, an *njiwa*-bird or ring-necked African dove, makes a plaintiff call. They're supposed to be sleeping. I wonder if this one knows we're leaving. It's the end of a lifetime for me. It was here, always here, my life took wings.

Fleeting, unsequenced wisps of memory breach the void. Green and white striped tablecloth, black front door, warm cosy bed, kiss on cheek. Need to compete with big sister. Trivia. Bigger things take time. The world is a mystery, my place and role baffle me. Where am I? Who am I? Where am I going? Where do I come from? Answers don't come. Big sister Becky tells me I came from Mum's belly-button. Mum says I'm her and Dad's son. Not sun in the sky, but a boy-child, born of love.

I will shine one day, bright as a star. Mum knows, because a fortune-teller told her when she was thirteen. At a fair in Johannesburg she went in the tent with the signs of the Zodiac. For sixpence her fortune was told. The old lady studied her palm and said five things:

9

You will marry a man from far away across the sea, but he will be already close. You will be separated by war. You will have five children. One will be a great disappointment. One will shine like a star. She married Dad, who came from far-away Cornwall, but was 'close' because he was her second cousin. They were separated for five years by war. She had five children. I'm the one who'll shine. She's sure. She doesn't say who's the disappointment.

I have entered the world at a time of great difficulty and struggle. It was the worst, but I'd like to hope the best, day of Mum's and Dad's lives.

Many things end with fire. I start with it. Roaring flames consume our wooden house. Only blackened foundations, ash and half-burnt timbers remain. That's the night I'm born. 1951, the Zulu town Nongoma, capital of Kwazulu, later the seat of King Zwelethini Zulu, and his uncle, Paramount Chief Gatsha Buthelezi, whose surname means *Blunt*. In 1951 it isn't as exalted. It has the only mission hospital for miles. We live nearby in *Hluhluwe*, or 'Who The Hell Are We?' as Dad first reads it. Now known for a game reserve. Mum and Dad run a concrete-block and corrugated-iron trading store. Sugar, soap, tea and cornmeal for tribal Zulus. Tragedy brought them here.

Rejoining the Royal Navy at the outbreak of war in 1939 as 'A1 fit', Dad was discharged in January '46 with leaking heart valves, epilepsy, and health grading 'E'. He was thirty-seven, and paid a terrible price for his loyalty to his country. (We all have.)

With intractable seizures, Dad languished most of 1946 in Tara Epilepsy Hospital in Johannesburg. They were very poor. No income, except a five pound a month naval disability pension, and four children to support. Bertrand was sixteen, Fraser thirteen, Rose three, and Becky nearly two. When Mum went to visit Dad in hospital she had to choose – raisin bun for tuppence and walk three miles, or bus-fare and hunger. After discharge from hospital Dad was very weak. He was offered and accepted a job where Mum could help him. Hence 'Nongoma' fills place of birth in my passport.

That blazing night the family takes another dive over the poverty cliff. Almost nothing is left. Not Dad's Purdey shotgun, nor his hard-saved box of silver coins. Not the paltry savings of copper coins in a jar. This, when found, is a rounded lump of yellow metal. Nobody's clothes, not even those carefully collected for the new baby, are saved. One prized possession, Dad's DSM, or Distinguished Service Medal, awarded to him for gallantry during the sinking of HMS *Turtle* by the Luftwaffe in 1942, survives little damaged – the ridged edge is slightly melted. Kept in a metal box under Mum and Dad's bed. It's a prize possession, one of only two of Dad's things I have. The other's his broken wind-up watch, the one he wore when his ship was sunk in 1942.

Those that have little shall have less, Dad says with gallows humour. It's the bottom. Can't have less now.

How the fire starts they have no clue, though rumour circulates that Mr Stevens, the landlord, torched the building for insurance. He goes on to become a wealthy businessman. He advises Dad not to renew his personal insurance, because the house and shop contents are covered. They aren't. Everything is lost.

Neighbours accommodate us, clothes are donated, and sympathy and largesse from both Zulu and European is heart-warming. There the saga of Zululand ends. After the fire Dad travels to Johannesburg. Waiting for a haircut, he reads the daily *Star* newspaper. On the second page is a headline: 'Murder In The Bush'. How can he know those four words are a signpost to the rest of his, and all our, lives?

A Mrs Williams, wife of a Welsh gold miner in Geita, somewhere in Tanganyika Territory, has been shot. She and an African driver are taking a week's gold production from the mine to a town called Mwanza, eighty miles through tsetse-fly infested swamp and jungle.

The killer, a German miner called Stroessner, *actually* dines with the Williams family the previous evening. They drink into the early hours, apparently not unusual in the bush. He discusses the shopping trip Mrs Williams is making with the gold transport next day. Asks her to visit the travel agent in Mwanza for him. Get a flight timetable to Germany. Mwanza to Nairobi with East African Airways, Lufthansa onwards. He's already given notice, after yet another row with the mine manager. Stroessner's got a drink problem, and often goes late to work. Now he's desperate to get out of this *scheisshaus* place. Wants to jump before he's pushed. Leaving the Williams' home at four in the morning, he drives out on the bush-road to Mwanza, hides his Land Rover in a thicket ten miles from the mine, and uses a shovel to dig a grave. He's prepared a story for the driver. He's broken down, and his vehicle is round the corner. Please come and help. He checks his Mauser 0.22 rifle, and lies in wait. With the gold in the transport Land Rover, he'll have a secure future. He'll work out a way to get it to Germany.

The gold transport drives up, and he waves. They recognise him and stop. He asks the driver to accompany him, then shoots him in the head. Mrs Williams is still in her seat when he shoots her through the windscreen.

Stroessner drags her body to the dead driver, and rolls both into the shallow grave. He douses them in petrol, and throws a match. They burn only partially. Not enough petrol. At five am, with the first rays of equatorial sun topping the treeline, he covers the charred corpses with a few inches of soil. He disguises the site with twigs and grass, drives the gold Land Rover off the road, and hides it. With six bars of gold bullion in his vehicle, he goes back to the mine. By six he's in bed. It's been a long night's work.

Stroessner feels unwell later that morning. Guilt, hangover, or both. He goes to the mine doctor, who admits him to the house which serves as a *Mzungu*, or European, hospital. British Tanganyika is racially segregated. His stomach pains may be caused by a stomach ulcer, the doctor says. Common with heavy drinkers like him. Rest and antacids are prescribed.

Hours pass. The driver and Mrs Williams fail to return from Mwanza. Mr Williams is worried. He wants to drive out and look for his wife. The manager orders him not to. Can't have a bush-novice out there alone. 'Bloody lions, for *Chrissakes!*' Next morning a radio-telephone call to Mwanza bank establishes that neither the couple, nor the gold, have arrived. A search party is recruited. Ten miles from the mine they discover Land Rover tracks into a thicket. Here is the missing vehicle, minus occupants and gold, bullet hole in windscreen. It is unmistakably blood and brain tissue on the front seat. The search continues. A shout is heard from a tracker. Half-cremated remains are found, driver's arm and lady's leg protruding grotesquely from the loose ground. The bodies contract first through burning, then rigor mortis. That's why they come up.

In Geita suspicion turns on Stroessner. There are only three Land Rovers on the mine. One is the doomed transport, and one belongs to the mine manager, who's been up most of the night drinking, in the company of several boozers. The third is Stroessner's. Sherlock Holmes isn't required. Before the manager and mine police-chief, Mr Higginson, reach Stroessner's hospital room, there's a sharp retort. The room stinks of cordite. There's blood, shards of bone and gloops of dripping brain on the walls. The bastard's shot himself in the mouth. Beside his bed is a written confession, and a hand-drawn map of where the stolen gold is. Buried on the golf course, next to the ninth fairway, not fifty yards from the club bar. They recover it. What is Stroessner's point? Why kill two innocent people to nick gold you'll never spend? Nobody knows. Williams goes mad. He and the children are sent home to Wales. They need three police escorts to stop him jumping from the train to Dar es Salaam. He's never heard of in Tanganyika again.

Dad, like others reading the paper in August '51, is shocked by the murders. He doesn't know how intimately what happened on that lonely bush road in the hours before dawn will be connected to our futures, and his own death.

By a strange twist of fate, two months after reading the murder report, Dad applies for a post advertised in a Durban paper. It's a ropeway manager's job on a mine in Tanganyika. He doesn't know where Geita is, and he's forgotten the bush murders. If appointed, he'll run a system of cable-borne carts transporting gold-bearing ore from a shaft in the bush to the mill at the mine. A medical examination before appointment isn't required. The interview in Johannesburg is brief. He's hired.

Meantime, against medical advice, Dad takes a short contract as relief skipper on a trawler in Walvis Bay, the South African enclave in South West Africa. We live in Swakopmund, a picturesque town on the sea a little north. Until 1916, when it became a UN mandate of South Africa, South West, or *Südwest,* was a German colony, and Swakopmund resembled a village on the Rhine. Dad goes fishing, and Mum looks after Becky, two, and me. Three months old, during a rare rainstorm, I am christened in the Lutheran Church.

There are scarcities in Swakop, and eggs are a rare luxury. A kind, over-involved elderly Prussian landlady, who speaks only German, goes to great lengths to procure eggs '*für das kinderen*', for which Mum feels she must show exaggerated gratitude. Foreigners probably expect that. Becky, who can speak Zulu, is a favourite of the *Frau*, and within weeks also speaks German. One day, frustrated by all the attention I'm attracting, she angrily declares that *gani,* Zulu for baby, *hold him big* – thinks he's important, and, for all she cares, can *hamba*, Zulu for go, *von wo ehr gekommen ist*, German for where he came from.

One day Mum takes us to a little park. There an elderly German war veteran is playing a violin. People give him coppers. He has a peg-leg. Shot off in a long-forgotten campaign. 'Poor old man,' Mum says to Becky, on whom the comment has lasting effect. That Sunday in church, at the end of a prayer, everyone says 'Amen'. Becky mumbles incoherently. When the next prayer ends Mum listens carefully. '*Pah-*

ole-man,' Becky shouts. Poor old man! She just can't forget him. Everyone laughs, it *does* sound a bit like Amen! Later, when asked why she feels so sorry for the fiddler, she explains 'one leg on, one leg off, and one stick-on!'

I'm three months old, born in one country, christened in another. It's an omen. Soon we'll be moving even further afield.

Dad is enthused about his new job. The mine belongs to the *Rhodesia-Katanga Gold Mining Company Limited*, registered head-office London. Because of Geita's remoteness, Dad's escaped a medical examination, which he would have failed. Difficult enough recruiting staff to the bush, without subjecting them to physicals. He works at Walvis until the end of December 1951. We return briefly to Johannesburg, then go by train to Durban. There we embark the Union Castle liner *Uganda Castle* for the ten day voyage north up the Indian Ocean to Dar-es-Salaam. Here we board the locomotive-drawn train to Mwanza on Lake Victoria.

We're going to Geita. We know little about it, 'cept it's deep in the bush. Won't be that bad, Dad assures Mum. Rent-free house, good wages. Soon they'll save enough to go home to Cornwall, and buy the small farm Dad's always dreamed of. At long last their luck is changing.

'Isn't *Geita* the place you told me about, the one in the paper, where that poor Welsh lady and her driver were murdered?' Mum asks.

'Well, scrub me with barnacles,' Dad exclaims, 'you're right!' He has a wealth of lovely naval expressions. Mum has a surge of foreboding. Better not tell him. He's so *desperate* to improve their lives.

Years later Mum recalls the rigours of that first journey to Geita, and how little they knew. In the local *Sukuma* dialect the place-name means 'Valley of Death'. Ominous. There's only one industry in a region of thousands of square miles, the mine. Fewer than two percent of the African population in the district work for money. Most live from subsistence farming, fishing and hunting. Others are limited to being *wa-omba*, or those who beg, because they are *wasikini*, or poor people. Geita is eighty miles south-east of the ramshackle and torpid lakeside town of Mwanza, on the hintermost end of the railway line from the Indian Ocean.

The train journey begins at Dar es Salaam. Mum and Dad have bottom bunks, Becky and me top ones. The story of the journey becomes a family legend. Dad is amused that the Africans call the

14

locomotive *gari-moshi*, smoking car. The narrow-gauge line heads north and west, away from the coast, into wild, hot country. For two days and nights it struggles and wheezes over ravines, across plains, up forested hills, through valleys of stark aridness, and surprising oasis-like patches of verdant green.

Stops are few, stations rudimentary. Wild animals abound, great herds of elephants loping lazily across the plains, prides of recumbent lions suspiciously eyeing the train, eland and wildebeest grazing beside small pools, endlessly flicking ears and tails at obstinate black flies. Hippos show dark snouts and bulging eyes above fetid water in muddy places. Repetitive scenes and unremitting heat. Occasional signs of humanity. Sudden clearings appear, clustered with mud huts and *makuti* thatch. Small children run naked, laughing and waving, scrawny chickens scratch dusty ground, elders sit impassively, wildebeest-tail fly-whisks in hand. They've seen the *gari-moshi* many times.

The engine struggles on, coughing and groaning uphill, wheezing over and over in rhythm, but ever more slowly, '*I think I can, I think I can. . .*' exuberant going down, '*I knew I could, I knew I could. . .*' Mean speed is thirty miles an hour. Walking pace approaching hill summits, galloping down.

Bigger stations like Dodoma materialise out of the shimmering heat. Sweat-streaked Europeans appear as pale ghosts among the *watu*. Most command porters in skins and rags. Some wave tiredly at their compatriots in the train. It's appallingly hot.

Forty-eight hours from Dar the locomotive, tiredly drawing six carriages, trundles across the last stretch to Lake Victoria. Proximity to the lake is declared in geology. Great smooth, cheese-coloured boulders grow like outlandish mushrooms, some big as a car, others taller than a house. After so long in the super-heated dryness of the interior, the nearness to a great expanse of cool water brings welcome movements of air, carrying exotic perfume. Heady essences of drying fish, cool water, rotting lilies and water-hyacinth, spices, woodsmoke, hemp, mangoes and guava are all on the cooling breeze greeting the train.

There's ten minutes of chaos at Mwanza station, when overheated passengers trundle luggage and greet suntanned, sweating, strangers. To get to Geita there's a bone-crushing ride in a Land Rover to come. Only eighty miles from town, but it takes over five hours.

The African driver is waiting at the station. He's tall and slim, erect, good looking, and late-middle-aged, smartly dressed in a light khaki safari suit, and he has a pencil-line moustache. That's how Dad recognises him. 'Safari suit and thin moustache,' the assistant manager wrote in his telegram. This driver is to become a source of mystique and humour. He doesn't fit any pattern – he's unique.

'Hello, I am Fritz,' he says, detaching himself from a knot of people. 'You are ze family *Penhaligon*, yes?' Mum and Dad are amazed. This black man speaks English with a strong *German* accent. There will be time to find out why. Right now it's just good to be off the sweltering train, though it's hot enough here too. We've been travelling a long time. Becky is complaining, and I've got a temperature. Time to get to Geita.

In 1951, few roads in Mwanza are tarred, and the dirt ones are only barely graded in town boundaries. As the road curves beyond the ramshackle outer-shops, it's forgotten. Potholes are everywhere, some three feet wide. We haven't seen anything as rough as this in Zululand or South West Africa. Elephant grass and thornbushes grow in the middle, bush closes in. On the best stretches maximum speed is a bone-jarring thirty-five miles an hour, which means not changing beyond third gear. Where the potholes are bigger or deeper, or where the middle growth exceeds three feet, we barely make twenty. Washaways from floods have cut gulleys or *dongas*. The driver slows to five, and engages four wheel drive. Like a traction engine, the Land Rover judders and growls, and crabs its way obliquely, even sideways, down one side, across uneven bottoms, and up again.

Fifteen hard miles later we reach a lake lagoon. Wooden jetty, vehicles queuing for the diesel-engined ferry. When the rusting relic isn't broken down, it plies across in daylight hours a dozen times. The load limit is two five-ton lorries and five cars, or ten cars if no lorries. There are four lorries in front, so we wait. Eventually we'll know the routine. We'll learn to rise early for Mwanza, to beat the hauliers. That, or wait for the second or third crossing. No fun waiting for hours by that sweltering, fetid bank.

Loading and offloading, the laconic crew are singularly unrushed. We learn a new word. *Badaai* means later, but Dad says it hasn't the same sense of urgency of *manana* in Spanish, or *dreckly* in Cornwall. It takes half an hour to cross.

On the far side the road is worse. We plunge into a tunnel of wild green, along a narrow track hacked from invading bush. The sky disappears above the tree canopy. Insects buzz, birds screech, the Land Rover snarls, down, up, round, precariously listing to left, right, front or back.

Ten miles, and an hour from, the ferry, we reach the 'Tsetse belt'.

Tsetses can read, Dad says. There's a painted wooden sign nailed to a tree beside the road. It declares:

**YOU ARE ENTERING TSETSE BELT. CLOSE WINDOWS.
HM GOVERNMENT, TANGANYIKA TERRITORY.**

The windows are hurriedly closed. Mum covers my face. The temperature soars. The tsetses attack. Fat, angry flies, four times bigger than a housefly. Always cross. One gets in, mocking closed windows. Bites Dad, and the pain is worse than a bee-sting. His cheek swells an angry red. We'll grow to loathe these demon-flies.

Four miles of unventilated heat later, a sign says:

**YOU ARE LEAVING TSETSE BELT. OPEN WINDOWS.
HM GOVERNMENT, TANGANYIKA TERRITORY.**

We open them. A fresh-air asphyxiation-reversal. The educated tsetses know when to call off the assault. They are confined to narrow strips. A 'riverine' species, they live close to water, trees and shade. Can't tolerate direct sunshine, unable to cross open ground. Used to control them in some parts. Infested areas are cut into parcels by removing vegetation. Restricts them to smaller and smaller zones, disrupting breeding and feeding. In some areas it achieves extinction of the pest. In 1951, and for many years after, it isn't done near Geita.

'Your accent,' Dad says to Fritz, 'is it German?'

'*Ja*, yes, *Ich vahr*, I mean I vos, in der *Schutztruppe* before.' That explains everything. Dad hasn't a clue what the *Schutztruppe* is. Sounds like shooting and troops. Either that, or doing something unpleasant *on* the troops! He forces himself not to smile. Fritz is a serious man.

'When?' he asks.

'In der vore.' Fritz isn't exactly talkative. The war, so he was a soldier.

'The last war?' Dad says.

'Nein, der forst vun.' I will learn a great deal about this war. World War I in Tanganyika, the British led by a succession of incompetent generals, the Germans by the legendary *Oberstleutnant*, or Lieutenant-Colonel, Paul von Lettow Vorbeck. Three and a half decades after it ended, the legacy of the campaign still lies heavily on the country, despite a second world war having come and gone. By Fritz's tone it's clear the conversation is ended. The ex-*Schtztruppe askari* is no small-talk man.

More miles, and hours, later, we emerge from the bush onto a huge plain fringed by rock-strewn hills, on whose slopes gnarled dwarf trees desperately cling. Mum says it's lunar. On the flat ground herbivores graze on sparse, dry grass, and drink from small, muddy, watercourses. When the monsoon floods erupt, they overflow and merge, and half the plain turns to chocolate-mousse. In the dry season the water evaporates, leaving huge expanses of slate-coloured sludge. In bad years even that dries to dust, and blows away on the hot, *djinn*-driven wind.

The local *watu* say evil *djinns* appear as dust devils, Fritz informs Dad, breaking his silence. First thing he's said in an hour. Judging by appearance, this is no place to spend a night. Skulls and bones of wildebeest, kudu, Thomson's gazelle and eland litter the landscape. It's a gigantic open-air ossuary.

This is the gateway to Geita. What will we find out here, cut off from civilisation? The open space narrows, the trees close in again, and then the Rover begins to painfully climb a very steep hill. When we finally reach the brow, we're overlooking Geita mine to the west.

Two

While Becky and I sleep, Mum and Dad are hot, eaten alive by *dudus,* a Swahili word they soon use for any insect, and they're exhausted. With relief they collapse into bed. In the morning, after sleeping 'like the dead', they emerge into glaring sunshine to survey their new home and surroundings. This is the crucible of our future.

Compound Hill has breathtaking panoramic views of the dense-green forested valley, with small hillocks rising in the medium distance, and faraway blue peaks piercing the horizon. So much for nature. Man is here. The ugly mine-shaft bores unsentimentally into the hillside. Like in a movie, the background sets the scene, but actors inhabit the foreground. The 'camp', or residential area, has three parallel roads running downhill a quarter mile apart, joining 'Top' and 'Bottom' roads. Top Road connects the camp to the mine workings, mill, head office, mine store and engineering and carpentry works. It terminates at Barrat Stores, a corrugated iron and wood, Indian-run, and only, shop. The other way leads to large wooden houses for the chief engineer, doctor, chief assayer, and, finally, general manager, most exalted, whose house is at the end, and biggest of all.

Bottom Road peters out into a footpath at one end, with dense bush beyond, and *Lone Cone Club* at the other. The club is named for the shape of the hill behind. An upside-down, thin, symmetric ice-cream cone, with arid, treeless sides, so steep I never hear of anyone ever climbing to the top. From the club the road runs a quarter mile to a tiny, church-like building all on its own. The mine mortuary. It continues past the church, the *kindergarten* school, and the 'African' hospital. From there it becomes the route to the '*boma*', four miles away. There is the nearest government police station, in the middle of a mud-hut village. It encroaches onto the *Boma Dukas*, a dozen Indian shops crowded into a long concrete and corrugated iron building, with a common verandah piled high with merchandise. This place will have magnetic power over Becky and I.

The roads connecting Top and Bottom road are half a mile long, with ten widely spaced wooden houses on either side. The houses grow sequentially bigger up the hill, the whole camp top-heavy.

All Geita roads are stone and dirt, and have to be frequently graded by a pre-war bulldozer, when they can get it to start. To prevent washaway by tropical rain deluge during the monsoons, there are three-foot deep ditches on the sides. Where roads cross, steel pipes the width of forty-four gallon oil-drums carry flood water under the intersections. Usually they are dry, and often the chosen abode of pythons, who like shade, and really *can* swim when push comes to flood, someone says.

Our house is at the base of the hill. We're minor miners, Dad says. There are two bedrooms, so Becky and I share. It's a pretty little wooden place, raised on four foot stilts because of monsoon *gharikas* or floods, and, more importantly, to prevent termites eating it. Those voracious little white ants have no preference when it comes to food. The stilts are soaked and regularly re-painted with tar-like insecticide, so pungently effective that even termites can't leg, or stomach, the climb.

The houses have electricity from a wood-burning generator at the workshop. Water comes from a concrete reservoir near the summit of Compound Hill. This is fed by a pipeline running four miles from a dam, which in turn takes water from Lake Victoria, ten miles away.

We don't need heating. Water for bathing is warmed in forty-four gallon diesel drums on concrete bases, where fires are lit in the evenings. There's only tepid water by day, which can't be drunk from the tap. It isn't only luke-warm, but carries bilharzia, typhoid, cholera and countless nasties, we're warned. It has to be boiled, passed through a slow ceramic filter, then bottled and cooled in the fridge.

Cooking is in cast iron *Belling* wood stoves, black and identical in all the houses. Like much of the equipment, they were bought and shipped as a job-lot from England in 1926.

Windows are open. Wire-mesh fly-screens keep insects out. Geita is a torpid, sweltering place. So bereft of man-made sound that buzzing bees or wings of fluttering moths are a racket. It teems with insects, and there's a constant background of scratching, fluttering, and crawling. For long minutes the throaty cooing call of the *njiwa* bird permeates the bush. In the cool of evening other noises begin. Frogs croak in throaty chorus in watery places, crickets screech in rising

20

crescendo, wild dogs bark. Sometimes the insane giggles of a *fisi* or hyena, or the thunderous roar of a prowling lion, drowns out other sound.

We arrive in Geita a day before I'm six months old. I'm a blank page, or book even, but not for long. Though lost to memory, the early months and years will shape me deeply, and I shall never escape them.

Dad takes up managing the ropeway. He rules over a double system of steel-wire cables which run, supported on pylons, to and from the mine in Geita, and a series of mine shafts seventeen miles away at *Ridge Eight*, known to all as 'Ridgate'. It's impressive. Every two hundred yards the cables are supported on huge steel tripods, which stride away like alien beacons into the heat-shimmered distance. On those cables, hanging on lop-sided arms, run car-sized, rusty red 'buckets'. The outlandish contraptions trundle squeakily on rusty bearings in close Indian file between their distant destination and the tipping station, where labourers wait to turn them over and discharge ore. From there a busy, smoke-belching front-loader takes huge bites to the mill for crushing. Becky is two and a half when she first spies the system. 'Swing-ang, swing-ang, daddy bucket, daddy bucket,' she yells in awe and delight. Any suspended thing becomes 'swing-ang', which embarrasses Dad when Becky spots him naked!

They give Dad a Land Rover. It's old in 1951, but she seizes my heart. She's an open olive-green short-wheelbase petrol version, registered MZ 202, for Mwanza. She'll still be around for fifteen years, and beyond.

The *waSukuma* and *waGallua* people in Geita are fascinating. Apart from those working for the mine, who wear shabby and disintegrating European clothes, male and female go topless, and generally wear short loincloths, or *kanzus*, round their waists. Both tribes have a love of bodily adornment, including many copper and elephant-hair bangles and anklets, and tribal scarring on the face. Many have pierced ears, through which they insert larger and larger, heavier and heavier devices, in Geita graduating to store-bought bronze-coloured padlocks, clearly a European addition to their culture, to stretch their earlobe-rings as long as two feet. The *Galluas* of both sexes, too, like to knock out their front teeth, considering the large gap *maridadi*, or pretty, and 'better for kissing'.

Mum often laughs about Dad's 'fresh Geita milk'. He craves a glass of real fresh milk, is fed-up with canned or powdered. He explains in sign-language to a passing *Gallua* what he wants. That it's liquid he demonstrates by running the outside tap. That it's white he shows by pointing at the white-painted house-wall. At last the bemused tribesman beams. An hour later he returns with a bucket of frothy white milk. Dad's delighted, and pays him twenty cents. It's so nice to have milk straight from a cow, even if the bearer doesn't look too hygienic. Heating will take care of that.

Dad boils the milk on the range cooker. He lets it cool, then pours a glass. He drinks greedily. It tastes shockingly unpleasant. He's drunk half when he begins to feel queasy. He's violently sick. The 'milk' is powdered *mahogo*, or cassava, mixed with water. The tribesman hasn't been dishonest. The *Mzungu* asked for white liquid, so that's what he brought!

When are my own memories first formed? Can't remember. Some 'early' recall has to be from later, recount confused with memory. Unable to discriminate between experience and legend, I 'remember' some things I never see. With time, direct and vicariously gained memories get stored together, blend to continuity.

In humans and sentient animals, vicarious, second-hand learning and memory, serve a vital evolutionary purpose. Without it each individual would need to learn everything themselves, know no danger not personally experienced. Vicarious learning, plus personal experience, is education. It starts at birth. Whether directly remembered or otherwise gained, Geita doesn't change, our house is the same for years, Dad only ever works in one job. If I fail to remember at two, there's time to learn later, gain explanations, create my own biography.

But the *bundi msitu* bird, or African forest-owl, *always* is. Its sonorous, haunted call comes at night from where the bush encroaches our garden. I never find where it hides, though it calls to me, just me, every time I'm alone in the darkness of my bedroom. It's a message I try to understand. What *is* it? *Pleading*, or *warning?* Owls *don't* go 'tu-whit-tu-whoo'. It's not a superficial sound. It resonates a deep and mystical mood, of ancient wisdom in the wild, and the eternal soul of the bush. I feel it in my heart and stomach, and even my bones. Sometimes, after the *bundi-msitu* has gone to sleep, from much further away, much, much further, comes that spine-chilling, half-giggling, almost human, sometimes jolly, sometimes alarmed, maniacal, racket from those creatures I'll get to know, hate, love, fear and dread, the *fisi*, or hyena.

Dad drives about in MZ 202, fixing or doing all day in the blazing bush. We're close to the equator. Mum works as a clerk in the mine store, where every nut, bolt, fan belt or cog for running the enterprise is ordered, kept, recorded and issued.

*   *   *   *

22

My older brothers, who have been in boarding school in South Africa, follow us to Geita three months later. They fly, landing on the way in Southern and Northern Rhodesia, then Nairobi in Kenya, from where they get a small charter-plane to Geita. Much quicker than our journey. The eldest, Bertrand, turns sixteen within weeks, and leaves for England to join the Royal Navy. Fraser, fourteen, will follow, but has to wait two years.

Fraser has informal school lessons from Mr Hessler, Mum's colleague at the mine store who, like Dr Weiss, is a German-Jewish survivor of Auschwitz. It's a strange concept: two survivors from Auschwitz having a chat, as one does. 'Tell you what,' one says, 'why don't we bugger off and live deep in the snake-infested, disease-ridden, sweltering bush in Tanganyika?'

There's someone else I should mention. My sister Rose is five, left behind in an institution in Cape Town. 'Deaf, dumb and mentally retarded.' I don't know till I'm twelve.

One day Dad and Fraser come home with a living nightmare for Mum. She retells it for years.

Dad drives miles to Nungwe bay, fifteen miles away, Fraser and a friend riding on the open back. They have shotguns for wild ducks. There aren't any, though Nungwe is usually crowded with them.

On the way back Fraser sees a huge male lion come out the bush behind the Land Rover. Dad hasn't seen him. Simba keeps pace behind, the Rover doing less than twenty on the bumpy road. Fraser tries to alert Dad. He shouts, yells, beats on the cab-roof. The engine's too loud. Simba's gaining. Fraser bangs frantically on the roof. Dad laughs. Boys will be boys. Anything that makes them happy!

The road's a little easier. Dad puts his foot down. The Land Rover speeds up. So does Simba. He breaks into what looks a gentle lope. The apparent slowness of this stride is deceptive. The gap closes rapidly. There's something about the hunch of his shoulders and angle of his head. He's only five yards away, preparing to spring. Simba wants Fraser and his friend for lunch.

Fraser's shotgun is loaded in case he sees wild duck on the way. Birdshot. He can see deep into the open pink cavity of Simba's mouth. He senses his moist, warm breath. Suddenly Dad sees the danger in his mirror. He jabs the accelerator violently. The Rover surges, Fraser falls against the cab-roof, and the shotgun goes off. Simba's face is peppered with birdshot. He swerves into the bush in blinded agony. The Rover plunges on, the lion is gone.

Fraser fervently tries to convince himself the shot was accidental. That reflex, not thought, pulled the trigger. But he saw it hit the lion in

23

the eyes. Probably blinded. What will happen to him? 'You had no choice,' Dad says. 'Him or you!' For the rest of his life Fraser worries about the poor Simba's eyes. Was he *completely* blinded? Make him easy prey for that most vicious of enemies, the hyena! Fraser is haunted.

Mum tries not to think what may have happened, and tightens her control over Rebecca, who's prone to wander off alone. This place is full of danger. Wild animals, poisonous snakes, scorpions and, for all Mum knows, cannibals.

Becky and I are given into the daytime care of a strictly instructed *ayah*. These are wives, girlfriends and daughters of African mineworkers, who supplement income by caring for European, Indian and Chinese children. The daily ritual is to be collected by *ayah* at seven am, and taken to a central point. There are two big trees standing in a clearing half a mile from the camp, where several *ayah*s congregate to while away the heat of day. One is a giant acacia, the other a baobab. Baobabs really *do* look as if they're growing upside-down. The branches are like enormous inverted roots. The acacia provides welcome shade. I'm carried there strapped onto *ayah's* back with a blanket, African style. Becky, two years older, walks, and never has that experience. We're home by six, exhausted and ready for bed.

Of my early playmates, Lutoli is the closest. Like me, he was born in '51, though nobody recorded the day or month. His father was killed before he was born, trying to defend a goat from a marauding lion. His mother lives on a *shamba*, or farm, between Geita and *Boma Duka*, and augments her income as *ayah* for a *Singa-Singa* family. *Singa-Singa* is what the *watu* call all Sikhs. When very young I think they must be performers, who serenade for a living. Turban must be stage-costume. Never hear one perform. Just their surnames are all Singh. This *Singa-Singa* family is nervous, and don't allow the *ayah* to take their child outdoors. Each morning on the way to work his mother leaves Lutoli at a cousin's shack. This extraordinarily fat lady brings him to the upside-down baobab tree to commune with other *ayahs*. One is mine, Amina, pronounced *Ah-mean-ah*. I meet Lutoli. By the time we can walk, run and talk we're inseparable.

Mum and Dad make friends easily in Geita. One day they're having a 'sundowner' with a surveyor. His name is Andy Sparks, and he's in Geita on short-term contract. Dad gets on with him, because he too was in the navy, which he refers to as '*The Andrew*'. Mum finds that amusing. The conversation which follows is one they never forget.

'Nice house,' Mum says.

'Yeah, nice,' he replies, 'but they won't give it to anyone to live full-time.'

'Why not?' Dad asks.

'The wives.'

'The wives?' Mum asks, intrigued.

'Too spooky!'

'What?'

'They say it's too spooky.'

'Why do they say that?' Mum asks.

'You don't know? I've only been here a month, and *I* know!'

'Know what?'

'Dick, you're sitting in Stroessner's chair!' says Andy.

'What?' says Mum.

'D'you mean. . ?' says Dad.

'This is the Williams' house. You're sitting in the chair bloody Stroessner sat in the night he killed Mrs Williams and the driver! Surely you know the story?'

'Read about it,' Dad says. He examines the chair. It's an ordinary wooden lounging chair with big cushions. Same as our house. They're *maninga* wood, made by the Chinese carpenters. Rough, but adequate. He remembers. Stroessner sat here, right here! He'd been drinking with his intended victim and her husband, while the children slept down the passage. All the time he knew, was making plans: soon he'd be lying in wait for his hostess on the lonely road to Mwanza. How could anyone be so cold blooded? It's a strange feeling. Mum has pins and needles all over. They could at least have got rid of the chair!

'Horrible,' Mum says.

'Awful, wasn't it?' Andy Sparks says.

'Cruel,' Mum says.

Dad thinks about poor Mrs Williams. One night he has a terrible nightmare. He's walking down a dirt road, all overhung with dense vegetation. There's a Land Rover up ahead, he can just see the back end – it's parked half-in, half-out the bush. The engine's running. He's also running, because he knows someone's going to be killed. He's going to be too late, no matter how fast he runs. He's approaching the Land Rover now. Getting very close. His breathing is laboured, because he's come a long way. A shot rings out, an ear-piercing

25

b

whiplash in the eerie silence before dawn. He's too late! He wakes up shivering.

Mum's superstitious. Poor Mrs Williams won't go away. First Dad reads about her. Then they come here, where it happened. Then the house, the chair. . . Now Dad has a nightmare.

'We should visit her grave,' Mum says at breakfast.

'And?'

'Put some flowers there, pay our respects. . .'

'But we didn't know her,' Dad says.

'Just let's do it,' Mum says. Perhaps she's a soul in torment. Maybe paying respects will help give her peace.

'Okay,' says Dad, 'I know when I'm beaten!'

Two days later Mum picks a huge bunch of flowers in the garden. The place is a horticulturalist's dream. Bougainvillaea, hibiscus, golden shower, azaleas, all grow wild. A riot of colour. Dad comes home half an hour early. They drive out along Bottom Road, past the African hospital, onto Boma Road, and then off on a branch to Samina, where the cemetery is. It's seventeen hot, bumpy, pot-holed miles, with midges and *tsetse* flies for company. Must be a stream nearby, Dad says.

They're standing by the grave. It's only been eight months, but already the jungle's reclaiming it. There's small bushes and creepers growing on the turned soil, and the wooden cross is already half-eaten by termites. Their little transparent bodies scuttle about in the holes they've made. A stone's been ordered months ago. Mrs Williams' parents sent money from Wales. They're slow workers at Lakeside Monumental Masons in Mwanza. Somewhere invisibly near at hand a *njiwa*-bird makes a plaintiff cry. *Hoo,who-hoo*. It's spooky here, even in daylight.

Mum feels a cold shiver down her back. Mrs Williams wasn't ready to die, she tells Dad.

'Superstitious nonsense!' Dad says. They put the flowers in a vase, leave it on the grave.

'Where did they bury the poor driver?' Mum asks.

'His family buried his body on their farm,' Dad says.

When a child learns to speak it is usually with one person, its mother. Only later, as many fathers testify, does the child talk to others. I am too young for that. Then, for most waking hours, I'm with people who speak only Swahili. Because there are two speechless babies, the *ayah*s are at pains to teach us. My first words are Swahili, which becomes my native language. Being constantly with Lutoli polishes my fluency. Soon we're talking continually, to the *ayahs*' delight.

Swahili is a colourful and beautiful language. Its name is derived from the Arabic word 'sawahil', or 'coastal plane'. It's the *lingua franca* of the coast, but the slave, and other, trade took it far inland, to the peoples of Lake Victoria, and throughout Tanganyika, Uganda, Rwanda, Burundi, Kenya, Congo, Nyasaland, and the north of Mozambique.

My Swahili germinates and puts down roots. It doesn't resemble the 'Kitchen Swahili' of Europeans, or *Wazungu*. Judging by the *ayahs'* glee when I use rude words and phrases, the ladies are pathologically crude. I don't mind. By two and a half I swear profusely. Hilarity in *ayahs* and their men, confusion and anger among *Wazungu*, depending how much they understand. The crudest, rudest and most colourful invective in my vocabulary is gained.

Swahili holds a special premium for vulgarity. I discover there is no shame *saying* things. What *is* shameful is bad actions, cruelty, meanness, plotting, snubbing guests, or being unpleasant on footpaths. Kindness, hospitality, generosity and reliability are esteemed. Coarse language doesn't debase social position or reduce affection. *Au contraire*, humour is the greatest delight, the funniest tales or jokes are filthy, the dirtiest speakers most esteemed. Everyone competes in ribaldry. Profound and specific indelicacy is used with abandon. Coarse and expletive repartee is endemic. The *watu* or people speak unadulterated truth. If asked what they're thinking, out comes every lewd and bawdy thought, pride and honour intact. Not even the young are spared broadsides of profanity. There's no discrimination by age.

To enliven matters, Swahili evolved slowly, borrowing from Arabic during the slave-trade, German, English, Portuguese and many local languages, including *Luo* and *Kikuyu* from Kenya, *Buganda* from Uganda, *Masai, Gallua, wa-Arusha* and many others in Tanganyika, and, especially in Geita, the *Sukuma* language. The list is not exhaustive. There results from all this a collection of swearwords and insults surpassing in quality all competition by an order of magnitude. The *watu* enjoy and celebrate the achievement gaily, excitedly, and with not a nebula of guilt or self-reproach.

I engage in colourful swearing all day, with phrases and words which would, if she understood, cause Mum to hyperventilate. My contribution to discourse earns me a reputation among the *watu* as theirs in mind, and the foulest-mouthed three-year-old they know. They adore me, and delight to hear me use my vocabulary against

27

Wazungu masters, who, unaware they are being abused, titter politely to hear a small white boy talk like a native.

'You have the face of a *samaki,*' I say in Swahili to Mum's lady guest, who's drinking tea in the garden. Fish-face. I'm smiling angelically, because it's my script. The *Mzungu* smiles back. My audience, the *watu,* giggle helplessly.

'Jimmy's so fluent!' the *Mzungu* lady says to Mum. I know it's a compliment, even if I don't follow the English.

'*Mkundu yako na nuka,*' I say. Your anus stinks. I put on a serious expression. You wouldn't swear looking serious. The *Watu* convulse, trying but failing to keep straight faces. The *Mzungu* lady smiles again. A little strained now. She senses, but is not sure, she is being grievously insulted by a three-year-old.

'Although I can't say why,' she confides in Mum, 'sometimes I feel Jimmy doesn't like me.'

'I'm sure you're wrong,' Mum says, but she looks worried. The *Mzungu* hastens to change the subject.

'It's amazing how *well* he speaks African.' Mum nods. She's blushing red. She's concluded I'm saying unsavoury things, but doesn't know what.

I learn to spit. Not artless de-gobbing. This is high science. Not just expulsive ejecting sound with pursed lips and tongue. I draw my lips back in a forced grimace, make a sucking 'tsch' against my upper front teeth. Through an impossible-to-explain mechanism, a drop of saliva ejects at high velocity. With time my accuracy increases. Most *watu* can hit a moving fly at six paces. Soon I'm pretty sharp myself.

I learn to blow my nose *Swahili*-style. This is a public act and, if you're accomplished, a spectator sport. One nostril is closed with a thumb. The head is projected slightly forward. Big blow out open nostril, ejecting *makamasi*, or snot. Doing well means making distance. Repeat other side. Wipe fingers on *majani*, grass. I'm getting good at this too.

'Handkerchief,' Mum says. Wouldn't a chief be upset?

Dad tells me my origin. 'We were sitting here having a drink in the early evening, when we saw a gang of monkeys up on they-there hill,' he says in his Cornish way.

'*Fanya nini?*' I ask. What you do?

'Well, Mummy wanted another baby, and we didn't have one, so. . .'

'Stop it Daddy,' Mum says, but he just grins.

'I took my big knife. I like *Nyanis*, monkeys, and ran up the hill, till I cornered one in front of a big tree.'

'*Fanya nini?*' I ask. What you do? Mum clicks her tongue. She knows what Dad's going to say. Said the same to Bertrand in Transvaal, years ago.

'I caught him, cut off his tail, and brought him home. Mummy shaved him for me.' Mum smiles. What can she do?

'And that monkey, Jimboy, is you!'

'*Nyani* ?' I ask in amazement. I'm a monkey?

'Yes, but don't tell anyone, or they'll send you back up *they-there* hill!' Here begins a long-standing idea: I'm really a shaved monkey in a human world.

There's a walk-in cupboard between the bedrooms in our house. It has no window, and it's pitch-dark inside with the door closed. Cockroaches. Big, black monsters who scuttle for cover when we enter. Becky and I call them *cockdies*. Mum and Dad don't like physical punishment when we're naughty. They don't need it. We're terrified of being locked in the *cockdie* room. It's an effective threat, because even though I don't speak much English, the word *cockdie* brings me to heel. They only ever put me there for half a minute, but terror of *cockdies* in darkness is powerful stuff.

'*Dudu mbaya!*' I say to Becky, '*mimi ogopa.*' Bad insects, I'm frightened. Dad and Mum overhear me. They crease up laughing.

'What *are* we raising?' Dad asks Mum. 'He's a savage, but he *can* put those Swahili words together!'

Honest swappings of casual profanities with the *watu* are everyday by the time I'm three. One day I sit alone on a big stone near our house. Along comes a freshly washed and dressed young man. He's going out for the evening. I recognise him as the chief engineer's cook. He stops to greet me. '*Jimu,*' he says, '*Jambo.*' Hello.

I reply: 'Where are you going?' *Una kwenda wapi?*

'*Kutembeya,*' he says. For a walk. He explains he's out looking for a vagina. He spits a long way through his teeth. I wish him speed and success, and he continues down the path, giggling. I block my nostril and blow my nose at a tree. I am reaching longer and longer distances.

I learn how to threaten people. '*Hi hospitali!*' I say, brandishing one fist. This means hospital. '*Hi Samina!*' I follow, showing the other. This is *Samina*. The graveyard. Works well on small *totos*. They don't know what a *Mzungu*, or white person could do. Even a little one like me. '*Nta zika ko ziara,*' I say. I'll bury you in your grave. A useful insult is to tell someone they're mad. '*Kwenda Dodoma!*' is shorthand. Go to Dodoma. Central Tanganyika, only mental asylum in the country. '*Kitchwa na penduka!*' I add. Your head is turning around. Insults like these are lightly given, laughingly received.

Meantime I notice strange things. Some people have one very fat

29

leg. So swollen the space between shin and foot is completely filled. Only toenails protrude at the bottom, like the elephant-feet they make into wastepaper baskets. I don't know how many are affected among the *watu*, but enough to suggest they're a different tribe. Not like other people. The sight, so shocking at first, becomes mundane. Here or there someone has a fat leg. This is 'elephantiasis'. Filariasis is the zoological term. A tropical parasitic worm blocks lymphatic ducts and causes grotesque swelling of the limb. I don't see a *mutu* with *two* elephant-legs.

'*Madudu,*' an *ayah* says. Bugs. '*Ngonjwa ya madudu mbaya.*' Sickness of the bad bugs.

Some people have scarred and pitted faces. Mostly Africans, but some Indians too. Smallpox before mass-immunisation. Kills millions, leaves many more scarred.

I'm four. Dad comes home with his stalwart Nyasa assistant, Wait, and takes two Whitecap beers from the fridge. Wait sits on the floor, Dad on an armchair. Dad offers Wait a chair, but he refuses. Having a beer with a white man is one thing, sitting on a chair is another. They speak about the ropeway, Dad in rudimentary Swahili, Wait in broken English.

I amble in from the garden, sit down. I love Wait. He's tall, light skinned, with finely chiselled features I later recognise as Nyasa. He always wears wellington boots, regardless of the heat. Some of the Wazungu call him 'Boots'. It's clear he dotes on Dad. I listen to them a long time. Mum and Becky are in the kitchen. Dad fetches more beer. Wait drinks from the bottle. Doesn't want a glass.

'Time for bed,' Dad says, pointing at me. I don't understand. My English is as poor as my Swahili is good. Dad sees my incomprehension.

'Wait,' he says, addressing the Nyasa, 'tell him to go to bed.'

'Jimu,' Wait says, 'father says you must go to bed.'

'*Siwezi,*' I say defiantly. It's posh Swahili talk. Shorthand, one word meaning 'I will refuse,' or 'I won't.' Before learning this I have to use lots of words. That's *kitchen*-Swahili. I'm slicker than that. Wait translates.

'He is saying. . . No!'

'I'll give him a hiding,' Dad says.

'*Baba na sema,*' Wait says, 'father says if you don't go he'll smack you.'

'*Ntakimbia,*' I respond sophisticatedly. I will run away! Shorthand again. One word saying it all.

30

'He says he will away run.'

'Mummy,' Dad yells, and Mum comes. 'Get this kid to bed before I lay into him. . !' He is choking on beer.

In bed that night he asks Mum, 'What kind of monkey are we raising? Jim doesn't speak English. He's a native. A cheeky one!'

Just up the road a furnace burns night and day, and its hunger for fuel changes our lives.

Three

Strange how everyday changes have impacts greater than we'd ever imagine. We wouldn't dream the mine's use of wild timber for electricity generation will lead to meeting our best childhood friends. Or the object of my long and deep infatuation. In Geita they use native forest timber as fuel to generate electricity. Cut at random in the bush, it's loaded on lorries and trucked to the mine. The lorries pass over a weigh-bridge both ways. After drying in the open, it's burnt in the furnace at 'Engineering Works' on Top Road. The heat boils water to power a huge steam-engine which drives the generator. It looks and sounds like a locomotive without wheels. Not surprising, as it's made from scrap salvaged from Singida railway yard. For a long time they can't get enough timber to feed the hungry furnace. Then a solution arrives. There's an old Sukuma saying: 'make a plate full, and a hungry man will come.' Geita's timber problem is a stranger's opportunity.

In 1952 a former *Afrika Korps* Officer called Eugen Blüger comes to Geita, with a contract to provide timber. We get to know his background well. Geita's like group therapy for the displaced and dispossessed. Everyone is expected to reveal their life story. In the *Korps* Eugen held the rank of *Hauptmann*. He's first cousin to Otto Müeller, a German former naval officer who runs a farm called *Lotanga* across a narrow lagoon from Mwanza.

Eugen acquires a fleet of four Bedford five-ton tipper lorries, and hires twenty tribesmen to cut and load wood. It's a lucrative business. His wife and two children arrive, and the family moves into a vacant house. They will be best friends to Becky and me, and play a big part in our lives. Gretchen will be my first love, but we're too young now.

In no time, the Blügers become an active and well-liked part of Geita society. 'Acceptable *Kraut*,' says Mr Snel. The war and its repercussions are still big in the people's lives, and even little Geita can't escape that.

During the retreat of the *Afrika Korps* after the battle of *El Alamein*, Eugen's tank hit a landmine, and he and two *kameraden* were reduced to walking across the North African desert. They stumbled into an American ambush, and Eugen's legs were riddled with heavy machine-gun bullets. It evokes ghoulish interest in Geita, particularly among the children. It's whispered fragments of lead still break through his skin eight years on.

Like other expatriates, Eugen enjoys a drink at the club. There is, in the early nineteen-fifties, residual tension between Germans and those who fought them in the war, but there's sufficient, if grudging, respect for this one, who fought bravely for his country, was wounded, works hard for his family, and behaves as a gentleman. The British and South Africans who served in the war make Eugen welcome, and engage him in friendly conversation, limited only by his poor English and guttural accent.

Eugen is strikingly handsome, a tall, slim, aristocratic man in his early forties. There's a framed photograph of him and another soldier, both dressed in the khaki uniform of the *Africa Korps*, hanging in the lounge of his house, which Becky and I admire when we visit. The other soldier in the photograph, smiling broadly, with his peaked cap at a jaunty angle, is Field Marshall Erwin Rommel. This is a heroic picture, and Eugen, not Rommel, the hero.

Late in 1955, when I'm four, the mine suffers another power failure, and the decision is made to change the ancient steam-driven generator for a newer, more reliable, model. The replacement is purchased and shipped to Geita, and four burly English South African engineers arrive from Johannesburg to install it. On the second night they go to the club. They're annoyed to see Eugen, a German, there. They remember fighting on the losing side at Tobruk. There they were disgraced for surrendering to a numerically inferior German force. To be fair, they didn't *know* they outnumbered the besiegers. Still, they hate *all* Germans. Exactly what takes place, or how it starts, is unclear. What I know I'm told later.

One of the South Africans calls Eugen a 'Nazi bastard' and punches him. Several people present report that all four launch a vicious and ugly attack. He's knocked to the floor, then kicked. Astonishingly, though later expressing shock and disgust, nobody intervenes. It's unfortunate Dad isn't there.

Eugen is badly beaten up. One of his lower legs, where the femur is weakened by old bullets, is fractured. When they stop kicking him, he's taken to hospital, which in Geita means that house with beds, the death-place of that murderer Stroessner, with visits by Dr Weiss, the German Jewish doctor, who, like Mr Hessler, who works with Mum at the mine store, is a survivor of Auschwitz. Many of his relatives have perished in the Nazi gas chambers, but he takes the Hippocratic Oath seriously, and doesn't discriminate against anyone, even Germans.

When I'm older, I hear people talk of how Richard, or 'Dick' Penhaligon, a Cornishman who fought Germans and saw comrades killed, 'nursed' an enemy back to health. Mum explains Dad's attitude by quoting him. 'If I was a German, I'd try to be a good one. I think Eugen's a good one.'

Dad believes all Germans love *advocaat*, made of raw eggs, brandy and *Demerara* sugar. Why he thinks that I don't know. From the day Eugen is carried to hospital, and for the next three weeks, Dad has a special routine. He drives home in MZ 202 after work, and dashes to the kitchen. He breaks eggs into a bowl, adds milk and *Demerara* sugar, pours in a hefty measure of brandy, shakes it up in a big beer bottle, tops it, then roars off down the road to see Eugen. Sometimes I go with him, and once Gretchen, Eugen's eight year old daughter, comes too. Even at this age I'm fascinated by her sky-blue eyes and long blonde hair. I have hopeful thoughts. If, like her dad, she gets into a fight, I'll save her and then she'll love me.

To others Eugene wincingly says he hates raw eggs, has never tasted *advocaat* before, and hopes he never will again. But, he says, how can he rebut the kindness of the Cornishman, whose accent makes it impossible for him, with fledgling English, to understand? So he puts on a grateful expression and drinks, only to have the glass refilled as many as three times. Eugen pretends to understand Dad, and Dad him. In truth no real communication happens, except that both men become deeply fond of one another.

Mum accompanies Dad sometimes. She recounts a conversation between the men.

'How is your wife?' Dad asks, passing a glass of *advocaat* to Eugen, propped up in his bed.

'Mein life, it is bad, ja!' Eugen says.

'How is that?' Dad asks.

'Zat ist brokken mein leg!' he replies, pointing at his plaster-cast.

When Eugen is recovered, three months after the assault, he takes his wife, Gretchen and Dieter, to visit cousin Otto Müller at Lotanga. He sings the praises of the '*Britischer* sailor' who has been so kind.

'A sailor?' Otto asks.

'A good one I think,' Eugen responds.

'Will you introduce me to this. . . *Dick?*'

'*Jawohl, der Dick,*' Eugen replies.

'I need a good sailor to fetch my boat, *Lotanga*, from Uganda,' Otto says.

Otto Müller is a German Tanganyikan of the old school. Eugen tells Dad about him, and his story is recounted many times at the bar in Lone Cone Club, in case anyone should forget. He was born in 1905 on the farm his grandfather established on the shore of Lake Victoria. The farm is *Lotanga*, a *Muanza* word Otto says means 'looking at the water'. He grew up there, went to primary school at a mission in Mwanza. When he was nine, his father, hailing from an old military family in Prussia, sent him 'home' to Germany to continue his education.

Prussia was alien. Otto hated the cold, disliked the people, longed for the friendly colours and faces of Africa. He only came home for short holidays in the next sixteen years. Eventually he graduated in agriculture and mechanical engineering. At twenty-five he returned for good, fresh-faced Bavarian bride at his side, to assume management of *Lotanga* farm, and the five year old *Lotanga* ferry service his father had established in his absence. It was 1930.

Eugen tells Dad about Otto over a beer on our verandah. I listen intently. The talk of war and submarines mesmerises me. Maybe I should be a submariner! When Otto returned to Lotanga after the war, things had changed since he left for Germany. So much happened here in Africa while he was away. In 1914 World War One broke out. Who'd think one Serbian gunman on a sidestreet in Sarajevo would cause such pandemonium!

At four I'm more obsessed with soldiers and war than I even am with Gretchen. I have little space for anything else. German, Japanese and British soldiers and war-machines crowd my imagination. Dad has difficulty convincing me I've not only missed the First World War, but the second too. I'm disappointed he won't start a third. What about U-boats, I ask. All at the bottom of the sea, he says. Isn't that where they're *supposed* to be?

So what about the First World War here, in Tanganyika? The year after the declaration of war in 1914, the British colonial army in Kenya prepared to invade *Deutsch Ost Afrika*. The gallant resistance of the German-led *Schutztruppe*, comprising German officers and native

35

askaris under the command of their legendary leader, Paul von Lettow Vorbeck, would deny the vastly superior invaders their predicted rapid victory, and divert hundreds of thousands of much-needed British and empire troops away from the western front in France. The British were not up against Dervishes in the Sudan, not pursuing someone like the crazed *Mahdi*, with his hordes of camel-riding tribesmen. They were facing the most cunning, wiliest enemy they would ever encounter, supported by well-drilled, dedicated, fearlessly brave askaris. Vorbeck wrote of his strategy in his book *My Reminiscences of East Africa*. He knew at the outset he couldn't win against such a numerically superior enemy, with so much *matériel* of war, but he could, and would, cause them a great nuisance, forcing them to deploy masses of troops and equipment against him, robbing the allies of much-needed resources for the European war.

Vorbeck's army was the *Schutztruppe* that the driver Fritz mentioned on that first road-trip to Geita. In a brilliant guerrilla campaign, they struck in unexpected places, then disappeared like shadows, to re-group, and attack elsewhere, sometimes hundreds of miles away. Cut off from re-supply from Germany, Vorbeck infuriated and humbled the British by ambushing convoys at will, even re-arming his *askaris* with captured British weapons. Lacking every type of heavy weaponry, he organised the salvage of the 4.2 inch guns from the German light cruiser *Königsberg*, after she was cornered and sunk in the Rufiji delta by Royal Navy Monitor-gunboats in July 1915. With the huge guns on improvised carriages, the *Shutztruppe* engaged the shocked British forces in long-range artillery duels.

This was supposed to be a walk-over against a small, isolated, ill-equipped colonial force, not a *real war!* To crown it, Vorbeck left infuriating 'thank you my English friends' messages nailed to trees. A gentleman! If he's ever captured, General Aitken angrily declared, he'd lose no time 'stringing the devil up, boots and all, from the nearest tree'. A *foreigner*, running rings round the imperial army! Not on, old fruit, simply not on! Not when the troops Vorbeck drew into this crazy bush run-around were so needed on the Western Front. He'd have to teach this impudent man respect! He didn't ponder how a hanged man will be respectful.

In the end it was events in Europe, not Africa, which determined the fate of *Deutsch Ost Africa*. Vorbeck didn't limit his campaign to the German colony, but exported it to the unprepared British and Portuguese settlers in Mozambique and Rhodesia. The armistice came when he was on the march in Northern Rhodesia. He got the news just after capturing another British fort, where he was planning further raids. It came with a captured British dispatch rider. At first the *Generalmajor* thought Germany had won! Then he was ordered by Berlin to surrender his East African forces to the British, to whom he'd so long given the slip. He agreed, only on condition he surrendered personally, but his 'undefeated' *askaris* didn't, and they kept their weapons. The *watu* still love him for that today. Vorbeck's campaign will be remembered as the greatest, most successful guerrilla campaign in history.

In 1946, twenty-eight years after his surrender to the British at Mbala, Vorbeck was living destitute in Berlin. When told, Field Marshall Jan Smuts was appalled, and with Montgomery arranged a modest British military pension for their tricky old enemy. Who says there isn't chivalry?

Vorbeck becomes my hero when I'm four. Oh how I wish for him to come back and lead another jungle campaign, with me in it. At least the jungle's still here, not at the bottom of the sea like the U-boats. Otto tells Dad that Vorbeck's Tanganyika story doesn't end there. He returned to visit Tanganyika in 1953. He arrived in Dar on the SS *Rhodesia Castle*. It's too early for me – I'm only 2 then. Otto says Vorbeck climbed down the gangplank onto the wharf, where he spied a gathering of *wazee*, or elderly, ragged men. He realised at once they were old *Schutztruppe askaris*, come to greet him. At first they didn't recognise him as their old commander, or *Obersti*. He's 83 years old. He's not only changed with age, but it's been forty-five years.

'Did you serve in the *Schutztruppe?*' he asked a great-grandfather in a ragged *kanzu*, or gown.

'*Lazima!*' the old man croaked. Of course! 'And I am here to greet our *Obersti!*'

'*Gina lako?*' Vorbeck asked him. What is you name?

'*Wilhelm,*' *replied the elder. A good German name. '*Gina Lako?*' he asked in return. *Your* name?

'*Pumbafu!*' roared Vorbeck, embracing the old bag of bones. Fool! 'Don't you even recognise your old *Obersti?*' The *mzee* fell to the ground and hugged Vorbeck's legs.

After the 1918 armistice, the re-named Tanganyika Territory, this huge former German slice of the continent they called *Deutsch Ost Afrika,* was joined to Uganda Protectorate and Kenya Colony, as the third part of British-ruled East Africa. All this happened while Otto languished in Germany, receiving between 1913 and 1918 only two letters from his parents in *Lotanga*. There's no point writing they said, when they knew, as Germans in East Africa, they were cut off and isolated from home by the Royal and allied Australian, American and Japanese navies, which had destroyed or captured all German shipping east of Suez.

There was a notable maritime exception, the raider-cruiser *Emden* and her indomitable *Korvettenkapitän* von Müller and crew, who wreaked havoc with British shipping in the Indian Ocean, famously shelling a sleeping Madras by night, and eluding a huge fleet of hunters from four navies, until her luck ran out and she was destroyed by HMAS *Sydney* in the battle of the Cocos Islands in November 1914. For the duration of the war, there was little mail between Germany and her East African outpost. In the last weeks of the war an attempt was made to re-supply the schutztruppe by air, using a zeppelin. Somewhere over Egypt the British intercepted her radio signals to Berlin, and cunningly sent a message, in German, that the war was over. The Zeppelin turned back towards the fatherland.

The Tanganyika twenty-five-year-old Otto returned to in 1930 was already adjusted to British rule. German East Africans were pragmatic. They accepted the new name for their country, and a King in London instead of a Kaiser in Berlin. 'Zey are both *scheiss!*' Otto said, 'so vot iss der difference?' The old colonists continued as before, intrepid workers, imaginative, tireless developers, and successful entrepreneurs.

Between 1930 and 1938, Otto and his wife settled into running the farm and ferry service to Mwanza, had two daughters, and replaced his parents as doyens of the budding Müller empire. In thirty-nine, overwhelmed by what he later called misplaced patriotism, he flew to Germany on the second last civilian flight for five years, to join his country's struggle against France, England and the 'Bolsheviks'. Same month Dad went home to rejoin the Royal navy. Strange, two white men from Africa going to join opposing sides in a European war. Otto was sent to the *Kriegsmarine,* the German navy, and due to his engineering qualification became second engineer on a destroyer.

Otto doesn't like to talk about the war. When he knows and trusts Dad, he opens up to him, who as a fellow-sailor he considers a comrade with similar standards. Otto is a veteran of both the Baltic and North Atlantic. He was only a few miles from *Bismarck* when she sank HMS *Hood*, causing the loss of more than twelve hundred British lives. He is now glad Dad had been transferred off *Hood* before that. From 1942 to 1945 Otto served as Chief Engineer on U-boats, mainly in the Mediterranean, and saw carnage on an awful scale. He lived day to day, never knowing when his last hour would come.

At this time Otto began to re-appraise the Nazis. They came to power on a wave of patriotism, promises of employment, and national rejection of the ruinous terms of the 'perfidious' treaty of Versailles. With time, they were revealed as something much more sinister. Paranoid individuals wrote their ideology, cadres ruled over things of which they were ignorant, brutal cruelty enforced loyalty and compliance, humanity was debased. Otto was in a war he'd committed to fight, but no longer felt right was on his side. He received the Iron Cross for bravery in action. He wrote in his diary 'Gott ist *nicht* mitt uns!' God is *not* with us! It was all so hollow, wasteful, barbarous. He pined for the sunsets and peace of home.

When Admiral Doenitz surrendered all German combat forces in April 1945, Otto was at sea in a U-boat. The crew heard the news when they surfaced to charge batteries off the coast near St Nazaire in France. After six months forced labour in an American POW camp, being called 'Fritz' by the guards, Otto escaped back to Tanganyika, his wife and daughters, *Lotanga* and the Mwanza ferry service. He picked up his pre-war life and set to energetically expand and improve the business. Dad says men like Otto are living demonstrations, that even here, in the remotest corner of equatorial African bush, enterprise and industry is possible. I will, in my early years, be much influenced by the presence of such men.

In 1954 Otto decides the twenty-foot motor boat of *Lotanga* Ferries is too small and antiquated for a forward-looking service. True, the British raised a German freighter, the *Graf von Gotzën*, which the Germans scuttled on Lake Tanganyika after losing the war in 1918, and restored her to service as the *MV Liemba*. Is it theft to take over someone else's ship, even if it's sunk? Anyway, Otto is a modern man, with modern ideas. He has the entrepreneurial frontier spirit so renowned in Tanganyika.

After consultations with boat builders in Port Bell, Kampala, Otto orders a new super-ferry, to be called *Lotanga* after his home. The new boat has an important assignment with Dad, though he doesn't know it. I'll also come to know her well.

Lotanga is fifty foot long. Otto is proud of her. She's traditionally built by '*Warabu*' or Arab craftsmen. Her hull is constructed of generous African hardwood ribs, assembled on a huge keelson. These are planked with inch-thick carved and joined *matunda* wood, hewn from the forest, sawn and matured for two years. The planks are fixed to the ribs by two-inch thick dowels of even harder wood, and, in traditional Lake Victoria style, smeared with *shamamu*, made with lime, animal fat and *dawa*, traditional poison from the forest, guaranteed to repulse invasion of the wood by insect or related life.

When the hull is complete, six months after *Lotanga* is first ordered, the engine arrives from Germany. It's made by Daimler Benz in Stuttgart. A five litre, passively aspirated marine diesel, it's a six-cylinder monster. With it come gearbox, propshaft, propeller, fuel tank and remote control assembly. Two German engine-fitters arrive under separate cover, and commence fitting out the engine and drive. After they have done their job, and disgraced themselves with local prostitutes, they go home, and the *Warabu* carpenters resume work, their task to build the deck and wheelhouse, with access hatch to engine, prop-shaft, fuel tank and bilge.

The planks for the deck are maninga, dark-rose coloured and fragrant timber which assumes, after sanding, the appearance of antique joinery. They're a foot wide, two inches thick, and the length of the beam where they are laid. The result is artistic, strong and ageless. With the deck in place, construction begins on the wheelhouse, strategically placed above the engine, to which the controls are inserted, using the skills of a mixed African-Italian electrician-cum-gambler-cum-pimp in Port Bell, who, when sober or not suffering the effects of '*bhangi*' or cannabis, is the best boat-control *fundi* on Lake Victoria.

The wheelhouse, resplendent and varnished, *shamamu* being too crude for that, is complete. Then come the thwart-seats, or pews. There are twelve, the longest in the middle, the others progressively shorter towards bow and stern. They're of solid hand-crafted Iroko, three inches thick and eighteen wide, supported on and bolted to legs of blackened angle iron in L shapes, a centimetre thick, six inches square. The longest seat is twelve foot, enough for eight passengers. The shortest is six foot and will seat four. The mean passenger-per-pew equation is six, so *Lotanga* will carry seventy-two passengers, a great increase on the eighteen of the old boats.

In May '54 *Lotanga*, rich timber-coloured of hull, glistening with *shamamu*, with a green stripe below deck and painted thwarts, is ready for launching. The wheelhouse, in glass and brightly varnished iroko, stands proudly astern, and the shining steel propshaft, three inches in diameter, emerges aft to meet the eighteen inch wide, four-bladed, bronze propellor, housed in a gap in the massively built rudder-stem. Behind that is the rudder, six inches thick, four foot long and five foot high. *Lotanga* is a noble sight.

Otto stares appreciatively at his new vessel. It's taken eighteen hard and frustrating months to build. He's had many problems in that time.

The German engine supplier dispatches the wrong gearbox couplings, and takes two months to send the right ones. The *Schwabian* engine fitters are arrested mid-job for refusing to pay for the services of those harbour prostitutes, while drunk on Nubian gin distilled by a one-eyed Kikuyu harbour labourer. The *Warabu* carpenters put down tools when told by a wandering *Ishmaili* prophet that the *shamamu* they are applying to the hull contains pork fat, which is '*haram*', or forbidden, not only to eat, but even to touch. Wrong nails are supplied by Patel, the hardware merchant, and he tries to rectify that by sending others even more wrong.

The paint isn't right. '*Verdamte* house paint!' Otto curses. Won't last a week in water. A Chinese 'chemist' at a Kampala branch of timber exporters suggests to Alefu, the boatyard headman, that he 'marinise' the paint by adding sulphuric acid. It's done, and results in a hundred litres of stinking brown sludge. Otto has to be restrained from attacking a cowering Alefu.

There are other problems. One by one he solves them. Anyone who weathered force ten gales in the Bay of Biscay in a steel cigar tube is equipped for adversity.

Now Otto has a new problem. How to get *Lotanga*, the boat, to *Lotanga*, her future berth, four hundred miles across the open waters of Lake Victoria? Otto is a former *Kriegsmarine* engineer, not a sailor or navigator. He's never taken a rudder in hand with intent. Never bothered with stars, other than viewing them as a pretty backdrop to courting his *freundin* on a summer evening by a lake in Swebia, bottle of *Riesling* in ice-bucket on the side.

He's pondering the dilemma when cousin Eugen, hobbling on injured leg, comes to visit.

'Introduce me to *der Britischer* sailor,' Otto tells Eugen. 'Maybe he will fetch *Lotanga*.'

Dad meets Otto with Eugen at Lone Cone Club. The three men get on well, and drink 'a herd' of *Whitecap* lager while sharing stories of the war. Otto's account of U-boat life fascinates Dad. He'd been on British ships which tried, sometimes with success, to destroy submerged U-boats with depth charges. He'd always thought how brave the crews were, cowering in long metal tubes deep under the water, waiting for charges to explode and crush them, powerless to do anything, just living in hope the enemy above would lose sonar contact. When oil and wreckage floated to the surface, meaning a hit, he felt distressed for the sailors who were dying so horribly. Otto is the first German submariner he's met. There aren't many who survived. Dad feels camaraderie beyond nationality or language.

Otto is equally keen to hear of Dad's experiences in the Royal Navy. He listens intently about HMS *Hood*, how Dad was transferred off her just weeks before she was sunk by *Bismarck*. He's intrigued about Dad's next ship, the fleet escort corvette HMS *Turtle*, her sinking by *Dornier* bombers off Grimsby in 1942, the Captain's determination to go down with his ship, how Dad saved him and a boy-seaman, and survived with five others out of a crew of sixty-eight. He remembers losing his close friend who grew up with him in Mwanza. A *Dornier* pilot. Shot down somewhere close to the north English coast in 1942. He admires Dad's Distinguished Service Medal, or DSM. '*Zis ist ein Britischer Eiserne Kreuz!*' he says to Dad, holding it close to read the lettering. Iron Cross. He has a German one.

By the time evening draws on, and the blood-red African sky plunges towards the horizon, sending crimson shafts of light and shadow across the polished bar top, Dad and Otto have forged a mutual liking and regard which will last till Dad's death, and for many years cause Otto to talk of 'der Cornish sailor vot I luffed'.

Before they leave the club, Otto tells Dad why he's come to Geita. 'Ritchie, *mein freund*,' he says, alcohol and camaraderie breaking down remaining boundaries, 'I vant you to go to Port Bell, Kampala, for me, und brink back mine boten!'

'What?' Dad says.

'Hiss boot,' Eugen says, slapping Otto on the back, 'ze big vun vot is builded fur das ferry.'

'You *what?*' Dad asks, trying to work out what they're saying.

'Let us take vun bottle visky und go to Eugen's house,' Otto suggests, 'zere ve talk more, yes?' He burps, immensely pleased with his *Englisch*.

By the time Dad staggers home, humming *Lilli Marlene*, which his drunk teutonic friends have loudly sung, he's agreed to ask for a week off work, go to Port Bell, and collect *Lotanga*. He has a crew in mind.

'I'm fetching a boat,' he tells Mum, who's never seen him so inebriated, and then he falls asleep, fully clothed, in an armchair. Mum covers him with a blanket, then leaves him. He's had difficulty sleeping ever since the head injury in 1945. She won't wake him now.

Three weeks later Dad flies on an East African Airways DC3, or *Dakota*, from Mwanza to Nairobi, and from there on to Entebbe Airport in Uganda. With him is his Nyasa assistant, Wait, and Umali, the servant he engaged in Geita. I'm bitterly disappointed he won't take me. So what if I'm only four, I want to go! From Entebbe they hitch a lift with a Scots government official, who kindly drives them all the way to Port Bell. A year later, purely by coincidence, the Scot is transferred to the Geita area as District Commissioner. His name is John McInlay.

At Port Bell they are met by the head boat builder, Alefu. Dad can't believe how old and wizened the Arab craftsman is. His face has the look of old leather, and he's completely toothless. He wears a filthy *kanzu* over his thin body, and a red *fez* on his head. Yet his eyes, grass-green, are much alive, as is his razor-sharp tongue. He speaks bad English.

'Ze best *dhow* in za lake,' he proclaims, 'I builded it!' German and Arab accents are surprisingly similar, Dad thinks. *Lotanga* is bigger than he expected. The timbers are finely worked, and to the knowing it's apparent each plank has been individually shaped and carved to fit in place, each wooden dowel inserted and driven in by hand, the caulking done so carefully as to be almost invisible. The joinery is, indeed, so detailed and perfect, it causes Dad to wonder how such a thing is possible in such primitive conditions, with such old-fashioned tools. The hull has the shine of mature iroko and *shamamu*, which is only seen on Arabian vessels. The maninga deck, dark rose coloured, contrasts strikingly with the gleaming hull. The wheelhouse is graceful and generous.

'You like?' Alefu asks, seeing Dad's amazement, sidling up and smiling toothlessly.

'I like,' Dad says, admiration for the old man growing. There are twenty *Warabu* workers standing around, watching the reaction of Dad and his crew to their work of so long. Alefu decides to introduce them.

As he calls their names, each man steps forward and bows his head. Dad says he's never experienced such a formal occasion before, including his decoration with the Distinguished Service Medal. After the last grinning man has gone back to watching, Alefu instructs a woman, who may be a daughter, but just as easily a junior wife, '*tuletee kahawa*', bring us coffee. From now on Mum has to get used to Dad only ever requesting coffee in Swahili, then adding that he needs more *bibis,* or wives, to bring it.

An hour later Dad, Wait and Umali motor out of Port Bell, Uganda Protectorate, en route for Lotanga, near Mwanza in Tanganyika Territory. I will hear the story of that voyage many times. The best account is from Umali, our servant, who achieves my highest esteem and affection as mentor and friend. His version of the voyage is colourful, not through untruth or embroidery, but perception. Umali is a tribesman from a small hamlet near Geita. Although he learnt the skills necessary to be employed by '*Wazungus*', or Europeans, he retains the magical and colourful thinking of his people, and is a

43

deeply entertaining, if superstitious, storyteller. I leave the story of the voyage to him, but something happens at home a week after Dad brings *Lotanga* to Tanganyika for Otto Müller, and I must digress.

It's late at night, and we're all asleep. Mum hears a sound from somewhere in the house and nudges Dad awake. 'There's someone in the house!' she whispers. Dad sits up and listens. Sure enough, he hears a bang, then a curse in German. Footsteps. Someone is walking round the lounge, crashing into furniture. Dad leaps out of bed and dashes to the bedroom door. He opens it deftly and flicks the light switch on the other side. He's encountered by a most curious sight. Caught in the bright light, holding an upside-down bottle of whisky in one hand, and pouring it into a glass, is Otto Müller, clearly the worse for wear already.

'Dick,' he proclaims, 'I am zo hippy you to see!'

'Otto!' Dad breathes, relieved but amazed.

'I vos brink you vun drink, but ziss *verdamte* glass ist licking der viskey!' says Otto, staring perplexedly at his now completely empty bottle. Dad sees the problem at once. Our house-breaking visitor has felt his way into the kitchen in the dark, and found a glass to pour his whisky in. Only it isn't a glass. It's Mum's pie-funnel, for holding up pastry on pies. It's got holes both ends. He has now poured the whole bottle of *Johnny Walker* through the pie-funnel, and all over the lounge floor. When he realises the gravity of the loss, Otto bursts into tears. Seeing his grief, Dad gives his friend his condolences. Luckily, he finds a bottle left over from Christmas, and the men console each other with it. It takes Mum a week to rid the house of the reek of spilled whisky.

Four

Umali is a villainous raconteur and opportunist. He always seems old to me, but never, in all the years, ages more. He's of the *Sukuma* tribe, those who settled locally in antiquity. The word *Sukuma* means 'let us abide in the north'. I decide I must be *Sukuma* too. Umali's in his forties when he comes to us as cook and kitchen help. He's slightly built, thin to the point of emaciation. He has a cap of short snow-white hair, and a wrinkled, hairless face. Unlike many of his tribesmen, he has no ear-piercings, tribal scars or bracelets. He is cantankerous and irascible, but possessed of a satanic sense of humour. He claims he's an accomplished *pishi* or chef, having worked in Mwanza for an Italian family for three years, and Indians for six. He's a *fundi*, he proclaims, in Italian and Indian *cuisine*.

So thin, so small, so bent, so dark, so white-haired, Umali gives the distinct impression, Mum says, of an irreputable, unreliable and untrustworthy garden gnome. But, she stresses, there's a likeable 'twinkle' in his eye. He has a mischievous, captivating grin, with big white teeth glinting in the wrinkled darkness of his face. Except for one tooth, which is missing. Umali is an *mpengu*, or gap-tooth-person. That's the raw beauty of Swahili, it's got wonderful, punchy, descriptive words, even for things like that.

From my earliest recall, Umali is my *rafiki,* friend. He loves my intransigent refusal to take orders from elders, my preference for 'African food' cooked outside, my fluent, poetic, swearing. To me, Umali is sent by a higher power, to encourage wilfulness, disobedience, profanity and non-conformity. And to ensure my Swahili vocabulary, including profanities, grows each day.

Umali becomes for me, not just lovable rogue, but wise and obturate elder of the bush, teacher, protector, story-teller, advisor, comfort, source of humour, not to mention cook, baker and boss of house and garden servant; the diminutive, dull-witted, but immensely strong *Tembo*, or elephant.

By the time I'm five Umali is my closest confidante, teacher and friend. It will be many years before I turn to anyone else. This friendship will largely shape my life. From it I learn to value my elders. They have more to offer than younger people. Wisdom, contemplation, experience, a balanced view and mature humour spring to mind.

I confide a great secret in Umali. I tell him I am going to marry Gretchen.

'The *Geremani* girly with white hair?' he asks. I nod. 'Five years is too young,' he laughs, 'but if you want her, you must never give up. Myself, I prefer someone fatter, and much darker.'

I can't defend Umali from one sad thing: he is a rogue of great stature. While he knows little of Islam, and has never left the environs of the Lake Victoria coast, he pretends to be *Hadji*, one who has made the great pilgrimage to Mecca. His tribe, late converts to Islam, are impressed, which opens a gleefully exploited commercial opportunity for Umali.

Many of the local *watu* are Muslims. Illiterate, far from Mecca and other holy sites, isolated in the bush, they practise very simple Islam. Their food has to be '*hal-al*'. There's a settlement of Ishmaelis, or followers of the prophet Ishmael, who butcher cattle, sheep and goats. Due to tuberculosis in the livestock, expatriates are wary of eating local meat, though fillet steak, well-cooked, is 'okay'. Pork, *haram* to Muslims, comes from the Müller family at Lotanga, and frozen mutton and lamb twice a month on a small *Caspair* charter plane from Kenya.

Chickens, or *kukus*, aren't sold by the Ishmaelis, but still have to be slaughtered according to *Sharia* law. This involves a prayer invoking the blessings of *Allah*, and killing by cutting the throat to let the 'haram' blood drain away.

Umali promotes and advertises his skill and authority to perform Islamic *makuku* executions for a fee, based on him being a *Hadji*. To us he admits he's never been further than Mwanza. I learn not to always trust a religious man. From infancy, I see headless *kukus* run amok in the garden, until, after a few crimson-spurting seconds, they collapse, quiver, and lie still, their smaller feathers wafting in the breeze. *Sumuni* is the charge per *kuku*. Fifty East African cents, or half a shilling. Forty *kukus* meet their maker to earn their killer a pound.

46

Surprisingly, Umali's claims about being a *fundi* in cooking Italian and Indian food are not so far-fetched. The dishes he prepares are excellent, whether Italian, Indian or English.

Umali's an innovator in cooking and baking. Because he never speaks English, the names he gives his creations are never quite right. Bread rolls, baked in the Belling range, are *sconzie*, or scones. Our *sconzie* are the finest, freshest, most wonderful-smelling, crispy, delicious rolls. Umali makes a dozen a day. His names for Italian dishes will lead me into many future and futile arguments. *Spangetti, Ravinoni, Fetevini, Bologniss.*

Rosti is his ubiquitous word for meat, whether fowl, mutton or beef, cooked in the range. It's not easy, because it's wood-fired and needs continual log-feeding. Umali loves to complain. I love his cursing and un-Islamic swearing as he chops wood. His profanity to inanimate wood or oven is both natural and hilarious. Here he invites an iron stove-door which has burnt him to have wanton sex with a lump of wood. Now he calls a too-slow-roasting chicken a base prostitute. The insults and suggestions never affect my appetite.

Umali's wife, my *ayah*, Amina, arrives after him at Geita. They have a tempestuous relationship. He's devoted to her, lusts after her, and believes she's a goddess among women. Our first memories of Amina, who becomes our *ayah*, is of the unforgettable *finya*, or 'pinch'. Amina's *finyas* are excruciating. If we challenge, or fail to respect her, out of sight of our parents, she *finya*'s us.

The action involves firmly grabbing a fold of skin between thumb and index finger, squeezing, then deftly twisting outwards or, in medical parlance, in external rotation of the hand. The pain is quite exquisite.

There's an incident with Amina which Dad notices. She causes one of us to cry. There's a fuss. He threatens her. She doesn't understand. He doesn't clock her bawdy riposte. She survives.

Amina has two large, rabbit-like teeth in front, and no others. She's a real *mpengu*, of many gap-teeth. She's thin and dark, like Umali. She has livid scars on her cheeks and forehead, her arms and neck. During a long and passionate affair with Nubian gin, drinking leagues above a reasonable quota, she engages in vicious no-holds-barred fights with other *wanawake*, or women, and even men. Becky and I have discovered domestic disruption through alcohol intoxication. We'll see much more in Geita.

Sometimes Amina turns her drunken fury on Umali. By the time I'm six it is a regular experience to open the back door to a wide-eyed, terrified, Umali, who gasps for sanctuary, lest he expire from the attentions of his wife. We let him into the kitchen, slam and bolt the door just in time to stop an axe or panga-wielding, wildly enervated, red-eyed Amina making his worst fears come true. Umali, cowering in the kitchen, says, '*yeye majinga.*' She's an idiot. '*Uso kama samaki!*' he adds. Face like a fish. Safe enough to say that with a locked door and a whole family of *Wazungu* between him and her.

Then Amina's sober again. Umali beams with happiness, his near escape forgotten, and regains the bounce in his step. She cooks for him on a fire outside their quarters, lavishes affection on him, and she seems, to the uninformed, a model wife. Umali, like his tribesmen unafraid of talking about such things to children, tells us '*jigi-jigi ana rudi.*' Sexual intercourse is back. Until next time. Reminds me of those spiders where the female eats her mate after sex. It seems like love for a while. . . It doesn't strike me as strange or unusual that I, four years old, should be discussing an adult man's sex-life with him.

Despite her proclivity to overindulgence and violence, Amina is, paradoxically, a kind and worthy woman. She keeps a close rein on Becky and me, and we know how far we can go. As we grow older, the *finyas* peter out and stop. Amina turns to persuasion, and finds it works better. She's kind to us, thoughtful and humorous. She has the loudest, most raucous laugh. Her spitting accuracy is Olympic gold-class.

In Tanganyika, as in many parts of sub-Saharan Africa, the *watu* eat a variety of insects. In Geita one is very popular. We call them 'flying ants', though the scientific name is *Pseudocanthotermes*. After heavy rain, as often as four times a year, they emerge *en-masse* from the ground. They're an inch long, a third in width, white, soft-bodied, plump creatures, with flimsy, transparent wings when they come out. They take to the air in huge swarms, and flutter about in what seems a meaningless frenzy, but to them is the mating ritual. After only a brief career as sexual aviator, they lose their wings and fall to earth, mounds of crawling food.

When they fall the *watu*, using pots and baskets, run around gathering them. The wispy, tissue-thin wings not already shed are plucked off. Heaving potfuls are cooked on fires.

Becky and I lack culinary inhibitions. We love the taste and texture of pot-roasted flying ants. They're buttery and salty, and have the texture of crunchy peanut butter. A mouthful is six to eight at a time. They add deliciousness to *ugali* or maize porridge.

Mum remonstrates with Amina and Umali when she sees us eat flying ants. It's her fault, she says. She should never have let us spend so much time with the servants. She allowed it against her better judgement, and what she gets is us eating insects! She tells Umali ants are *off* our menu. He pretends to agree. Becky and I become the keenest gatherers of the fluttering bonanza. Mum gives up. Like Napoleon, she chooses battles she can win. She never tells Dad. The thought will make him ill, she says.

He would be ill too, if he looked at some of the other food. The *watu* love eating, but don't restrict their diet like the *Wazungu*. The furry lower legs of goats or sheep, roasted on a fire until the hair's burnt off, are delicious to gnaw on. Fish heads, complete with eyes and tiny brain, go well with ugali, as do huge, chewy, sheep's eyes. I spit a small hard bit out when I eat an eye. Someone tells me it's a lens, whatever that is. Intestines, barely cooked in boiling water, and dipped in a homemade chilli sauce, are great to tear 'tween hand and teeth.

Every town has its memorable street-characters. The bearded one-eyed tramp scaring small children, the loud vegetable hawker, the threatening beggar, the over-aged prostitute pounding her well-worn beat. Geita has Mlozi. He's between twenty and thirty, people think. According to his late mother, he was born in the year of the 'great rain'. This pins it down nicely. The monsoons bring big rains *every* year. Maybe her roof leaked, or water ran under her door. Who knows? Something to do with rain. Mlozi's age is approximate.

He sits on a huge *mwamba* or flat granite rock at the end of Top Road, next to the turn-off up Compound Hill. *Mwamba*s like this are the sort of places where chiefs stand to talk to their tribe. They're sacred, so Mlozi must think he's important. He's there every day, from sunrise till after sunset. He sleeps somewhere in the compound, although nobody knows where. Somebody's sheltering and feeding him, because Mlozi does nothing except sit and talk to himself, yet, though filthy and odoriferous, he looks in good health.

He wears strips of cloth. Not just old rags, like many *watu*, but purposefully torn ribbons of fabric, of every colour. Where he gets it, nobody knows. He wears a *moochi* made of strips of green, red, orange and blue cloth, all knotted together, only just preserving his modesty. Sometimes. There are torn coloured ribbons plaited into his thick, overgrown, hair and wispy beard. More round his forehead and neck. He is truly Ribbon-Man.

He has *mifupa*, or bones. At least a dozen are tied round each ankle on thin rawhide cords. They're dry, make a rattling sound when he moves. Lutoli says they're chicken bones, so they don't really count in *ishara*, or omen, terms. Real witch-doctors have bones from scarier

49

c

animals, like *fisis* or hyenas, or lions. Some even from people! *They* have strong magic. Not Mlozi.

He talks to himself constantly. A whispering commentary, which sounds like two different voices, one male, the other female, giving different views about mundane things. I find it strange, because everyone can *see* the sun's up, the birds are in the sky, *watu* are walking past, the hills are all around. Say something I *don't* know, I think, as Lutoli and I stand and listen. Sometimes he reads my thoughts, leaps to his feet, violently shakes a *Kimbo*-tin full of stones, producing a very loud rattle, and shouts. '*Kwenda wewe!*' He continues 'go you, don't come here, return home!' His eyes bulge like a frog's, veins stand out on his neck. The *Kimbo*-rattle alone is enough to send Lutoli and I running. Yet we find Ribbon-Man irresistibly magnetic. It becomes a game of dare. How long dare we stay before we run? Dread, fear, delicious panic. Beats boredom.

As time passes, we flee less quickly. This drives him to ever louder stone-in-the-tin and ankle-chicken-bone rattling and shouting. Lutoli says Mlozi's possessed by a *jinni* or *djinn*. Bad spirit or demon. His fat aunt told him. Amina says he's just mad. Umali reserves his judgement.

We go past Mlozi often. The road's perfect for our *garis*, or cars. These we make ourselves. We get steel wire from the mine-store dump. There's long pieces in lengths and coils, all discarded. First we make two wheels. They're circles of wire, with a middle bit forming a foot-long axle. Then we make little wire loops to attach the middle of the axle to a long stick. On the top of the stick we make a wire steering-wheel. When they're finished, we walk about pushing the contraptions in front of us. It's amazing how well they work. Turning the steering wheel immediately turns the wheels on the axle. Over time, we make better and better models. Technology marches on. Top Road's the best place to drive our *garis*. It's smoother than all the other roads. That's why we see Mlozi so often. A couple of times he scares us so much we run off leaving our *garis* behind.

There's an open-air dump on the ground near the engineering works. There's all kinds of discarded rusting iron things there. The most interesting are the 'war helmets'. There are hundreds of them. They're World War II British army helmets. They're so old, and have been exposed to the elements so long, that none of them have any webbing or straps left. Some have neat round holes in one side, and some have two holes on opposite sides. Lots of people on the mine take un-holed ones home, to use as water-basins for their dogs, or their chickens. Umali tells me how they came to be here. After the war, an enterprising Arab, or *Mwarabu*, bought them from wandering Dervishes who found them on old battlefields in the North African desert. He put them on a *dhow* and brought them south to Dar es Salaam, where a *Mzungu* from Geita mine bought them for underground use by African mineworkers. They were so uncomfortable, the *watu* refused to wear them, and hence they were dumped next to the engineering workshop. These helmets, and lots of other things we find on the dump, are, to Lutoli and me, the nearest equivalent to Aladdin's cave. We will spend many happy hours hunting in this treasure trove. Lutoli cuts an interesting profile, bare-foot, dressed in rags, carrying a spoked motorcycle wheel, and sporting a rusted, holed British army *tin-hat* which covers his eyes and half his face!

At home I discover the *wasikini. Masikini* is a poor person. *Wa* is a plural prefix in this case, though plurals have varying rules in Swahili. In Geita *wasikini* don't only lack goods and money, but also have visible and pity-provoking physical defects. It seems *wasikini* always have a crippled leg, shrivelled hand or cast eye. They're invariably thin and emaciated, and have a skin disorder. With these attributes, the *wasikini* are qualified to beg from the *Wazungu*. Only *they* have the right, they believe, and, though other, healthier, *watu* may try, there's an informal, but very efficient, *wasikini* trade union which will go to great trouble to stop them.

Stories abound of this or that *mutu* being given a pair of old trousers or a bag of sugar, only to be ambushed, assaulted and robbed by several cast-eyed, withered-legged and psoriatic *wasikini* on the footpath. They always seem to know. Mum says it's bush-telegraph, but I don't know what she means. There's 'telegraph poles' sticking into the sky in Mwanza, so maybe it's to do with the sky. Communication through the sky, one pole to another. But I haven't seen telegraph poles in the *bush*!

The *wasikini* call one at a time. Knock on door, open it, *masikini* outside, leaning on withered leg, eyeing me through good eye, cast eye staring blindly over my head. '*Masikini*,' he or she says in a special voice, as if it isn't evident. Said this way, the word doesn't just mean poor person. It's a whole sentence, which says 'I'm a poor, *pitiable* poor, person, look how unlucky and miserable I am, feel pity, Oh Great One, and lessen my suffering by showing generosity.' It's accompanied by a carefully cultivated sob. The cruel world is causing heartbreak.

'*Jambo*,' I say. Hello. It's a brash response to a thespian masterpiece.

'*Jambo Bwana Mkubwa*,' he or she answers, still whining. Hello Big Master. I like this. Nobody else says I'm big.

'How are you?' I ask, knowing the answer.

'Bad, Master, very bad!' These people should be on the stage.

Mum comes to the door. She takes pity, gets distressed by the *wasikini*'s tales of woe, which are slickly adapted according to audience response. The *wasikini* discover losing young infants presses Mum's pity-button, and now all *wasikini* at our door have been preceded to the grave by their cherubic, loved *watotos*.

Mum tries to ease their pain by giving generously. The recipient changes to business-mode, examines the spoils efficiently. 'This has a hole in it!' he or she might proclaim, or 'Is this *all* the sugar you have?' When satisfied, or realising there's no more today, the *masikini* prepares for next time. He or she becomes a mystic and sorcerer. The cast eye is fixed. The other glazes over. 'Good luck will be yours, God will help you, and the fortunes will favour you,' the *masikini* says, with the air of one who decides. It adds superstitious fear. You'll be nice next time.

Mum's a *wasikini* gold-mine, Umali complains, '*I* wanted that jug and blanket!' Mum hunts around, finds something else for him. Between the *wasikini* and Umali, it's an expensive thing.

One day when I'm four, Becky falls out the big tree in the front garden. I don't have a clue what she's doing up there. At least when boys climb a tree it's for *proper* reasons! Someone runs and tells Dad. He arrives so quick it's like a miracle. I've just come out of the house to see why Becky's screaming, when MZ202 careers into the dirt driveway in a cloud of dust, scattering small stones. I'm taken by surprise, and Dad misses me by inches. If not for Becky's screams and the bright blood pouring from her left ear, he'd rebuke me for nearly being hit. He gathers her up, puts her on the passenger seat, orders me off the driveway and roars off to the hospital.

Becky's injury isn't as serious as it looks. A small stick's penetrated her eardrum and burst a blood vessel. She isn't going to miss the opportunity to get everything she can. Dad has to take her to Barrat's store on the way back from Dr Weiss. She returns to the house, turban-like bandage on her head, and a huge packet of sweets in her hand. She gives me a few, but not many.

A few days later Dad takes me along for the ride when he calls on a big-shot on Top Road. He stops MZ202 outside the big-shot's house, pulls up the handbrake and tells me to wait. He's barely gone when I decide to give the handbrake a try. I take it in both hands and try to push it down. It won't budge. There's a spring-loaded black button on the end. I try pressing it in, then pushing the lever down. It gives way with a sudden jolt.

The Land Rover begins, ever so slowly, to run downhill. It gathers speed. Then Dad's running beside it, yelling. He manages to yank open the door and jump in my side, frantically reaching over me to grab the handbrake. We're going faster, nearing a thirty foot precipice, when he manages to do it. MZ202 slows and skids to a halt, back wheels locked, front wheels inches from the edge.

'Don't ever do that again!' Dad exclaims when he stops puffing.

'*Nini?*' I say. What?

Dad tells Mum. 'First he gets in my way in the driveway, then he tries to go over a cliff in the Land Rover,' he says. 'Has Jimboy got a death-wish?'

Five

In July 1956 we travel to Europe. For me it's the first of many trips to the 'old country'. Dad's contract includes two weeks' annual leave in East Africa, and three months abroad after two years. Dad's been asked to combine his long leave with buying advanced winding engines for the ropeway. These are manufactured in Munich, Germany, and he has to go there to discuss details with the manufacturer. I turn five at the beginning of the month, and am so excited by the prospect of going on a big aeroplane that I can hardly sleep the last two nights. I've longingly watched the *Caspair* mail-plane fly overhead most weeks when it comes to Geita from Nairobi in Kenya. It's a single-engined Cessna, and lands on the grass runway a mile beyond the club. I've never been in a plane. Dad says we're flying in a DC4 *Argonaut*, a very big aeroplane. The anticipation is almost more than I can bear.

We drive by Land Rover to Mwanza, where we catch our old friend the *gari moshi* to Dar. Forty-eight hours of jolting, blazing daytime heat and dust, welcome night-time cool, soot in the eye looking out the window. Sometimes the hissing locomotive does it out of pure spite. '*Take that, take that, take that!*' it wheezes jubilantly when I recoil to rub smarting eyes. Wild game, African villages, sweltering water-stops at desolate, seedy stations like Tabora and Dodoma.

Other stations are even more forsaken, where, though there's hardly any evidence of the hand of man on the countryside, scraggy, half-naked hawkers fight to get to our windows, screeching the virtues of proffered animal carvings, patterned *kanzus* or loincloths, bananas, mangoes and oranges. At each stop another tribe. Who cares? The only thing which matters is the big plane, and soon we'll be on it.

In Dar I have to wait two more whole days. There's been a delay. Plane needs a spare part, somewhere called Benghazi, Dad says. We book into the *Inn By The Sea*. It's a small collection of round huts and rusty iron roofs, just above the high-tide mark on the beach. The huts are bedrooms. There's one big one with bath and toilets.

Becky and I are only interested in the sea. The beach is on the side of the sheltered harbour entrance. There are no natural waves here, but when a ship goes in or out, the wake sends mountains of water rolling our way. Mum makes us wear a water-safety-thing she's constructed. It's a jacket-cum-armband, of stitched canvas, filled with hundreds of bottle-corks. Got them from the club. It goes all the way from my neck to my belly-button, and as far as my elbows each side. Wearing it I feel like a tree, I'm that stiff. When the ship's-wake-rollers come, I have to stand and jump vertically, because I can't bend.

One morning I find a thing of stunning beauty on the beach. It's at the high-water mark, where driftwood is piled high by the receding tide. It's a car's steering wheel. I have no idea how it got there, but I am immediately smitten. It's a spoked, chromed wheel, with a big bright-red boss in the middle. A logarithmic improvement on the wire steering wheels I play with in Geita. Not that I understand logarithms. I run up and down the beach, steering my imaginary car, making engine and gear-changing sounds. I get encouraging shouts from *Warabu* fishermen. '*Upesi, upesi!*' they shout. Faster, faster!

I persuade Mum and Dad to ask the hotel manager to look after my steering wheel while we're away in England, so I can collect it on our way back. Only when he's agreed do I relax. The manager tells Mum and Dad I've spent too much time with natives, because European kids don't get attached to garbage. Have to watch it, or I'll be speaking Swahili in preference to English. Mum and Dad laugh. It's too late for Jimboy, who's careering about the beach, steering with the wheel, shouting Swahili abuse at other imagined drivers, to the delight of several elderly *Warabu* fishermen.

The delayed *Argonaut*'s even bigger than I imagined. I spot it when we emerge from the concrete airport building onto the tarmac. It stands sideways-on, with an iron staircase going up from the ground, so long I think of Jack and his beanstalk, which Mum has read to me lots of times in her attempts to improve my English. Only it doesn't end in cloud, like the illustration. Instead, it leads to an open door in the huge, gleaming silver fuselage, which suddenly looks, to me, far *too* big. *BOAC* is emblazoned in huge letters above a row of square windows. *British Overseas Airways Corporation.* The behemoth's wing is so long it almost touches the terminal building. The shadow it casts is as dark as the sky is bright. Slung under it, side by side, are two engines, each as big as Dad's Land Rover. The propeller blades are like gargantuan art-statements,

55

pointing at sky, ground, building, and me. Suddenly I realise this thing *cannot* fly!

I stop walking and announce to my family that, though I'm very grateful for Dad's kind intentions in taking us to Europe, I personally have now had enough holiday, I've got a lovely steering wheel, this aeroplane definitely cannot fly, and I'll appreciate being taken back to Geita immediately. It's said in Swahili, but they get the gist.

'*Hakuna barabara ju!*' I add for completeness. There's no road up there! Umali says so. Flying is impossible, even though he's seen the small planes at Geita *kiwanja ya ndedge*, landing place of the bird, or aerodrome. Sorcery or trickery, one or the other. He's a strange Muslim!

'Of course it flies,' Dad says, putting an encouraging hand on my shoulder and squeezing, 'it'll be alright Jimboy, really!' I look up and see his confident smile. He looks relaxed. Who am I to believe, him or my instinct?

'It's really okay,' Mum says, also smiling. She doesn't look frightened.

'Don't be silly Jim,' Becky says. She's holding Mum's hand. She doesn't look as sure as she sounds. She's very loyal to Dad. Are they in cahoots? Or is a cahoot a kind of cigar I've seen some men smoke?

'This plane flies every day,' Dad says, bending down to make eye contact. He puts his hand on my other shoulder. 'There's nothing to worry about, Jimboy, really.' He kisses my cheek, then stares me in the eye. 'Would I lie to you?'

'No,' I say uncertainly, searching his eyes for giveaway signs of dishonesty. I don't see any. 'Alright,' I say after a long pause, 'I'll go.' There is no option. Dad gives me a soggy toffee.

We're strapped into our seats. I have to admit they are nice, comfortable seats. There are clean white covers on the back tops. To stop Brylcreem staining the seats, Dad says. Why do men put greasy stuff on their hair? Before Dad can answer, there's a retort from an engine exhaust. One by one the four Rolls Royce Merlin engines cough, splutter, then roar into life, and the huge propeller blades disappear into a whir. I'm amazed I can see through them. The tarmac, for example, or a *mutu* with what looks like two red ping-pong bats.

In turn the engines roar louder and louder, reaching a crescendo, shaking the huge plane like a leaf, before cutting back to guttural grumbling. Testing, Dad says. Doesn't sound good. Testing for *what*? Even the pilot doesn't know if this thing can fly! My misgivings grow. Before I can tell Dad I'd like to reconsider, the four engines bellow together, too loud for talking. The monster begins to roll.

After a long time we turn onto the runway and stop. The engines thunder again, and things outside begin to zoom past, faster and faster. It's a race to nowhere. Suddenly the angle changes, and the ground leaves us. Up and up, everything below smaller and smaller. Patchwork. Cloud. White cotton wool wafting across the windows. Sun breaks through. Cotton wool below. Blue sky, bright sunlight on shiny wing, toy-land way down there. I fall asleep cuddled into Dad. They laugh. At last I've worn myself out.

The BOAC route to England is by five dog-legs in a general northerly direction, each four to six hours long. My memories are patchy. First stop Nairobi, Kenya Colony. Evening, getting dark. Small bus to airport hotel. Early morning, board again, fly to Khartoum, Sudan. Waiting in steaming terminal for someone important, 'running late'. Finally comes. Hot and bothered, fat and bald, white safari suit, speaks French. Stinks of *mavi*, or poo. Mum says it's garlic, but I'm sure it's poo!

Next stop Benghazi, Libya. Overnight again. Hot, smelly room in strange hotel. Incense, Mum says. Walk in bazaar. Arab men sucking smoke up tubes from big bottle, making gurgling noise. *Hubble-bubble,* Dad says. Smells like a bonfire. Shifty grey-bearded character in *dishdash* offers six camels for Becky. Blonde girls, premium prices. Dark hair, only four camels.

By this calculation, Gretchen is worth more than Becky. I agree with that. I tell Dad it's better we sell Becky than Gretchen, even if we get less camels. 'You say price Meester,' the shifty man says when Dad doesn't haggle. 'I good man, I look her good!' he pleads as we walk away. We remind Becky of the Arab who looked-her-good for years. And Dad reminds me I was ready to sell my sister. To make up, I tell Becky that, when she marries, I wish her husband looks-her-good. We leave at midday. Rome. Evening. Stay in lovely room with balcony overlooking the Tiber. Lots of little boats. Last leg to London. Arrive early afternoon.

Most of our leave is in Cornwall. I meet granny, Dad's mum, for the first and only time. Strange old lady. Very thin, one eye looking sideways. A white *masikini*. Squint, Mum says. Not her fault, so don't stare. I never meet Dad's father, Edgar. He died before I was born. Houses in Cornwall are small, poky. Gardens tiny, wet, slippery. It never stops raining. It's misty too. They call it *mizzle*.

Germany. We stay in a small hotel in Munich, where Dad is seeing people about ropeway engines. Two things are clear. One is whatever we see or do, it's offered '*mit music*'. Applies to buying a jewellery box for Mum, clock for Dad, doll for Becky, toy car for me. The Germans have decided to put music into, or adjacent to, everything.

Indeed, we are asked, when Dad books a table for dinner, if we want it *'mit music'*. For a fee of fifty *schillings,* the restaurant manager puts a record on. Will the other diners object, I wonder. They don't. Dad pays, and we are serenaded with gusto by Germans singing along to *Um-pa-pah* music.

Dad goes off somewhere about the ropeway engines, and Mum takes Becky and me for a walk. It's eleven years after the end of the war, but much of Munich is still scarred and broken. It was the carpet-bombing of 1945, Mum says. Many bombed out ruins are boarded off. Construction is everywhere, great cranes dissecting the skyline. We come to a place where the pavement runs beside a park hit by a big bomb.

On one side is a massive crater. At the bottom, standing axle-deep in muddy water, is a child's pram. The metal parts are rust-red, but the blue and white striped canopy still looks new. We can see inside. There's a piece of blanket, green with mildew, but with patches of red and white pattern still visible. Half in, half out of the pram is a doll, its head turned to one side, glass eyes staring. Mum says the pram was for the doll. Becky and I can see it's too big. The doll was in the pram when the bomb struck. Held by a baby!

I have a nightmare about the pram. Pretty lady, like Mum, pushing pram with baby clutching doll. Whistling sound, louder and louder. I saw a film once about the London blitz. Bombs whistle as they fall. Bang. *Ka-boom*, Pretty lady blown apart. Baby, pram, flying high in air. Pram lands on wheels, doll half in – half out. Blood all over. Isn't that what happens? There's *always* blood if you get hurt.

'Can I see General von Lettow Vorbeck?' I ask Dad. After all, we're in Germany, and I'd like to ask him to come back and start a new war, with me as an *askari*.

'Out of the question!' says Dad, who's busy looking at a brochure, in German, of steel cables.

We go home by mail-ship. Board MS *Windsor Castle* at King George VI docks in London. First port of call, Gibraltar. Stop at Barcelona, Genoa, Port Said, Egypt. We enter the Suez Canal. At the southern end is the sweltering and dusty town of Suez. We continue south into the Indian Ocean, to Mombasa, Zanzibar, and, finally, Dar es Salaam. I see too many things to remember, eat lots of ice-cream and swim in the ship's salt-water pool.

The rolling waves look like beaten copper at dusk, with the plunging sun turning everything golden. Then it's daylight, and the water is blue or green. I never tire of staring at the hypnotic, restless sea. Blue, golden, green. Never the same. Soapy suds froth in the ship's wake and there's bleached-white on the tops of breaking waves.

They call them 'white horses', though I can't see an equine connection. Big people have odd notions.

In Dar I haven't forgotten my beach-found steering wheel. The manager at the *Inn By The Sea* has kept it safe, and I'm joyously reunited with it. He says it belonged to an American car. Chevrolet.

The *gari-moshi*, through the same countryside as I knew before. It's a comfort to be back where the land isn't uniform peppermint-green, marshmallow-soft and wet, where the sky is wide and blue, not closed and grey, where rain, when it briefly comes, is sudden, flooding and oh-so quenching, and doesn't gently weep in wind-driven icy misery all day long. That's how I remember our trip to *Uriah,* or Europe.

Now it's Mwanza, Land Rover, home, steered all the way by me, with my shiny Chevrolet wheel. 'Der kind iss liking der veel!' Fritz remarks, surprising Dad by talking. Geita, at long, long last. The big aeroplane to England did fly, I have to admit, but I like it not one bit. It isn't how it should be. Too big, too heavy, too noisy. I'm amazed we survived, that we're back, still alive. Never again, I promise myself. The ship was altogether better.

It's strange how quickly life returns to normal after a long time away. Within days our epic journey to England and Germany, and all the places *en-route*, are distant history. It's just like old times when I go with Umali to Barrat Stores. We're walking along Top Road when we see a big group of *watu* standing near the turnoff up Compound Hill. It's where Mzlozi, *djinn* or *jinni*-possessed ribbon-man, hangs around on his flat rock or *mwamba*. We join the crowd, who're in jolly mood and much-entertained.

Mlozi's predicting the future. He's got even more colourful ribbons and stripes on his hair, forehead and neck. He's more animated than we've ever seen him. He's jumping from foot to foot on his *mwamba*, making the dry chicken *mifupa*, or bones, sound like galloping hooves, at the same time rattling his *kimbo*-tin and stones. His knotted-ribbon *moochi* is loose, and we can see his *mboro*, or willy. If it was only Lutoli and I here, we'd be running for safety by now. Umali senses my anxiety, takes my hand in his. '*Pole*, Jimu,' he whispers. Be restful, Jimu. The surety of his hand calms my fears. With Umali, no *djinn* or *jinni* can get me.

'The world will end, all will die in months three!' Mlozi shrieks. He rattles louder. Several *watu* giggle.

'A long snake will bite you while you sleep at night!' More giggling. Entertainment like this is rare.

'Whose snake?' a woman asks. More *watu* giggle. Mlozi's ill-fitting moochi has been noticed.

A laughing young man in a mine-helmet and very shredded shirt takes the stage. 'Is it the snake of your pants?' The crowd erupt in merriment; one fat *mama* actually falls over she laughs so hard. Her *kikapu,* or basket, bursts open and oranges roll down the hill. This is Geita cabaret. Even Umali and I are laughing. We haven't thought of an *mboro* as a pants-snake before.

'Just mine, just mine,' Mlozi mutters, suddenly deflated, stopping in mid-dance, sitting down on his rock, returning to his soft, rhythmic muttering monologue. Just mine, just mine. Is he saying his *mboro* is going to bite while people sleep? That's funny. . . but he looks so sad. He begins to mumble descriptions of the sky, the hills, the trees. Why does he always do that? Can't he see we've *all* got eyes? It's difficult to hear him after all his yelling. It seems he's talking to someone invisible, answering questions. I wonder why he shakes his *Kimbo*-tin-and-stone-rattle when he makes a speech.

The *watu* begin to drift off. Umali says he thinks Ribbon-Man *is* mad after all, like Amina says. He personally doesn't believe in *djinns* or *jnnis.* It's un-Islamic, and he's a *Hadji* after all. As we walk away, I see Mlozi's crying. There are fat tears streaming down his face. Until now I haven't felt pity. Suddenly I do.

I see Gretchen. I didn't notice her arrive. She looks pretty in denim dungarees and a floral shirt. She's sad. 'Vy zey they make fun uff him?' she asks.

'Dunno,' I say.

Six

They come with a soft, high-pitched drone, in the torpid air of night. The female anopheline mosquito seeks a blood meal, and the unwilling donor is human. While drinking, she unknowingly injects a terrible parasite. *Plasmodium Vivax, Ovale, Malariae* or *Falciparum* are the agents of malaria. It's endemic in sub and equatorial Africa. The fly-screens on the windows give false security. The mosquitos get in, and navigate up the concentration gradient of exhaled carbon dioxide, to find unprotected skin to pierce with hair-thin, needle-sharp, probosces. Then they drink.

Dad complains of a headache in the morning, and by afternoon develops high fever. For the first time in almost five years in Geita he comes home early from work. He's been used to poor health since the war. He takes tablets for epilepsy, and can't exert himself because his heart won't keep up. Rheumatic fever after the loss of HMS *Turtle* off Grimsby, and four hours in the North Sea, is the cause.

Dad works on, refusing to go off sick, often when he should. He's been unwell ever since the war. 'Don't say anything to anyone, Mummy,' he says when she pleads. 'They'll fire me, then just *what* shall we do?'

Today's different. He can hardly walk. Mum sees him get out of the Land Rover, and knows something's wrong. She opens the door and helps him to the bedroom. He lies down. Becky and I have been playing in the garden, her with a doll, me with my Chevrolet steering-wheel and a rusty army helmet on my head. We see Dad stagger to the house.

'Daddy needs to rest,' Mum says when we try to see him. We have lost interest in our games. We sit in the lounge and watch Mum walk from the bedroom to the kitchen and back. She takes him a drink.

'Is Daddy alright?' Becky asks.

'He'll be fine,' Mum says, voice strained. After an hour she decides to call the doctor. 'Stay here and be good,' she says as she goes. The doctor's house is half a mile up the hill. Mum can't drive, so she walks. There are no telephones, apart from the radio-phone at head office.

We wait a long time. We don't hear any sound from the bedroom, and are afraid to check. Finally there's a crunch of tyres on gravel, and Dr Weiss's car is outside. Mum hurries up the steps, through the lounge to the bedroom. Dr Weiss follows.

Josef Weiss. As mentioned before, a German Jew, doctor, Auschwitz survivor. He comes to Tanganyika, of all places, in 1948, looking for a new life. Mother, father, two brothers, a sister, all perish. He meets his wife in a resettlement camp in 1945. She's a survivor from Treblinka. In 1957 he's a portly sixty, with thin grey hair, round steel-rimmed spectacles, and, despite life experience, a wicked, even warped sense of humour.

Josef tells Dad two things when they meet in '51. Dad is, he proclaims, the 'spitting image' of Edward, Duke of Windsor. Come to think of it, he isn't wrong. When Dad meets Marina, Josef's wife, she gasps and says, 'You iss der double uff zat luffly man!' The second thing Josef tells Dad is that he shouldn't have taken a job in such a disease-ridden place as Geita, given his poor health. Dad pleads with him, says it's his only chance to support his family. Josef, against his better judgement, relents. He lives to regret it.

Now Josef shuffles past Becky and me, winking as he goes. Last time we saw him he made hand signals of giving us an injection, and we ran away screaming. He laughed to bust his gut, the sadist! He enters the bedroom. We strain to hear the voices.

'It vood be best,' we hear Josef say. No humour. Serious.

'Do I *have* to?' Dad answers, sounding tired.

'Best do as Josef says,' Mum says. The door opens. Dad comes out in a dressing gown, leaning on Josef, who looks grave.

'I'm going to hospital,' Dad says, 'be good, you two. Jimboy, you're the man when I'm gone, look after your Mum and Becky.' He gives me a wink, but I see pain in his eyes. He stumbles to Josef's car, like a very old man. Josef closes the door for him. They drive off ever so gently.

Mum tells us about the next hours. Dad is gravely ill. Josef says he's got malaria, but that's not all. His scarred and damaged heart valves, from rheumatic fever after the sinking of HMS *Turtle*, are an ideal site for bacteria to grow. They've thrived, and now he has bacterial endocarditis. Emboli from the infective growths on the valves shoot off all over his body, causing small bright-pink blemishes on his skin. Josef knows the signs.

Dad becomes conscious and looks at Mum's face, leaning close to hear his voice. 'Bring me seven beers,' he says. Josef is close. Why *seven* beers?

'Do it,' he says, 'geef him vot he asks.' Mum goes to the club, comes back with a bottle of Whitecap. She feeds it to him with a teaspoon. He sucks greedily, like a small infant. Suddenly there is a quiver through his whole body. His pupils begin to dilate.

'Becky and Jim!' he says, and his breathing begins to take a strange rhythm. Mum is sitting at the head of his bed, and holds him tight.

'Please Ritchie, darling baby, please don't leave me,' she sobs in his ear. He stops breathing. She holds him even closer. After a long time Josef coughs.

'He vill not suffer any more,' he says.

He can *not* be dead! Not Dad. He can *not* be dead. It's a mistake. A lie. Blackmail. They don't need to do this. There are two women standing ten yards away. One is saying, 'He's dead, Jim,' and the other is Mum, wiping her eyes with a hankie. *Apana*, no!

'He's gone to be with God,' the woman says. 'He's happy now.'

'God?' I say, 'Happy?'

'Yes, God Jimboy,' Mum sobs, reaching for me. She hugs me, I can feel her stomach heave.

'He'll be alright,' the woman says, bending down and putting her arms around me. I pull away. Becky is there. I haven't noticed her. I was playing with a Dinky-car on the ground, driving it up a little road I'd made. What is happening? What do they mean? Dead? They are fibbing. . .

'Daddy's dead!' Becky cries.

'What?' I say.

'He's gone, Jimboy,' Mum says, choking.

'Where's he gone?' I say. He's in hospital. It isn't far. I'll go see him. He's alive. He can't be dead.

'Daddy's gone to be with God,' Mum says, trying not to sob. This is getting serious. They are all saying Daddy is dead. I begin to panic. What if they're right? They can't be! Maybe I should try a different tack. Surely that will show they are making a mistake.

'Why?' I say.

'Nobody knows why,' the woman says. She's Mary O'Rourke.

'But why should Daddy be dead?' I say, my voice becoming a whine.

'God decides,' Mary says.

'I love you,' Mum whispers. Becky sobs. Her face is white, her eyes red. They've known an hour, were terrified to tell me because I'm 'highly strung', and they don't know what I'll do. Vomit. That's what I feel like doing. They can't *all* be acting. Something's happened to Dad. While I was playing with my stupid toys, God's attacked him. He won't get away with it. No! He's *my* Dad, not God's. He can't have him! I don't care if he *did* create the world.

Wesley-Richards is an old London firm of gunsmiths. They're posh and expensive. I know, because Dad paid a hundred guineas for his gun, had to go to the gunsmiths in London for a 'fitting' when it was ordered, and a 'sighting' when it was ready.

The rifle's a 375 Magnum, one of the biggest, most powerful guns in 1957. The calibre makes it an 'elephant gun' in African terms, though Dad doesn't shoot elephants. He buys it because he loves guns. He wants to shoot targets, and maybe defend us from charging rhinos or marauding lions.

I'm four when he first takes me shooting. I'm too small to hold a rifle. Dad kneels on the ground and aims at a tin can. He tells me to pull the trigger. I ask what he means in Swahili. Exasperated, he takes my hand and places my finger on the trigger. I clock him and pull as hard as I can. The gun bellows, the tin leaps brokenly into the air, I shriek in fright, and black smoke belches from the barrel. It smells like a firecracker. I'm shivering. Mum admonishes Dad. 'Make him a man, get him used to loud noise,' he says. He wets the corner of his handkerchief and wipes soot from my cheek. Now my face smells of pipe tobacco. I will always associate that saliva-and-tobacco smell with him. I calm down. Mum returns to sitting on the picnic blanket.

Dad shows me how he loads the gun. He opens it by pulling the knobbly bit upwards and back. He says it's the bolt. A shiny hollow he calls the breech appears. He drops a huge bullet in, and closes the breech again by reversing the bolt. Up to five bullets go into a metal box he calls a magazine, clipped underneath. How can it be a magazine? Mum reads those. Old ones from England, with pretty ladies on. Pulling the bolt back after firing ejects an empty bullet-case or 'cartridge', and inserts a new one.

Suddenly I'm not frightened anymore. It's very loud, true, but I'm not hurt, am I? I pull the trigger again. Another tin jumps skywards. Dad works the bolt. I fire. Again. And again. This is fun! Eventually, despite jumping at every retort, even Mum is grinning. She tells me I am a *fundi* at shooting. Swahili for expert.

Dad takes me shooting many more times in the next year and a half. When he dies, I know exactly how the Wesley-Richards is operated.

'He can't be dead!' I say again, still refusing to believe.

'Now, look, Jim,' says Mary O'Rourke, 'it's no good going on like this. . .' Mary is a close friend of Mum's. She's always popping in for a cup of tea, constantly smoking. I won't forget her brand of cigarettes, because they're very popular in East Africa. *Sportsman Filters*. Made in Kenya.

By five, I'm infatuated with smoking. Lutoli, other African friends and I pick up cigarette butts thrown away by big *Wazungu*, and try smoking them. No amount of coughing or spluttering puts us off. We want to be big people too. I don't know my smoking is noticed. It is, I find out now. Everyone knows Jimmy's a smoker. Mary O'Rourke is holding a full packet of *Sportsman Filters*, in her hand. A red and white packet. Her lips move, and as if from a distance I hear her say, 'You can have these, Jimmy. . .'

What? Is this woman trying to *buy* Dad with cigarettes? Is she crazy? Has she helped God kill Dad? Something stirs deep down. Anger. I look at Mum's pale face, Becky's red eyes. I know what to do. Take action. Fight this. I know how to work Dad's gun. I know where it is, the bullets too. *Piga risasi ko Mungu!* Shoot God! That'll change things. . ! I'm running towards the house. My cheeks are wet, and I can hardly see through my tears. It's a hot day, but the air feels cool on my face. My heart's banging wildly, like it wants to escape my chest. They don't have a clue what I'm going to do. Mum says I just want to be alone. I'll show them. I'm not giving up on Dad.

I get to the bedroom. The gun is in the wardrobe, behind the clothes. I know, because Umali told me that's where Dad keeps his *bunduki*. I pull it out. It's heavy, and the barrel almost hits me on the head. I put it on the bed. The bullets are in a shoe box, under Dad's side. Bullets are called *risasi* here. I take three, stuff them in my shorts' pocket. I heft the gun on my shoulder, holding the butt with both hands. Down the passage to the back door. I don't want to be seen, or they'll stop me.

Down the kitchen steps, across the back yard, into the elephant grass. Need cover. It's taller than me. I disappear. Now! I drop the back end of the gun on the ground, barrel pointing up. God is up there. Holding the barrel between my knees, I take the bolt in both hands and pull it like Dad did. It's stiff. Try again. Moves a little. Massive effort. Snap. Up. Pull back. Slides open with ease. Reach in pocket for *risasi*. Slot into shiny breech. Push bolt forward, down. Easy. Notches into recess by itself. Ready. I reach for the trigger. Hope my aim is right. Have to hit God. See how *he* likes it.

Mum and Becky will speak about that gunshot for years. A 375 magnum is one hell of a gun. The explosion of its cartridge is like the sound of a small bomb. A cracking, whipping, fierce crack. In Geita it shatters the stillness of midday, and bounces off surrounding hills. Cacophony. It echoes and re-echoes for several seconds.

Mum has heard the sound of that discharge many times before. She's recoiled in terror at its venom. She freezes.

'Jim's got the gun,' she shouts at Becky and Mary when the echo stills. 'Oh God, he's got the gun and he's shooting!'

'*Hupo!*' Umali yells, gesticulating as he runs down the steps. 'There!' He points at the grass, where a tendril of black smoke coils into the air.

They start running together. It's only thirty yards. I'm pulling open the breech, fumbling for another bullet. God may not be killed by one shot. Another may do it. I'm sobbing, angry, determined. '*Nta uwa yeye!*' I shout. I'll kill him.

Umali reaches me first. I am still trying to load when he scoops me up, sending the gun clattering onto the ground. He holds me tight. I struggle. My face is wet with tears. I try to lever myself from his chest. He's too strong. Suddenly I notice his face is also wet with tears, his eyes red and swollen.

'*Pole, Jimu,*' he says, '*Pole mtoto!*' Sorry Jim, sorry child.

'I'll kill God!' I sob.

'*Ana jua,*' Umali whispers as I stop struggling. He knows.

'He knows?'

'*Lazima.*' Of course. He's walking now, carrying me back to Mum and Becky, and Mary O'Rourke.

'I'll get the gun,' I hear Mary say. Then Mum is holding me, and we are all crying.

'What were you doing?' Mum asks.

'Shooting that *Mungu*,' I say. I am exhausted. The running, the crying, the shock. I'm asleep almost before she puts me where I want to be. Dad's side of the bed.

I wake in the dark. The crickets are screeching. Far away a single hyena giggles. There's moonlight outside. Mum is talking with someone in the lounge. I hear a man's voice. A gravelly low tone. I don't know who. The gun has to go. Mum agrees.

Something stirs in my chest. We're going to starve! Mum always says Dad's the bread-winner. I've thought it *was* bread he won, loaves, in a curious food-game. Then she explains it means *all* food, and 'winning' is another word for earning. Did Dad die because he didn't eat enough? Starvation's the only thing that can kill a person, isn't it? If only everyone would realise that, nobody would ever have to die. What's *wrong* with people? Anyway, Dad has gone to be with God. Oh hell! If I've killed God, Dad's all alone up there! A bit late now. But food. . . *I* will have to win it, or Becky and Mum will also die. I hold my breath. I can hear the man's voice. Something about 'Little Jim'. They haven't heard me getting up.

I climb through the window. It's six feet from the ground that side, the house being on a slope. The other side's ten foot. Shorter stilts here. There's a patch of sandy ground below. In the pale moonlight it looks a long way down. My throat still aches from crying, and I've a pain in my side where the gun jerked. No time now. I can't let us starve. I drop silently to the ground, the impact buckling my legs. Sprawled out, both knees and hands skinned. I try to ignore the pain, not cry again.

At the far edge of the garden are some untended yards between us and the neighbour. Elephant grass, a few thorn bushes, an anthill. Beyond, the Hewitts have a vegetable garden. The moon slips behind a cloud, everything goes black. I feel my way through the grass. My hands and knees are stinging. I choke on a sob.

I reach the garden. I've been here before. Then it was light. I grope my way to where the carrots grow in rows. By feel alone, I begin to pluck them. I make a pile. Then potatoes. More difficult. They won't come up when I pull the leaves. I feel for a stick. Dig at the ground, scooping away soil with my other hand. In a nearby tree my invisible old friend the *bundi-msitu* bird, that most spooky-sounding of African owls, hoots. What's he trying to tell me? A hyena giggles shrilly, not so far away. I shiver. The crickets are silent. Are they frightened, like me? The moon slides back round the edge of the cloud. Light again. Good. I can see what I am doing. Bad, I can also be seen. The Hewitt's house is quiet. There is only one light on. They don't know.

I have enough potatoes and carrots. I take my shirt and lay it on the ground. I put my haul on it and tie it in a bundle. Time to go.

I haven't thought about going back. I'll never reach the window. I'll have to go in a door. Back door is best. Straight into the kitchen. The voices still come from the lounge. I open the back door and collide with Mum. I drop my bundle, and the carrots and potatoes spill on the floor.

'Jim, what've you done, where've you been?' Mum demands, shocked to see me shirtless, muddy, bleeding from hands and knees.

'I want. . .' I begin, but my voice breaks.

'What's this?' Mary O'Rourke says, bending to pick up my vegetables. The carrots are inch-long, the potatoes marble-sized.

'To get food for you,' I finish, ' 'cos Daddy's gone!'

'Darling,' Mum gasps between sobs, 'we won't starve, I promise.'

Next day she apologises to the Hewitts for my piracy. They understand. My foray has a result. When their vegetables are ripe, they give us some.

Later that night I wake up shivering, as if covered in ice. I'm in bed with Mum and Becky. We cry ourselves to sleep. My throat aches and I shiver so violently my teeth chatter. Mum turns the light on. I'm bathed in sweat, my skin is hot to the touch.

Within hours of the fever I go into a coma. I have seizures. Dr Weiss says it's cerebral malaria, that it's 'bad', that there's little chance I'll survive. He gives Mum a sedative. They say three seizures with cerebral malaria, and you die. I have five. They say malarial coma of more than three days is fatal. Mine is five days. If, by miracle, I survive the coma and seizures, there'll be brain damage. I can't disprove that. Am I brain damaged? Who knows? Can I blame life's failures on *Plasmodium Falciparum* and its *anopheline* carrier? Don't know.

Dad's funeral is during the worst of my illness. Mum talks about it so many times it feels I was there. On that grim day Mum doesn't know if she's going to lose me too. It's a dreadful time for her. The grave has been blasted out of the granite, which is too hard to dig. The rough wooden coffin has rope handles. It's carried by white men, while a knot of *mwanaume*, or men, Dad worked with stand at a respectful distance. Wait's face is streaked with tears. Anand Singh, the Singa-Singa who will replace Dad on the ropeway, is visibly traumatised.

Dr Weiss stands beside Mum, supporting her. It's like a dream. Last time she was here with Dad, he was still alive, and they came to pay their respects to poor Mrs Williams. Mum had a bad feeling then. The murdered woman had, in death, strangely impinged on Dad's life. He'd read about her murder in Johannesburg. Taken a job here, not realising it was the same place. He'd unknowingly sat in her killer's chair, in *her* house, here in Geita. The open grave, waiting to swallow Dad, is right beside Mrs Williams. It doesn't seem real. What chance all this is just coincidence? Is Mrs Williams satisfied now, or does she want others? Mum's upbringing among the deeply superstitious *Pedis* in the Transvaal has affected her deeply.

The priest from Mwanza is talking. His voice seems to come from far away. A time to put away childish things. A time to gather stones together, a time to cast them asunder. . . a time for war, a time for peace, a time to live, a time to die. . . Insects buzz, perspiration itches. Committing departed brother to the earth, in the certain knowledge of resurrection. Coffin is lowering on ropes. *Mwanaume* allowed to do this. Mum takes the first handful of soil from a shovel proffered by a tearful Wait. She lets it fall through her fingers into the grave. It resonates on the lid. What a dreadful thing to be doing, she thinks. Mary O'Rourke hugs her.

The priest starts to sing. A strong baritone. Other voices join. *Nearer my God to thee. . .* More handfuls of earth are dropping. Led by tear-stricken Wait, the *mwanaume* take up shovels. Earth and rock cascade. The last bit of coffin-lid is covered. Mum can't stay. She doesn't want to go, but there may be a new tragedy at home. As they drive away they hear the *mwanaume* singing as they fill the grave. It's a sad sound. An old German hymn, from the days of *Deutsch Ost Afrika*. It's called *Gott is die liebe*, or God is love. They're singing in Swahili.

> *Mungu ni pendo*
> *Apenda watu*
> *Mungu ni pendo anipenda*
> *Sikilizeni furaha yangu*
> *Mungu ni penda*
> *Anipenda*

> *God is Love*
> *Loves his people*
> *God is love, he loves*
> *Listen my friends*
> *God is Love*
> *He loves you*

At home Mum finds Umali and Amina surprised and overjoyed because, after five long days and nights, I open my eyes and ask for *maji baridi*.

'He wants cold water,' Umali laughs delightedly. Amina's doing a little jig.

Mum calls Dr Weiss, who says it's a miracle. 'I haff niffer seen anysing like it!'

I'm sitting up drinking an ice-cold Pepsi, when Mum tells me I've got a visitor. It's Gretchen. She's eight, and a big girl now. She's pretty, with long blonde hair, light blue eyes and even white teeth. She smiles a lot. She's visited every day I've been sick, and just sat by my bed. Mum thinks it's very sweet. One day before I wake up she says to Mum, 'Jim vonte die, like hiss vader, *vill* he?' She's crying, and still has a strong German accent when she's upset.

Dad didn't believe in life insurance. Said nobody should ever benefit from someone's death. He had a point. But Mum is left in the Tanganyika bush with two young children, and two hundred pound sterling in the world. All that stands between us and the 'poor house', she says, is that two hundred pounds. And the tenuous goodwill of Geita Gold Mine. I will test that to the extreme.

Seven

I've never thought about death till now. I turn five in July 1956, Dad dies next February. I'm kept from the realities, never see his body or attend his funeral. I only see his grave months after he dies, when my eldest brother Bertrand drives us there.

They put him in the mortuary near the club. They keep him there two days, while the Chinese carpenters make a coffin, and a grave is blasted from the granite of Samina graveyard. The mortuary or *kifo nyumba* looks like a tiny church. It's twenty foot by ten, and has slit-windows high up to stop peeping.

Kifo nyumba or 'dead-house' is two hundred yards downhill from our garden, and its red tin roof is visible from there. It stands in a small clearing, surrounded by gravel, beyond which wild trees and bushes grow. A footpath leads round the clearing to the door on the far side. Lutoli says the *Wazungu* take bodies there in darkness. He refers to Europeans like I'm not one.

After Dad is dead and buried some weeks, *kifo nyumba* becomes pressingly important to me. I am morbidly fascinated. *Mzogas*. Dead bodies. What are they like? Why don't they move? Do they really smell as bad as they say? How long till they become a 'skelington'? Do 'skelingtons' get up and dance? Seen dancing 'skelingtons' in a cartoon. Not becoming for Dad's 'skelington' to be dancing! That would look happy. Can't dance in a coffin, can you?

Two things happen to exacerbate my curiosity about death and *kifo nyumba*. First is Tembo's puppy, second the passing of Mr Valari (senior).

Tembo is a semi-mute, miniature Gallua tribesman. He's four foot six tall, hardly more than my height at six. He's intellectually challenged, an outcast from his tribe. He works for us from the outset,

71

and lives in an outbuilding in our garden. He has no friends, but is slavishly devoted to Mum who's been very kind to him. It is her who named him *'Tembo'* or 'elephant', and not as a joke. He's small, but prodigiously strong. He has shoulders and arms like a weightlifter, and can lift rocks his own size. He works tirelessly and uncomplainingly. I never know Tembo well, because he rarely speaks, and briefly then.

I don't know where Tembo gets his puppy. It's a curious little dog. Black and almost hairless, it has a fat tummy, and a pencil-thin tail. It never looks healthy. Even as a tiny puppy with half-open eyes, it lies languidly in the heat, and doesn't chase its tail or play. It has an aura of impending death. Something is wrong. At only six, I sense another call from that terrible servant of God the visiting preacher talked about. Angel of death. Not like nice angels. A murdering one.

I come into possession of a glass syringe and needle. I find it in the grounds of the African hospital, litter from a spilled dustbin. I think how unwell Tembo's puppy is, and decide to help. I will give it an injection, like Dr Weiss. What does he inject? Water. Obvious. What else goes through a needle? I'll fill the syringe, and inject Tembo's puppy. It will fix him, whatever's wrong.

Tembo, surprisingly, doesn't countenance my cunning plan. In his limited way he says I shouldn't. I look at his puppy lying listlessly, and decide I *have* to, Tembo or no. I fill the syringe, a five-millilitre one, with tap water, put the needle on, and await my chance. At midday Tembo disappears into his quarters. I strike. The puppy doesn't even wince when I plunge the needle into his thin buttock. He squirms weakly when I press the plunger to force water in. It's over. I flee the scene, my good deed done. He is my first patient. I never imagine the day I will become a doctor, move to England, specialise, and lecture at medical school. . !

I don't know exactly why the puppy dies that afternoon. Was it going to anyway? Has my injection done it? Tembo finds him lying dead, and brings his *mzoga*, or corpse, accusingly to me. I haven't expected my patient to die, at least not so soon.

I'm stunned and sobered. Mixed feelings. On one hand I'm horrified, and feel for Tembo and his puppy. On the other, there's a dawning realisation. If, indeed, I killed the puppy, that makes me less than powerless regarding death. When Dad died I had nothing to do with it. I neither saved nor killed him. I was only told it had happened. I was totally and completely powerless in its presence. Death is an independent, overwhelming, insurmountable force, over which I have no control or influence. Only God has that. That's why I shot him.

This is different. Whether causative or failing-to-treat-successfully,

I'm instrumental in a death. Horrible, but exciting. A glimmer into a power I wanted when Dad died. With it I can *reverse* his death.

I help sad Tembo dig a grave. He lowers the tiny *mzoga* and covers it with soil. I fashion a cross from two sticks and one of Dad's remaining pipe cleaners. The little mound and cross is all that remains. It is not the end of the matter. I've found an opportunity to research a question which has haunted me: how long till a *mzoga* is a 'skelington'? I'll revisit Tembo's puppy.

Mr Valari (senior) is in his sixties. I'm not sure why he's in Geita, because he doesn't work. He lives with his son, Mr Valari (junior), and his wife and children. They're Italian. His son is an electrician.

It's shortly after I turn six, five months after Dad's death, a month after Tembo's puppy, that the news breaks. Mr Valari (senior) is dead. I don't know what he looks like alive, because he's a recluse who seldom ventures beyond his son's wood-built house. Now he's joined the legion of the dead. This time I'll not be sidelined and denied the knowledge. On the day he dies, I resolve to peep into *kifo nyumba*. I'm determined to see a human *mzoga*.

From the age of two I've been trying to make things from wood and nails. By six I'm an accomplished *fundi*. In Geita, it seems, everyone's a *fundi*, or expert, at something. I find some discarded planks and begin to build a ladder. It's so poor, Tembo, uninvited, comes to help. He neither asks, nor seems interested, what it's for. It's five or six feet high, with a step every foot. Interestingly, it's later used by Mum to reach ripe pawpaws in our garden, and is still around ten years later.

It's still the day of Mr Valari (senior)'s expiry. Before nightfall I drag the ladder through the elephant grass next to the road, and hide it in the bushes next to *kifo nyumba*. When they put Mr Valari (senior) there, I'll climb up to the slit windows. Then I'll see how a dead person looks!

I don't know if they'll put him there that day or the next morning. Either way, I am resolute. Maybe, even, my new-found power around death and dying, which I've found with Tembo's puppy, will enable me to bring Mr Valari (senior) back to life. If I can do that, I'll find out more about my power. Using that, I'll get Dad out of his grave at Samina. Isn't that what happened in the Bible? Jesus came back. Someone else must have been involved. Anyone who can bring a dead person to life must at least have killed a puppy.

Next day, when I'm sure Mr Valari (senior)'s *mzoga* is in *kifo nyumba*, I creep there under cover of the bushes and elephant grass. It's around noon. Most people are sheltering from the sun.

My ladder's heavy, and I struggle to place it against the wall.

73

d

Nobody can see me from the road. The only moving thing is a *mwewe* bird, or hawk, a miniature black shape soaring high in the sun-scorched sky. He's like a small black crucifix against the pale blue. I wonder if he can see me. With the ladder in place, I begin to climb. The top of the ladder is just under the sill of a slit widow. It's very wobbly. I reach the window and look in. For a few seconds I see nothing but darkness. Outside it's fierce sunlight. Inside it's gloom. Slowly my eyes accustom. Shading them with one hand, I begin to make out shapes.

There are two shelves along the opposite wall. On the bottom one there's a long white parcel. A human *mzoga*! At one end it's partially unwrapped. His head. Someone's been here to look, and left without re-covering his face. It's fate. I'm *supposed* to see him.

Suddenly this doesn't seem such a good idea. He's there, all right! His pinched dead face is peering out of the cover. What shocks me is he looks *alive*. Not as I imagined a dead person. There's a yellow waxiness about his thin face, but nothing, to my mind, pronouncing death. I expect a sign. Swelling, bruising, blood. . . Tembo's puppy wasn't bruised or bleeding. Just swollen around his tummy. Surely people, being more important, should have more outward evidence? Mr Valari (senior) doesn't. I've never seen the old man close up, but he looks very much like his son, Mr Valari (junior). Both are thin, rangy men. Like rope, I think. I don't know if they closed his eyes after he died, but they're wide open now, and staring when I peer through the high window.

His eyes are accusing. There's a resigned grimace on his face. He *sees* me, accuses me of killing him. Not fair. I haven't injected *him* with water. I am innocent. I feel my power evaporate. I can't bring *anyone* back to life!

How I don't break a leg I don't know. It's not recoil at his staring eyes. True, the ladder wobbles, but I don't fall. It strikes me I can't revitalise the *mzoga*. Then my concentration lapses. The ladder moves backwards in slow motion. I'm free-falling, clinging to my ladder. I thump into a thornbush. I'm knocked breathless. I lie gasping. The pain starts slowly. My chest, my back, everywhere. I've bruised my ribs, scratched all over with thorns.

As I fall Mum and Tembo run up. He tells her where I've gone when she asks. She's alarmed to see me in the thornbush. She sees the ladder and what I've been up to. 'Shame,' she says, 'you shouldn't be looking in there!' Tembo gives me another of his accusing looks. His eyes say he knows this is connected to his puppy. They help me up and carry my ladder home. Josef Weiss puts iodine on my scratches.

'You vant to be ze Frankenstein, yes?' he laughs, hugely pleased at his wit. No, I don't want to be one of those horrid tinned sausages from Barrat Stores!

If I can't bring people back to life, there's something wrong with what I know about death. 'Skelingtons'. . . they're the key. Becky says they're *skeletons*. I don't believe her. It's from the 'skelingtons' I'll get magic to raise Dad from his grave. I'll dig up Tembo's puppy.

Tembo, for all his quiet ways and untrammelled views on life, has made a shrine. He's planted flowers, and is often seen in the evening sitting on a stone, staring quietly. When I dig up the *ziara,* or grave, I can leave no trace. Tembo will look accusingly at me again. No matter, I *have* to see if the puppy is now a 'skelington'. Or is that really a *skeleton?* English, or *Kiingereza,* isn't easy!

Before I can dig, a surprise comes from Europe. My brother Bertrand has heard of Dad's death while serving as able seaman on HMS *Ark Royal*, an aircraft carrier, in the Mediterranean. He's seventeen years my senior, twenty-two years old. It takes time to arrange compassionate leave, then he flies via Cairo and Dar-es-Salaam to Mwanza, where he catches a lift on a timber lorry. He arrives early one evening at our front door. Mum lets him in, and there's a tearful family reunion, made up of bereavement and loss, and joining of survivors, or whatever happens at such times. I don't feel connected. I neither know nor recognise the tall, gaunt young man in white tropical naval uniform. He left to join the navy when I was one. I haven't seen him since.

Bertrand is feted and treated like a celebrity. It's not every day they see a young sailor here. They queue to buy him beers at the club, and Mum has to help him home several times. Big people are strange. They seem very strong, being able to enjoy themselves so much when someone's died.

Bertrand takes time out from the club to borrow a Land Rover and drive us the seventeen miles to the cemetery at Samina. The road has tall grass and bushes growing in the middle, and potholes the size of dustbins. The going's slow and hot. When, after two hours, we near Samina, we're assailed by midges, tiny flies which zoom down our noses and into our eyes.

I'm standing by the grave, where I've never been before. It's horrible. How can Dad be here, under the ground? Mum said they buried him, but somehow I didn't expect this. The disturbed earth and stone are not yet covered by thornbush and elephant grass, as the other, older graves are. There's another exception. Mr Valari (senior)'s grave

75

is even fresher and starker than Dad's. I'm being mocked by God. Here they both are, Dad and Mr Valari (senior), and there's absolutely *nothing* I can do. I feel unpleasantly that day I've killed Tembo's puppy *and* Mr Valari (senior). I've no clue how to bring Mr Valari, Dad, or even the puppy, back to life. Have I somehow killed Dad too? I was angry with him sometimes. . . Painted in fading black on Dad's cross is:

RICHARD PENHALIGON
1909-1957
Darling Husband, Father & Hero
'Home is the Sailor'

I see, when Mum points it out, that Dad's buried next to Mrs Williams, who was murdered by Mr Stroessner before we came to Geita. Mum says Dad read about it in a newspaper while waiting for a haircut in Johannesburg. Her grave, alone in that cemetery, has a stone. Cursive letters are carved on it.

SANDRA WILLIAMS
Dearly Beloved Wife
Devoted Mother
1922-1950
Cruelly taken from us

Mrs Williams reached out long ago to Dad, in a newspaper article about her murder. Now she's drawn him from so far away, to lie beside her forever. That's what Mum says to Bertrand. Strangely, I understand every word. In English. Why would this unknown lady do such a thing? In the heat, I feel a tingle of dread running up my spine. To compound it, a three inch scorpion, tail held scimitar-high, stalks across the top of the gravestone towards a slowly-moving centipede, oblivious of the danger. Life, and death, go on.

Midges invade mouths, noses and eyes. They drive away all thought. We keep our visit brief. We set off back to Geita. How can I ever make dead people alive? I'm desperate.

Bertrand's handsome, toothy, lanky. It's funny to think I've got such a big brother. I'm sorry when he goes.

I return to my plan to dig up Tembo's puppy. Surely, when I discover how long it takes to turn into a skeleton, which I now accept is the right word, because Gretchen says so, I'll be wiser about death. I'll re-visit the concept, and find how to go to Samina and bring Dad back.

A golden opportunity arrives. Tembo goes away. Although eschewed by his tribe for his small size and diminutive wit, they send him a message that his mother has died. Another death. This time an African woman in a village called Biharlomoulo, sixty miles from Geita. I wonder if they put her in another *kifo nyumba*, and if her eyes are open. It's a sign. Death keeps signalling. The message is clear: dig up the puppy's *mzoga* and see if he's a skeleton yet.

One evening during Tembo's absence I carry out my grisly plan. I take the spade and dig up the puppy. It's still wrapped in the red and white dishcloth I stole from Mum. She's been looking for it everywhere. The earth-stained parcel stinks even worse than the *machula*'s bucket. It makes me choke. Determined to discover the truth, I persevere and unwrap it. He *is* partly 'skeletised', or is that *skeletonised?* Some bones are exposed. Some parts still furry. His face is dried out like a mummy, giving him an appearance of an older, wiser being. Everywhere there's fat earthworms, sliding about unaware and uncaring to be pulled from the earth. What does this teach me? I put the little parcel back in the ground, smooth the soil so Tembo won't know.

I ponder for days, without resolving the problem or answering the question. But the thought of finding out about death, skeletonisation and resurrection never goes. I retain a morbid fascination for death and dying. It colours my growing up, and gives different meanings to many things, not least religion. Jesus was resurrected, and before that brought the walrus, or was it *Lazarus,* back from the dead, didn't he?

Eight

The legend of *Lotanga*'s voyage from Port Bell, Uganda, to Lotanga, Tanganyika, is told and retold in Geita for years. Umali's the first to tell me, when I'm able to understand Swahili. That's when I'm two. I hear the story from Wait at four, and Dad tells me snippets when I'm five. My English is so poor, I don't take much in. The tale of the voyage is clearly important. After Dad dies in 1957, Mum frequently mentions the epic voyage, and other adults make comments about 'your father's narrow escape on the lake.'

By six, I want to know the whole story, from beginning to end, in sequence and detail. I need to own it because it's part of Dad. I ask Umali, not only as my most trusted historian, but also as Dad's companion on that trip, to tell me.

We're in a circle with Amina and Umali around a fire by the servant's quarters. Supported on three big stones, a pot of *mboga*, or vegetables, with a lump of fatty goat-flesh floating in it, is boiling furiously, smelling delicious. A little distance away Tembo whittles a piece of wood with a knife blade. He likes to be part, yet outside, gatherings like this. Amina will see he gets a generous helping of the *chakula* when it's ready.

The moon is full, the bush illuminated in yellow light. The crickets are still. It's an extraordinarily quiet evening. The light from the fire flickers on Umali's face. He adopts a distant, philosophical look. Amina watches him closely. When he's like this, he's in the mood to tell a great story. Even Tembo notices, and stops whittling. Umali, as always, speaks in Lake Swahili. He gives his account in dramatic style, voice rising and falling, speeding up and slowing, with long pauses for effect, and to make the listeners long for what's next.

'Lake Victoria is very big,' he begins, holding out his arms. 'From

78

Port Bell to Lotanga is two hundred and fifty miles as the great black *kunguru*-bird flies. The crow. But there are many shallow places, and islands, some with people, some without. To make this journey you have to go here and there, weave your own course, or road, to avoid many dangers.' He lets the silence hang. 'Crocodiles as big as three or four men, great floating logs, ready to puncture a boat. Bad people, *mwizis,* thieves who board at night to *chinja* you, cut your throat, steal your money.' He whistles between his teeth, and spits. 'There are more dangers than you can imagine.'

'We left Port Bell, your father, the Nyasa Wait, and me, as the sun went down in the west, and the moon rose on the other side. Your father was brave to set out so late. I would have waited for morning, but who was I to tell the *bwana*?' Umali shakes his head. 'Your father was a courageous and clever man.' He sticks out an arm, straight at shoulder level, with index finger pointing into the dark. The light and shadow from the flickering fire play across his face and illuminate his eyes.

'We headed south. The engine went *pap-pap-pap*, bubbles came from the water at the back, and smoke went from the big pipe on top. Your father stood at the wheel. He had a pipe in his mouth. He looked happy. He said he always loved boats.

'As we travelled, the moon went behind a small cloud. It didn't come out again. The cloud must have joined its bigger, fatter brothers. For some time we didn't see the moon, or enjoy its light. We motored on. In the darkness it was impossible to see anything. Your father the *bwana* was the only one who knew where we were going. He wasn't worried. He had that gold and glass thing he said was a '*compasi*'. I didn't understand how he could trust that little thing in the dark.' Umali looks wistful.

'It grew black, like I never saw. There was no moon. Even the stars were gone. It had been a hot, very hot day. I had the feeling I get before the rain. A pain in my right knee, I just knew. . .' Umali rubs his knee as if feeling the pain. 'The wind started gently. A cool, welcome breeze after the heat. Your father was at the wheel, and the Nyasa Wait and I made tea on a primus. Your father was grateful. Know what he did?' Umali shakes his head and smiles. His eyes glint.

'He was a great man, the *bwana*. He took out a silver flask from his pocket. The one your mother keeps on the sideboard. It had whisky. He called it *Scotchie*. Like petrol. It burns, I know because I tried it before.' Umali grins wickedly. Dad said his whisky disappeared quicker than he drank it. 'He poured it into our tea, just a little. It tasted wonderful. It strengthened the tea and sugar. Like drinking the *maji* of *Mungu!*' God's water.

Umali smacks his lips. He turns to Amina, who, like me, is enthralled. 'You have never made *chai* like that one for me, sweet one of my longing!' She slaps him on the shoulder. He laughs delightedly.

'We enjoyed that tea,' Umali resumes at length, grin making way to stern expression, 'but by then that baby wind, that cooling breeze we so appreciated, began to blow harder and harder, colder and colder, no longer pleasant. Then the fattened clouds, far above and unseen in the darkness, burst above our heads, with thunder like the roar of *Shataan*, the devil, and lightning came to split the sky to the water, and made such light it was brighter than day!'

'A storm?' I say.

'Not *just* a storm, the worst I've seen, and it happened then, at the exact time when I, who had never before been on a boat, apart from a *mtumbui* hollowed from a single tree, at Nungwe Bay, went on the great water with those two.' Umali addresses Amina. 'Is the food ready?' he asks. '*Chakula tiari?*'

'It can wait,' she replies in Swahili, 'I want to hear the ending.' She's heard it many times before. That's the beauty of old fashioned story telling around a fire. Excitement and newness never diminish.

'Now I began to feel fear,' Umali says, taking Amina's cue, his eyes closing to express his feeling. 'I felt an unpleasantness inside, here, in my chest.' He pounds his thin ribs. 'My heart began to say it was not happy with this boat, this water, this thunder, this lightning, those waves, which rocked us like the high branches of a mango tree when boys throw stones to release fruit. I began to think this, my first time on the great water, is a mistake, and if I was not so frightened I would *kunya* over the side to relieve my groaning bowels.' Umali breathes deeply. His nostrils flare, and he opens his eyes. He spits three yards through his top teeth. A great spitter. Only Amina is better.

'Your father stayed at the wheel, his pipe clenched in his teeth, and he turned the wheel left, right, left again. But the boat was like a dry leaf in storm water. It went where the water said, and no man could control it. By now the waves were higher than the deck, and broke over it, trying to drive us down into the black water. The tops of waves came away in the wind, which shrieked with the voice of *Shataan* himself, and shot like small stones from a catapult, to hit me and the Nyasa with painful force.' Umali opens his arms, his eyes wide. It must have been terrible, I think, to hear the very voice of the devil! Umali continues.

'We thought we had come early to our end. I even beseeched *Allah*, if he would only let me live through this storm, I would blind one eye and break one leg, and become a *masikini*, a poor man.' Amina chuckles.

'I'd like to see you a *masikini*,' she says. Umali pouts.

'What happened then?' I ask. Umali is still here, and Dad didn't drown, nor Wait.

'Your father somehow kept the boat facing the wind and waves. The engine went *pap-bwaaf-pap-bwaaf*, as the back heaved in and out of the water and the propeller turned, now in the water, now in the air. . .' Umali draws an open hand across his face to illustrate panic. 'Then *Mungu* gave us a death sentence. Maybe it was *Shetani*, I don't know.' God or the devil, one or the other.

'What happened, *Mzee*, old one?' Amina says, adding to the tension. The pot's boiling furiously on the fire. She leans forward and deftly lifts it and places it on the ground. 'Tell us what then became of you.'

'It was then the engine died,' Umali sighs, '*Ari Kufwa*. . . it left us completely without control.' He turns his face to the moonlit sky. The firelight illuminates his features, craggy and mysterious, his eyes reflecting deep distress. I follow where they are looking. High in the sky a cloud drifts in the direction of the lake, revealing the full moon. I remember, Umali said Ramadan ended yesterday evening, with the first sighting of that moon.

'It died – *ari kufwa?*' Amina says, emphasising the words. She knows the story. But the expression of wonder, or asking for confirmation by the audience, is integral to story telling.

'*Kabisa!*' Umali shakes his head. It died *completely*. His expression says, 'Where was my God when this happened?' He lets the silence hang a long time.

'Your father knew it was big trouble – *mbaya*, *hatari!*' Bad things, danger. Umali purses his lips. 'It was then he showed me and the Nyasa he was truly a man of the sea. . .'

'What did he do?' I ask, my heart beating with tension.

'The boat turned sideways on to the wind and waves, and the water struck at us in fury, waves taller than a Masai cattle-herder breaking over the deck, submerging the seats, while the big wind pushed the boat leaning on its side so we had to grasp the handrails with all our strength, not to be hurled into that shrieking, *Shetani*-inspired blackness. We hung there, in fear and in hopelessness. But your father didn't panic. He struggled uphill out of the wheelhouse, carrying a coil of rope and three blankets, which were for us to cover ourselves at night. He bought them at the *Boma Duka* near Geita.'

'*Blanketi?*' Amina asks dutifully, one huge tooth shining in the firelight. She stirs the pot of *mboga* cooling on the ground, replaces the lid. She makes that sucking 'tch' sound and spits fully ten feet. I'll never be able to match her range.

'*Blanketi*,' Umali confirms. 'I thought he was mad. What could we do with them? Did he want us to sleep while the deck heaved and bucked like a drunk and angry rhinoceros trying to copulate? With water up to our knees?' Amina laughs and slaps her thigh. A drunk and angry rhino trying to do *jigi-jigi* is funny.

'But our *Mzungu* had a plan. He gave the blankets to the Nyasa and me, and told us to make knots in the corners. We obeyed, for there was nothing else to do. While we struggled to tie the knots in the wet blankets, he cut the rope in pieces. With these he joined one knotted blanket corner to another. After several minutes fumbling, because of the wet and the dark, the three blankets were finally tied together, corner to corner. Then he fastened long lengths of rope to the corners of the whole. He told us to help him, and we carried the blanket-and-rope-thing to the back of the boat. He secured the ropes to the bollards used for tying up the boat, and threw the blankets into the raging water.'

'What for?' I ask, intrigued.

'Your father said it was a '*sea anchor*', and I was amazed what happened. The ropes went tight, and the boat began to turn, bringing the point to face the anger of the storm. The bucking and rolling reduced, just like that!' Umali snaps his fingers. 'The trouble was not over. We didn't know how long before the water tore the blankets away. We no longer feared we would sink, but we were still in a mad storm, without an engine.' Umali shook his head and smiled. 'Do you know what amazed me most of all?'

'No,' I say.

'The *bwana* kept his pipe in his mouth the whole time!'

'*Bwana* loved that pipe,' Amina murmurs softly, looking sad, placing her hand on my knee, 'he was a good *Mzungu*.'

'The waves stopped swamping the deck, but the *bwana* said *Lotanga* had taken water. We took up a hatch, and shone a torch. There was water, as deep as the height of Tembo.' He inclines his chin at Tembo, who, to hear better, has moved closer to, but not into, the circle round the fire. Tembo grins sheepishly. He enjoys stories. He's stopped whittling.

'I had to go down with a bucket, fill it, and pass it up to the Nyasa, who emptied it over the side. It was hard work, and slow. The boat wasn't bucking like an injured gazelle now, but it still moved this way and that, and I fell many times, hurting my shoulder and my head against the sides, which, in the blackness, I could not see. At first the water was above my waist.'

'He was in trouble!' Amina laughs, tapping my knee, 'who knows, but you may never have seen your Umali again!'

'That is true,' Umali says gravely. 'I was down there a very long time, perhaps an hour. . .'

'Then?' I ask.

'The storm ceased. Just like that!' He snaps his fingers. 'It seemed to go on a long, long time. But the whole thing started and finished in two hours. The *bwana* checked on his watch.' Umali smiles. 'We had covered only twenty miles from Port Bell. Now the lightning and thunder stopped. The scream of the wind died, and the moon came out from hiding, to light up the world like day.' Umali shakes his head in wonderment. 'I later heard several fishermen coming home in dugouts lost their lives that night. The lake, it can be evil, a playing place for *Shetani*, where he destroys people and takes them down to hell. It's not always as it looks, a peaceful glittering thing of beauty.'

'Now we were on a vast flat plate of water, shining in the moonlight, and the air was still, like we had died and gone somewhere else. We were still in trouble. We had no engine, we were just sitting there, wondering what to do.'

'What did you do?' I ask. *Fanya nini?*

'The *bwana*. He said there was a loss of diesel to the engine. He took his torch, still sucking his pipe, and went down to the engine underneath the wheelhouse. After a few minutes he came out and said he'd fixed the problem. A fuel pipe had come off and he'd put it back. He turned the key. For a few seconds the starter motor made a sound, *whee-whee-whee-whee,* and smoke came from the chimney. Then, like a great buffalo which wakes from sleeping, *garum-garum,* the engine began to roar, and *pap-pap-pap*, the propeller began again to stir the water. We were so happy. I even hugged the Nyasa, in spite of his ugliness!' Amina giggles and pokes him in the ribs.

'The Nyasa is better-looking than you, you wrinkled, dried out fish!' she laughs.

'*Hau*, I am again insulted!' he quips, making his best sad face. He continues. 'The rest of the journey was easy. It took three more days to get to Mwanza and Lotanga. On the way we saw fishermen in their dugout *mtumbui*s, islands with people and islands without people. In the shallows close to Musoma we saw house-sized hippopotami lying with their snouts just above the water, watching us with evil eyes. In one place there were crocodiles, great reptiles as long as three men, or four of Tembo.' He inclines his head at Tembo, who grins hugely. Unlike Umali and Amina, he has good, white teeth. When he smiles there's something of a *fisi,* or hyena about him.

'Eventually we arrived at Lotanga, and *bwana* Müller, the *Geremani*, was very happy to see us. He had heard of the sudden storm in the north of the lake, and feared we, and his beautiful boat, were lost to the evil *djinn* of the waters.'

What a great man Dad was! I can see how much Umali admired him. Dad sailed many oceans in different vessels. The *Lotanga* and her crew must have been very different. Yet he coped, and won Umali's admiration. It fills me with pride. But why, oh why can't he be here with me now? I feel tears running down my cheek, and I sniff loudly. Amina notices, as she always does. She puts her arm around me, draws me to her. '*Baba iko ndani, toto, hawezi ku acha!*' she whispers. Your father is inside, child, he'll never leave you! I wipe my tears on her *kanzu*. It's used to it.

'*Tu-ile*,' Amina says at last. It's time to eat. She lifts a buttock on the log she's sitting on, and lets out a loud *jamba*. It sounds like a trumpet. We laugh. Amina farts with aplomb. She upturns the still-steaming *ugali* onto a huge steel platter, then pulls the dish of *mboga* and fatty goat close. We reach out as one, take handfuls of ugali, roll it in one practised hand, and make deep dents with a thumb. Then we scoop it into the *mboga*. It's delicious.

Just then Lutoli appears. It's amazing how he senses there's freshly cooked *chakula* in the offing. I move up on my log. He sits next to me and reaches into the ugali pot. He isn't shy. Nor am I. Umali and Amina regard us with obvious affection. To them we are *their* children. I feel so happy. These w*atu* are my family. I'm a bit guilty about Mum, but decide you *can* have two families.

After eating till our stomachs are full, we drink *chai*. It's tea, brewed, together with milk, and lots of sugar, in a pot. If the *watu* can afford a tin of condensed sweetened milk, that's a very good day. The *chai* is stewed, because the pot's left to simmer awhile with the ingredients in. It's delicious.

Nine

Long, hot days. Nothing stirs. No sound. Everything alive sleeps. The leguaan in his hole, hyena in the fastness of his hide, leopard in the branch of canopied tree, python in overgrown ditch or *donga*, frog under leaf at water's-edge. Pet dogs skulk from sun's furnace under houses, *watu* hide in windowless mud huts. Every breathing thing tries to live out the day. Even insects avoid the heat. In the distance objects shimmer, like through a bonfire. They dance, change shape, change again. How can a hunter aim if the object moves like this? This is why they don't hunt in the day. *Jua kali!* The sun is angry! The laconic greeting of a *mutu* to another if they chance to pass. '*Kali sana!*' is the response. Very angry! No one looks up. Can't say 'Good Day' if it isn't. Too *blurry* hot.

I'm lying on my back in tall grass. Life's suddenly very quiet. At least it's cooler here. Somewhere invisibly close by a *njiwa*-bird breaks the silence with a tired and throaty *ooh-oor-oor*. The sound of torpid midday bush. Even the *njiwa* is tired. It falls silent again. African siesta-time. High in the wide, shimmering, aching, sky are small drifting black shapes. *Mwewe*, the hawk. They, alone, move on this canvas. Soaring on thermals from sun-blasted ground, they float far and effortless over hill and bush, wings fixed, deep-set yellow eyes searching. *Mwewe* see miles, swoop from nowhere to carry off prey their own weight. Rabbits, baby sheep or goats, puppies and kittens, have met sudden nemesis in sharp talon and beak. Beautiful but deadly, I think, awed by the graceful aerial display.

It's more than awe. There's continuity here, a never-ending expectancy that tomorrow, like today, at precisely. . . what *is* the time? I look fleetingly at the sun, but have to close my eyes. Everything goes red, like blood. You can't see the sun more than a second. It's high, near the top of the world. A *mwewe*-bird is directly between me and it. A small black silhouette framed in white heat. It's *saa sita*. Time six, or six o'clock. Swahili time-keeping is six hours behind English. Six o'clock is twelve midday. Sensible. For the *watu* the sun comes up at twelve, goes down at twelve. Back to my musing. I expect that, precisely at *saa sita*, or midday, tomorrow, as today, in this sun-scorched place, absolutely nothing will happen! It's boring, but comforting. Yet I wish I had something to do.

I don't know where Lutoli is today. Sometimes his fat aunt sends him on errands which seem to last all day.

A dog, that'd be nice. A reliable friend to share these quiet moments. If, that is, I can coax him out from under the house. Some people with dogs can't. Most hounds round here won't brave the heat of day.

Feral, or wild dogs are all over Geita. Product of uncontrolled breeding between all the diverse kinds of domestic dogs brought here by expatriates, mixed with African wild dogs attracted by the smells of man and easy food from his garbage. The half-breeds and quarter-breeds breed again and again, until Wild Dog, Alsatian, Boxer, Afghan, French Poodle, Rhodesian Ridgeback, Pointer, Corgi and Bloodhound are all represented in what becomes known as *Shenzis,* or 'rubbish', dogs.

In 1955 Mrs Snel imports two pedigree Daschund, or *Sausage-dog*, puppies from Germany. Brother and sister. She names the boy Fritzie, and the girl Mitzie. The German breeder hasn't bred morals into his little dogs. Fritzie grows to be an unbounded canine philanderer, and Mitzie a whore. First they practise incest, producing six more Daschunds of equal immorality, then they turn to low-life, or *Shenzis*, for good measure. Soon Mitzie gives birth to six low-slung *Shenzis,* while Fritzie fathers several dozen more.

A sea-change in the genetic makeup of Geita *Shenzis* takes place. Short legged *Shenzi* breeds with short legged *Shenzi,* then they breed again. The mixing genes fancy each other, and, from the epicentre in Geita, ever shorter legs and longer bodies spread out to the district like ripples in a pond. Out of this epi-phenomenom, in 1957, on a *shamba* ten miles from the camp, Sandy is born.

Sandy is ten weeks old when she's offered for two shillings by a wandering *Gallua*. She's a furry, hand-made, teddy bear. She's low to the ground, and has the hanging ears of a Daschund. There's seams running up her legs, and down the middle of her belly, like she's been stitched in a factory. We fall in love instantly. Mum gives in easily. Truth is even she can't resist the little *Shenzi* who licks our faces the moment she's close enough. Mum insists she do a lap-test before agreeing to buy her. She has to prove she's old enough to be separated from her mother. She puts a saucer of milk on the ground, and Becky and I watch with bated breath. The little fur-ball stumbles on short legs to the saucer. When she gets there she sits down and stares at us in turn. Finally she's staring intently into my eyes.

'Drink, girl,' I say. Her deep brown eyes don't blink. 'Drink,' I urge. She turns to the saucer and puts her mouth to the milk. A tiny pink tongue begins to lap. Becky and I applaud. Mum goes inside and comes back with two shillings. Sandy has joined our family.

Meantime, there are other matters in mind. I'd like to use the word 'venerable' when talking about Puncture Car, though I never know if the old car has been a distinguished or expensive model. I notice the discarded car when I'm three, Mum says, and fascination for the rotting wreck never leaves me. I still don't know what make she was, or the year she was built. Nobody says who she had belonged to, or why the owner pushed her off the side of the road a quarter mile from the club.

She's from the nineteen thirties, or forties at the latest. She was once black, but now she's a patchwork of black and red rust. She has massive mudguards back and front, with a running-board between. There are two doors, making her a *coupé*. Her bonnet's long, and opens on the sides, hinged to a chromed part down the centre. There's a two inch deep pool of rusty rainwater on her floor, and she reeks of oxidising iron, a sharp, acrid mustiness.

Her seats are cracked brown leather, green in creases where algae thrive. Her steering wheel is huge. It has chromed, but rusty spokes, and a big black boss in the middle. Nothing like as pretty as my Chevrolet wheel. Her gear lever has no top, and is unmovably seized. The pedals are flat on the floor, submerged in red water, with rotting leaves floating in it. There are round dials in the dashboard, which remind me of the Grundig radio in our lounge. Her tyres are not only flat, but have largely disintegrated, leaving black lumps of gloopy rubber, with shiny green stuff growing from it, hanging about the rusting spoked wheels like eccentric strings of pearls.

Never mind her state. Never mind there's a small tree growing through her boot, forcing the lid open and buckling one side. Never mind the smell of rust, the vines and creepers which envelop her windscreen and interlace the wipers. Puncture Car's blurry magnificent!

Before he dies, Dad humours me by stopping MZ 202 every time we pass where the abandoned car lies. He lets me look and admire her many times. After he's gone, Mum tries many things to console me. She knows how angry I am with God, and everybody. One day, seven months after Dad dies, she speaks to Mr Snel, the manager, about me and Puncture Car, and he decides to tow her home to our garden so I can see and play with her every day.

He takes his Land Rover down to her, secures a chain, and drags her, screeching in complaint and trailing branches and leaves, to our garden. It's a great day, and I'm bursting with excitement.

Lutoli's also driving, using my shiny Chevrolet steering-wheel, which I've cherished ever since I found it on the beach in Dar-es-Salaam. It's only now, since I've got a whole car, I can let anyone else play with it. Three of his *rafikis,* tribal friends, stand on the running board on the left. Perched on my right are Becky, Gretchen, and her brother Dieti. Gretchen seems as excited by the old car as me. Sitting on the boot are two more *totos,* and another is perched on the bonnet. For a reason I can't discern, I've insisted everyone wears one of those rusty World War II British army helmets. Gretchen's blonde hair and her chin are about all we can see of her.

With all passengers aboard, or clinging on, I announce we're 'off'. We make a great roar of engine noise, grating gearbox, hooter and collisions with small objects, and the side passengers rock the car. Mum tells us we'll wake the dead. I file the idea away for later. Maybe *noise* is the secret I've ignored for resurrection. We aren't loud enough to wake our hidden, secret passenger. He sleeps through the cacophony.

His Latin name is *Dendroaspis Polyepsis*, but everyone calls him black mamba. He's been given many pseudonyms, but most chilling is 'widow-maker'. He belongs to the genus *Elapidae*, and has fixed fangs, unlike many lesser cousins. He can grow to great lengths, and examples eight feet long are not rare. Such specimens have a diameter of up to two and a half inches.

The black mamba's a shy, unassuming reptile. He's known to be timid, and avoid contact unless cornered. Then, in a desperate attempt to escape, he will try to get away, and, in passing, make several lightning-quick bites. His poison is an extremely potent neurotoxin. Tiny amounts are enough to paralyse the muscles of the throat and respiration. Death, which is said to be quick and agonising, is by asphyxiation.

I don't know this the day Puncture Car comes home. I also don't know mambas are deaf. Explains why he doesn't hear the racket. Doesn't explain why he doesn't feel vibrations, because mambas should have sensors for that.

The others have tired of playing and gone off, leaving only Lutoli and I. We take off our helmets, because we can't see properly with them on. We survey our limousine. I'm in the passenger seat with my Chevrolet wheel, Lutoli's in the driving seat. He pretends to work the gears. Puncture Car's lovely. I reach and press the knob on the glove-box. It falls open.

The mamba's awake. The pupils of his hooded eyes are dilated in the twilight of evening. His black head is coffin-shaped, and I'm drawn to his slit-like reptilian mouth. A long forked tongue darts in and out. I see only part of him in the glove-box, for the back's missing. The scaled brown body extends into the engine compartment. The inside of his mouth is coal-black. I don't know how long we stare at each other. My arm dangles over the glove-box. Time is frozen. An urge to leave the car rises in my breast. Have to do it gently, quickly. I draw my arm back slowly, and even more slowly reach for the door handle. It's stuck. I've put my Chevrolet wheel down the side of my seat. Lutoli has stopped playing driver. His eyes are wide. I hold my breath and shove the door with my shoulder. It creaks open. Then I'm out, running, screaming. Lutoli's almost as quick. He's only a yard behind.

'*Nyoka!*' I shout hoarsely when I spot Umali peeling potatoes on the steps.

'Snake, where?'

'In the car!' Lutoli and I yell hysterically.

'Snake in car!' Umali bellows as he runs, a panga magically in his hand.

I learn there is nothing which galvanises the docile and peaceable *watu* more than the word *nyoka*. Where they come from, or how they get there so quick I don't know. Suddenly there are four, then eight, then more, all bearing pangas, sticks or rocks. The wild-eyed mob, led by a manically energised Umali, get to the car. And stop.

'*Wapi?*' Umali breathes, nostrils flaring, panga raised high, 'Where?'

'There!' I shout. I point to the glove-box. It's empty.

He must have retreated backwards into the engine compartment. Before Umali can comment, there's a commotion amongst the *watu* behind, and I see them yelling, cursing, and striking at something on the ground. Then I see him. He's made a dash for safety and dropped out of the engine. He's quick, but they're quicker. He's fully seven foot, but as I watch he's chopped into pieces only inches long. It's over in seconds, and his head, forked tongue still darting in and out of his mouth, spins, attached to a six inch piece of body, to lie twitching in the dust next to my bare foot.

89

The *Wazungu* adults don't swear in front of children. But they do swear at the *watu*. The victims of their invective don't understand the words, but they know when they're being abused. Always keen to add to their own repertoire, they use English swearwords blindly, without understanding, but with even greater flair and venom than their teachers. A large boulder mashes the snake's head into the dirt.

'*Blurryfuckenblackbastar!*' screams the thrower. He's clearly a good English-learner, but hasn't a clue what he means.

'*Blurrystupidbitch!*' shouts another, vigorously trampling the mangled remains. Like them, I don't understand the words, but they seem right. In time I'll incorporate them in my vocabulary. This is vicarious learning with a twist.

With much shoulder-clapping and congratulations, the *watu* disappear as magically as they came, back into the elephant grass and thorn trees surrounding our garden. Umali, Lutoli and I stare at the remains of the mamba. Some bits are still twitching. I discover two things that day: the *watu* hate snakes, and there really *is* a bush telegraph. I retrieve my beloved Chevrolet steering wheel. I don't know why, but I've got a feeling it's got magic, and that's why the mamba didn't bite me. Later I tell Umali, and he agrees. 'Some things are *hirizi,*' he says. A charm against evil. Everyone knows *nyokas* are in cahoots with *Shetani,* the devil. You need charms.

Funny how things come in twos or threes. The Puncture Car mamba saga is only a month ago, when I decide to conduct an experiment with a coir rope, an old wicker chair, and a branch high on a tree in our front garden.

Lutoli joins me. He's an ever-smiling, game little chap, and we have been hanging around forever. We've learnt Swahili together, in the company of *ayahs* under the baobab tree. He's proud of his well-spoken *Mzungu* friend.

'If we throw this stick, with the rope on one end, over that branch,' I say, 'we can bring it back down and tie it onto a chair.'

'*Sababu?*' he asks. Why?

'Sit in the chair and pull ourselves up,' I say.

'*Ndio,*' he beams.

We take turns throwing the stick, but our arms and muscles are not man enough. Tembo arrives and asks what we're trying to do. We explain. He doesn't say anything, just takes the wood and rope from Lutoli, and hurls it high into the sky. It flies past the jutting branch, and falls down the other side. He lets out rope, and brings the stick down.

We thank him, but he just shrugs his shoulders and walks away.

I fetch Mum's wicker chair from the verandah. It's one of those with close-woven reed, and it has armrests with holes. Lutoli and I thread the rope through the armrests, and tie it back on itself three feet above the chair. Now it's time to winch ourselves up. On this occasion, as it's my idea, Lutoli votes I go first.

It isn't possible to pull myself up in the chair. My weight pulls the rope too tight round the branch. I find that by pulling on the rope, and lifting myself out of the seat, I can raise the chair a foot at a time. By increments, I labour up the side of the tree, the ground moving further and further away. In later years, I note the branch is only thirty feet up, but it's higher at six.

After much effort I arrive under the branch. There's something not quite right with the rope. It's been looped over the top, not wound around it. The rope is brown coir, not green. Now it's coiled three times round the branch, and it's green. Grass green. Then I see the head. It's smaller than the black mamba's, but a similar shape, and its eyes are red and staring unblinkingly into mine.

My face is eighteen inches from a green mamba. I release the rope very slowly. My heart beats so hard I think it might burst. The snake doesn't move. I go down, foot by foot. When I am halfway to the ground I yell, for the second time in four weeks. '*Nyoka, nyoka!*'

By the time the chair's legs meet the ground there is a mêlée of axe, panga, stick and stone-bearing men and women, and a teenager who fits a pebble to a long sling. He hurls his sling round and round, then dispatches the stone at the snake on the branch. It hits him, or frightens him, for, rapidly uncoiling, he falls heavily to the ground in a tight bundle of convulsing green. He's dispatched just like his black cousin. Congratulations ring out, backs are slapped, and the *watu* go whence they came, leaving Lutoli and I speechless.

'Snakes are bad,' he says.

'*Ndio*,' I say.

'Shall we try again?' he asks.

'*Lazima*,' I say. Of course.

The next few hoists up the tree are fun, and uneventful, though Lutoli and I get blisters on our hands, and a telling-off from Mum when she comes home to find Lutoli dangling high in her beloved wicker chair.

About this time Geita is treated to one of its comedies. Major William Bigginsbottom, late of the British Army in India, latterly of Bexhillon-Sea, in his sixties and unmarried, has kept in touch with several wartime colleagues. Coming from an aristocratic and wealthy family 'at home', he's spent the years since VJ day in 1945 travelling old haunts, looking up old comrades. Higginson's is one of the addresses he's kept, and he finally makes his way to Geita to reacquaint himself with his old Colonel.

He arrives, this colonial relic, in an open Land Rover driven by a faithful but aged Gurkha from his Indonesian campaign, sporting a sunburned red face, six inch twirled grey moustache, pith helmet and smartly tailored, if sweaty, short khaki safari suit, plus polished army boots and white socks. He actually carries a swagger-stick.

Higgs is delighted to see him, and Major Bigginsbottom is not fazed by the mixed-race marriage of his old friend. They settle into fond reminiscences of the Burma campaign, and invite Kaizer, who fought in the Kabaw valley, to join their evenings. In the spirit of camaraderie and past adventure, they drink enormous toasts to one another, and eternal calumny to Japs, Nazis and communists. Higgs, Maria and Bigginsbottom drink from glasses, Kaizer straight from the bottle. Like Wait.

One afternoon the Major goes outside to the little fenced shower enclosure. He's forgotten to take the latch key to regain the verandah. One of Maria's young female cousins is helping around the house.

'*Wewe!*' the Major shouts from outside, naked from the waist-up, towel around his waist. He pronounces it *way-way*. It means 'you'. From the verandah only his top half is visible. To the young girl, there's a naked old man out there.

'*Mimi*?' she asks. Me? What does he want in his state of undress? He smiles appeasingly. He wants to be let in. The message is misconstrued. She's affronted. '*Mimi, apana!*' she says, me-no! She turns and flees into the house. The amorous major and shy *kijana* tale spreads like bushfire.

Lutoli and I decide to establish our own republic when we're six. The *Wazungu* are too repressive. Andrew Miller, a Yorkshire boy, son of Mum's friend Mary, wants to take part. We set out up the hill above Top Road one morning, supplies of food and drink in a *kikapu*, or woven basket. We carry it in turns.

I'm on a mission. I'm angry, I don't respect the posh-speaking, dishonest *Wazungu*. They're *wenwe's*. Not Swahili. Just 'when we were in Kent', or 'when we had a mansion in Surrey', or 'when we were in Devon'. That's how all the big *Wazungu wakoloni*, or colonials, start their stories. They sit on barstools at the club, drink locally brewed beer, smoke local cigarettes, breathe local air, go home to a local house, eat local food, and sleep in a locally-built bed. They get their wages because of local gold, and use local *watu* to dig it. But they only talk about 'home', and '*wenwe*'. They tell everyone who'll listen how wonderful it was in Brighton, Somerset and Canterbury. Geita, Tanganyika? They denigrate it with gusto. The worst thing ever. Just look at the *watu*. . . they're *animals*. These *wenwe's* don't *think* so, they *know!* Anyway, 'it's far too hot, old bean!' Wipe streaming brow with handkerchief, take long draught of cold *Whitecap*.

Yet they stay, these unredeemed habitual moaners, contract after contract. They always return here after visiting their wonderful 'home'. There's no pleasing them. They'll complain, and hate, as long as they breathe. I'm ashamed of my white skin. Lutoli is right. Our own republic is what we need. I'm not sure about Andrew.

The hillside above the houses on Top Road is densely wooded. We wind our way upwards between the trees. It's much further on than we expect. After over an hour, we emerge onto the rounded summit. There are trees here, but not so densely packed. I find a flat and shady space under a large acacia. The sun's very hot. We beat the elephant-grass flat with sticks. Lutoli gathers dead branches, and makes a barricade.

With solemn ceremony, we declare the eternal independence of our *Republic of Kichoncho*. The word means nothing. It just comes to us. It must be fate. We feast on dry *ugali* and water. The cuisine isn't up to much. But the view of the mine and camp is panoramic, and independence is liberating. 'One day all Tanganyika will be free,' Lutoli says. I stare at him curiously. He's a strikingly handsome chap, always smiling, with deep dimples and brilliant white teeth. There's more than looks. Pride. Refusal to be suppressed. I feel a surge of affection for him. 'The *Wazungu* will go,' he adds, grinning.

'*Mimi?*' I ask. Me?

'No, *Jimu, you* will stay!' He pauses, then says '*Wewe ni yetu.*' You are ours. He strikes his chest with a closed fist. Good enough for me. *I* can stay when the *Wazungu* leave. It will never really happen, so I don't have to think about Mum and Becky.

'What's he saying?' Andrew asks. His Swahili is rudimentary, and he's deeply suspicious.

'Says there'll be *uhuru* one day, and Europeans will leave.'

Andrew cuts his eyes dangerously at Lutoli. They'll never be friends. 'No we won't,' he says.

Lutoli shrugs. He knows Andrew disagrees.

Lutoli and I visit our home country often, without Andrew. We

93

agree he's a bad *Mzungu*. We choose a two-president solution to the question of government. That's the entire population, which we think fair. We paint a national flag onto a square-foot piece of hardboard, which we nail to a stick. It's a bright red star on black. Becky's Christmas-present paints. We decide on a set of rules by way of a constitution. It will be handed verbally down through the generations, as neither of us is a writer. Donning oversized rusty WWII British army helmets, we stand at attention, salute our republic, and recite our constitution. The rules are simple:

1) *No girls.*
2) *No grown-ups.*
3) *No bad Mzungus.*
4) *No Mzungus except me, who is not a Mzungu.*
5) *No bad anyones.*
6) *We are independent.*
7) *Our country first, everything after, enemies last.*
8) *We will pigana, fight, to the last boy to preserve our freedom.*
9) *We will attack other countries who threaten our freedom.*
10) *Spies must be killed. Violently.*
11) *Girl spies must definitely be killed.*

Secretly, I resolve that one girl, even if she spies, won't be killed. How can I kill Gretchen? I think I love her. It's her blonde hair and trusting blue eyes. I've told Mum, but she says I'm silly. Far too young.

On our third trip to our home country, we discover Becky and Gretchen have established their own country only twenty yards along the hillside. They call it *Chola*. Also a meaningless word. Love would have gone out the window, if there was one. Is there nothing we can do without copycats? As soon as they leave, we raid. There's little to plunder. Like *Kichoncho*, *Chola*'s a bankrupt state. The best we can do is use a helmet to gather up hyena and jackal droppings on the hillside, and leave them as calling cards. That'll teach them! It doesn't strike me as strange to leave feral faeces as a present for the girl I love.

We're coming down the hill from *Kichoncho* when we walk into a near-riot on Top Road. There's a crowd of more than twenty at the turnoff to Compound Hill. I've never seen so many *watu* together in Geita. They're in an ugly mood.

Mlozi has finally realised he is, in fact, God. The one and only. He's unwisely elected to announce his decision at the top of his voice, yelling over and over that he is *Mungu,* who created everything in the world, all the way from Geita to Biharlomoulo, forty miles distant. There, as everyone knows, the *dunia,* or world, ends. Where does he think the *Wazungu* come from, I wonder? Or the *Wahindi* or Indians, the *Wachina* or Chinese?

It's gone down badly. A small group of *wasikini* beggars is one thing, but this crowd is different. He's still performing when we get there, jumping from foot to foot on his flat rock, technicolour ribbon-hair flopping, Kimbo tin rattling, ankle-bones jingling, and froth bubbling from the corners of his mouth. He's blissfully unaware of the effect of his words. The crowd is not having this blasphemy. There is no humour here.

'*Tu chinje!*' a furious man says. Let's kill him! Several bend to pick up rocks. There's going to be a stoning. Right here in front of us! A *masikini* was stoned to death nearby a year ago. He was a *mwizi,* thief. He stole a Kimbo-tin of *karanga,* or groundnuts, from another *masikini,* who hysterically denounced him. There were no convictions, because the only witnesses were living participants, and. . . Mlozi's life is in the balance.

'*Ngoja!*' shouts a *mzee,* or old man, in a *kanzu.* Wait! I *know* this old man. He brings chickens for Umali to kill. He's a Muslim, but squeamish. Umali says he's got a big *shamba* and at least three wives. The stone-gathering stops. Some pebbles drop. The *mzee*'s got authority. His printed *kanzu,* or loincloth, is clearly expensive. Umali says he has *phedha mingi*, a lot of money. Based on a herd of *ng'ombe*, the strange hump-backed, long-horned local cattle. They say they're immune to sleeping-sickness, transmitted by tsetse-flies, which kills horses and most breeds of cattle. We never see those in Geita. The *mzee* in the expensive *kanzu* is an important supplier of animals to the *Ishmaeli* butchers. The crowd falls silent.

'Who said *you* are God?' the *mzee* shouts at Mlozi. He's cunningly shifting this from an execution to an interrogation. Clever. There are some disappointed murmurs, respectfully muted.

'The sayings said,' Mlozi yells.

'What sayings?' the *mzee* spits.

'The sayings of God!' Some *watu* chuckle. Others are indignant.

'*Blurryfucken-dammit!*' one shouts.

Another joins the refrain. '*Gotohellyoubastar!*'

'*Blurryfuckenbitch!*' a young man in a red shirt yells. Becky's told me what bitch means. It would be funny in a different situation. How can they call him a female dog?

'You hear God?' the *Mzee* yells above the rising clamour.

'I hear!' Mlozi says. The *Mzee* turns to the others.

'*Pumbafu!*' he announces with authority. A fool! There's murmuring of agreement. '*Lazima*', naturally, '*ndio*', yes, '*Kabisa*', absolutely. Some are amused. 'He's *not* evil,' the *mzee* adds. Whispers of reluctant agreement. It's not as if it's a *normal* person saying such things. They've always thought Mlozi's mad. Or is he possessed by a *Jinni* or *djinn*? Some stalwart *watu* still look angry, but the fury of the moment is broken. They begin to wander off. Lutoli and I too.

Ten

Growing up without a father is not only sad, it's arduous. It's worse if fatherless status is unique to you. Unfair, unkind, poignantly lonely. The *wakoloni*, or colonial, community in Geita is patriarchal, macho, both. Only men are given contracts to work on the mine. When wives are employed, it's strictly 'off contract', meaning they have no rights, and can't even expect notice if their services are terminated. That said, a contract doesn't stop management from summary firing of anyone, nor does it mean *anyone* can expect a pension. All it does is give men status, and 'proper' permission to work, at the same time sending a message that women are less.

When Dad dies, the 'contract' matter should, in normal circumstances, ensure we'd leave the country on the next mail-ship. Two hundred pounds won't last long in Cornwall, Mum says. Then it'll be the poor-house. Becky and I live in terror. I won't even have a gun, I think. How will I protect them? *Poor-house* sounds awful.

For once, and never again, Mr Snel, the manager, decides to alter the rules. He does so, he says, out of respect for Dad, whom he admired. A pity he never said so while he was alive. He gives Mum a contract, meaning she keeps her job, remains in the house with free water and electricity, and has the benefits of a contract-holder. Crucially, the mine pays children's fees at boarding school anywhere in East Africa. Mum becomes an honorary man. Many years later in South Africa, I see 'honorary white' status applied to black people by the government when it suits them. Hypocrisy in race. Echoes of gender hypocrisy in Geita. Meantime, the poor-house threat recedes.

Despite her status, Mum's a woman. The expat community know that too well, and some people treat us with disdain, patronisation and sometimes overt cruelty. Mum is vulnerable. Having gained a unique

97

e

favour, it can be taken away with ease. She can't afford to make enemies of 'higher ups' on the mine, or their wives. She has no choice but to keep her counsel, sometimes in vexing circumstance.

Mum lectures Becky and me ceaselessly about the goodwill of the mine, and its necessity for our survival. How we, as children, should behave in exemplary fashion, and never be impolite or naughty in front of Europeans. If we behave badly, or swear, the consequences will be our doom. She'll lose her contract and job. We'll be 'packed off' out the country, and end up on the street somewhere. We'll starve. I'm only five, and begin to develop real aversion to my own race.

Contrasting with my feelings about *Wazungu*, and particularly the English, who occupy nearly all senior positions in Geita, is my unbridled love for the *watu*, with whom I can fluently, and often vulgarly, discuss any topic without fear of anger or retribution. Further driving this is the cruelty of some children. Particularly those of people on Top Road.

Dad has only been dead some weeks when posh white kids from Top Road use his death against Becky and me. 'Your Dad's dead, and my Dad can beat your mother up,' is typical. 'He's just a skeleton now', or 'worms are eating him'. I never get that from my *rafikis*, nor their elders. They never even mention Dad's death, or that I have no father. Their own life expectancy is short, and most of the *totos* have lost one or both parents. They know what it's like. Especially Lutoli.

Despite trying to obey Mum's orders about deportment and behaviour, I fail. I suddenly find myself *the man* in the family. My duty, I believe, is to protect the others, like Dad did. Protection means vigorous response to threat or unpleasantness, not beating a retreat. Mum's messages to me are ambiguous. On one hand she ceaselessly praises Dad's courage, his heroism and strength, and tells me to be like him. Then she says I shouldn't challenge people, I should walk away from confrontation, be sworn at and not swear back. The two don't go together.

I'm taught to deal differently with difficulty by my real friends, Lutoli and the *watoto rafikis*, into whose company I am more and more driven. I learn from them not to start a fight or argument. If I'm on the receiving end of unkind attention, however, there's only one way to deal with it: vitriolic, abusive, profane and, if necessary, violent riposte. My playmates are arbiter on the contradictory instructions from Mum. That suits me. I'm angry. Cross with God, furious at the taunts of white kids, afraid for the family, morbidly curious about death, confused. I'll fight for survival and dignity, against anyone threatening either.

I'm less that six when it becomes apparent to all that 'Jimmy is a tearaway', he swears in Swahili at anyone he disagrees with, he stands his ground, and he argues with adults. Mum can't control me. I don't know then, but those early days after Dad's death are a crucible for future anarchist tendencies. I will always hold a jaundiced view of authority.

'*Speak Swahili, Dammit!*' I yell at Mrs Snel, the manager's wife, when she orders me to stop slashing the club's flowers with a stick. Not only does she only speak English, which is bad enough, but she's got a strong, nasal Canadian twang. I can't understand a thing she drawls. It's Sunday, and I'm callously rearranging the club garden-bed with roundhouse swipes. I'm very good at this. *Swish* goes the stick, decapitating ten blooms. She shouts something in gobbledygook. I stand my ground. I'm not frightened of God, so who the hell is *she?*

'I will *not* speak Swahili,' she answers, 'but *you* will stop cutting down the flowers!'

'Eat your willy!' I swear in Gallua, taking another ten blooms down. The only Gallua I know are swearwords. Just like the *watu* here. They *say* they hate Galluas, but they admire, and therefore adopt, their invective. I don't care if Mrs Snel *doesn't* have a willy. I add she has a vagina like a snake, in Swahili, and round it off with '*youblurrybitch!*' My fluency and diction leave her flummoxed. But my tone and expression, and the last word, don't. She knows it's open rebellion. Later, I'll damage my reputation further through the game of *uchi maji mti kimbia*, or naked-water-tree-running.

I have oaths and swearwords for every occasion. My *rafikis* witness my outbursts, giggle, laugh, clutch their sides in glee to see me abusing powerful *Wazungu*.

In *watu* circles, and among villagers, my name is known. I am '*Jimu*', the '*Piri-Piri*', or Chilli-Pepper. I cause much laughter. Unlike other *Wazungu wakoloni*, or colonials, I'm fluent in Swahili, having learnt the language so early, and used it ever since. I can converse about every manner of thing with elders, have good knowledge of local things and customs, have an obvious preference for African company, am not fazed by matters of biology or sex, and am more dismissive and opposed to *Mzungu* authority than even they are. I am a hilarious anachronism. I have also moved to the centre of Umali and Amina's lives. They never have their own children. Now they have me. White, but un-white! I am aware of ever closer bonds between them and me. And, of course, Lutoli.

My connivance with servants, plus my abusive and dismissive attitude, makes me widely unpopular with *Mzungu* adults. They are undermined before their hirelings, angry, but powerless. They take the only open courses: they discuss me among themselves, 'report' me to Mr Snel, the manager, or make forays to talk to Mum. It becomes a regular part of life: 'Mrs such-and-such says you swore at her,' or 'Mr such-and-such says you threatened to burn his house down.' I develop *kiboko*, or rhino, skin, and unhearing ears. I don't expect kindness from those quarters. I'll give as good, or better, than I get. It's a dangerous path, and will lead to unpleasant consequences.

It becomes habitual and inevitable that Jimmy is blamed for anything untoward, conceivably caused by a child. If a window's broken in an empty house, Jimmy threw the stone. If a plant's destroyed, Jimmy did it. Sometimes the allegations are justified. Often they aren't.

My notoriety grows. I'm ever more alienated from the expatriate society to which I allegedly belong. My only solace and comfort is with Mum and Becky, Umali, Amina, Lutoli and the *watu*, who the *Wazungu* call 'natives'. And Sandy.

Sandy becomes my closest friend and constant companion. She follows me everywhere. Bedroom, where she sleeps, head on pillow, much to Mum's annoyance, toilet, kitchen, chicken run, even swimming pool, where she dives in and swims abreast of me. For Christmas Mum buys me a high quality, four foot long rubber dinghy, in which I'm frequently to be seen furiously paddling or languidly floating on the green lake water of the huge pool, Sandy perched half inside, front legs raised on bow, head held like a commander viewing the vessel's progress. She loves being with me, and never chooses to disembark when I give her the chance by paddling to the pool edge.

One day when I'm six I need a theme to live by, a rationale and philosophy to sustain me in this world grown colder and harsher. It comes to me in bed, while I'm thinking about Dad and how I'm going to survive without his warm, friendly face, his manly-tobacco smell, the confidence his strong hands gave, the surety that with him I was protected and safe.

A homespun proverb comes to me. It's simple. 'I am my *own* father', it says. It has three meanings. One, Dad's within, because I'm his son. Amina said that. Two, anything I do is with his authority, which I inherited. Three, even if he isn't with God, who I may have killed, if I am *him* I can watch over myself in his place. Sad though it is, it gives me direction and hope. I have the right to fight adversity. I have licence to stand up for myself. Who else will? I resolve never to run away from anyone. *They* will have to run away from me.

Umali's a bush psychologist. He knows how disturbed I am by Dad's death, and shows great compassion. He's always trying to make me laugh, sometimes using filthy Swahili, of which I am so patently fond. His expletives are unparalleled. Why should he say he 'went to the bathroom', when he can graphically pronounce he's defecated, urinated, and passed wind to blow a hole in his trousers?

Poor Umali. He has an irritable bowel. He has diarrhoea so often, Mum resorts to giving him raw flour stirred in water. 'To bind you up, *kufunga,*' she says, her Swahili always improving. It does. Three days of constipation, a day or two in-between, then diarrhoea again. He's never completely well.

Despite trying never to show emotion, it's evident Umali dotes on me. He's constantly amazed at my Swahili, flattered by my returned affection for him, Amina, the *totos* and *watu*. When he sees me looking sad, he cracks jokes to make me laugh, or tells stories of lions and *fisis*, the fearsome hyenas, striking delicious terror in my heart. Humour and terror. Better than emptiness. He avoids Dad's death. I think he knows about Tembo's puppy, and Mr Valari (senior), but never broaches the topic.

I ask him a grave and serious question.

'Where do people go when they die?' I ask.

'This is a big thing,' he says.

'Tell me old one. *Tafadhali.*' Please.

'They go up to meet with their elders.' What kind of Muslim *is* he? Ancestor worship?

'*Sababu?*' I say. 'Why?'

'*Showeri ya mungu,*' he says, looking into my eyes. A matter of God. Umali knows me well. What if he does know about Tembo's puppy and Mr Valari (senior)? He witnessed my attempt to shoot God. '*Mambo ko Mungu.*' The business of the all-powerful.

'*Sababu?*' Why?

'*Nimesema,*' he says, 'I have spoken.' He will be drawn no further into my morbid thoughts. '*Sikiliza,*' he says, changing the subject. Listen. 'I will teach you to bait fish.

'*Wapi?*' I ask. Where?

'*Ko dam.*' The dam which brings lake water to the mine, halfway from Nungwe Bay.

'*Ndio,*' I say delightedly, yes, my thoughts of death evaporating. I really want to learn. From that day our relationship takes on another dimension. Mum says what an old rogue Umali really is, how he goes fishing when he should be working, on the pretext of teaching and looking after *Jimu*.

101

Our equipment is basic. Sisal, a kind of cactus, grows wild in Geita. Making a fishing line begins with chopping off one of the great thorn-tipped leaves, then beating it with gusto against a tree trunk, until the pulpy green skin is removed. By then fibres are visible, and are plucked out, then rolled together on the thigh. It's incredible how a little rolling can connect lengths inseparably. We continue until thirty foot of line is made, then hang it to dry overnight.

Our hooks we fashion from thin nails. We cut off the heads with pliers, then beat the lower shaft to a U. At the top a closed bend makes an eye. At the other end, using a rusty file, we sharpen the point and cut a barb. It's hard and tedious. Floats are a balsa-type wood. Weights, ingeniously, are discarded spark plugs from the garage. For fishing poles we cut lengths of wild bamboo. Our kit is environmentally friendly.

There's a catch. The dam's five miles away, a long walk in the hot sun. Umali persuades Mum to take us in the morning before work, and to fetch us after five. She agrees because she knows Umali will never let anything happen to me, and because she welcomes my interest, at last, in anything other than death and dying. Mum's learnt to drive since Dad died, and has bought an old car. She drives us to the dam in that elderly Morris Minor, Maisie. The little black car has had umpteen owners, and is held together more by serendipity than science.

There isn't much choice of cars in Geita. Only two are sold in fifteen years. Mostly they're thrown away, completely worn out, like Puncture Car. Maisie, for all her shabbiness, is the only entertaining thing we have. There's no television, and the shortwave radio can't pick up signals beyond Congo due to magnetic iron ore in the ground. Bends radio waves. Mum takes us on little drives, sometimes just two or three miles. Barrat stores. The club. Sometimes, daringly, to the grass airstrip down the bottom of the wooded valley two miles from the camp. We love Maisie. Particularly when she starts.

Mum leaves us at the dam, with strict instructions not to drown. Sandy, who refuses to stay behind, takes the warning seriously, watches me like a *mwewe*-hawk, and whimpers when I approach the water's edge. The dam's huge. A half mile long reservoir, where the builders cast a concrete wall across the valley, and installed a pump to bring water ten miles from Nungwe Bay. All round is dense green bush. To approach the water I have to take off my sandals and squelch through thick, glutinous mud. Umali never wears shoes. He digs with bare hands in the mud for fat blood-worms. We put them on our hooks, toss our lines out, and make dry seats from banana leaves.

Tilapia only grow ten to twelve inches long, and rarely weigh more than a pound. But they're pretty fish, and, for their size, give quite a fight. Umali tutors me. He shows me how to sweep my fishing pole overhead, and get the line far out on the water. When I try to rush things he gives me a singular and valuable piece of wisdom. '*Haraka-haraka, habina baraka!*' he says. Speed-speed, is without blessing! He watches my float, and tells me to strike when it bobs under. When I catch my first fish he whoops with delight, and takes it off the hook for me. It's small, and he calls it a pygmy's anus. The next one is better. I catch five fish that time.

Sandy shows a true spirit of cooperation. Each time I pull a fish onto the bank, she grabs it in her mouth and brings it to me. While I'm removing the hook, she makes spitting noises. It's the funniest thing. Sandy doesn't fancy raw tilapia. Umali says she's a person who died and came back as a dog. He's a Muslim who believes in reincarnation.

After just a few trips to the dam, I'm a *fundi* at tilapia fishing. Umali prefers catfish, which live on the bottom, so he doesn't use a float. These fish are sometimes as big as his calf, and appear most hideous to me, whiskers and strange mouth, like a deformed cat in a horror show.

Eleven

We bring home fish, small and large. We don't throw them back like people in England. Why catch them? That idea wouldn't work here. Amina cooks. Umali's friends, and passing strangers, come to share. Amina boils the tilapia whole in a heavy-duty iron pot, called a *sufuria,* with wild spinach gathered in the bush, chillies grown next to the hut, onions and sweet-potato chunks. When it's ready, she takes it off the fire, and places it beside a steaming mound of *ugali*, or stiff maize-meal.

We sit in a circle on the ground, dip fingers into a bowl of water, take handfuls of *ugali*, and roll them one-handedly into balls. We dent them with our thumbs, and fill the recesses with fish and gravy by scooping into the fish-pot. Popped in the mouth and chewed, it pleases both by taste and texture. No other food satisfies like this. It doesn't matter how many *watu* there are. Somehow, there's always enough.

The fish meals exacerbate our habit of eating with the servants, and Mum sometimes begs us to eat with her for a change. One day we decide to acquiesce. There's been a torrential rainstorm that afternoon, and the flying ants have erupted from the ground to flutter briefly before losing their wispy wings and falling in a heaving, squirming carpet of life. They're eagerly collected by the *watu*. Becky fills a china pie-dish. She's just come in the front door with her writhing pot when Gretchen calls from the garden. Becky puts the dish on the dining table, covers it with a lid to stop the ants escaping, and goes out. She completely forgets her dish. I go out with her. I haven't seen my blonde Gretchen for a long time.

The dining table's laid. Mum's friends, Mrs Moore and Margaret Miller, a prim and upright expat wife from Darlington in Yorkshire, are coming. Mrs O'Rourke, of *Sportsman* cigarette fame, has left Geita. In the kitchen, Umali's been labouring for hours. A fine roast chicken, potatoes and cabbage are in the offing. Becky's covered pie-dish is from a set, and a matching salad bowl's also on the table. There's nothing out of place.

After washing our hands, Becky and I take our places at the table. It feels strange to eat so high up. The big people greet us. They've been talking about us, Mum says. 'Going native' and 'running wild' have been mentioned. She's been at pains to deny it.

Umali enters, carrying the delicious-smelling roast chicken on a platter. Mum takes the lid off the salad bowl. Margaret Miller lifts the lid off the pie-dish. Pandemonium ensues.

'Maggots!' Margaret screams in her Yorkshire accent, recoiling so violently she tips her chair backwards and falls, striking her head on the floor.

'Oh God!' yells Mrs Moore.

'Jim!' yells Mum.

'Not me!' I shout.

'Sorry,' Becky whispers.

'Oh, my head. . !' groans Margaret, sitting up, probing a gash in her scalp, where a thin arterial jet of blood pulses three inches high.

The dinner party's a resounding failure. Our notoriety grows. We aren't going to see much of Margaret Miller for a while. Umali can't hide his delight. He finds the repugnance of white people to good food amazing. He and Amina dine in style on roast chicken.

It's shortly after Becky distinguishes us with flying ants that I make my own contribution to Mum's sense of unease. Mum's asked, in addition to her job at the mine store, to 'run' the guesthouse, a small building with a big verandah on Top Road. This means supervising Thelemani, the *pishi* or cook, cleaner and do-it-all, and ensuring all's as it should be for important visitors. Sir Gordon Wearing is a 'bigwig' in the mine head office in London. He comes to Geita once a year. Mum finds Thelemani can't cook at all. Umali can. When the big man comes, meals will be prepared in our kitchen, and Thelemani will take them to Top Road on a covered tray. Thelemani's a very tall and agreeable man, much younger than Umali.

Sir Gordon arrives by Land Rover-taxi from Mwanza a little before four in the afternoon. He's been told Mum's name, and his driver asks a *toto* playing beside the road where to find her. All the *watu* know where each *Mzungu* lives. Mum's still at the mine store. I'm whittling a stick in the garden. Sandy's sleeping on the ground beside me, twitching when flies bother her. The big *Mzungu*, dressed in a fancy white safari-suit, introduces himself and asks for Mum.

Sandy growls and shows her tiny teeth, which seems to amuse him. Standing, she's less than a foot high. I tell her to *nyamaza*, be quiet, and say Mum will be home soon. He's welcome to wait for her, or I can give him a tour of our house. I'm determined to do the right thing. Mum's told me a man is coming from London, and Mr Snel asked her to show him around. She isn't home, so I'll do it.

When Mum comes home she's met by a very amused, if slightly embarrassed Sir Gordon. 'Jimmy gave me a wonderful welcome,' he says, a glass of orange juice freshly squeezed by me in his hand, and with a strained smile. He tells her what I've shown him. The lounge, the dining room, the bathroom, and the bedrooms. I've told him the history of each piece of furniture.

I've shown him the washing basket where we put dirty clothes. All my toys. The chest of drawers in Mum's bedroom. I've explained what she keeps in each drawer, and opened them to show him. I've displayed her 'posh' knickers and bras, as well as her 'normal ones'. Mum says: 'I didn't know where to put my face.' I just can't get things right. Abuse the *Wazungu*, trouble. Be nice to them, still trouble! Sir Gordon has a lovely tale to tell at the club. Jim, his funny little dog, orange juice and Mum's knickers!

Thelemani, meanwhile, is a philosopher. He speaks of many strange things. One day he introduces me to the concept of bisexuality. '*Iko watu,*' he proclaims. There are people. 'They go and do *jigi-jigi* to others, then return and *are jigi-jiggied* themselves.' I muse on this a long time. When I ask Umali, he says Thelemani is a *majinga*, fool, and speaks out of where he should only *kunya* to relieve his obviously over-full bowels. Thelemani's going *too* far for a six year old. Even Umali, as profane as he is, has limits. He tells Thelemani his mother is a *fisi*. Thelemani is most affronted. He says his mother doesn't even look like a hyena, whereas Umali's mother has a distinct resemblance to a catfish. Everybody laughs. Umali has met his match.

From five, the expatriate children attend the mine 'junior school' in the mornings. The building has one big room, with a cloakroom in one corner. The number of children varies from six to ten, aged five to six. It's on Bottom Road, between the African hospital and *kifo nyumba*.

There's only one teacher at a time. Before I go, there have been five young ladies from England in four years. Each time, the 'peaches and cream' faced arrival has been spontaneously pounced upon by sex-starved bachelors. Geita never lacks for those. They're pregnant, married, or both, 'before the *jogoo,* or rooster, crows', I hear them say, and not necessarily to their impregnator. Another replacement is found. Another bachelor, and at least once a married man, steps forward.

My teacher is Alice. She's from Hampshire. I'm five and a half when she comes. My memory of her relies not only on then, but years after, when she's married to Bob Hawk, surveyor, thirty-five years her senior, and until then a sworn single man.

Alice is plain. She lasts in post a year, unlike her predecessors, because young bachelors think her too plain. Mice frolicking in the absence of cat means sixty-year-old Bob tries her charms, in spite of boozily declaring he 'wouldn't let a woman' in his life. Geita is amused. Soon Bob's gathering wild flowers in his garden, and people note what time Alice's light goes out. 'She's marking your work', Mum says, embarrassed when I suggest they're doing *jigi-jigi*. Umali sagely says I'm right. Of course it's *jigi-jigi. Lazima!* Naturally! It takes six months before the swelling of her belly heralds a not-so discreet trip to Mwanza, from where the Derby and Lolita of Geita return as Mr and Mrs Hawk.

Before and during her pregnancy, Alice tries to teach me for a year. She isn't used to children 'run wild', and, though impressed by my Swahili, she finds it has disadvantages. I express profane opinions of her and old Bob to the cleaning maid, knowing it's safe. When Alice complains 'Jimmy's saying things in African,' Mum's alarmed.

'What have you been saying?' she asks.

'Bob likes her *kuma*,' I say. Her vagina. Mum laughs in spite of herself, and calls Umali. He's the only person I listen to.

'*Usisema*,' don't say it, Umali says, turning to me when Mum has finished regaling him with her fears. The teacher will tell the manager, Mum will be fired, we'll have to go away, he'll lose his job and quarters in the garden. He's trying not to laugh.

'*Sababu?*' I ask. Why?

'*Watanifukuza*,' he says. They'll chase you.

'*Nisemaje?*' I ask. What *should* I say?

'*Vitu nzuri*,' he replies. Nice things.

'But isn't a *kuma* a nice thing, Umali? Don't you like Amina's?' Umali loses control, hoots with laughter. Mum digs him in the ribs.

'You're as bad as him!' she exclaims, unable to keep her face straight. Her Swahili is coming on, I have to admit. I'll have to be more careful.

It isn't Mum, nor Umali, who take action to curb me. The next time I speak Swahili at school, though I'm only telling the maid I don't like the teacher, Alice grabs me by an ear, drags me to the bathroom, bends me over the low basin, turns on the water, and forces a piece of

Lifebuoy soap between my lips. 'That'll wash the filth from your mouth!' she says when she lets me up. It doesn't. I tell her what to do with her fat vagina, and her tits while she's at it. She doesn't understand, but gets the gist. From now on we're sworn enemies.

I'm thrilled to hear of Alice's bust-up with Mrs Snel, the manager's wife. It's just days after the soap incident when, sunning herself topless in what she presumes is the seclusion of her garden, she causes an accident. Driving down from Top to Bottom Road for an early sundowner, Vito Parelli, an Italian bachelor who's shunned her virtues before, applies his Land Rover's brakes to prolong his view of her naked bosom from his high vehicle. Unaware of the go-slow ahead, Mrs Snel drives her Volkswagen Beetle into the back of him. Instead of lying about why he's stopped, the terrified Vito points out Alice.

'What *do* you think you're doing?' Mrs Snel yells at Alice from the road. 'You're that new teacher, aren't you?' Alice leaps to her feet, holding a T-shirt in front of her chest.

'This is *Africa*, you know!' Mrs Snel yells. 'You can't go naked round here!' Soon the story of the *oochi,* or naked, English teacher is old news in Geita. Not really fair, she was only topless. I don't care. Alice and Mrs Snel are never to be friends. It may have been hard for Mr Snel and Bob Hawk, but, being old drinking pals, they decide to ignore the petulance of women. For me the bust-up is heaven-sent. Talk about *schadenfreude!* I don't like either. They can kill each other for all I care. I don't know then, but I'm anticipating the thoughts of Mao tse Tung. Somewhere in his little red book are the words '*my enemy's enemy is my friend*'. If it ever comes to it, I'll help either kill the other.

I'm six, Becky eight. Umali and Amina are run ragged during the day, too exhausted to look after us at night if Mum goes to the club. In desperation they introduce Jackson, Amina's long-lost nephew, tell Mum he's a super chap, and persuade her to employ him *ad-hoc* to babysit. Jackson's in his early twenties when we meet him. He's always dressed in clean shorts and shirt, which in a district where most *Watu* wear *Kanzus*, long wrap-around cloths, or tattered, filthy remnants of western garb, is unique. Unlike his aunt, he has a mouth full of brilliant white teeth. He plays the guitar. An old, battered, much-repaired one. He strums it with enthusiasm, if not skill, and sings, in what he thinks is *Kiingereza*, or English.

Once, sometimes twice, a week for two years, before I go to boarding school, and later during holidays, Jackson is our evening companion. He's always gleaming and freshly bathed, smelling of carbolic soap, wearing a wide grin, and carrying his beloved guitar. We welcome him, Mum gives him instructions not to let me run around with a knife, or stick nails into electric wall plugs, and to keep the doors bolted in case of lions or *watu mbaya*, bad people. Then she drives the half mile to the club in Maisie.

We love it when Jackson plays his guitar. At least two strings are usually missing or replaced with fishing line, and the other four aren't in tune. He strums it, beats a drum-sound with his thumb, and sings. That's the best. His English, which he insists on using, is atrocious, mispronounced, non-understandable and wonderful. We sit in a circle on the floor, and listen.

Jackson sings lots of songs. Popular ones throughout the British empire, ubiquitous and defining Englishness. He's heard them on his crackly wireless. For me the real words, meanings and pronunciations will take years to permeate, let alone replace these first renditions. Everything I hear later is, to me, fake, a re-make, and a less likeable version of the 'original'. '*Gorde Sieve Our Greasious Quinn*' is my favourite. Sieving the greasy queen would get the bad bits out. I also like '*We'll mate again*' and '*Tack a massage to Miree*'.

About this time the BBC begins random-time broadcasts to Geita in diverse style, manner and smell. I don't know who starts it, but the craze sweeps through the camp like a locust-storm, and soon we're all doing it. The rule is, when you feel you're going to break wind, you clench your buttocks, hold it in, stand to attention, salute, shout 'London News!', then let it go. We are updated by the news at random times of the day for several years. There are foreign, as well as British announcers.

'Der London Newses!' Dieter shouts. 'Pffffpfff.'

'Newsa da London!' It's Antonio. 'Bwaaapff.'

'London News,' Gretchen says sweetly, 'pfff.' Girls are always so gentle, even when they *jamba*. Specially Gretchen.

Even Lutoli gets into it. '*Newsi ya Congo!*' he pronounces before he lets rip. Perhaps this news coverage explains my early take on world affairs.

Jackson's so relaxed and tolerant, we begin to take advantage. We tell our friends we can do anything we want when he's minding us. They come to see for themselves.

There are evenings when the Blüger pair, Sophia Fortuna, Becky's Italian friend, and the two of us congregate at our house and listen to Jackson's songs. Then we play games, usually starting with good old hide and seek. When we tire of that, we make up others. We play doctors and nurses, which means we ask each other what's wrong, health-wise, then flash our private parts. It's quite cursory, and I wonder why we bother. It hasn't got any real meaning. Unless I can look at Gretchen.

Our most exciting game is Becky's invention. It's called *ruka chini*, or 'jump down'. She pulls the mattress off her bed, and puts it on the floor under the built-in wardrobe. Then she empties the shelves on one side, and leaves the door open. This forms a ladder, which we climb in a queue, to sit on top of the wardrobe, then launch ourselves into space. We have to shout the name of a wild animal in mid-air, then emulate the sound it makes before crashing onto the mattress.

'*Nyani-wah*-thump!' monkey, '*Fisi-hee-hee*-crash!' hyena, '*Simba-roarrrr*-bump!' lion, '*Tembo-woo-hoo*-bang!' elephant, '*Chui-arrrghh*-wack!' cheetah, '*Twiga-chew-chew*-biff!' giraffe, '*Nyoka-sssss*-wallop!' snake. We live charmed lives. Not one broken limb in hundreds of jumps.

One evening we again persuade trusting Jackson to let us play *ruka chini*. We file into Mum's bedroom, unpack half the wardrobe, drag the mattress off Mum's bed, and start jumping, to jungle sounds and hoots of laughter. Unnoticed by us, the door opens and in steps Umali. He's heard the racket and come to investigate. Sometimes time stops. This is one. For a frozen moment he stands staring up at the top of the wardrobe, where Dieti, too late to stop, is launching into space, the trumpeting of an elephant breaking from his pursed lips. Umali's eyes go wide as baked-bean-tin-tops, and his mouth opens and closes like a freshly landed tilapia. Time catches up. Dieti thumps into his chest, knocking him sprawling.

'*Scheise!*' Dieti exclaims, rolling off Umali's body.

'*Shetani!*' Umali wheezes, struggling to sit up. Devil! When he recovers he tells us his thoughts in graphic terms. He's unamused. He tells Mum he went to investigate loud noises, and '*Geremani ndogo ari ruka ju mimi!*' A small German jumped on me. It takes a long time for Umali-relations to thaw.

'Tell that Dieter not to jump on Umali!' Mum says.

Twelve

I prefer Lutoli's company to anyone else's, except Umali. We get along so well, and play inventive, amusing games together. The *Wazungu* don't understand or sympathise. They say I've 'gone native'. It makes me mad. I won't be forced to abandon my oldest friend just because the *Wazungu* say so.

One of our best games involves 'volunteered' animal participants. In Geita there are huge trees which produce eight-inch long seed pods. When they fall, and dry in the sun, they split into two brown, boat-shaped, halves. They have sharp prows, and perfectly shaped hulls. There's even a squared-off transom. They float, and are completely waterproof. Lutoli says they are *Mungu*'s, or God's, little *mashuas*, open sailing dhows, like the fishermen's ones on Lake Victoria. We make holes and insert sticks for masts, then attach bits of rag for sails. Faithful to the *mashua* design, we attach a flat stick to one side aft, as steering-oar. Mashuas don't have central rudders.

With boats ready, we head for the dam above top road. We check which way the breeze is blowing, then look for passengers. There are always ants in Geita. Termites, safari ants, little brown ants, red ants. They're never difficult to find. Using a stick or leaf, we deposit several angry little passengers in our *mashuas*. Then we launch them downwind. The craft are surprisingly fast. Within minutes they're fifty yards away. Sometimes they go all the way to the far bank. We run round, and watch our seafaring ants disembark. As they step on land again, they look confused, and fan out into defensive positions. I can imagine their thoughts. What the hell's happened? Sometimes the breeze dies when the boat's in mid-water, and our passengers are becalmed. We don't know if any swim for it.

One day my *mashua* is sailing along with its un-choosing

111

passengers, when there's a sudden disturbance on the surface of the water. To our astonishment a big frog leaps into the boat. We don't know if he's after the ants, or likes sailing. He crouches there, in the middle of the deck, his thick throat billowing, watching with slit eyes as his commandeered craft continues into the middle of the dam. He's a frog-pirate, I say. Lutoli doesn't understand.

Just then there's a huge splashing sound, and something like a long, undulating black rope flashes out of and back into the water. It's gone. So is the frog. The *mashua*'s swamped. It's sinking. '*Nyoka ya maji!*' Lutoli screams, retreating from the bank. Water snake. '*Blurryfucken!*' he adds for completeness. Even Lutoli's learnt from the English. With blurryfucken snakes like that here, we go in search of other adventure.

Later, at Mum's office, I tell Mr Hessler about the snake. I leave out our adjective. Hessler knows everything, Mum says. At his request, I describe as best I can what Lutoli and I saw, and what happened to the frog, which was stealing my boat, and. . . Mr Hessler holds up his hand.

'Ach zo,' he says, peering at me over his half-glasses, with the sunlight from the window illuminating his bald head, 'zat iss der Barotse vorter snake. Der proper name iss *Crotaphopeltis barotseensis* – I know ziss von!' He's triumphant. I've stumbled onto his passion, water-snakes! 'Zey eat small sinks, like leetle fish und frogs, but, to us, zey are harmless.' That might be, I muse, but I'm not *ever* going in that water! Lutoli's waiting outside. He agrees with me. What does the bald *Mzungu* know, anyway? Does he know the *watu* call him *Kiwanja,* for *Kiwanja ya ndege,* or landing-place of the bird? An airport, really. It's an abusive name for bald people. We head for my house.

On our way along Top Road, we come to the junction of Compound Hill. Mlozi's there, sitting on his *mwamba,* or flat rock. It's been a while, maybe more than a year, since he narrowly escaped stoning for blasphemy. We're so busy, we don't go this way often, and usually we keep to bush-paths. Mlozi's changed. He's slimmer, looks older. He's got even more coloured ribbons braided into his locks, and there's more *mifupa,* or bones, around his ankles too.

More importantly, he's built himself a home! It's only six foot by four, and four foot high, made of sticks and mud, roofed with bundles of tied banana-leaf. There isn't a window or door. It's just behind his *mwamba*-stone, which now serves as front patio. When he sees us he does a little dance, shaking the bones, but he doesn't rattle the dreaded *kimbo*-tin and stones. Lutoli says some *watu* are beginning to be afraid of Mlozi. Say he's not mad, nor *jinni* or *djinn*-possessed, but an *mchawi,* or witch. He shudders saying it.

The *machula* is a collector and carrier of *mavi*, or faeces. That's his occupation, like many people did before water-borne sewage.

The camp has separate water-borne systems for each house. They built them the same, and the length of transit is twenty yards. The destinations of the outlets are concrete-covered septic tanks, with vents lidded by concrete stoppers. They say expanding and explosive gasses force the lids up, thus venting and reducing pressure. This amuses us, and we want to hear our septic tank fart. We'll take a whiff, get a thrill, run away, breathe fresh air, and laugh. Problem is, despite equatorial heat, supposed to exaggerate and expand foul gas, venting never happens when we want. Must occur gradually, unexplosively. Maybe at night. Or it waits till our backs are turned. We have to prise the lids off, stick our noses in, and inhale deeply. There isn't a smell at all. What a let-down!

The *machulas* are different. The *mavi* they carry is raw, rotten, stinking, nauseating downwind. In the grassy waste between the houses are eight corrugated wood and iron privies, with steel buckets under the seats. These are removed, emptied, and replaced through a rear trapdoor every week. This is *machula* work.

The post is undesirable, the waiting list short. Incumbents are placed by fate on the lowest rung of humanity. All have, at least, squint, cast eye, partial blindness, old age, bent posture, abnormal gait, small stature and low self-esteem. They are the real *wasikini*.

I'm six when *machula*-baiting begins. It's to become an obsessional pursuit for me, my *Mzungu* friends and African *rafikis*. A game of *machula*-baiting can't be pre-arranged like other sports. The *machula* is wily, knows his terrain, and that his best defence is to reduce exposure by randomising his timetable according to chaos theory. A serious mathematician when not carrying *mavi*. We never know when he's coming, before, unexpectedly, the cry of '*machula, machula*', sung to the tune of '*I'm the king of the castle*', rings out.

We can rely on one thing. The *machula* comes by day. The task of emptying buckets of *mavi* into bigger buckets is precarious enough, without doing it in the dark. To top that *fisis* or hyenas, the object of great fear among '*watu*', are keen diners on *cordon bleu* human excrement, and can smell a thimbleful from a mile. They can't open the privies to gain their culinary delights themselves. A *machula* doing it for them, in the dark where they alone can see, would be a *fisi* dream come true. They'd dine on the delicacy, and wash it down with fresh *machula!* The crafty machula comes by day, and generations of wistful *fisis* live out their lives in eternal hope, but ultimate disappointment.

He comes in the shimmering heat, with a dark three foot wide halo, faithfully following above his bent head. These are the *bluebottles*, or 'shit-flies', moving like the '*Interahamwe*' of Rwanda in later years, 'as one'. There's a low buzz, which by ears unabused by modern life can be heard for hundreds of yards.

Closely following, like the second horseman of the apocalypse, is the honk. Not a stink, not a stench. Worse. Faeces stink. Faeces rotted more out of the bowels than in, stink worse. Rotted in temperatures above 40 degrees, mixed with urine, carried in open buckets, garlanded with shit-flies, it produces an olfactory sensation for which there is no word. *Honk* has to do.

Under the moving, humming cloud, and out of the nose-banging honk, the struggling *machula* staggers into range on thin legs, yoke over shoulders, buckets swinging, breathless from exertion, heat and toxic fume. With enough warning, we can be in position, out of sight in the grass, waiting with breath baited by anticipation and revulsion. The range closes.

In an ambush you shouldn't open fire too soon. You should hold your fire 'till you see the whites of their eyes'. John Wayne said so, and he can't be wrong. When you open fire, the enemy must be in range, unable to retreat without suffering significant casualties. Hence subterfuge, camouflage, and careful placing of artillery and machine-gun out of sight. Military strategy. John Wayne's a trusted expert. He always wins against Red Indians. We take his words seriously.

We have to let the *machula* into range before we attack. That's rule one. Here, Sandy proves, for the first time in her life, to be an unreliable ally. Though she creeps with us silently to our ambush positions, she finds it impossible to contain her excitement as the *machula* comes closer, and, before he's in range for the attack to begin, she leaps on her short legs from the cover of grass and thornbush to deliver a wild, yelping bark, and high-pitched snarl, giving away our position and sacrificing our element of surprise. She sabotages two ambushes, and I am prevailed upon to lock her in the house when a *machula* attack is planned. When I do, Sandy ignores me for an hour afterwards. But she can't keep it up.

Sandy-less, we're able to concentrate again. After maintaining the surprise element, the second matter of importance is to have lots of ammunition ready, so to deliver a sustained fusillade. Verbal abuse, like anything else which may give the game away, has to be withheld until the last moment. The *machula* must 'walk into it'. This is vintage John Wayne. Gretchen tells me a joke she heard about him. Someone told her dad. John Wayne wants to have an Indian squaw, which is *IS*. He goes to the Indian Reserve, which is *IR*. He enters the Indian Tepee, which is *IT*, and asks the Indian Chief, which is *IC*, for an Indian Squaw, *IS*. He gets badly beaten up by the *FBI*, which is a *Forkin Big Indian*. I laugh, because otherwise she'll think I don't understand. I've heard the word *fork* used like this before. When a car engine doesn't go, it's *forked*. That's what Spiros the mechanic says when he throws his spanner down and gives up.

There are five, sometimes six or even seven of us. We need sufficient combatants to outflank and surround our quarry. Our numbers depend on how quickly we can recruit after a warning. All are sworn to join if called, and close enough. Sometimes we are only *Mzungu* children, but at other times several *totos* join us. There are never more than five minutes to get organised and into position. The *machula* shuffles determinedly. He stops at each privy. If uninterrupted, he can move between all of them, and be gone in ten minutes. Timing's critical.

In the early evolution of the sport, our artillery comprises only pebbles picked up and pocketed *en-route* to the battlefield. This is unsatisfactory, and serves only to harass and annoy our target. Soon, however, technology being what it is, we make catapults. This changes not only the results, but the rules of engagement. Now we can award points for hitting particular targets, on or off the *machula*.

Top points go to knocking his bucket off the end of his yoke, or causing it to overturn. Lesser points are for striking the *machula* himself. There's kudos too, in missing, but putting him to flight, particularly if he knocks over or spills his buckets on his own. A negative or 'minus' point is awarded if the *machula*, responding to the attack, hits you with his own ammunition, a handful of *mavi*.

Battles occur up to ten times a year. There are so many that the exact disposition of troops, position of the enemy, accuracy and success of the fire, and final outcome, can't be recalled for each occasion. What can be recalled is the predictable diction of an ambushed *machula*.

'*Blurryfuckenbastars, fokin you. . !*' he yells, scooping the contents of a bucket and hurling it in our direction. I think he'd use the same words even if he *did* know the meaning.

One day in 1958, a year after Dad died, it's school holidays, and everyone's at home in Geita. I'm a little over seven, which makes Becky and Gretchen nine, Dieti seven, and Antonio Barelli eight. We're playing cops and robbers in the garden of the Barelli house. The girls have little choice. If they want to play with *us*, they play *our* game. Dieti's being a robber who just happens to be hiding, after a bank-heist, in the branches of a very large tree. This affords him a great view over the camp, and particularly the open ground and latrines.

Dieti, unlike his sister, still has a strong German accent, and suddenly, instead of being quiet and maintaining his hiding place, he yells, 'Ze *machula* ist Komink!' This is the end of cops and robbers. We drop our toy guns, grab handfuls of stones, and dash headlong into the elephant grass to set up our ambush. The girls are as keen as us, and collect stones in held-up skirts.

'Jeem, eef I heet the *machula*'s bucket weeth thees stone,' Antonio whispers as we lie peeping through the grass, 'you must geeve me one chicken-gum!' He means chewing gum. On this occasion, we're too slow. By the time we get our ammunition ready, and deploy, the *machula*'s gone. We decide we have to plan ahead, not leave the initiative to the enemy. We'll get him, before long, and it'll be us who choose both time and terms of engagement.

It's Christmas holidays of the same year, when we decide the time has come to spring a major ambush. Thus far we've only held sporadic skirmishes against the *machula*, and the outcome's been undecided. It's time for a strategically planned, devastating attack, to teach him a lesson.

Dieti's father was in the Afrika Korps, so there's military talent in the family. Dad was in the Royal Navy, and I'm bigger than Dieti, so I also qualify. Antonio's dad surrendered with thousands of other Italians in Ethiopia, so Antonio comes along as a simple trooper, not to partake in strategic planning.

'Anyvay, yor fadder iss ein *alcoholic!*' Dieti adds for good measure.

'Why you says thees?' Antonio asks.

'I hearded him singink in der club,' Dieti says, 'und he vos singink "arrived drunk in ze *boma!*" '

'Thata wasa "*Arrivaderci Roma*," Goodbye Rome!' Antonio mutters.

'Vell, he shood say zo!'

Antonio's brother Stefano is only five, too small for action. Gretchen and Becky are nine, and keen, though they've no weapons-skills. Girls! They don't even know how to shoot a catapult!

The offensive has to be bold to be effective. We anticipate the 'shock and awe' American bombing campaign of Baghdad more than forty years in the future, in 2003. We have new weapons, in addition to tried and tested stones and catapults. It's Dieti who comes up with our gunpowder plot. In those days in Tanganyika there are problems with baboons raiding the *shambas* or kitchen gardens of the *watu*.

116

Someone imports large red fire crackers, or bangers, from China, which the *watu* buy to throw at the baboons, who, it is hoped, will flee and never return. They're called '*bobejaan bangers*', from the Afrikaans for baboon. In fact, these giant three inch long bangers are bought more for fun and frightening people than by baboon-harassed *watu*. The buyers in chief in Geita are us, the Anti *Machula* Front.

Dieti, adopting his best military planning pose, draws on the ground with a stick. We've seen films where generals do that. 'If ve take big bamboo,' he says, 've can empty powder uff four oder five bangers in it, und make vun cannon.'

'How will we set it off?' I ask.

'Vid der fuses,' he says. 'Ve make a hole in der back, und pull der fuse out. Zen ve light it!'

'Whata willa we shoota from ita?' Antonio wants to know.

'Anysing. Stones, hoont-sheet. . .' Dieti says.

'How many cannons?' I ask.

'Two. I make zem. Ve haff big bamboos at mein haus.'

Dieti goes off to make his cannons. Antonio and I collect smooth round pebbles from the stream near the club. For the cattys. The girls say they'll come to shout abuse, and maybe toss a few stones. That's a worry. Stones chucked by them may go in any direction. Including ours. I tell them to stick to abuse.

Meanwhile I consider the enemy. The *machula* always comes from the west. We know this, because he collects *mavi* in the evenings, when the sun is going down behind him, throwing long *machula*-shadows on the thorny ground to the east. With the enemy in bold outline against the orange East African sun, there's a disadvantage. The sun'll be in *our* eyes, not his. How to overcome that? I decide to consult an old military advisor. Umali.

'*Sababu, mdogo wangu?*' he asks when I explain our mission to disrupt the local sewage system. Why, little brother?

'*Ninapenda,*' I say. I like it.

'*Atatosha,*' he says, smiling wickedly and showing his teeth. It will suffice. 'If that's what you want to do, I'll advise you how.'

Umali draws on the ground with a stick. Also a bit of a general. 'The machula comes from here,' he says, pointing to one side, 'and the sun's behind him?'

'Yes.'

'You have to attack from behind. Wait until he's half-way up the slope, then attack from downhill, where he came from. That way the sun will be behind *you,* and will blind *him* when he turns.'

'*Asante,*' I say. Thanks. I relay the revised plan to Dieti, who's delighted, because shooting cannons into fierce evening sunlight can't be accurate.

Unfortunately, our latest, and boldest, attack has to be postponed because of the intervention of a scorpion. Dieti and I are intricately planning the attack. It's a hot, sweltering day, and we're sitting on the floor in our lounge. We don't like the wooden armchairs because our feet don't reach the floor. I yawn and stick my right hand under the edge of a big rug. It's so strange how, in the heat of day, it always feels cool in the space created by fingers between wooden floor and rug.

The *Buthidae* family of scorpions are the most dangerous to man. The genus *Parabuthus*, of which there are several species, are commonest. *Parabuthus granulatus* is the culprit in most fatal scorpion stings in East Africa. They grow up to three inches long. They're light brown, with paler striations across the body. They hold their tails high, and on them are hook-like extensions to deliver the sting. The poison they inject is a neurotoxin, which, in sufficient dose, causes difficulty speaking or swallowing, inability to pass urine, a rapid heart rate, incoordination, panic and respiratory arrest.

Scorpions don't, as a rule, choose humans or large animals to sting. Their prey is other insects. But they seek out cool, dark places in the heat of day. Places like the space between our wooden floor and the rug.

It's difficult to describe the sensation. Everyone knows what it's like to hit a finger with a hammer. This is indescribably worse. Like someone's injecting petrol into my fingertip. I scream in agony, and pass out.

I come to with a bumping, rocking movement. I look up to see the underneath of Amina's face. She's running, breathing like a locomotive, carrying me. It's the road to the hospital. Her mouth is open as she gasps for breath, her two big teeth protruding. We're almost there, and only seconds later I'm staring up into the worried face of Dr Weiss.

'You vill be fine,' he says, as I feel a sharp prick in my left shoulder, 'zis is ze treatment for ze scorpion sting. Ze maid vos very clever.' He holds up an empty, lidded jam jar, with a crushed scorpion at the bottom. 'Zis is vot stinged you, and I know zis von. Today iss your lucky day.' He pricks me with another syringe. 'Zis is adrenalin.' He puts his stethoscope on my chest and tells me to breathe. 'If I didn't know vot stinged you, zat vood be bad, but ze maid she kilt it, und bringt it. She iss *very* goot!'

The sharp pain in my finger has subsided, but now a throbbing begins. I lift my hand and am shocked. My finger's dark purple like a *bringali* or aubergine, swollen to twice its normal thickness. I wince more with alarm than pain. Beside me Amina tut-tuts. '*Pole, Jimu, Pole.*' Easy, Jimu, easy. I feel her hand on my shoulder. Good old Amina! Not the wicked witch I once thought.

'Das ist fur der pain,' Dr Weiss says, injecting me again. It's my first experience of morphine. The pain recedes like magic, and I enter a pleasant, dreamy world. It's almost worth being stung by a scorpion. Pity I couldn't just have the morphine. As I drift into euphoria-land, I giggle to think of the scorpion working for the *machula*. It has stopped our planned attack before it began. With what would a *machula* pay a scorpion? Obvious, isn't it?

Convalescence is so boring. Josef Weiss orders I stay in bed, without friends, for five days. Mum insists I obey, and persuades Umali to police me. I'm not feeling well the first two days. I have a banging headache, and my finger still throbs. I lie with Sandy, listening to the sounds of the bush at night, of *watu* talking and Land Rovers going up and down the road in the day. I'm woken each morning, as always, by the raucous crow of our rooster or *jogoo*.

By the third day I'm fatally bored, and Umali finally agrees to let me sit outside, while he and Amina hover, just in case. They keep an anxious eye on the road, lest Mum come home early and catch me out of bed. Equally concerned for my welfare is Sandy, who at a year old looks like a shortened Daschund, a brown teddy bear with a big black button-nose. She's lain on my bed since I was bitten, and now sits solicitously close, studying my face with unblinking, doleful eyes. Together we watch the *kukus*, or chickens. I've never paid them much attention before.

The *kuku* run is huge. Twenty yards by ten, fenced by wooden poles and chicken-mesh. We have thirty fowls, all hens except one. The exception is the *jogoo,* pronounced jog-awe, or rooster. The females are small and drab, but the *jogoo* is magnificent, proud, and twice as big as his ladies. He's black and white, with a collar of reddish brown, and a scarlet comb like a ripe pomegranate on his head. There's a cruel curve to his beak, and his beady black eyes glare with menace and disdain. As I watch, he stalks the run like a slave master, stopping either to drink from an upturned WWII helmet, or to briefly mount a hen.

'*Na tengeneza mayai,*' Umali says. He's making eggs. Doesn't make sense. We only get two eggs a day, if we're lucky. As I watch, the *jogoo* mounts his sixth hen in an hour. He knows I'm watching him. Between thrusts, he glares at me. He wants to be my enemy. He came after me last time I fetched eggs, but thought better at the last second. A coward, despite his crowing and posturing. I'll teach him one day.

I don't need to bother. Only a few weeks after the scorpion, Mum buys a young male turkey from a chicken and orange merchant.

Moses is from the *waGallua* at a shamba near Biharlomoulo, a large village forty miles away, where many *Gallluas* live. He's a serious *mpengu* or gap-tooth. His top front teeth are missing because, in the age old *Gallua* custom, he's knocked them out with a rock, because gaps in the teeth are deemed *maridadi*, attractive to maidens, and allow 'better' kissing. His remaining teeth are badly decayed, and two are only black stumps protruding from his gums. His short curly hair is as white as the distant snows of Kilimanjaro, and his face as wrinkled as dried fruit. He's very slim and stooped. He broke his back as a child, he says, when he fell from an *umstafehli* tree. Not everything about Moses is decrepit. His dark eyes, always darting about, as if looking for danger, are bright and mischievous, and he has an enchanting, if lopsided and dentally challenged, grin.

There are twenty orange trees, six lemon trees, five *umstafehli* trees, and a grapefruit tree on his *shamba*. When the fruit is ripe, Moses trundles it to Geita. His transport is an aged bicycle without handlebars, pedals, chain or seat. Just the metal frame and wheels which were once part of a bicycle. The front wheel forks are wired to the frame to prevent turning. Attached to the top bar there is a *baruti*, or dynamite, box. Moses fills it with fruit, and pushes his strange two wheeled cart all the way. It makes sense, in fact, because the footpaths to Geita are narrow and overgrown, and won't allow a four-wheeled cart to pass.

Becky and I like Moses, and he finds Mum a compassionate, and therefore gullible, customer. By the time he emerges from the dense bush, and pushes his contraption up the hill, he's exhausted, parched, and breathless. He comes to expect that he will be given cold water from the fridge to drink, and Mum will surely buy all his fruit to save him further labour.

The average load in his box is fifty large oranges and half a dozen lemons. The oranges are huge, almost the size of a grapefruit. They're green on the outside, and never change colour, no matter how ripe. Inside they're a rich orange, almost red. When cut in half and squeezed, one produces half a tumbler full of sweet, tangy juice. In Geita we don't buy *Coca Cola* or other bottled drinks, except at the club. Umali squeezes the oranges, and fills several pint glass bottles,

120

which are kept in the spare fridge in the pantry. We drink glasses full whenever we're thirsty.

Once a year the *umstafehli* trees each bear a single fruit. A massive dark green thing, twice the size, and roughly the same shape, as a rugby ball. The green skin is soft, and the fruit easily bruised or burst by contact. There are inch-long green spikes on the surface, but they're illusory. Like the rest of the skin, they're soft and fleshy, and easily bent or crushed. Nature using trickery for protection. They *look* like thorns, but don't have the same effect. Must keep *some* gullible fruit eaters at bay. The *umstafehli* is linen-white inside. The soft flesh is separable into spindle-shaped segments, each with a large black pip in the centre. If a segment is squeezed, milky white juice runs out.

An *umstafehli* has to be chilled in the fridge for maximum enjoyment. When it's sufficiently cool, we gorge. The taste cannot be likened to any other. Sweet and sour at the same time, fragrant and tantalising to the taste buds. Once eaten, never forgotten, and the next *umstafehli* is longed for passionately. That's the problem. One tree, one fruit, one year. Not exactly available. Only favoured customers get one, and we get two, sometimes three, each year. We're lucky indeed!

In addition to tending fruit trees, Moses rears chickens on the *shamba*. When they are half grown he forces them into little baskets made of twigs and twine, six to eight at a time, leaving them so little room that their heads protrude and they can't move their wings or bodies. A basket is suspended from each end of a long pole, which he hefts on his shoulders for the trip to Geita. Moses knows Mum won't let him continue to carry a burden in the hot sun, and can't see animals in distress without rescuing them. Fortunately for us, he's usually sold half his chickens before he gets to our house. Mum buys the rest, and they're set free in the chicken run. After, that is, the little black lice which stick to the outer edges of their eyes are removed, using a fine cloth and a dab of turpentine.

Our chicken run's a flat piece of wire-fenced ground twenty metres square. There are two chicken houses, made of wood planking, raised from the ground on stilts a foot high. They're roofed with corrugated iron. Each has an entrance just big enough for a chicken to squeeze through. Inside there are wooden perches running across, where the fowls cuddle close to each other at night. On the ground there are six upturned army helmets, filled with water. It's hot in Geita.

The number of *kukus* varies. At times there are as many as forty, at others as few as fifteen. In Geita you can't buy an oven-ready chicken. Squeamishness and sentimentality are out. Our *kukus* are for eggs, and eating.

121

f

One day Moses brings a different kind of bird, a *batamzinga*, which strangely translates as cannon-duck, but is known to *Wazungu* as a turkey. It's a feisty, very angry young male. He's a handsome thing, all reds and browns, with huge hanging bits on his chin and under his fierce, curved beak. He has tail feathers all the colours of a *can-can* dancer's skirts. He's contorted in a tiny woven-grass cage. Of course, we buy him. When he's released in the *kuku* run, he does a high-speed dash around the perimeter, scattering sand and pebbles. He's relishing his freedom. The *kukus*, and even the *jogoo*, look taken aback. Life's going to change round here.

From the outset, the *batamzinga* dwarfs the *jogoo*, and he continues to grow. The *jogoo* tries to ignore him, but the hens overlook his gigantism, and adopt him as one of their offspring. It's hilarious watching Snow-White, our favourite hen, leading her six newly-hatched chicks round the run, with a huge gawky turkey youth in tow. Sometimes, when she digs up a worm, she even gives it to him! People don't believe us till they see it. We've had the turkey three months when he first makes the call by which we'll name him.

He stands in the centre of the chicken run, spreads his magnificent tail feathers like a huge technicolour fan, thrusts his head back, opens his beak wide, and shrieks. 'Gooloogooloogooloogooloo,' in an unbroken challenge to all. A *coup d'etat*. The *jogoo* is supplanted. From now on, though he still announces the sun's rising, and services the hens, he'll never strut again. His eyes lose their threat. The dictator of the *kuku* run is Gooloogooloo now. The *jogoo*'s a broken bird.

Moses has a brother, Iwe, pronounced *ee-weh*, which means 'you' in Gallua. This causes much hilarity. If he says, 'I like you', he'll be saying 'you like you!' There are many delightful possibilities. You could *marry* you. You could even do *jigi jigi* with you! I wonder why his parents named one son *You* and the other after a Hebrew Patriarch. The brothers live with their wives and children on a shamba six miles away in the bush. Iwe is absent much of the time, as a guest of the Tanganyika Territory Correction Service. He pursues a more nefarious occupation than his brother. We're all hugely amused by him.

Iwe is even older than Moses, and is a notorious criminal. His crime is illegally producing a poisonously alcoholic drink from maize and sugar, distilled to a potent spirit called '*moshi*', or 'smoke'. This he sells to tribesmen and women far and wide, including those at Geita. The *selekali* or police try to stamp out illegal brewers and distillers because, being so potent and so cheap, illiberal consumption is at the root of many murders and maimings, and, more importantly, Her Majesty's Colonial Government in Dar es Salaam receives no excise.

Caught red handed many times, Iwe has just as often moved the location of his distillery, each time rebuilding it deeper and deeper in the bush. He disguises his enterprise by sinking the bins in the ground, planting vegetation, and only lighting fires in deep holes. His efforts only protect him briefly, because he only ever gets one production to market before the *selekali* pounce, smash his equipment, and remove him to jail. Iwe doesn't remember how many times he's been locked up, but knows it's a lot.

Mum takes pity on Iwe, and finds him a likeable rogue. She asks him why he's always in trouble. Iwe can speak no English, but he has heard the words of the magistrate many times, and he takes them as total explanation for his woes. 'I didn't got the line-sense,' he says, and the meaning is unclear. What sense *is* there in a line? I ask Mum. He means a *licence*, she says. He doesn't have a brewing licence, so he isn't allowed to distil alcohol. Many times over the years he disappears because, yet again, he's in jail. Each time we see him again he gives the same explanation. Mum tries to get him to look at the matter more broadly.

'If you haven't got a line-sense,' she says, 'why do you do it, and get into trouble?' He cocks his head and looks confused. Maybe he wonders if the *Mzungu* woman hasn't imbibed too much *moshi* herself, talking in riddles like this!

'Because,' he says at last, 'it's my work.'

'Yes, but the *selekali,* the police. . .'

'They won't give me the line-sense, *blurryfucken!*' Mum blushes, but controls herself.

'But you have to stop. . .'

'*Memsahib*, are you, too, working for the *selekali*?' He eyes her quizzically. 'Do you want Iwe to become *masikini,* a poor man, and blind him in one eye so he can beg?' There's no winning. Each time he's freed from jail, Mum makes him a big mug of sweet tea, and he regales us with the latest chapter in his continuing infamy.

We've got to give Iwe his due. He's an entrepreneur. Doing his own market-research, he branches out into growing *bhangi*, or cannabis, beside his jungle stills. It's noticed the known drunkards among the *watu* seem even more detached and carefree than before. As a consequence, Iwe's stays at Her Majesty's pleasure are longer, and we see ever less of him. Still, he steadfastly pleads, it's all simply due to the lack of a line-sense.

Thirteen

In January 1959, at seven and a half, I go to boarding school. There's no school in our district at the time, and Arusha is a long way from home. Becky, two years older, has been boarding there for two years. Now I'm going with her. I don't know how far it is, nor how long three-month terms will seem. I have no inkling how different it will be to live in close company with other boys, nor what discipline is like. Such is the naivety of youth. I'm excited. I'm going on a journey. It's going to be an adventure. Becky and Mum don't try to persuade me otherwise. I wonder why Becky cries when she has to go back after the holidays, but that's girls for you!

Buying clothes for school is a new experience. The uniform for boys is short khaki trousers, dark green short-sleeved shirts, grey stockings and brown lace-up shoes. Most of these are available at *Boma Duka*, a collection of Indian shops strangely isolated in the bush six miles from Geita.

The shirts are only available in white. Mum's a *fundi* at dying clothes, and dyes the white shirts green in a cauldron heated on the Belling range. I'm measured for my khaki shorts, which are stitched in the hour on a Singer treadle sewing machine by an ancient Indian lady dressed in a flowing pink *sari*. There's a red dye-mark on her forehead. She's Hindu. The dot means she's married. She speaks continually as she deftly pushes the cloth under the whizzing needle, and pedals the machine. Beautiful Swahili. So I'm going away to school! She wishes she'd been to school. Could have succeeded in life. Too late now. She's just a poor old widow. Has to work her fingers to the bone. Do her children care? Not at all! All they want is money, which she earns with her life-blood.

I'm called back into the *duka* by Mum. Plimsoles or *tackies*, stockings, underpants, vests. I've never worn a vest before. Too hot in Geita. Arusha's colder, Mum says. She isn't buying shoes. Margaret Miller says I can have Andrew's old ones. They're a size too big, but what the heck!

My clothes are packed in a tin trunk. Last night at home. I'm excited, and don't heed Becky's dark warning. 'It's really going to be horrible!' she says. I can't understand why, as the end of the holidays comes nearer, she becomes more and more morose, or why sometimes she has puffy eyes, like she's been crying. On the last night we go to bed early, though I take ages to fall asleep because I can't wait for morning. Even Sandy sleeps fitfully, her little legs pummelling my side as she chases an imaginary *leguaan*, which she never catches.

Mum wakes us at four. It's black outside, cool and strangely quiet. There isn't much sound in the bush. The crickets, cacophonic at night, are sleeping. The maniacal giggle of the hyena, the screech of the crickets, the mating calls of bullfrogs, all are absent. Chill, dark, impenetrable silence. The jungle waits for the day. Everything sleeps. Except us.

I'm up, washed, dressed in my new uniform. Becky's slower getting ready. Umali, bleary eyed and cursing, is clanging about in the kitchen, making a cold breakfast. There's no fire in the range, just ash in the grate. You can't cook this early in Geita, unless you get up even earlier to chop wood and light a fire. Umali looks really funny. It's his shirt.

Umali's shirt has died and decomposed, and would have gone to meet its maker if it were not that its fragmentary, string-thin remains still adorn his scrawny neck, and briefly extend to cover one nipple. It *was* a shirt once. Over time it grew holes. They merged. Now the whole thing's a hole. Mum buys him three new shirts. He's so happy. He wears one. And wears, and wears it, until it, like it's predecessor, is all string-and-hole.

'Why don't you put on another shirt?' Mum asks.

'Because,' he says, 'I haven't finished this one yet!' His short trousers aren't much better, and Mum's many attempts to improve them meet the same fate. Umali is a dedicated rag-wearer.

At five to five a loud horn honks in the darkness. It's Fritz, the non-talkative driver with a pencil-line moustache and German accent, with his long-wheel-base Land Rover. Someone says he's sixty-four years old, though he doesn't look it. His history is known to Eugen Blüger, who tells Dieti, who tells me.

In World War One Fritz was an *Askari* in von Lettow Vorbeck's *Schutztruppe*. His father was a staunch ally of the Germans, and gave him a German name. During the war, when the Kenya-based Kings'

African Rifles invaded *Deutsch Ost Africa*, now Tanganyika, Fritz fought against them with detachments of African troops and German Officers. They harassed and harried the far superior British forces throughout Tanganyika, and as far south as Rhodesia. In an outrageous display of cheek, they actually seized, and, for some days, occupied a British fort there.

Fritz was involved in many ambushes and skirmishes, sometimes followed, when the British brought overwhelming force to bear, by strategic withdrawal across the Rovuma into Portuguese East Africa, or Mozambique. Frustrated and outwitted, the British forces were ordered to respect Portuguese sovereignty, and only cross the frontier in pursuit on negotiated terms with the Portuguese. That bought the *schutztruppe* valuable time.

In this way von Lettow Vorbeck's guerrilla troops, one of whom was our driver Fritz, tied down a force several times their size for four years, and only surrendered to the British as World War One ground to an end, and the *verdamte* order came from Berlin itself. Fritz, after having given his all for so long, was perplexed and bitter. He'd worked hard at becoming German, then, after not losing a single engagement, his beloved *Obersti,* or *Oberstleutnant,* had to ignominiously surrender to the enemy!

Fritz speaks fluent German, and everything about him, apart from his African ethnicity, is Aryan. He's tall and slim, and has a proud and arrogant bearing. He shaves his moustache in a straight line on his upper lip, and he's always immaculately turned out in military-style khaki safari suits. He speaks little, very guttural, English.

Fritz even tells Eugen an amusing war story. One day close to Kilwa, a hundred miles north of the Portuguese East Africa border, the *Obersti*, as the *Schutztruppe askaris* fondly referred to *Oberstleutnant*, or Colonel, von Lettow Vorbeck, was asked to exercise his jurisprudence in a tribal dispute. A villager brought a complaint against his neighbour, that this man ate his grandfather. Understanding that cannibalism wasn't quite as eschewed here as in Europe, Vorbeck reached a judgement, and ordered the offender to pay the complainant a dozen hens. Plaintiff and defendant walked off 'as good friends', the one 'with the other's grandfather in his stomach.'

'*Parp-parp*' the hooter goes impatiently, cutting the dark silence like a bursting balloon.

'That Fritz is so impatient!' Mum exclaims, sitting on Becky's bulging suitcase and trying to close the zip.

Then he's loudly knocking on the door. He isn't from the Geita area, and his tribal language is Gallua, though he resembles his tribesmen

126

not at all, not having the usual tribal scars, pierced and stretched earlobes, nor even front top teeth knocked out. He's a stranger to his tribe, every bit as much as he's a convert to German-ness. He *can* speak Gallua, but prefers not to. He understands Swahili, but thinks it common. German's his choice, and he seizes the chance to speak it when Eugen Blüger comes to Geita. When not out driving the Land Rover, Fritz has become Eugen's shadow, they say.

'Ve vill be late!' he barks when Mum opens the door. He grabs a suitcase impatiently, and carries it lightly in one huge hand. On the way to the car we hear him mutter crossly, 'Vy zey say ve go early, zen be late?' He's not as chatty, or friendly, with us as he is with Eugen. Only likes Germans!

Five minutes later, luggage aboard, headlights carving glowing yellow shapes on the surrounding bush, the Land Rover growls from our uneven driveway, and gathers speed as Fritz changes gears and stabs the accelerator to show his impatience. Framed in the verandah window, Sandy cocks her head on one side and looks bereft. Umali says she whimpers for hours after we leave.

I sit back, thrilled at everything. The darkness, the stillness, the expectancy of the road to Mwanza, the prospect of a train ride for a whole night and day, a night in the railway hotel in Dodoma, and a twelve hour bus ride to Arusha, which is the 'big school', where I'll feel important and fulfilled, and have exciting adventures.

Fritz drives the Land Rover up Compound Hill in four wheel drive. No two wheel drive vehicle ever makes it to the top. The engine whines and groans. Then we're at the summit, and Fritz free-wheels the heavy vehicle down the other side.

Soon we're in deep bush, the Land Rover rattling and banging as we hit potholes, with rustles and thuds from leafy branches on roof and windows. Tsetse territory, the peeling black and white warning signs giving us just enough time to close the windows before the aerial assault. It seems shorter between Her Majesty's 'close windows' and 'open windows' signs. Happy anticipation does that. I fall asleep.

I wake up to find we're going even slower than usual. In front of us is a lorry, piled twice its height in bundled raw cotton. It's from the ginnery twenty miles away, where the freshly-picked cotton is threshed, washed and deseeded. This one treats cotton from plantations in a radius of a hundred miles. Then it sends the cotton on a 'gin-lorry' to Mwanza, from where it's shipped on the lake to Kenya for further processing. There are several ragged *watu* perched on top of the high cotton cargo. It's a tradition here – lorries pick up *watu* on the road. As always when we're behind a struggling gin-lorry, our trip is badly slowed.

The ferry's waiting, and there's room. I get out and walk about, watching the water boil on one side, where the big engine thrashes its propeller round, the blades just exiting the surface of the green water.

I amaze the crewmen with my Swahili, and amuse them with my bawdiness. Mum laughs. Her understanding of the language, though better than most, is limited to 'kitchen Swahili'. She enjoys seeing me 'talk like a native'. I think she'll enjoy *anything* I do. That's mothers for you.

Mwanza is only twenty miles after the ferry. My excitement grows. We reach town at ten-thirty, five and a half hours after leaving Geita. That's good time. Fritz drops us at the Mwanza hotel, and goes on to the bank for Mr Snel, the manager. The train leaves Mwanza station at six pm, so we have time to kill.

Down the road, two hundred yards from the hotel, is an iconic shop, the 'Lake Printers'. We always take Becky there before she catches the train. She buys comics, and Mum's always generous at these times. She won't be seeing Becky for three months. Now she won't see me either. This is my first opportunity to share in 'off to boarding school' largesse.

In 1959, and for years after, there's a comic series whose passing will leave the world a colder, poorer place. *Illustrated Classics* tell the greatest stories in the English Language, in script and beautiful coloured drawings. *Treasure Island*, *Twenty Thousand Leagues Under the Sea*, *A Christmas Carol*, *The Man in the Iron Mask*, *The Three Musketeers*, *From the Earth to the Moon*, and *The Amazing Tales of Baron von Munchausen*. Becky calls it the Astonishing story of Policeman Higginson, after the boss of the Geita police force. I don't know what astonishing means. She must have heard it from big *Wazungu*. Lake Printers always have some *Classic* titles, and we buy every one. They also have *Beano*, *Topper*, and other comics. On the train, and at Arusha School, these'll be our treasures, until we swap them for other treasures.

At the hotel we sit on the verandah, drink ice-cold Pepsi's through straws, and begin reading, while Mum fusses that our cases are properly packed, she hasn't forgotten toothpaste, soap and shoe polish, that her letters to the headmaster are properly sealed, and protected from crumpling. From the verandah the turquoise-blue of Lake Victoria is visible down a palm-lined avenue.

At six o'clock that evening the train pulls out of Mwanza station. The locomotive wheezes and chuffs, and blows a stinking column of greasy black smoke into the air as it gradually, and very slowly, builds up speed. Becky is crying inconsolably, sticking her head out the window and trying to keep Mum, standing waving on the platform, in view. I'm not sad at all. This is my great new adventure.

Including Becky and me, there are six children, and a teacher has come from Arusha as escort. We're in two compartments, each with four bunks. Becky and I share our compartment with Gretchen Blüger and the teacher, a very old-looking, wrinkled lady called Mrs Shuter. Dieti Blüger is in the compartment next door, with two boys who live in Mwanza. Gretchen looks lovely in her dark green uniform. Her golden hair is in a pony tail, and she looks older and more grown-up than her ten years.

From the outset Mrs Shuter stamps her authority. Firstly, she says pointedly to Becky, there's to be no sticking heads out the window. If you do, you'll get soot from the engine in your eye. Secondly, we're not to go anywhere, not even to the toilet at the end of the carriage, without asking permission. Lights out is an hour from now, so there's just time, if we hurry, to go to the dining car and have supper. Listening to her, I begin to realise that, adventure though it may be, there are negative aspects to this experience.

East African Railways & Harbours, with the *EAR & H* badge and logo on its trains, has rolling stock from the early twentieth century. The carriages are fitted out in beautiful teak and oak. They're real masterpieces of craftsmanship. The furnishings, like the wall panels and windows, are hand-made for the trains. Must have taken a long time for the builders in far-off Birmingham and Northampton to complete a single carriage. These trains are symptomatic of a different time, when things weren't rushed, mass produced in plastic or chipboard, or hurried to market without pride.

The dining car's a spectacle. The oiled teak panelling glows like filigree gold. Velvet drapes on the windows, tied back and hooked, are ocean blue, and bear the *EAR & H* logo in gold italics. The tables have snow-white tablecloths and starched napkins in shiny silver holders. The cutlery, also silver, is confusing in number and complexity. Small and large knives, a fish knife, a spoon, small and large forks, and a very small fork with one prong shaped like a knife. This, Mrs Shuter says, is a cake-fork. Salt and pepper pots are silver, and have *EAR & H* embossed.

The waiters are solicitous and friendly. They carry several hot plates at a time, and remain upright as the train bumps and sways into the gathering gloom. Despite my misgivings about Mrs Shuter, I feel a deep thrill of excitement and anticipation. This *is* still my first great adventure.

129

The four hundred miles from Mwanza on Lake Victoria to Dodoma in the southeastern hinterland is a sixteen hour journey. The train stops at lots of lesser stations, as well as Shinyanga, a hundred and twenty miles, and Singida, three hundred miles from Mwanza, before the last hundred miles to Dodoma. After dinner we get into in our bunks. We'll arrive in Dodoma next morning at eleven. Meantime it's thrilling to hear the locomotive chuff, the wheels click on the rails, and to feel the surge and sway of the train.

Dodoma's a dusty town of no importance, apart from the railway which links Lake Victoria to Dar-es-Salaam on the Indian ocean, and the lunatic asylum which is the only facility for mental illness in all Tanganyika Territory. Here we disembark. The bus which will take us the hundred and thirty miles by dirt road to Arusha is only expected next morning at six, so we walk the quarter mile dirt road to the Railway Hotel.

The hotel, the only one in town, is a beautiful old German building, built of red brick at the turn of the century. It still sports long arched verandahs on each of its three floors, with a crenellated outer wall resembling the battlement of an ancient Hapsburg castle. It originally served as a regional social centre under the German colonial administration of *Deutsch Ost Afrika*. After the British accepted von Lettow Vorbeck's, but not his *Schutztruppe*'s, surrender at Mbala on the shore of Lake Tanganyika on the twenty-fifth of November 1918, the territory changed hands. The hotel became the social centre for British incomers in the district.

The lounge has faded grandeur. A great portrait of von Lettow Vorbeck, in *Schutztruppe* officer uniform, ostrich feather in hat, and Mauser pistol in fastened side-holster, still hangs imperiously on the long wall. It's dated in the corner, in German. *Neunzehn funfzehn.* Nineteen fifteen, Gretchen says authoritatively. Funny, I think, German military pictures on the wall after all these years. This here, from the first war, that other one in Geita, of Eugen Blüger, Gretchen's dad, and Ernst Rommel, chief of the *Afrika Korps,* from the second. I'm in the company of German war-heros wherever I go. 'A nice painting,' Gretchen says beside me. Not as nice as you, I think. Someone says they never take Vorbeck's picture down because he's still so fondly remembered.

There's a large dormitory with two metal beds and six bunks, in three tiers of two, which open through a heavy wooden door onto the verandah overlooking the main street, which, though tarred at some distant time, has all but decayed to a dirt road again. On either side are rusting corrugated iron 'shops', where *Wahindi* and *Warabu*, Indian and Arab, traders sell a limited range of wares. The teacher, Mrs Shuter, takes one of the beds, and assigns us to bunks. After a shower and a change of clothes, we have a dinner of hard fried eggs and baked-beans on toast, in a shabby dining room which was once grand. Then it's time for bed. We have to be up by five in the morning. The bus to Arusha is at six.

The bus is ancient, and gaudily hand-painted in all the hues of the rainbow, and some not in the rainbow. On the door-side there's a logo in hand-painted purple. '*Duma Upesi!*' Fast Cheetah. We board with blustering people of diverse origins. Indians on business, tribesmen and women travelling to villages *en-route*, with sacks of maize flour, live chickens in grass cages, and a couple of unhappy-looking goats. There are two very weathered and haggard white big game hunters, complete with bolt-action rifles, who take great care that their elephant tusks and other trophies are securely attached to the rusty iron rack on the roof. I wonder why they don't have a Land Rover.

As the *kunguru* bird flies, it's a hundred and thirty miles from Dodoma to Arusha. But the Fast Cheetah lacks the freedom, and speed, of a crow.

The Pienaar Heights lie on the edge of the Masai Steppe in the Kondoa district, halfway from Dodoma to Arusha. A great windswept, barren escarpment looms after a grinding, gut-wrenching ascent from the wooded plateau. Here, a winding road snakes along the lip of a vertical fall of thousands of feet. Clouds drift past, a long way down. The heights are named for Major General Dan Pienaar of the *SAOEV*, or *South African Overseas Expeditionary Volunteers* force which joined the fight against von Lettow Vorbeck's *Schutztruppe* in the fourteen-eighteen war. Not even Pienaar and his huge South African army could corner the wily Vorbeck.

The bus hurtles down the stony road to terrifying oblivion. After an hour of pure panic we level out onto the valley below. I relax, then fall asleep again.

When I wake we're cruising along a straight, level dirt road on the approach to the town named for its original inhabitants, the *wa-Arusha*. Finally we roll onto the tar road. It's a small place, with some western-looking shops in the centre, less salubrious buildings of corrugated iron, wood and adobe everywhere else. From there it's a short way to Arusha School.

The school's a privately run institution, a pleasant, and, for Tanganyika, cool little town in the foothills of the great twins, mounts Meru and Kilimanjaro, or *Kilima Njaro*, as the locals call it. *Kilima* means hill. I never find out what *Njaro* means. Unlike Geita, the land's lush and green, and cold rivers and streams formed by melting snow on the mountains criss-cross the land.

The school takes boarders, the only reason we're sent there. In the nineteen fifties less than one percent of African children go to school. The European and Asian population in Tanganyika never top ten to twelve thousand. Thus there are very few schools of any description. Arusha school is the biggest and best in the country, and caters for the children of the expatriate community from all over Tanganyika Territory.

The school's modelled on an English public school, I'm told, though nobody says which one. The headmaster in 1959, and for the five years I'm there, is a very upper class English don by the name of Mr Houghton. His deputy, the assistant head, is a mild tempered and pleasant, baritone-voiced, sports-loving, Welshman, known to all as BL Thomas. Someone says BL is short for 'bloody'. A worrying thought.

The buildings are typical English-styled, late Victorian in design and construction. The main buildings are built around two large quadrangles of lawn, a hundred square yards. On one side is a row of classrooms. At the two far ends are boys' dormitories, juniors one side, seniors the other. Facing the classrooms is a linen store and tuck room. Between the grassy quadrangles is the dining room, with big windows, and kitchen. This part of the school is joined to the female dormitories by a curved and covered walkway thirty yards long.

I sleep in the junior dormitory. Sadly, my memories have more to do with enemies than friends.

I meet Marais. For a long time I don't know his first name. He's a rarity in Tanganyika – a *Boer,* or Afrikaner, from South Africa. The *watu* call Boers *Kaburu*, because they can't pronounce *Boer*. Plural is *waKaburu*. I don't like Marais. He's a thug and a bully. There is a family of Afrikaners, or Dutch as we call them, in Geita. The van der Westhuizens. All I know about them is our *ayah*'s always give their place a wide berth or they get abused. Boers don't like the *watu*.

I'm six and a half when I'm shown to my bed. I'm choked with homesickness, ill from crying. Realisation has dawned: this is no holiday, it's banishment. Becky and I are here, Mum's alone in the house in Geita. How did I get conned into this? I'll have to do something about it. If I survive the twelve long weeks of this term, and I've never thought about such a long stretch before, I won't come back! My throat aches and I have a pounding headache. Dr Weiss said I'd have headaches after the cerebral malaria. I find I only get them when I'm upset. I'm screwing up my eyes to avoid the sun's glare through the big glass window, because it makes my head feel worse.

I instinctively dislike the matron, a middle-aged spinster called Miss Baxter. She's very businesslike, and not at all friendly. She's also stout, ugly and lacking personality. But she's in charge, and determined to thoughtlessly exercise her duty. To begin with, she lets me know who's boss by calling me Francis. My name is Francis James Penhaligon. I rather like it. But I'm used to being called by the abbreviated form of my second name, James. I'm Jim in Geita, Jimu to the *watu*.

'Francis,' she announces, 'this is your bed.' She grimaces, like I learn to expect. I have encountered the 'put-down'. Marais is in the next bed.

From the outset, Marais bullies me. He's older, in third year. He's eight, a foot taller than me. He's lanky and tough. He has a strong Afrikaans accent. His parents farm a hundred miles away and speak no English. His only weakness is asthma. For that he has a bell-shaped glass bottle with a rubber tube sticking out the top. On the end is a hollow rubber ball. When he gets wheezy, he puts the bottle near his open mouth and squeezes the ball. This produces a liquid spray, which he gulps into his lungs. I have no compassion. Marais is irritating in all ways. I hate the way he looks and talks. I can't stand his wheezing, and the sound of his spray-bottle is like hard dry chalk screeching a blackboard. I'm to have this for company every night, eighteen inches from my bed.

Marais knows I'm not his fan. He sees me wince when he speaks, feels my agitation when he wheezes and splutters. He can't miss me sticking my head under my pillow as I attempt to escape Marais-ness. Despite his poor health, Marais has advantages. Age and size. He uses them against me.

It begins with a shove in the back. I'm standing in line to enter the dining room. Breakfast time. I'm not happy. I've had a horrible night. My worst nightmare for a long time.

Mum's buried the other side of Mrs Williams. She's trying to get to Dad, but can't, no matter how hard she tries. Mrs Williams's coffin's in the way. It's made of something stronger than iron. Digging under it's no good, because it moves. It's determined to keep Mum and Dad apart. There's a horrible sound. Cruel, evil laughter. Stroessner, the murderer. Half his head is missing, and there's brains and gore on his leering face. 'You can't, you can't. . !' he laughs satanically. '*Kaa peke yako Memsahib!*' he continues, switching to Swahili. Stay on your own, Madam! Mum's getting desperate. Her fingers are torn and bleeding. It's normal for the dead to bleed.

I'm awake for several minutes before I'm completely sure it's just a dream. When I get up I feel so sad. It's physical, like there's a heavy bag of potatoes on my back. My legs feel leaden. I'm nauseous. I'm depressed, but I don't know the word.

Marais shoves. I'm forced to take a half-step forward to stop myself falling. I almost collide with Miss Baxter. Marais's face is impassive. Miss Baxter says I'm playing the fool, and sends me back to the dormitory. I miss breakfast. I don't care because I'm not hungry. But Marais has just started. There'll be more, much more. Other boys have told me what he's like. From the outset it's clear to all new boys that 'snitching' is not allowed. Whatever happens, you never snitch on anyone to teachers or matron. Particularly not older boys. This serves Marais well. When he returns from breakfast he's not only wheezing, but gloating as well.

'*Ja, Rooinek,*' he says, '*dit sal jou leer!*' Afrikaans. Difficult enough having to talk English! Still, I get to know his sayings. 'Redneck, that'll teach you!'

I resent the English bit. I'm Cornish. Dad said we're British, not English. Loyal, not Royal. Cornwall's only 'cledged' onto England by a tiny spit of land at the river Tamar. A couple of sticks of gelignite, and we'll be an island. Stick together, us Cornish. '*One And All!*' That's the motto. Mum told me. I can see myself manning a machine-gun on the west bank of the Tamar. I'll be like Dad. Fierce and brave. The enemy will be the English. Odd that. Dad fought *for* them against the Germans. Why did he do that? He liked Eugen, and fetched the Lotanga for Otto. I like Germans too. *I'll* never fight against them. Now the Afrikaners, the Marais of the world, that's different!

There's tons of gelignite in the cold-store at Nungwe Bay near Geita. A man-made tunnel at the water's edge leads to a cave right *under* the lagoon. Ingenious. Cool like a fridge. A perfect store where explosives won't explode. Brainchild of a man called Harold Norris, who has a jutting chin, and tells stories which never go anywhere. The under-lake explosives magazine comes to him in a dream after two Gallua miners are blown to smithereens by *baruti* left in the sun. Dynamite. I wonder if I could pinch some and send it to Cornwall. How much is needed to blow Cornwall from England?

Starting now, life gets worse. Marais likes destroying my Saturdays. After applying *Blanko* to my tackies, I turn to find they're streaked with brown polish. It's inspection time, too late to re-*Blanco* them. After inspection we're allowed access to our 'tuck boxes', can take five sweets. That's a week's allowance. If shoes or *tackies* are found wanting I miss out on tuck. Marais celebrates! '*Verdamte Soutpiel,*' he wheezes. This is worse. Damned Salt-Prick. One foot in England, the other in Africa. Prick hanging in the salty sea. Afrikaans is endearing itself to me. Prick means willy.

Sand in my bed, mud on my shirt, and worse, comes my way. I'm a bed-wetter. It only stops at nine. It's infrequent and irregular, and usually happens when I have nightmares, invariably containing jumbled stuff about people, animals and death. In the dreams I'm visited by intense anguish, like on the day Dad died. I see Mr Valari (senior)'s waxy face and accusing eyes, the half-skeletonised *mzoga* of Tembo's puppy, and visions of Mum, Becky, or Dad, dead and rotting in the ground. I'm told I moan, grind my teeth and thrash about. I wake to find I've wet my bed. In Geita I've been bed-wetting about once in six weeks. It continues.

Bed-wetters are treated in a special way. I have to tell Miss Baxter. I'm given a harsh talking-to in front of everyone, then have to strip my bed. I carry the wet mattress, on my head, into the centre of the quadrangle and place it on the grass. The timing is for when the boys on one side, girls on the other, are queuing for breakfast. They enjoy a grandstand view. It's morning cabaret.

It's hard carrying and scrubbing a wet mattress to the giggling attention of boys, and more so girls. Marais leads the mocking. 'Jimbo has peed his bed again!' he says in his heavy accent, just loud enough for the children, not Miss Baxter, to hear. He imitates a hyena's giggle, which infects the others. When the matron turns and asks why everyone's sniggering, Marais says, in a husky voice, 'Nothing miss. . . nothing'. My hatred grows. Somehow, sometime, I'll teach him!

My unhappiness and disappointment at Arusha school extinguishes my excitement and optimism like *mvua ko moto*, or rain on fire. Becky told me, and I didn't listen. Now I know she was right. From this time forth, I will never want to go again. I'll stay in Geita, no matter the consequences. This decision will have consequences for me, and for what I'm beginning to think of as 'them', or authority.

135

Fourteen

In 1959 Arusha is a small market town in the heartland of the *wa-Arusha* tribe, not yet a national Capital. The snow-capped peak of Mount Meru, the smaller sister of Kilimanjaro, is visible from most parts of town. From elevated positions the blue-grey slopes and white hat of Kili, though almost forty miles away, interrupts the sweep of the horizon. The *wa-Arusha* have an ancient belief. Meru and *Kilima Njaro*, or Kilimanjaro, were twins, but Meru got arrogant, and tried to out-do her big sister. In response, Kilimanjaro hit Meru on the head with such force that Meru's been shorter ever since.

The surrounding countryside, four thousand six hundred feet above sea level, is alpine green. Pines and conifers cluster in groves between vast expanses of green, luscious grassland. To me, from the arid, hot flatlands by Lake Victoria, the countryside can't be more different. Arusha town is a motley collection of buildings, some European-style, others built of a variety of materials, including stone, mud, corrugated iron and wood.

On Saturday mornings after shoe inspection, providing we haven't 'blotted our copybooks' during the week, or failed to properly clean our shoes, we're allowed to go into town. We line up in rows, boys one side, girls the other, smallest and youngest one end, biggest at the other. We find ourselves facing our age or size-equivalent of the opposite sex. Then, at an order from the escorting teacher, we hold hands, and fall into a column, teacher in front, smallest children behind him or her, biggest at the back. In this formation we walk the mile into town.

I'm a junior misogynist. The touch and feel of a girl's hand is more repugnant than a snake. It takes willpower not to throw my little lady-partner's sweaty hand aside. With the cloying touch and feel of a keener grasp than my own, I proceed into Arusha town. I make it clear small-talk is not allowed. It would be different if Gretchen was my partner, but she's ten, and I'm seven, so she goes with another group. The thought of her holding another boy's hand brings a hard lump of jealousy to my throat.

There's a pattern to our Saturday morning town trips. First we're taken to a little take-away where we buy burgers. The sign on the window says *MISTREES YUM-YUM-TUM SPECIAL BURGER BAR. TASTIE AND DILICUSS.* Yum-yum I understand, but not dilicuss. Someone says it means nice tasting. 'Oh,' I say, '*tamu!*' Being here's a welcome break in loathsome hand-holding, and maybe it's because these are my first burgers, or just because they're not school food, that they're simply the most delicious burgers in the world. *Tamu sana!* I love them. They're scrumptious, and I never miss the opportunity to gorge at Mistree's Dilicuss Burger Bar.

Next is Arusha Printers, a bookshop with all the regular comics from England. We buy *Beano* and *Topper*, and the boys get war comics about heroic British troops fighting Germans and particularly evil Japanese. The Germans shout '*Blitzen*', '*Englander*', '*Achtung*' and '*Schweinehund*', and the Japanese yell '*Banzaai*'. Becky says that's a small tree. She's mad. Having stocked up on reading material, we proceed to the most important shop of all, *FATTI ALIDALI'S NICE-SWEETS EMPORIUM*.

Here is a magical cave, full of Rowntree's fruit gums and pastilles, sherbet fountains, Crunchies, Cadbury's chocolates, and things dreams are made of. We're only allowed a shilling each on sweets, so we form syndicates, buy as many kinds as our money allows. There's bickering and argument later, when it comes to dividing spoils. Generally the silly girls come out worse. What they deserve, holding our hands so keenly!

We're told to pray for forgiveness of sins. The bearded preacher keeps saying we must, from the pulpit of the little church near the river. Suddenly, aged six and a half, far from home, feeling very lost and lonely in this foreign, colder, greener place, almost as bad as I remember England, I undergo a spiritual awakening. So it seems. It's apparent to me the preacher knows all about me. He knows what I've done. My spying on the corpse of Mr Valari (senior), killing Tembo's puppy, and above all, shooting God! How can he, who has never met, or talked, to me *know* all that? Only one explanation. God knows everything! Obviously I have not killed him. Just made him very, very angry. And he's told the preacher. Instructed him to tell me from the pulpit to repent and mend my ways.

At bedtime in the junior dormitory we have to kneel beside our beds and pray before lights-out. Until now I've closed my eyes and thought of Geita, Mum, Dad, Umali, Lutoli, Amina, Sandy. Now I can't afford such indulgency. God's on my case. *Ata Kamata mimi*, I think. He'll catch me. I still think in Swahili. It'll be years before I can think a whole thought through in English, and not mentally translate. *Mungu* has found me out now, and I have to make peace. Dodging my bullet hasn't gone down well.

I kneel by my bed in awakened knowledge of my evil and badness, and try to find a proper prayer to do the job. Difficult. I'm not even sure I'm sorry I missed God. He took Dad, didn't he? Then he presided over me leaving Mum so far away, to come to a hell-hole. But I *have* to apologise. The bearded preacher has talked about hell and punishment. What if God decides to take Mum, or Becky, or Umali, seeing taking Dad hasn't taught me my lesson? I had better put my ideas in order. Apology beats apocalypse.

'Dear God,' I begin, 'please forgive me for all my sins. Please help me never to sin the same sin again. . .' I don't realise I'm praying for *variety* in my sinning! After asking for forgiveness and avoidance of sin, I decide it's okay to ask a favour. After all, I've humbled myself, apologised. If God is merciful and kind, the other thing the bearded preacher keeps saying, when not threatening us with hell, then surely he can grant a little wish to an apologetic sinner.

'Please look after my mother and father,' I begin. Can't leave Dad out because he's dead. He's up there with God, isn't he? He still needs looking after. 'And my brothers and sisters, and Gretchen and Dieter, especially Gretchen, and Umali and Amina, and Lutoli, and Tembo, and his dead puppy, and Sandy, and all my relations and friends, and everybody who I know and who I don't know, even the *wasikini,* who are poor, and the *machula,* who stinks. . .' I'm casting the net wide, asking a lot. But what if I don't pray for someone, then something happens to them? I can't bear the guilt. I can't bring myself to pray for the *Wazungu*, or Europeans, as a group. I don't like them. I don't like being one. I pray all the harder for those I choose.

'Let them live a long, long time,' I pray, knowing it's strange to ask for Dad, who's dead, to live a long time, but not prepared to relegate him to second class-ness. I can't pray 'let him be dead a long time', can I?

'And let them be happy,' I conclude. A happy *machula* seems a contra-something. Mission. No, *dission*. I don't know. I give up.

138

'Amina,' I say, not yet knowing 'amen', then I hop into bed. It doesn't strike me as odd that I end my prayers with my old *ayah*'s name. Just to be sure God has heard me, I pray everything all over again, three times. Hello, Obsessive-Compulsive Disorder! Isn't there something obsessive about monks chanting the same thing over and over? It's from now I'll have to resist an urge to re-do things several times, then check I've done them. Over and over. Before ending my praying session, I allow myself one extra prayer I'm not too sure about. God might think it's opportunistic and greedy. On the other hand, if I don't ask, I certainly won't get. Recklessly, I ask for it: an ever-lasting lollipop.

That done, I allow myself the luxury of imagining I'm at home in Geita. Walking in the bush with Gretchen. I wallow in this for ten or fifteen minutes, before moving on to imagining something else, which is my own, unencumbered by other people, and gives me a great sense of peace. It's amazing how powerful the imagination of a child can be. I create something all mine, with vivid colours and real sounds, replete with everything I need, and without all the things that trouble me.

My imaginings in bed at night, with my head under the blanket to cut out the noise of Marais snoring, are simple. I'm with Lutoli in our hillside republic of *Kichoncho*. The only sound is the peaceful cooing of the *njiwa* bird. We're lying on the ground, looking up at the aching blue sky. High up there on a rising thermal current drifts a magnificent *mwewe,* its great wings immobile, its all-seeing yellow eyes searching hundreds of square miles for prey. It's great to be here watching this. That lasts a while, then I need to conjure something else.

My restless mind searches for ideas. That's it. . ! I have a canoe. Very strongly built, closed in on top, with a small hatch for access. I have stores of things to eat and drink, and the inside is cushioned with foam rubber. I get in when the rainstorms begin, and seal the hatch. Everything that can possibly go wrong has been thought about, and prevented.

After a while in the darkness, I imagine the canoe begin to move as storm-water nudges it towards the river. Then the rocking of flotation, and a sense of drifting downstream. I'm safe in my canoe. Nobody can touch me. There are no teachers or matrons, or Marais, or anyone to worry me. I'm alone. I feel better. The rushing thoughts slow down, and calmness descends.

Eventually my drifting canoe reaches the sea and is swept far out into the blue vastness. I eat sweets and biscuits and dried fruit, drink from a bottle of lemonade or Coke, and take a peek at my whereabouts through the hatch. When storms brew on the horizon, and the sky

139

darkens, and the winds begin to howl, I batten down the hatch, make myself comfortable, and enjoy the feeling that, though the elements and world conspire and try to kill me, I'm safe and indestructible in my canoe.

I fall asleep enjoying the feeling of enclosure and inviolability, then my dreams take over and continue with more of the same. When, that is, dead people dripping blood and gore don't suddenly come at me.

Only much later do I realise what I'm doing in these perambulations of my mind. Vicarious escape from intolerable circumstances, in which I have no control of what happens. I don't want a life without Dad. I don't want Mum to be a widow. I don't want to be away from her, or Geita. I don't want to be terrorised by Miss Baxter, or the teachers, or Mr Houghton, the headmaster. I don't want to sleep next to wheezing, nasty Marais. I want nothingness. Only my canoe, out there on my imagined sea, offers me the refuge I seek.

As the end of the first term approaches, there's a mood of excitement in school. The first sign is a reduction in bullying of smaller children by big ones. Like a miracle. Suddenly they stop calling names, shoving in line at pre-dinner inspection, and streaking mud on whitened plimsoles, which we call *tackies*. Why are they so unkind in the first place? Why do they change, just because it's close to end of term?

Suddenly there's a relaxation of rules. Lights-out is no longer so strictly enforced, and Miss Baxter leaves them on as long as twenty minutes after eight. She doesn't pounce out of the dark to catch us talking after lights-out or 'playing the fool', with her usual frequency or ferocity. The last Saturday shoe inspection isn't as rigorously carried out. The biggest boon is that, on the last Saturday, we're allowed, after shoe inspection, to empty our tuck boxes. This leads to gorging, which is, I think, what went on in Sodom and Gomorrah. Excess. The bearded padré is obsessed with this. The evil ones practised excess, and the Lord struck them down. It's obvious the Sodomites ate too many sweets. I pray to God to make me like sweets less, to avoid Sodom, 'cos it's awful what the priest says.

There's a rhyme I learn at the end of the first term. It has to be used only two days before term ends. 'Today's the brush, tomorrow's the comb, next day I go home!' There's never sweeter poetry. The older kids have a rude version. 'Miss Baxter's bush, Mr Houghton's bum, take me home – I want to come!'

Finally the last night comes, and we're given our cases and trunks to pack. By this time law and order has completely broken down. People call each other by first names. Miss Baxter laughs and jokes,

140

instead of shouting and threatening. There's a festive spirit. We pack our neatly pressed clothes, our shoes, comics, and whatever toys we still have. That night supper is informal, and there's no queuing for hand inspection. Even the food's different. Edible.

Last night. It's impossible to sleep. I don't need the canoe. Just thinking about going home, after twelve never-ending weeks, is enough. In the small hours I drift to sleep. Then Miss Baxter's shaking me awake. 'Your bus leaves in forty-five minutes,' she whispers, not to wake snoring Marais. His father's fetching him later. 'Bath before you dress,' Miss Baxter says. Three quarters of an hour go by in a flash. Bath, dress, quick bowl of porridge in dining room, collect case, check trunk has been put out front.

The headlights of the bus illuminate the main building, where I meet Becky, Gretchen, and Dieti, and the boys from Mwanza. It's six in the morning, and dawn. An icy wind from Meru and Kilimanjaro penetrates our clothing. We board and the bus glides out the school gates, *en-route* to Dodoma. I make sure I'm sitting next to Gretchen. Does she know how I feel about her? She doesn't say.

Dodoma at six pm. We don't stay at the Railway Hotel, but meet the Mwanza train at seven. On board the *gari moshi* we sleep as if drugged. At six next morning I look out the window. Only four hours to go. The train has descended to flat country, and there are signs Lake Victoria's near. In the early light I see the great, smooth, cheese-coloured boulders strewn on hillsides and perched on plains. Igneous rock, or granite, submerged for an eternity by a much higher, deeper Lake Victoria, before, also aeons ago, it finally broke through at Jinja in Uganda, to form one of the sources of the Nile. Then the lake level fell by over a hundred feet, exposing the rocks eroded smooth by such long submersion. They have huge emotional content. They say I'm nearing the water, and, more importantly, getting close to home. The sun rises above the horizon, beaming down its intense white heat, and it is day. Soon, in a few hours, I'll see Mum and Fritz, and we'll set out for Geita.

By nine o'clock we see glimpses of blue lake as the train snakes on towards Mwanza. My beloved boulders are everywhere. Our excitement's too much to contain. The escort rasps her voice telling us to stop leaning out the windows. We don't want to miss any of this.

The train splutters into the station and squeals to a halt. Becky and I spot Mum on the platform. Fritz is beside her, teutonic and black. While the locomotive hisses and exudes steam and black smoke, we're locked in an embrace of three. Fritz stands alone, aloof, impatient. His moustache is shaved straighter than ever. How does he avoid cutting his lip? I can almost hear his thoughts as we hug. 'Vy you do zis?' Doesn't he ever hug anyone? He's impatient to drop us in town and go off on mine business. He'll collect us from Mwanza Hotel at two o'clock. That gives us time to buy anything we want not available at Barrat Stores or *Boma Dukas*.

We're in a state of high excitement and bliss for the next four hours. After stocking up on comics at Lake Printers, and sweets from two different shops, we lunch on the verandah of Mwanza Hotel. Cool and shady here, red cement floor, wicker tables and chairs. Homely atmosphere. Apt, I think. Home!

Fritz drives up at precisely two o'clock. He wordlessly helps us load our luggage in the back, and then we're off, Geita-bound. Exit Mwanza, car ferry across lagoon, into bush and tsetse belt. The Land Rover groans and creaks, sometimes almost losing the struggle along the rudimentary road. In spite of our excitement, Becky and I lose our epic fight to stay awake.

Mum wakes us as we fight towards the summit of Compound Hill. The Land Rover's positively groaning. It must be the steepest hill in the world. It's seven thirty, and the sun has gone. A moonless night, only the yellow lights from the Land Rover piercing the black cloak of night. It's cool at last. Even cold. The back of my shirt is still wet with sweat, and now it's like an ice-pack. The engine whines in a final agony as we reach the top of the hill. It's visceral. As the engine relaxes, so do we. Like an apparition in a magical fantasy, the fairy-lights of Geita camp appear before and below us. We free-wheel down the steep road, Fritz applying brakes to prevent a headlong plunge. The houses separate as we approach. Then there is just one house before us. Our house, *home!*

The Land Rover crunches on the gravel of the driveway, and has not rolled to a halt before the front door opens. Silhouetted against the light, the unmistakable form of Umali appears. He runs down the steps towards us, the prancing shape of Sandy at his heels. Now we're really home!

As I step from the car I'm embraced by Umali, then Amina. Sandy jumps up and whimpers in happiness, the little bell Mum put on her collar tinkling merrily. Fritz bids us a guttural farewell, and drives off in a cloud of dust and a shower of small stones. He has a family at home. I hope he's more avuncular with them.

The house looks so daintily decorated and furnished, so clean and polished. I've forgotten how house-proud Mum is, how hard Umali works. From the kitchen comes a delicious aroma of roasting chicken and potatoes. Umali has made a special effort. I'm almost

142

overwhelmed with happiness. I'm home for four whole weeks. I won't even let myself think about going back. That will spoil the holiday.

Gooloogooloo, our *batamzinga*, has entrenched his hegemony over the chickens. The lady *kukus* haven't suffered. Before the coming of the turkey, they're subjugated by *Mr Jogoo*. Then it's he who has first choice of tasty morsels cast over the fence, to him they give way at water basins, and his is the right to ravage them at will. The ravaging continues, but *Jogoo's* rule over the *kukus* is now only as vassal to Gooloogooloo.

The days whizz by too quickly. In a frenzy we re-establish our Geita lives. It's never going to be the same, no matter what we do. There's a calendar now, a countdown to disaster. That's what we think about going back to school.

I try valiantly to put the horrible thought out of mind. I visit old haunts. The club and swimming pool. The golf course, the African compound, the many *watu* who know me. I enjoy Sundays when we go to the club. We swim, eat crisps and drink bottles of icy Pepsi. We sit and wait for Sunday night cartoons, newsreels and black and white movies, with great excitement. We play Germans and English at war, or cowboys and Indians. When we tire of that we spring a poorly-planned and unsuccessful attack on the *machula*, hitting his full buckets with a few stones but singularly failing to overturn them or delay him in his determined limp from privy to privy.

Dad has been gone two years. 'Uncle' Adrian, a dashing Afrikaner with huge handlebar moustaches who manages the mine 'reduction' works, begins to visit Mum, and accompany her to the club. Becky doesn't mind. At first I'm incensed. He's taking Dad's place. Yet Mum looks less unhappy than before. I'm torn. He's an Afrikaner. Like Marais and the van der Westhuizens, that strange and reclusive 'Dutch' family on the other road. But I have to admit he's not really like them at all. Firstly, he's nice-looking. Becky says he's handsome.

There's something gallant about Uncle Adrian's moustache. It's huge, just like his car. That's a two-tone blue and white Chev with big wings, like a spaceship. He drives that, while all the other men drive beaten-up Landys. He's also very generous. Always sending Pepsis and crisps out to us kids on the verandah at the club. What can I do? What *should* I do? In fact, Uncle Adrian is so generous, he spends all his money every month. Mum says he hands over half his pay to Ishmael, the club barman, and the other half to Barrat's stores. Asks them to tell him when it's finished. It's just like that song that's popular these days: '*I Owe My Soul to the Company Store.*'

Uncle Adrian just buys things for people all the time. He's always 'standing rounds' at the club, or buying presents at Barrat's. He wears crisp new white shirts on Sundays, and he never wears the same one twice. Sunday nights he gives them to his 'house-boy' who makes a small fortune selling them to the *watu!*

I decide to do nothing about Uncle Adrian for now. Anyway, due to his generosity we're able to buy more sweets at Barrat's store, as well as more Pepsis and crisps at the club. Also, in a strange way, it feels good to have a man around. Less empty, less lonely for all three of us. With a sense of guilt about Dad, I decide I won't do anything to drive Uncle Adrian away. At least, not now.

I'm woken by blood-curdling shrieks. They're coming from the *kuku* run. Pandemonium and panic from thirty straining *kuku*-throats, and as many pairs of wildly pounding *kuku*-feet. They're zooming about the run, squawking as loud as they can. Something's very wrong.

'What's happening?' Becky shouts above the din. It's woken her and brought her running to my room, which overlooks the run.

'Dunno,' I shout.

'Stay there you two!' Mum yells, dashing past my door to the kitchen. That's the way out. Torch there. On shelf, for going out in the dark. We're a yard behind. Won't let her go out alone. Sandy's at my feet, barking. The *kuku*-shrieks and foot-pounding is louder. Mum flicks on the torch. She opens the door. We're running down the steps, following the pencil of light. No way will we let Mum go on her own.

'*Memsahib!*' It's Umali. Invisible in the dark. Mum swings the beam. He's naked apart from a *kanzu* round his waist. There's a glint of *panga*-blade in his hand. We're at the *kuku* run. They're dashing about like creatures possessed, colliding with the wire mesh, bouncing off, dashing the other way, shrieking at the tops of their voices. Mum shines the torch. Under the wire near our feet is a mound of earth that wasn't there last night. A tunnel. Even as we watch, something mottled brown and black, a foot high and three long, torpedoes from the hole and disappears into the elephant-grass. Umali hurls his panga after it. It clatters uselessly against a rock.

'*Nguchiro!*' he shouts. Mongoose! No point going after it. It's gone. The *kukus* are thoroughly spooked. Takes them ten minutes to stop dashing about. Three lie dead in pools of coagulating blood. Their throats are torn open. Later we realise one's gone. A black and white speckled hen. The killer must've carried her off when he dashed past. One young hen has her wing half-torn from her body. She's a pretty

144

one, white all over. She's feeling very sorry for herself. Her wing-bone's broken, and there's a scarlet streak of blood on her snowy feathers. Standing together silently on one side are the *jogoo* and Gooloogooloo. There's no posturing or crowing now. In the torchlight both look bewildered and frightened.

'*Wapumbafu!*' Umali shouts at *them*. '*You fools!*' He stamps his foot. 'Why do you just stand, *blurryfucken?*' He stamps again. He does that when he's angry. 'What kind of guardians are you?' He's disgusted. They should have *done* something! Not just stood around as if this is entertainment. He's right. These two are bigger than the other *kukus*. Particularly so 'Emperor' Gooloogooloo, regent and show-off *extraordinaire!*

We take the injured hen into the house. She's in shock. She's the one who adopted Gooloogooloo when he first came. Mum wraps strips of torn sheet around her body, holding her broken wing in place. There's little chance she'll survive. Umali cuts some grass with his panga. In the dark, he cuts his leg too. Mum wraps another piece of sheet round his shin. We put the grass in a cardboard box, and make a bed for Snow-White. That's the hurt *kuku*'s name now. She lies in the box and stares at us unblinkingly. Mum opens her beak and puts a tiny piece of aspirin on her tongue. She tries to eject it, but swallows instead. May as well try something. She's going to die anyway. Mum gives her a handful of chicken-food mix. Dried maize, groundnuts, sunflower seeds. It's in a little dish. Another's got water. Snow-White looks pathetic all bound up.

'Mongoose?' Uncle Adrian says next day. 'No, don't think so. They take what they kill. Don't kill so many and only take one. This is the work of something else. I'd say a Civet Cat. That, or a honey badger. Much more likely.'

'*Nyegere?*' Umali says. Honey badger? He shakes his head emphatically, '*Hakuna hapa.*' There aren't any here. '*Ngawa?*' Civet Cat? '*Labda. . .*' Maybe. . . He shakes his head again. '*Alakini ni nguchiro!*' But it's a mongoose! Umali's not one to admit he may be wrong. '*Blurryfucken nguchiro!*' he spits.

'Enough of that!' Mum says threateningly. Umali grins. 'Solly *Memsahib*,' he says.

We nurse Snow-White in turns. She's a model patient.

There are naughty pawpaw trees in our garden. Two of them produce rude-shaped fruit. One may look like a bum. Then a lady's privates, or so Becky says. Then one like a man's willy and testicles. Mum wants

145

g

the offending trees cut down, but Umali says the fruit's the sweetest he's ever tasted. So she gives in.

One Sunday afternoon the Mwanza priest who conducted Dad's funeral pops by. Mum sits with him and Becky at the garden table made from a wooden cable-drum. Just five yards away is a huge hanging pawpaw in the shape of a lady's privates. It's very detailed. The priest and Mum look assiduously the other way. I arrive home after a walk in the bush with Lutoli, and announce the unannounceable.

'That looks like. . .' I begin.

'Yes, Jimboy please get the sugar,' Mum says, her face reddening.

'But you've got sugar!' I exclaim, 'and that pawpaw. . .'

'Yes, now could you check if Sandy's okay?'

'Sure, but the pawpaw is just like your *thing!*' I say. The priest chokes on his tea, coughs into his handkerchief. Mum takes time forgiving me.

'You showed me up,' she says.

'It's the tree that's naughty,' I say, 'not me!'

There's that peculiar family living in a house down the road and off to the left. They're quite reclusive, though not as bad as the Valaris, the 'secret' Italian family further up the hill, who nobody ever sees, apart from Mr Valari, who's seen at work, but nowhere else. The van der Westhuizens are from the Orange Free State in South Africa, home of the 'Dutch'. Like Marais. They're *different*, everyone says. 'Only speak Afrikaans,' someone explains, 'they're common as muck!' Muck *is* common, I admit, it's everywhere!

They *are* a strange family. Unlike the Valaris, they don't hide in their house all day, but always seem to be in the garden. Our *ayahs* give their place a wide birth, because these *Wazungu* don't like the *watu*. When they walk anywhere near, they're shouted at. By adults *and* children, of which there are several, all dirty and snotty-nosed, Becky says.

'*Kaffir*' is a word the van der Westhuizens like. It means nigger. '*Ek sal jou bliksem*' means 'I'll lightning you'. How will they do that? The *watu* don't like the abuse, and don't like the van der Westhuizens. Nor do I.

'They shout me *blurryfuckenkaffir* every time I walk past,' Amina laments to Mum, 'Why they *blurryfucken* do that?'

One of the sons is nicknamed '*Skokie*'. Afrikaans for 'Shock'. He put his thumb into a big electric plug-thing on an outside wall near the head office. I don't know what it was for. He got a 'helluva shock',

146

they said, and the end of his thumb was burnt off. The plug-thing was removed from the wall.

There's worse. The van der Westhuizens cut off puppies' tails! I don't believe Dieti and Gretchen when they tell me. The van der Westhuizens' dogs have puppies. They're Boxer-lookalikes, because there's no pure Boxers here, and the mother's tail's off. All she's got is a funny little stump she wags furiously. They're going to cut the puppies' tails off today, Skokie tells Dieti when he walks past the house. Why does he do that? Why tell *him*? To frighten us, says Becky. That's why. They're horrible.

Becky and Gretchen refuse to come. They don't want to see puppies' tails chopped off. It's cruel. We agree it's cruel, but is it worse if we see it?

Dieti and I watch the house. At four o'clock Mr van der Westhuizen comes down the back steps. He's a big, bald man. His kids are bald too, at least the boys are. They really *are* strange! He's carrying a big basket. Three of his bald sons are with him. He walks to a tree stump, puts the basket down. He takes a big knife from a sheath and extracts a little brown bundle from the basket. It's a puppy. He puts it on the stump, positions it. There's a glint of steel in the sunlight, then there's a spurt of bright blood, and a pitiful whimper from the puppy. He's cut its tail off. There's shouts of delight from his kids. Dieti and I are sick in the grass. Told you so, says Becky.

During my absence at school, they've built a concrete circular, above-ground children's paddling pool next to the club pool. It's just two foot deep. In the middle is a concrete plinth with a big steel pipe in the centre. Topping that is an upside-down steel bowl six foot wide. Water shoots out the top, jets down the inside curve of the inverted bowl, and cascades in a solid curtain to the pool, where it hits the surface with the force of hail. It's so loud we can't hear someone shouting from inside. Indeed, the water-sheet's so thick we can barely *see* anyone inside. This is 'water-cave', and becomes the venue of secret meetings when we don't want anyone to know our plans. We can go anywhere for secret meetings, but *anywhere* doesn't have the glamour of water-cave.

I choose water-cave to tell Gretchen I'm planning to run away.

'Run a *what?*' she yells, trying to make herself heard above the thunder of the water.

'Run *away*,' I shout in her ear.

'*What* away?' she yells.

'*Run!*' I scream.

'*Okay*,' she shouts, '*let's!*' What an offer she's making! I don't seize

147

the chance. I'll regret it one day. Not now. All I can think is water-cave's not an ideal place for conversation!

In the last days of the holiday we invent a new game. *Uchi maji mti kimbia*, or naked-water-tree-running. It starts in our garden, when someone turns the hose on. In panic, we dive for cover. Big trees. The trunks are two foot wide, and the icy jet can't get round. At first Sophia, Antonio, Andrew, Gretchen, Dieti, Becky and I take turns to be *Shetani maji,* or water-devil. Soon, like all games, it needs spicing up.

Dieti shows great imagination by suggesting running for cover should only be done *visout clozes*. In addition, taking turns is too predictable. Gretchen suggests anything be allowed. You shouldn't know who'll be the next ambusher. This introduces new, exciting, danger-elements. From now, the rules go, hose-ambush can happen anywhere, anytime. When it does, it's forbidden to find cover unless naked.

A further development in the game of naked-water-tree-running occurs and teaches me an important lesson. It's Dieti, again, who decides it has to be more challenging. It isn't enough to strip off before running for cover from water attack. Boring. What we should do under attack is not *run* away naked, but nakedly *hop* on one foot. It's a hop too far.

The gang have slavishly obeyed the rules thus far, but now sheer complexity make it impossible. Failure to comply, along with interest, is lost. The game withers and dies under the weight of bureaucracy. I find out that complicating things can kill them. Like they say, *KISS*, Keep It Simple, Stupid!

Snow-White is making remarkable progress in the kitchen. She hasn't got an infection in her wound, which is amazing, because her wing is not only broken, but badly lacerated. Mum's given her a bit of aspirin every day. She's convinced that's why she's doing so well. She doesn't seem to mind having her broken wing strapped to her body, and she's really taken to living in her cardboard box. She lies there quietly, but clucks gently when someone approaches her. She only gets out her box to relieve herself. After a few days we experiment. We leave the back door open.

Snow-White gets up, exits her box, walks to the door, goes gingerly down the steps. Stares disdainfully at her erstwhile companions in the run, until Gooloogooloo spots her and comes to the wire. It's amazing. They stand like prisoner and visitor on either side of the barrier, making gentle clucking sounds at each other. It's like real

148

conversation. Tiny adoptive mother advising overgrown adopted son. Eventually she walks away, relieves herself, wearily climbs the steps, pads across the kitchen floor, and gets in her box. She clucks. A job well done.

She's eating and drinking, and starting to look positively happy. The wing's very stiff, and she'll never be able to fly. It won't matter. We trim the feathers on one wing of all the *kukus* anyway, to prevent them flying up in to the tree. Learn that early in Geita. When Mum and Dad had their first *kukus*, and wanted to eat one, they were all perched on high branches. They'd invited someone for a dinner of roast chicken. Dad had to shoot one out the tree.

Snow-White is endearing herself to us. She's got a physical defect now, which makes her *kuku masikini*, or poor chicken, Umali says. But she hasn't got a cast eye, I say. Not yet, Umali replies. Many chickens in the bush have cast eyes. She'll have that, and worse, if she doesn't vacate his kitchen soon. When Mum's out he whispers that, even though Mum doesn't like his language, Snow-White is a survivor of an attack by an *nguchiro,* or mongoose, and a *blurryfuckenbitch*-one at that!

Fifteen

The holiday draws too soon towards an end. The last week is spent getting our things sorted out and packing. I try not to think there's only days left. Something will happen to prolong our stay. Maybe we won't have to go back at all. If I pray hard enough, maybe God will intervene. If he's got round to forgiving me shooting him. Also, if I ignore the matter, maybe it won't be true. But going comes closer. Soon it's the second last day. Umali has noticed my growing depression. He suggests we go fishing.

'Why you cross, *Jimu?*' Umali asks on the bank of the dam. Lying beside us are our bamboo fishing poles, lines stretching out parabolically to the floats. We're lazy fishers. 'Why you angry?' Sandy whimpers. She wants to know too. I turn to Umali.

'I don't want to go back to Arusha!' I say fiercely. I spit several yards into the water. There's a long silence. Umali considers my words. Suddenly my float disappears beneath the still surface, and I grab my pole and strike. Flash of silver near surface. Fish on hook. I run up the bank, tugging. Sandy barks. A fat tilapia glints in the shallows, then I haul him onto the bank. Sandy grabs him in a deft movement, runs a few steps, stops and drops him at my feet. He's at least a pound and a half. Sandy makes that spitting sound. It's amazing she fetches them for me, when she hates the feel in her mouth. She's almost as good a spitter as the *watu!* Can't let myself laugh when I'm in serious conversation with Umali.

'*Samaki muzuri!*' Umali says, breaking his silence. Nice fish. He grins. I take the fish off the hook and throw it further up the bank. He hasn't even taken the worm off the hook. I cast again, landing my float almost in the original spot. I'm getting very good.

'You fish well,' Umali says. Big compliment. When he first took me

150

fishing I hadn't a clue. He's a good teacher. I concentrate on my float, or try to. The thought of going back to Arusha causes tightness in my throat, pounding in my chest.

'You don't want to go back?' Umali says.

'*Sitaki!*' I say with feeling. I *don't*. I spit again. This is serious business.

'*Jimu*, that is your school, if you don't go, how will you know to read, to get work of a *Mzungu*?'

'*Sitaki,*' I say. I don't want.

'*Usi pigana, Jimu,*' he murmurs gently. Don't fight, Jimu.

'*Nta kimbia!*' I threaten. I will run away.

'*Apana,*' Umali tuts. No. You won't run, and you won't fight.'

'*Sababu?*' I ask. Why not?

'Because your mother cries a lot. She works long and hard for you.'

'I want to stay with her and you,' I say.

'Think *Jimu*. All the *totos* here stay at home. They won't read, they won't get good work. . .' I'm silent. Umali is agreeing with Mum. I have argued and pleaded with her so many tearful times, to no avail. Here's my best friend in the whole world taking sides against me. I decide it's time to stop fishing and go home. Umali comes too. He's caught two fat catfish. There's little conversation on the road. I walk ahead, my fish in a bag tied to my pole, Sandy at my heel. It's a long walk home.

That night I lie in bed and think about this place, Geita, my home. Anyone from outside would imagine that a little mining camp deep in the African bush would be a backwater, cut off and isolated from the world. But nothing is further from the truth. You only have to scratch, and the world outside is with you, either in the present or in history.

There's the local *watu*, of different tribes, Indians, Chinese, Germans, German Jews, British, Italians, South Africans, Seychellois, and Mr Snel's wife is Canadian. All these people have different backgrounds, languages and ways, and that colours the culture here. Then history: there are *askaris* who fought in WWI with von Lettow Vorbeck's *schutztruppe* against the British. There are three German-Jewish survivors of German extermination camps in WWII, Dr Weiss and his wife, and Mr Hessler, who works with Mum at the mine store. There's Eugen Blüger, Dieti and Gretchen's dad, who served with Rommel in the Afrika Corps in WWII, and his cousin Otto Müller at Lotanga, who sailed in German *Kriegsmarine* submarines. Then there's Higgs and Kaizer, the mine *askari*, who fought with the KAR in Burma, as part of General Slim's army taking the war to the Japanese between 1942 and 45. Several of the British people on the

151

mine also served in theatres of the war, though none with such distinction as Dad.

Geita is no backwater. The important events of the first half of the twentieth century are all represented here, in the memories of living, breathing people. I love that about Geita. It looks isolated from the world, but nothing could be more untrue. Where else, I wonder, could I actually talk with the very people who were involved in so many momentous, world-shaping events?

Next day I go in search of my old friend Kaizer. There's no television, nor clear radio reception apart from Radio Congo, but Kaizer's wartime tales more than compensate. He's a mine *askari*, or policeman, and served with the King's African Rifles in the war. They're affectionately known as the KAR, and have roots in Nyasaland, or modern Malawi.

In 1899 a British Captain Lugard, of the Norfolk regiment, founded a small army called the Central African Rifles, in order to defeat a notorious slave trader called Mlozi, just like our Geita ribbon and *kimbo*-tin man. Was that earlier Mlozi as crazy as our one? I wonder. Was his insurrection also due to madness?

After the rebel Mlozi was dealt with, 'natives' from colonies in West, Central and East Africa, were recruited into the KAR to serve under British officers. In post World War I Tanganyika, sixteen battalions of the KAR were raised, many from among ex-*askaris* of von Lettow Vorbeck's *Schutztruppe*. I wonder why Fritz, the German-accented driver, didn't join the KAR like the others. Did he dislike the British *so* much?

I ask Kaizer to tell me about the war in Burma. He scratches his greying hair, smiles, and begins. He loves to tell stories as much as I love to hear them.

In World War II the KAR was deployed in Abyssinia, Somaliland, Madagascar and Burma. I find it so compelling. My *watu*, from right here in little Geita, fighting in big wars far away! In Burma battalions of the KAR formed part of the Eleventh East African division, in General Sir William Slim's Fourteenth Army, the largest army of Commonwealth troops in the war. In all over a million men were deployed through different phases of the war. In 1944 General Slim's army launched a major offensive against the Japanese in Burma. The East African Division fought its way down the great river system of Burma, one brigade crossing the Chindwin, another striking the Japanese in the Kabaw valley. It's in the Kabaw valley that Kaizer won a commendation for bravery.

Do I know, he asks, that Mr Higginson, the chief of the mine *askari*-

152

force, fought in Burma too? That's interesting, even if Kaizer's own story is delayed by telling me this.

Kaizer smiles. Then he begins again. Captain Reginald Higginson, known even then as 'Higgs', was an officer in a Tanganyika-based battalion of the KAR, in which, by 1944, there were only a few former *Schutztruppe askaris* left from 1918. But the tradition of their gallant predecessors was evident in their fighting prowess. When Higgs was disbanded from the army in 1946, he got a job forming and running a small private police force for the gold mine in Geita, Tanganyika. Half a dozen of his *askaris*, from the area originally, came with him, to form the backbone of the new force.

They say about Higgs that his years serving with African soldiers turned him into an African himself. Soon after arriving at Geita he was stricken with malaria, and would surely have died if not nursed back to health, in a tent, by an African woman. She was Kaiser's sister, and an ageing spinster at twenty-two. She thought so because her mother said she was born six years after Vorbeck's tragic surrender in 1918. They say Higgs was so indebted to her he married her. I doubt that was the only reason, because I get to know Higgs and his *bibi* very well, and find them a very close and loving couple.

Higgs committed the worst transgression in British Africa. He dared to marry a black woman. While they decided to keep him as police chief on the mine, it was a unanimous decision to socially black-ball him, and, of course, his wife. They couldn't ban him from the bar at the Lone Cone Club, because that would be 'going too far'. The drinkers knew how thirsty it gets in that heat. To deny a man a cold beer was inhuman, old bean. Nevertheless, he was told his wife was not welcome, and he must avoid too much conversation with 'decent white women'. They may catch something.

Kaizer, so-named by his *Schutztruppe askari* father, is a man in his mid forties in 1959, when I'm eight. He served in the King's African Rifles with Higgs, in Somaliland and Abyssinia, and finally in Burma. There has always been an *askari* stationed outside the Lone Cone Club, why I don't know. In Geita the *askaris* are armed only with a wooden baton, which won't do much against a rampaging lion or a man with a gun! Kaizer insists on the club posting. There are two reasons. One is he loves Higgs more as a brother than a brother-in-law, and thinks his former officer, and current boss, may get so drunk he'll need help to get home to his *bibi*. The other is that Higgs, who also loves Kaizer, has a habit of bringing him out an icy bottle of *Whitecap* several times an evening.

Kaizer sits on the low stone wall outside the bar. He loves to talk.

His English is very limited. Army commands, mostly. Even in Burma he was posted with other Swahili-speaking *askaris,* and the British officers spoke good Swahili. He's fond of me, and enchanted by my fluency in his native tongue. I sit outside with him on many occasions, from as young as five. By the time I'm eight we're old *rafikis*, or friends.

One day I ask how they march in the King's African Rifles. He jumps to his feet, smoothes his khaki shirt and shorts, and, stamping his right foot mightily on the ground, raising dust knee-high, stands to attention. Shouting '*kushoto, kulia, kushoto, kulia,*' lifting his knees almost to his chin, he marches towards the flower bed. *Kushoto* is left, *Kulia* is right. He reaches the edge of the bed, and executes a high-stepping, stomping about-turn. He's so proud, so erect, so correct, so enthusiastic, even though he wears car-tyre rubber sandals, not boots and puttees. A born *askari.*

'Tell me about fighting the Japanese,' I say to him. This time he'll tell me about himself, I hope, not Higgs.

'*Hawa,*' he says, 'them'. I relax. This is what I want. Fighting the Japs is what I'd like to do, and I pretend the war isn't really over. Soon as I'm big enough, I'll be off. Hearing Kaizer's story will prepare me for future battle. He found the Japanese formidable fighters in the jungles of Burma.

'In the Kabaw valley I was with a small patrol, sent to find how close the Japanese were. We walked carefully, hiding behind one tree, then another. It had been raining days, and mud sucked at our boots. Sometimes my boot came right off, stayed there in the mud, and I took my next step in my sock!' I nod my head in empathy.

'There were flies and small insects everywhere, and we had to be quiet, not smack them on our faces or legs. A slap can be heard a long way. We had to pick the insects off one at a time. Couldn't keep it up. Just left them, even though we felt them crawling. We were even afraid to breathe.' He smiles at me.

'It's hotter and wetter than here. The sweat runs, the insects crawl and some bite.' I shudder. Suddenly I have an itch on my cheek, and have to scratch. Kaizer laughs. Then he continues.

'We'd been walking, and hiding, for four hours, when we found the Japanese.'

'You found them?' I ask.

'They found us!' he laughs. 'These Japanese, they cover themselves with leaves, and crawl through the jungle. You can't see them at all.' He shakes his head in remembered surprise. 'We said they had narrow eyes to stop the bush getting in.' He laughs. Then he's serious again.

154

'Suddenly a machine-gun opened up. . . *kak-ak-ak-ak-a,* bullets were spitting on the ground about us. *Plop-plop-plop* they went, leaving round holes in the mud. One *askari* screamed. He got one through the knee. They had to cut his leg off.'

'Did you shoot back?' I ask, captivated.

'At what, little *Mzungu*, at what? We couldn't see anything!'

'What did you do?'

'We fell on the wet ground and nearly *kunya'd* in our trousers.'

'And?'

'There was a huge explosion, right near us.'

'What was it?'

'Mortar bomb. Blew one *askari's* head right off, like a chicken. His name was Arozi, and he was a friend. Came from Geita, like me.'

'Then. . ?'

'I, and another *askari,* crawled to the right, to get behind those Japanese *nyokas*. That's what they were, snakes with narrow eyes. It was slow work, and the insects wouldn't leave us alone.'

'And?'

'We came up behind 'them', but there was only one. He was lying in the grass, between two bushes, and had a mortar-launcher and three bombs. He didn't know we were there. I took aim with my Lee Enfield, and, *ka-boom*, I missed him!'

'What happened?' I ask, the tension overwhelming. Kaizer smiles.

'It's alright *Mzungu ndogo*, little European, can't you see I'm still here and healthy?'

'Yes. . .'

'The Nippon, he rolled over and tried to get to his feet when my bullet hit the ground by his head. The other *askari* shot him with his Sten-gun, Brrr-aa-a-ppp, six bullets in the chest, knocked him backwards like a toy. Nine millimetre.'

'Dead?'

'Completely dead. *Na kufwa kabisa!* He died completely. Can you believe, he had strings in his hands going to triggers on two machine-guns, which were tied to trees, sighted where he knew we would approach! Just one Japanese!' Kaizer shakes his head. 'They are very clever people.'

Kaizer smiles and gets to his feet. The story is over. Those Japanese are tougher than they look in the war comics. In them they're all thin, short, knock-kneed, buck-toothed and bespectacled, and the only word they yell is *banzai,* which means 'charge'. Perhaps I shouldn't really fight them! I tell Kaizer this is a great story, and one day I will learn to write, and make a book about it.

'*Asante, ndugu ndogo,*' thank you little brother. 'You have *hakiri,* brains, you will do it one day.' On the way home my throat feels really tight. Distraction from going back to Arusha only works momentarily. It's still there, getting closer each minute.

At home a visitor's waiting in the compound. Lutoli. I haven't seen him since I've been home. We're delighted to meet up again, and for a couple of hours I almost forget my misery. He tells me he's been away with his mother, visiting his late father's relatives in Biharlomoulo. He knows I'm going back to Arusha soon, but hasn't realised it's tomorrow. We talk, practise shooting with our home-made catapults, and eat a meal of *ugali* and *mboga* with Amina and Umali. When we part, Lutoli cries shamelessly. 'You're my best friend in the world,' he sobs, 'a friend to beat all.' That makes *me* cry. There's something very sad about Lutoli.

Umali doesn't show anger about my temper tantrum at the dam. Instead, he tries lifting my spirits by telling me one of his funniest jokes. A Swahili one.

'There was a man with two penises, or *mboros*. His wife was tired, because when one lay down, the other stood up. Finally, exhausted by double *jigi-jigi*, she sent *Two-Mboros* to the doctor to have one amputated. When he reached the clinic, after many days on the road, the nurse told him to wait, as *Three-Mboros* and *Four-Mboros* had come first!'

Reality returns brutally. It has been a break to think about something other than going back to Arusha. Kaizer's stories distract me from the harsh here and now, as do Umali's jokes. For a while. Maybe I can get help from another source. I've tried praying, begging, hoping for a *novus actus interveniens*. None has worked. I'm still going back to school. My scheming and plotting have come to nought. Perhaps I should take a completely different tack. What about Mlozi? It's not just Lutoli who says he's a *mchawi,* or witch. There are others.

Just behind his flat rock or *mwamba,* is Mlozi's tiny hut. It's so small, not even tall enough for me to walk in without bending, if I wanted to. It's made of bent sticks, twigs and mud, and roofed with banana-thatch. He sits on his rock all day, then crawls into his hut at night.

There are mutterings about Mlozi among the *watu*. It's been a long time since the *ng'ombe,* or cattle-rich, *mzee* intervened to stop the crowd stoning him to death. Since then, some *watu* have begun to believe he's neither mad nor possessed by *jinni* or *djinn*. That leaves only one explanation for his lifestyle and appearance: he's *mchawi*, witch-sorcerer. Some think no further, others avoid him, lest he curse them. Then there are the *wasikini*. Begging for a living is an insecure occupation. They need all the luck they can get.

One day Mlozi tells a *masikini* that if he begs at the green house beyond the baobab tree, he will receive blue trousers. The *masikini* does, and it happens. The *wasikini* oracle is born. How, or with what they pay him, I don't know. But *I've* got money. Of my fifty shillings pocket money for next term, Mum's already given me five. Suddenly I know how I must spend it.

'*Jambo,*' I say next morning. It's my last day in Geita. Time is running out. I'm standing before Mlozi's flat rock or *mwamba.* It's one o'clock in the morning. Swahili-time for seven am. Once I got the idea last night, I couldn't wait to get here. The sun's already scorching, and Mlozi's sitting in his usual place. He's bent over, and his ribbon-tied locks obscure his face. He's murmuring softly in there. The murmuring stops. A hand on the end of a wrist heavy with copper-wire bracelets reaches up and parts his plaited locks. Coal-black eyes are staring.

'*Nini Mzungu?*' What, white person? asks that strange, reedy voice. This is not simple. It could be 'what do you want?', '*what* white person are you?', or even 'what *now?*' implying I've been before. Suddenly I'm struck with dread. I can see why the *wasikini* fear and respect him as *mchawi.* Anyone who with just two words can bring such confusion has very strong *dawa*, or medicine! How do I answer?

'I have come. . .'

'You have come?' His voice is spooky. High-pitched, yet gravelly. He can see I have, yet he asks. There's more to this. He *knows* why I'm here. Just wants to hear it from me. I feel a tingle in my spine. What am I doing here, seeking out this strange, strange man?

'*Ku ulisa,*' I say. To enquire.

'*Aw omba?*' Or beg, even pray? He's playing a game with me.

'To ask *hekima!*' I blurt. Wisdom. I'm not *praying* to him!

'My *hekima?*' A thin laugh. The anorexic figure suddenly straightens, and he sweeps his locks aside. His face is even thinner than I remember. Bony. Amused, he looks like a laughing skeleton. I want to leave this place. It's eerie, even so early in the day. But I've got a mission.

'I don't want to go back to Arusha!' I plead.

'*Uta rudi!*' he says, you *will* return. He adopts his faraway look and begins a mumbling speech with no one. It's like I'm not here, as if he's consulting the sky. 'You'll go back!' he suddenly says. He spits expertly at the ground. 'You'll return both *there* and *here.*' He loses

157

interest. That's it. He's not even looking at me. I'm dismissed by the *mchawi*. My hand's in my pocket. I feel the five shilling-coins. I'm devastated. He's just robbed me of hope.

There's a crippled *masikini* standing nearby. He's been waiting, watching with one bright eye. Clearly he's next in line. I extract a shilling and place it on the rock. Mlozi doesn't move. The *masikini* does. For a cripple, he moves with dazzling speed. The shilling disappears into the folds of his ragged clothes. Mlozi doesn't notice, or care. He is not a material man. I go away to nurse my disappointment.

After two hours of wasted tearful pleading with Mum, though she's as distressed as me, I go to bed. But I can't sleep. I lie in the dark, trying desperately to hatch an escape plan. I can't run away in Geita, because all directions lead into the bush. Foolish anyway, because Geita's where I want to be! This is the opposite of breaking out from prison. I want to break *in* to where I already am! How can I do that?

I wrestle my thoughts. The only chance I have of changing things is to change Mum's mind. If *she* decides I can stay, that'll be that. How can I persuade her? All my pleading, all my tears, have failed completely. Out of all the confusion I have an idea.

If I escape on the way to Arusha, and disappear for a while, that'll make Mum realise how serious I am. I *don't* want to go back to Arusha! I have to make my move *between* Geita and there. Geita to Mwanza is no good – jungle. Mwanza to Dodoma, on the train? That's difficult, because when the train stops there are always lots of people on the platform, and everyone on the train looks out the windows. The hotel in Dodoma? The dormitory – difficult to sneak out. Someone's sure to wake up. I'm getting desperate. I'm thinking myself closer and closer to Arusha, without escaping. It will have to be the bus. It's the only option. I'll jump out the bus when nobody's looking.

I force my mind off the subject. It can wait till Dodoma. There are so many other things to think about. What about Higgs and Heathfield? Thinking about them will take my mind off my dilemma.

Higgs and Heathfield are reprobates in the eyes of the *Wazungu*. Higgs because of his black *bibi*, Heathfield because they say he's 'homosensual'. Something like that. Thelemani told me about it. Men doing *jigi-jigi*. The *mutu* who does *jigi-jigi*, then gets *jigi-jigied*. Not that I really understand. At this time I know, yet I don't. It's a no-man's-land of knowing. Higgs, on the other hand, doesn't only live with his *bibi*, but has a troika of half-caste children. People say this in lowered voices. The shame of it!

Being socially unacceptable to other club members, the semi-outcasts come, nevertheless, reliably and regularly, every time the sun tips the western hills, to drink at the great maninga-wood bar at Lone Cone Club. The far right hand end, because everyone else occupies the middle and left, and proximate tables and chairs.

They drink heavily and share only each other's company, except for the occasional interlude when a more sympathetic and less bigoted member of the middle-to-left assembly forays over to show slightly embarrassed solidarity with the outcasts. A joke, a pat on the back of one, usually Higgs's rather than Heathfield's, his folly being less reprehensible, for 'homosensuality' is worse than miscegenation, a beer ordered against the tab, then a retreat to more hallowed surroundings. Quizzical looks and 'tut-tut's' from those who remain unpolluted from mixing with the unmixable.

Higgs and Heathfield are always last to leave, ordering more Whitecap when Ishmael, the barman in white *kanzu* and red fez, rings the bell for last orders. They drink till the beer's finished, the lights are turned off, and everyone's gone. They stagger outside, and Higgs takes Heathfield home on his Harley Davison, before finding his way down the dirt road to his own house .

In 1958 I hear a most curious story. It's one which will live on in Geita folklore, and something so strange I have difficulty persuading people in Arusha it's true. The drunken outcasts, Higgs and Heathfield, lurch out the club into the parking area. They're even drunker than usual. Higgs finds his motorbike and pulls it off its stand. He straddles it and kick-starts the engine. Heathfield has disappeared, and Higgs calls for him impatiently, gear engaged and clutch held in. He feels a weight alight, Heathfield's warm body against his back, his moist breath on the nape of his neck. Heathfield can get rather clutchy and a little pathetic after ten quarts of Whitecap. Higgs is used to that. He lets out the clutch with his left hand, and rolls up the revs with his right. The big Harley Davison roars, and the twosome ride unsteadily away, up the gravelled road towards their homes.

Then Heathfield *really* starts to exceed himself. At first Higgs feels Heathfield's arms move up from holding him round the hips, to grasp his shoulders. 'What the hell you playing at?' he shouts above the roar of the engine. No answer. Now Heathfield begins to dig his nails into Higgs's shoulders, and the pain is excruciating. 'Stop that, you fool,' Higgs yells, but the nails dig deeper, and begin to scratch painfully down his back. The agony is so extreme that Higgs, rounding a corner, loses control, and he, Heathfield and bike plummet off the road into dense undergrowth.

159

Higgs hears his bike hit something. He finds himself on a bed of soft branches, and feels suddenly very inebriated. To hell, he thinks, and falls asleep. His last thought are 'where the hell is Heathfield?' and 'I'm not taking *him* home again.'

At seven in the morning Higgs awakes to searing tropical sunshine, the buzzing of myriad insects, and a skimpy memory of last night. When he tries to rise, he finds his back and shoulders are in agony. Gingerly he feels the scratches on his back, and discovers deep lacerations running from shoulder-tip to waistline. He limps to where his bike lies on its side by the trunk of a *Mbuia* tree, and is astonished to see the near side of the petrol tank has four deep dents. He pulls the bike up, and finds the same on the other side, but one dent has a hole in it. Protruding from the hole is a very large, bloodstained claw-nail. Higgs's clingy passenger of last night was not Heathfield. He, on staggering into the fresh air, feels awfully tired. He sees an inviting flowerbed, and subsides into it.

Higgs's passenger is a full-grown leopard. The news spreads like bush fire. Some *Wazungus* say he's making all this up. Whites who marry blacks are probably liars, and worse. But how can they explain his lacerations and the holes in the tank? The claw? Why does Heathfield admit sleeping in a flower bed? Higgs brought him to the club, and the bike was undamaged then.

Did Higgs sneak out between drinks, disable and puncture his own bike's tank, insert what was undeniably a leopard claw into the hole, severely lacerate himself, then sidle back in and act normally? Wouldn't someone notice the blood? Even if not, how did he get rid of Heathfield on the road? Unless he and Heathfield are making this up together. But why? Why would these two men, no matter their faults, play a prank like this? It doesn't make sense.

Three days after the incident, while Higgs is still receiving daily injections and dressings for his wounds, a leopard is shot just two miles from the club by Marcello Barelli, Antonio's father and our great white hunter. His rear right foot is missing a claw, and the toe-pad is torn and septic. When his back feet are placed against the fuel tank, the claw positions match the punctures. The incident is closed. The leopard weighs two hundred pounds, and is fully nine foot from nose to tail. He will be remembered for years as the 'Geita-Night-Rider', who hitched a lift with the constabulary. When Higgs recovers his limited dignity, he's often heard to brag, after several Whitecaps, that 'I gave that sod a lift half a bloody mile!' The legend of *The Astonishing Tales of Higgs the Policeman* grows. I think 'astonishing' means funny.

Higgs isn't bad, I muse. In fact, he's a good man, a kind one. Yet the cruel *Wazungu* make him an outcast. During this holiday I go to his house. I meet his *bibi*, Maria, Kaizer's sister. She makes me lemonade from a fresh lemon she picks off her tree, squeezes, mixes with sugar and cold water. Higgs comes home and is hugely pleased to see me. Doesn't get white visitors. I ask where his children are. At Kaizer's *shamba*, visiting, he says. 'You're a big friend of Kaiser, aren't you?' I confirm I am. 'He's Maria's brother, you know?' I do know.

I notice a whole wall in the lounge is filled by a built-in bookshelf. It's crowded with books. All sizes and colours. I've never seen so many together. Higgs is a big reader. How many of the *Wazungu* know that? He's cleverer than them by far!

I can't sleep. I don't want to let my mind wander back to my Arusha-school-escape plan. Too much thinking, and I'll be terrified before I start. I'll have time aplenty for planning on the horrible train, and in the Railway Hotel in Dodoma. There are other things about Geita I can think about now. Anything to stop thoughts of Arusha. I fall asleep trying to think what to think.

I wake while it's still dark. I know what I should have thought about. There is this other story, the coffee-planter's one, which is funny and sad at once. Such things don't happen anywhere else than in the Tanganyikan bush. The Land Rover may be coming for me, but not yet, and I've got my mind to play with as I want. It's a defence against the coming dawn, which will see me on the road away from home again. A road I don't want to travel. They can't stop my thoughts now.

Higgs and Heathfield are not at all unusual in Tanganyika. By comparison with some people, they're pillars of propriety and conservatism. I turn over in bed. Geita is such a wonderful place. I don't want to go tomorrow. Why can't I just stay, like Lutoli? I feel sad when I think about him. Why do I have to be a *Mzungu*, and go away to school? It's happening again, I'm thinking about Arusha.

I force my mind back to Geita. There's no end to interesting things which happen here. The coffee planter's story for example. That's a good one. It's stories like this which give Geita, all Tanganyika, that special something which makes it home to me. Not like that soft, green, wet place with tiny houses, which is all I remember of Cornwall, or England. This place is a man's country, I think, and that suits me because I'm a man!

*   *   *   *

161

In 1959, a visitor comes. Don't know why, but he does. Probably because he likes his beer cold, and the word is out there's a good fridge at Lone Cone Club. Terence Worthing is his name, and he farms coffee a hundred miles from us. Ex-servicemen have been encouraged to start the industry in yet another attempt to make the colony pay. Terence stays a week as a personal guest of Mr Snel, General Manager. They met long ago in the war. Snel was in Gibraltar, where Terence was a Navy diver.

Terence is a big, bearded man, who smokes a pipe, drinks prodigious amounts of *Whitecap*, and loves recounting his escapades. He tells several stories at the bar. One stands out, and becomes an addition to Geita folklore.

The coffee plantations were three years old, spread out in a crescent over ninety square miles of sun-scorched scrub. A dozen new ventures halfway between Mwanza and Musoma, and ten miles inland from Lake Victoria. Young coffee plants stood in long rows on cleared fields; living conditions were basic. Most planters still slept in tents, or huts of corrugated iron and wood. Their energies were focused on bringing irrigation from small rivers which fed the lake, grading roads, planting coffee.

Blistering hot days in the open, and bush-loneliness, led to a meeting of planters at one's *shamba*. A decision was reached. At a point equidistant from their properties, designated *Timbuktu*, a clearing was cut. A huge round mud and wattle hut, open above the waist, was built, roofed with *makuti*-style elephant-grass. A bar was made of rough-hewn maninga planks, and tall stools of hides and sticks were commissioned from local *watu*. The *pièce de la résistance* was a large paraffin refrigerator, which arrived by lorry from Dar-es-Salaam, five days distant. Club Timbuktu was in business.

Hard-working men shouldn't drink every day, the four planters' wives declared, so the club only opened Sundays. The sabbath mutated to a riotous, happy and very drunken occasion.

Early in the history of Club Timbuktu, the Sunday revellers saw a most curious sight. 'We were thoroughly under the affluence of incohol, really sizzled,' Terence says, 'and didn't know if it was real or imagined. Sun and booze, deadly together!' A dozen tribesmen and women emerged from the bush. They weren't from tribes the planters knew round there. These were the much feared 'bush-people', of whom the *watu* spoke with dread. They were cannibals, they said, and worshipped a monkey-king, or, some thought, a great crocodile. No one was quite certain. They wore animal-skin *moochies* over their genitals, and nothing else. How can a cannonball eat people, I wonder.

Carried at shoulder height by the leading four apparitions was a stretcher of wooden poles and plaited grass. Regally perched on the platform, perfectly balanced and smiling a greeting, was a white man. He was unmistakably European, despite his deep-copper tan and black fur *moochi*. Apart from that diminutive garment, he was stark naked.

'Hallo,' he said in an Oxbridge accent, 'I'm Joe'. The planters burst out laughing. This was comedy, a joke by one of their number. They were always playing tricks.

'Good show!' one shouted, clapping. They played the game, greeting Joe and offering him a drink. Joe gave a command, and his bearers set him on the ground. While his entourage watched, Joe joined the *Wazungu* drinkers in a 'bender to end benders'.

It turned out Joe was, in a previous life, an Oxford law graduate who went into colonial service after university. He was helped by contacts of his wealthy family, who lived in a grand estate in Hertfordshire. 'It'll make a man of you, show you the world, and teach you responsibility,' his crusty barrister-father told him. 'Oh, and don't come back until you've got yourself a real woman, not a floozie like before. And get that woman to show you how to do up that damnable tie!'

Joe joined the colonial office, underwent two weeks' training, which comprised polite cocktail parties in Chelsea, and drunken debauched forays into Soho with six colleagues and two heavy-drinking 'trainers'. He got sent east as a junior in the legal section of Hong Kong's colonial administration. There he met his first wife, daughter of the third most powerful man after the Governor General. Married, and with a baby due in an indelicately short time, the couple moved into their own home.

By this time Joe was twenty-six, and deeply bitten by the 'booze-bug'. He began to have symptoms of alcohol dependence. He told the planters, who listened in rapt concentration, 'I began to have a drop in the morning, to smooth the shakes.' He took a swig of neat gin, grimaced, and swallowed. 'Then I started to hide a bottle in the drawer at work.' Then he was topping up his alcohol level throughout the day. His young wife, now with daughter, whose only occupation was 'screaming and shitting', finally began to resent his drinking. Arguments flared. He started to lie about his drinking, to hide bottles where she wouldn't find them. He avoided going home when he couldn't face the rancour. 'Office floor's comfortable when you're pissed!'

After another 'bender' with a friend in the Chinese bars of Kowloon, Joe returned home to find two things. 'She'd up and left, with the baby, and written me a note saying sorry Joe, can't take this anymore. Melanie.' There's another envelope, a brown manilla one with a seal. 'Know that anywhere. Bloody colonial office! I'm informed that, due to unprofessional and thoroughly reprehensible behaviour. . . my services are no longer required by this administration.'

Joe grinned. 'At the bottom it says I'm being given two months severance pay and a second class ticket home on the steamship SS *Orion*. Departing Hong Kong for Cape Town, Mombasa, Dar-es-Salaam, Suez, Port Said, Genoa, Barcelona, Gibraltar and Southampton, on 27th instant. That's three days.' The planters were impressed. None of them could reel off a list like that. Not 'affluenced' as they indubitably were.

Joe drank his money before *Orion* reached Dar-es-Salaam. Desperate for a drink, he tried his luck ashore. For a few pennies he bought enough home-made Nubian gin to slay an elephant. 'And so,' he said, grinning a black-toothed grin, 'I decide to hell with the ship. I don't want to see Mombasa, Suez, Port Said, Genoa, Barcelona, Gibraltar or bloody Southampton. I have my paradise, here in Tanganyika!' There's applause from the planters, who all think Tanganyika's a good place. They pour him another glass of neat gin.

Joe hung around Dar a few months, found he didn't need a fixed abode while the *Warabu* and *Swahilis* offered food and a floor-mat to sleep on. But he 'began to be noticed' by the 'damnable Brits'. It was unheard of for a white man, an Englishman to-boot, to mix with the natives this way. . . 'First I'm arrested, thrown in a cell for a night, and lectured on race-mixing by the superintendent in the morning. Bugger them!' It failed to reform him, and a policeman broke his arm with a baton. '*Stronger advice*, the bastards!'

Joe decided to head inland, away from authority. It was 1936, and there was a lot of construction work in different parts. Every day lorries left Dar, loaded with cement and material for places with exotic names, like *Shinyanga, Dodoma, Iringa and Musoma*. The first driver he asked offered him a ride.

'I don't give a bugger,' he said, 'all I want is peace and quiet, and something to drink!'

Somewhere near Musoma, ten miles from where he was telling his tale, the lorry blew a head gasket. Joe was no mechanic. He thanked the driver, and took his chances on a footpath into the hills, a bottle of Nubian gin in one hand.

'That's 1936,' one of the planters says, 'now it's 1959, twenty-three years. . .'

'Exactly,' says Joe, 'time flies when you're having fun. I even managed to avoid the war. Only heard about it in '51.' He held his glass out for a refill. The planters appraised him. If he was twenty-six or seven when he left Hong Kong, he was fifty or thereabouts now. Okay, he wore nothing more than that *moochie*, and his teeth were black, but there wasn't a grey hair, nor a single wrinkle on his face.

'I think you should meet the *bibi* and kids,' Joe pronounced. '*Marina, kuja hapa, leta watoto.*' Marina, come here, bring the children. A dark, wrinkled, bare breasted, elderly looking woman detached herself from the watching clan, and several light skinned men and women, plus a couple of teenagers, joined her. 'This,' Joe said proudly, 'is my family.' His family smiled, but looked bewildered. According to Joe, he was the only *Mzungu* they'd seen before that day.

'To what do we owe this visit, Joe?' a planter finally asked.

'Gin,' he said. 'Ivory for gin.' He snapped his fingers and yelled, '*Leta meno ya tembo.*' From the edge of the clearing two young men came running, bearing between them a huge elephant tusk.

'You shoot elephants?' the planter asked.

'Naw. Find dead ones. Elephant cemetery, you know. Have to die sometime.'

'Well,' said another planter, eyeing the tusk. 'Ivory's selling for. . . what is it. . . several pounds a pound. This one's heavy. . . I think we can do business.'

Then began a most unusual commercial and social relationship. Native Joe, as they named him, had to wait a week for his first two cases of gin, but he and his *watu* didn't mind. They camped beside *Timbuktu*, and waited. Next Sunday the planters came back with the gin. Someone had a delivery of irrigation equipment from Dar, and contacted his supplier. After another drinking binge with his '*Mzungu* tribe', Joe embarked imperiously atop his stretcher, bottle of gin in hand, and waved goodbye. Everyone shook their heads as the strange procession filtered back into the vastness of the bush.

'We were onto a good thing,' Terence Worthing tells his audience. I'm listening raptly. I'd love to meet this wild man of the bush. I have much in common with him. 'Native Joe brought us tons of ivory. Tusks like we'd never seen. By George it paid! All our booze, and more. He came every six weeks, ten times in all, his poor sweating devils divided between those carrying him on that ridiculous litter, and those lugging ivory. All the time he sat swigging gin from a bottle! Never saw anything like it!'

'What happened?'

'All good things have to end, I suppose,' Terence muses, staring into his empty beer glass. Someone takes the hint and buys him a

Whitecap. He pours, takes an appreciative swig, and continues. 'One day Joe kicked the bucket, out in the bush. His adopted *watu* didn't have a clue what to do. See, they're ancestor worshippers, have rites and rituals when one of them croaks. With Joe, they didn't know what to do.'

'What did they do?'

'Trussed him up under a pole, like a deer, carried him three days through the bush. We'd know best, they thought, how to send Joe to his ancestors. Joe liked us, and we were his *kabila*, or tribe. 'Course it was the gin he really liked, but what the heck. 'Course it was a bloomin' Sunday, like they arranged it specially. They came out the bush, carrying the stinking corpse on a pole, flies all over. . !'

'They brought him to the club?'

'Too right. Luckily we'd had a few by then, made it easier. Once we understood the poor heathens had carried him through that bush, in that heat, we thought we'd better do something. We dug a big hole, or they did, three foot deep, 'cos that ground's as hard as bloody steel, then we put Joe in, stuck a bottle of Johnny Walker with him, covered him up, and made a show of praying to impress them. My oppo, Bruce the Aussie, held a friggin' exercise book, the one we kept the tabs with, upside-down, and made a speech. 'G'bye Joe,' he said, 'hope there's shitloads of gin where you've gone!' Joe's *bibi* never stopped wailing, nor his youngsters. We gave them the cash in the kitty, and that's that.'

'That's it?'

'Not really. Same evening, all boozed up, we ran out of grog.'

'And?'

'Well, we wanted more booze. . .'

'You didn't. . ?'

'We did. Dug the bugger up again.'

The digging up bit doesn't worry me. I dug up Tembo's puppy, didn't I? But I'm worried about Higgs. He married a *bibi*. Joe married a *bibi*. Joe's dead. I hope that's not going to happen to Higgs. Please God, I pray, don't let Higgs die too. I wonder how much he'll listen to my prayer. Can someone who killed Dad have mercy? Or someone who makes me go to boarding school?

Sixteen

Finally I fall asleep, Sandy's head beside mine on the pillow. It seems only minutes before it's five am. Fritz's hooting outside. Quick wash, get dressed in school uniform. Lug my trunk to the front door with sleepy Umali. Get in the Land Rover. By the time we get to Arusha I'll have firmed up my plan. I'll escape. It'll be before the Dodoma-Arusha bus. I'll pretend I've given up the struggle for now, act normally, buy comics for school at Lake Printers, get on the train with only limited emotional display. Don't want anyone pre-warned of my intentions.

The same children as before, with parents seeing them off. Mrs Shuter is escort again. Horrible old bag! Becky sobs a lot. I sob a little, though my feelings are mixed. Gretchen sits next to me and tries her best to engage me in conversation. Mum asked her. Mum knows how I feel about Gretchen.

'It's not so bad, Jim,' she says.

'It is!' I say. As much as I adore her, I'm too busy thinking to have a chat.

Competing with the dismay and foreboding I've felt the whole holiday is another feeling. Excitement. Anticipation, exhilaration almost. I'm going to turn this thing on its head, and only I know. I'll put an end to the nightmare. When I've been gone a few days, they'll know I'm not prepared to go to Arusha under *any* terms. They'll give up and let me stay in Geita. They'll all know soon enough, I think, watching Mwanza Station and the distant figures of Mum and Fritz growing smaller. Mum's looking so sad. He's erect and, as always, aloof. I noticed, this morning, that on shaving the pencil-line of his moustache, he's nicked the edge of his upper lip. There's a scab. Did he say *Himmel!* when he did it?

167

The train journey's the same, only this time I've changed attitude and intention. As the miles roll by, the sun's glare hurts my eyes. After several blinding hours comes the welcome sunset. The landscape grows more gentle in early twilight. I think how different this journey is to last time on the same line. Then I was keen, excited about the adventure. Now I know better. There's nothing to be happy about. They're taking me where I don't want to go. A place where I'm alien, where I don't fit, where I'm unhappy. All for my 'own good'! Why don't they listen to me? Mum. . . surely she, of all the people in the world, should listen? But she hasn't, no matter how I pleaded, cried, begged. It's seven thirty, Becky says, showing off her new watch.

The sky grows dark as the blood-red sun plunges off the edge of the world. A three-quarter moon softly lights the arid land. Trees cast eerie shadows. Somewhere ahead the locomotive belches. The brakes clunk on, iron wheels screech on iron rails. The train judders and slows. A naked light-bulb attached to a wooden pole, surrounded by giant fluttering moths, beams jaundiced light on a disintegrating cement platform. A station.

We squeal to a halt, and judder again. Why is that? I don't know. Nobody gets off or on, and the locomotive doesn't need water or coal so soon. Not that these are here anyway. Gretchen is fast asleep. Her head has slipped to one side, and is resting lightly on my shoulder. Her breath is sweet and warm. The only people on the platform are two tired-looking women vendors in *kanzus,* trying to sell roasted *mahogo*, or cassava, chips. I don't see takers. The train shakes and groans, and starts to go again. The vendor-women look disappointed.

At eight thirty Mrs Shuter says go to bed. I lie on my narrow bunk, listening to the clicking of wheels on track. It comforts me. That and the gentle roll of the carriage. Tomorrow's another day. I'll show them I mean business! But I can't sleep. My mind's somewhere between ensconcement in my imaginary canoe, and the train trying to rock me to sleep. Even the *gari moshi* is in on the plot. The thought keeps me from slumber.

I'm awake when we roll to a halt in all the little stations, as well as Shinyanga and Singida. I remember the sounds well from the last trip. Noisy bartering. Women's shrill voices, deeper tones of African rail-crew beating prices down. Swish of water feeding locomotive boiler. Clanging boots on steel plate. Hissing from restless engine.

I doze, then it's morning. The dazzling white sun-orb is up already, beginning its relentless obsession with cremating creation. Breakfast in dining car. A tatty one this time. Faded, fly-blown, hand-written *EAR&H* sign. I hardly eat. My brain's grinding out a plan without me.

168

It's visceral, involves the gut. I always think important things there. We sit in our compartment more searing hours. I doze again, and wake, my head aching from heat and discomfort. Trouble with sleeping sitting up. Head lolls all over the place. Lips dry too, cracking. Taste blood when I suck them. Nobody has lip-ice or Vaseline. I just lick them. Becky says it'll make them worse. Gretchen agrees.

Four in the afternoon we pull into Dodoma station. The Railway Hotel's the same. Miserable. Can I escape from here? Von Lettow Vorbeck's painted eyes look stern. Does he know my plans? I consult my stomach-brain partnership. No answers. Not many routes out. Just the rail-line we've come on, and the road to Arusha. Last place I'll be running to! Cross country. Where that will take me, I've no clue. Seen glimpses from the train. Dry, arid places, no water anywhere. Dust-bowls. Could get lost out there. Like Lawrence of Arabia, only worse. He had a camel and a gun. Places where it's green, but no road, just windy footpaths back to the railway line. No point. I'll go round in circles, come back to the rails every time.

There are other places, where lions lie sunning themselves, flicking their tails at flies. Look like big pussycats, but they aren't. Don't fancy a one to one with them. Not without a gun. Rhinos, they're about too, massive grey tanks with pointy fronts and big bums. Bad tempers too. Wish I could have Dad's Wesley Richards 375 Magnum. Not that I could carry it far. The *watu* don't even speak Swahili round here, they say. Can't tell them 'Speak Swahili, dammit!' Not in English either. What will they do with me, a small Swahili-speaking *Mzungu*, or whatever they'll call me? All in all, escape prospects are lean.

Morning. Surprisingly, I've slept in the old hotel. Not even a dream. Must be mental exhaustion. We've had breakfast, though I only managed half a dry bread roll and a glass of juice. The gaudily painted bus is parked out front on the dusty circular driveway. Same one, the *Duma Upesi*. Only I know it's *not* so *upesi!* More like *pole-pole*, slow. The driver's a young chap in blue overalls. He's flirting outrageously with a nubile cleaning maid. He speaks Swahili. I don't know if she does. She's giggling as he reaches out and squeezes her breast. '*Nina penda ku tomba,*' he says. I'd like to do *jigi-jigi* with you. I *would* laugh, but this is Last-Chance-Saloon. After this it's Arusha. I don't fancy trying to escape from there.

'Everyone on the bus,' the old bag shouts. Why she has to be so loud, I don't know. Likes bullying smaller people. Becky and Gretchen get on with the others. I don't. I'm glued to the spot. Don't *want* to get on. My plan's not ready. I haven't got it sorted out. How am I going to escape? Can't let this bus carry me even closer to school. My plan's

h

going downhill, approaching irretrievable. If I don't act, do something, it'll be too late! 'You, Francis,' the ugly one says, noticing my lack of movement, 'on the bus, sharply now!'

'Yes Miss,' I hear myself say. It's automatic, not considered. Unknown to me, my brain-stomach partnership has reached its limit. I climb the two iron steps, enter the bus. Becky and Gretchen have kept a seat for me. The diesel engine roars into life. The driver's parted from his sweetheart cleaning-lady. He doesn't believe in formalities. The gearbox grates, the old bus roars out the drive, scattering pebbles and raising a cloud of dust. I'm still standing. I hold onto the seat beside me. Then something happens. The secret conspiracy within takes over. I'm amazed to feel myself start running, bumping against metal seat-sides.

The bus plunges forward. I accelerate the other way. At the last moment, just before I collide with the back, I jump. Breaking glass, flying, still running, hit the road, dragged backwards by momentum. I'm still trying to run when I tumble and fall. I hit the unyielding ground with my face, and roll.

I'm lying there, bleeding. The bus is braking, skidding on the road. The pain! I get to my feet. I feel dizzy. Blood drips from my cheek. People are running towards me. I've got to get away. I take a step. Sharp pain sears through me. I've twisted my ankle. Mrs Shuter's there. She's gasping, breathless. 'What happened?' she says. Becky's just behind her. The blue-overall driver's behind Becky.

'Ouch,' I cry, and fall back on the stony ground in a faint.

I awake with a throbbing face and a fierce headache. There are sword-fighters fencing in my head, I tell Mrs Shuter. I'm lying on the back seat of the bus, which is going again. The window I've broken is above me. Becky and Gretchen are standing by the seat in front, staring anxiously.

'Are you okay?' Becky asks. Her face is very white. Just like when Dad died.

'My face and head,' I sob, 'they're sore!' I notice there are long cuts on my arms too. Not deep, but they burn.

'He'll be just fine,' says Mrs Shuter. 'Now sit down, you two. We don't want more injuries.' Becky and Gretchen look very worried.

'Is he okay?' Gretchen asks Becky. Just then the bus swerves alarmingly, and there's a rumbling vibration shaking everything. We roll unevenly to a stop. A tyre's burst. It takes the driver an hour to change it because he can't find the jack-handle.

*   *   *   *

We arrive in Arusha, and I'm expecting the worst. Or is it the best? I'm in trouble, all right. What will Mr Houghton do? *Fukuza*, chase, me? I hope so. *Expansion* is the word they use, I think. He'll expand me from school and I'll have to go home! That'll be a result! I'll have succeeded, though not the way I thought.

They must have made a decision not to punish me. I don't know why, because I've broken the bus window. They put me in the sick bay and everyone is strangely kind. I've got a huge scab covering my whole right cheek and it looks scary in the mirror. I can't believe it. No lessons, no sermons, nothing. Just the sweet nurse-lady, and the visiting doctor. They give me tablets for my headache. My ankle's only sprained, not broken. I have four days lying in a comfortable bed, reading comics, and sleeping when I feel like it. I like this.

All good things end. On the fifth day I'm sent back to the dormitory. Okay, I didn't get into major trouble, but now I realise I failed completely in what I planned. It's as if I never tried.

One good thing happens. Everyone in the dormitory knows I jumped through the bus window. They respect my courage. Even Marais, though for him retribution will come. I know it.

Arusha. Saturday afternoon. Swapping comics with Andrew Miller. He gives me a Classic. *Mutiny on the Bounty*. Bought at Lake Printers in Mwanza. Their stamp is on the back. Tanganyika advertising. I've never heard the word 'mutiny' before, but it resembles 'mutton'. That's the red meat we eat most in Geita. Unlike the cows, local sheep aren't infected with tuberculosis. How or why seizing a ship from the captain is likened to mutton, I don't know, but there it is. Surprising, though, 'cos what I know of sheep is they're sort of timid, not rebellious.

These white people are very strange. I know I'm one, but that's different. The *Bounty* author must mean mutton is somewhere. I even have secondary delusions on the topic. Perhaps eating *too* much mutton causes sailors to seize ships from their captains. Maybe something in the mutton breeds rebelliousness. Life's confusing, and I can't expect to know everything at seven and a half. Not with my English.

I give Andrew *Around the Word in 80 days*. 'Here's *Mutiny on the Bounty*,' he says. He pronounces it 'mewtiny'.

'It's muttony,' I correct him, 'like *mutton.*'

'It's not,' he says. A bad-tempered argument ensues. Finally it's settled by Miss Baxter.

'Muttony, indeed!' she laughs, shaking with mirth. I hate them both. Why do *they* always have to be right?

Marais has gained other enemies. Andrew Miller, for one.

'We've got to get him!' Andrew says. Marais put mud on his tackies once too often.

'How?' I say. He's a lot bigger than us.

'I've got friends,' Andrew says. He stares at me. 'Are you in?'

'I'm in!' I say.

Next day is Sunday. Everyone goes to play down by the river. We wade in the shallow, cold mountain water, throw pebbles, try to skip them off the surface, dig tunnels in the soft riverbank. People say a boy was suffocated when a tunnel collapsed. It doesn't stop us.

After breakfast Andrew sidles up to me. Behind him are two others. English twins. Jed and Jack. I can't tell them apart. They sleep on the other side of the dormitory, and keep to themselves. I wonder how Andrew has befriended them.

'We're gonna do it now!' Andrew whispers.

'Do *what?*' I say.

'Marais!'

'What we gonna do to him?'

'Tie him up, shove him under his bed!'

'What?'

'Teach him to mess with us!'

'How?'

'Just come with us, you'll see!' We're walking towards the dorm. Jed or Jack saw Marais go in. The other one's pulling a long piece of string out of his pocket. I'm thinking as we go. I don't like Andrew. But I like Marais less. Perhaps using one enemy against another is a good idea. Once again, like Mao-tse-Tung said – my enemy's enemy is my friend!

'What you want?' Marais says as we walk up to his bed. He's sitting on it, looking in his locker.

'You!' says Andrew .

'Me. . ?' Marais sees the other three of us. His voice is different now. Sort of quavery. This is it. . . this is something I've longed for. All four of us jump on him. He's lying down on his bed. He's not resisting. The twin with the string is winding it round his wrists, tying them together. Andrew pulls Marais' dressing-gown cord out and gives it to me.

'Tie his ankles,' he says. I do. I wrap the cord round and round. Marais is trying to speak. He's quite wheezy. We don't care. Jed or Jack's got one of Marais' socks. He's forcing it into his mouth. He's also got a roll of sellotape. Must have pinched it from art class. These boys are organised. He pulls tape from the roll, puts long pieces across

172

Marais' mouth, forcing the sock to stay in. It's a gag, he says. Andrew's putting Marais' belt round his knees, tying it tight. Marais is completely still.

'Right,' says Andrew, 'under the bed!'

We lift him between us, and push him under his bed.

'Counterpanes!' Andrew says. Jed or Jack pulls one side of the counterpane down so Marais can't be seen by anyone coming in. The other fetches his own counterpane. Shouldn't be noticed where his bed is, in the far corner. He puts it on the bed, pulls it down to cover the far side.

'Let's go!' Andrew says. He should be an army officer, a *kernel* maybe. Or is that maize? Maybe an *oberst!*

The sun's shining down at the river. We join the other boys. They're doing what they always do. Chucking pebbles, wading, digging, arguing about nothing. We've got a secret. We've got a prisoner. While we're strutting about here, we're punishing someone we hate. It feels great. Only, what if his asthma gets bad. . ? He sounded wheezy when we were tying him up, and then there's the socks in his mouth. I don't like Marais, but I start to get really worried.

'Maybe we should go and check on him,' I say to Andrew .

'What for?'

'Well, he might choke or something.'

'Good if he does!' Andrew says. Jed and Jack grin widely. They don't talk much.

'But we can't just leave him. What if he *dies?*' Andrew frowns. Suddenly he looks worried too. The twins look anxious, though not as much as Andrew.

'Okay then,' Andrew says, 'you go check on him, we'll wait here.'

Marais has been lying trussed up under his bed for half an hour. He's been completely unable to move, and the gag has made it difficult for him to breathe. His asthma has, fortunately, not got worse. He had an attack just before we jumped him, and took his spray.

I pull up the counterpane and bend down to him. I see he's breathing. By now my own heart's beating like a drum. I've had horrible thoughts. What if I find him dead? His pupils are dilated from being in the dark. He blinks in the light. Thank goodness. I breathe more easily.

'Now then,' I say, trying to sound as if I'm not panicking myself. I've got to set him free, but I've also got to make sure he knows the new order. 'Now then, if I untie you, will you promise to stop bullying me, and the others too?' His head nods, his eyes still blinking. ' 'Cos if you don't, we'll tie you up again and, and. . .' I search for something we'll do. I should have asked Andrew.

173

'We'll throw you in the river!' I say, pleased at my inspiration. He nods. I get down on my knees, and start by dragging him out from under his bed. It's difficult getting the sellotape off his mouth, and it leaves a nasty red mark. He spits out the sock. He doesn't speak. His mouth's too dry, and he doesn't know what to say. It takes forever to undo the knots the others have tied. Finally Marais is undone and sitting on his bed. I leave. Andrew's angry I let Marais go. I was only supposed to check on him, not spring him!

There's no more Marais-trouble. After a while I even feel sorry for him. It's difficult for me when he starts following me around and offering me his sweets. I've never made friends with an enemy before.

'You helped me,' he says one day, staring at the ground.

'Well,' I say, embarrassed. I did help him, but then again I also helped tie him up.

'I won't forget,' he says. He sees me as a friend now, because I'm the one who came back and set him free. I don't know what's worse, persecution or adoration, by Marais. I tell Becky what we did to Marais, and she tells Gretchen. Gretchen says she doesn't want to get on the wrong side of me. I take that as a compliment, or is it *complement*?

At the end of term we are flown back to Mwanza instead of going by bus and train. I think it's because they've decided it's safer with me. I won't jump out a plane window. The plane is an East African Airways DC3, otherwise known as a *Dakota*. It's a twin-engined aircraft of World War II vintage, and is fitted out to take thirty passengers. It never has that many, and most seats are occupied by mailbags. It comes from Nairobi, lands at Arusha, goes on to Mwanza, then returns to Nairobi. I'm about to discover air-sickness.

The door to a Dakota is at the back, where the steps go. After climbing them, I am faced with a narrow aisle between the seats. It's very steep. The Dakota stands very high at the front, very low at the back. There's a strange smell. I come to know its ingredients. Aviation fuel, pressurisation, and previous passengers being sick. I struggle to my seat. Becky, Gretchen and the others are in theirs. The rear door's closed. Pilot and co-pilot squeeze past. Smile at us.

The engines explode into life one at a time. The plane taxis, speeds up, then we're up in the sky. There's buffeting, rising and falling, sideways jolts and every kind of movement. I'm terrified. This is worse than the Argonaut. But, before my panic can reach crescendo, nausea intervenes. As the plane drops into a sudden trough, it leaves

174

my stomach up there, and I vomit all over the back of the seat in front. I wish I'll die, quickly. Two more hours of unmitigated hell of heaving stomach and burning throat. Becky's ashamed. Gretchen is kind and wipes my face with tissues.

'It's horrible to be airsick,' she says. Her German accent is long-gone, unlike her brother Dieter. The others in the plane are amused at my illness. None of them feel even a little sick.

At Mwanza aerodrome Mum sees how pale I am. It takes a long time to feel better. I get the first real smile I've had from Fritz. 'Ze plane iss make you sick-yes?' he says. I smile weakly back. I think he likes people to suffer.

Seventeen

First day home in Geita, Becky, Gretchen, Dieti and I capture a *shenzi* dog, and give it a bath. We corner a little black and white one against the mine-store wall, and rush him home. He's only a few months old, but already jumping with fleas and festooned with fat black ticks. Like Sandy, his Daschund genes are declared by the shortness of his legs and his small size. First we pull the ticks off and pop them underfoot. Black, inky blood squirts out. We dust him with Sandy's flea powder. After allowing a few minutes for that to work, we run a warm bath, and pour in half a bottle of Mum's treasured bubble bath.

The bewildered and quaking captive makes no effort to resist. We scrub him from end to end, inside his filthy ears and under his tail. All the while Sandy stands up at the bath, watching with interest. We use one of Mum's best towels to dry the trembling waif. Finally, Becky and Gretchen use Mum's hairdryer and a brush to finish the job. Sandy watches it all.

We take our glistening prisoner to the kitchen, and give him a tin of braised steak and a bowl of diluted Nestlé's milk. He stops quivering and laps with gusto. He doesn't look *shenzi* now.

'Let's keep him,' Becky says.

'Yes,' I say.

'Our *Vati* vill go mad if ve take him in our *haus*,' Dieti says.

'We can call him Dickie,' Becky announces, clearly having thought about it.

'Why *Dickie*?' Gretchen asks.

'It's a nice name,' Becky says simply.

Just then Mum comes home. She sees the little dog, the wet towel, the hairdryer, and makes up her mind.

'He can't stay,' she says, despite our pleading, Dickie goes back to the tough *shenzi* life. But his story isn't over.

It's Christmas Eve 1959, and the astonishing saga of Higgs the policeman marches on. Gretchen and Dieti's parents get a special Christmas parcel from Germany each year. It's filled with goodies, and *makes* their festive occasion. Today a couple of *totos*, who are also caddies for the *Wazungu* on the golf-course, climb in through an open *dirisha*, or window, and make off with the special parcel. When its loss is discovered, a distraught Mrs Blüger sends her *haus-boy* running down the footpath to fetch the police. In Geita this means *only* Higgs.

The redoubtable Geita constabulary roars into the Blüger driveway on the battered and rust-streaked Harley Davidson of leopard-riding-fame, petrol-tank still deeply dented, and Blüger's *haus-boy*, riding pillion, wide-eyed and struck dumb after a wild, erratic, deafening projection up the dirt road. There's no headlight. It came off when Higgs ploughed into the bush. He dismounts and strides purposefully to the front door. The sway in his gait declares his inebriation, standard by six-thirty of an evening, but he's determined to act professionally. The *haus-boy* found him where he predictably would, in the club. Ishmael the barman said someone outside had a *seryus massage* for him. And serious he deemed it was, to be so summoned. He knocks loudly, as officially as he can, on the door. Eugen opens it.

'A robbery, is it?' says Higgs, trying but failing to suppress a beery belch.

'*Ja!*' says Eugen, astonished at the wild-eyed, red faced and moustachioed spectre of the *askari*-chief.

'Tell me,' says Higgs, extracting a tatty notebook from his shirt pocket, 'do you have a pencil?'

'Come in, I haff vun som-vere,' says Eugen. Dieter, Gretchen and Mrs Blüger sit glumly in the lounge.

'Vood you like *ein* nice cold *Vitecap?*' Eugen asks, passing Higgs a pencil and motioning him to a big German armchair with ashtrays built into the wide wooden arms.

'What a *capital* idea!' says Higgs, collapsing delightedly into the deep chair.

An hour, and six bottles of *Whitecap*, later, Higgs has forgotten why he came. He has thoroughly enjoyed himself, taken no notes, but has bonded with this affable, if difficult-to-understand, man, who, though German, and therefore the enemy, was a soldier, like Higgs himself, and therefore a 'good sort', not to leave out his generosity with beer.

Higgs returns the pencil to Eugen, not sure why he's got it anyway, gets up, makes for the door, trips over the rug, and falls over another chair. When he sits up he's clutching his arm. His left radius is broken.

Credit where it's due. Somehow, despite the Plaster of Paris lumpily applied by an annoyed Dr Weiss, who himself has to leave the bar to go to the hospital, Higgs somehow apprehends the guilty *totos* next day, which is Christmas, and the parcel, or most of it, is returned to its grateful owners.

'Zese *totos*,' says Mrs Blüger, 'you chust can't trust zem!'

'But Higgs is goot, even iff he iss alvays trunk!' says Dieter.

'Ja, he iss,' says his father, shaking his head, 'but how, I chust don't know!'

Important to us is our Cornish heritage. Though patriotically 'British', in his whole life Dad never called himself 'English'. As I had already learnt, Cornwall is only 'cledged' onto England by a tiny bit of land next to the river Tamar. It has only been ruled by the English six hundred years, and is a separate '*Duchy*', not county. Mum learns to make Cornish pasties from her mother. She makes a short pastry, using flour, butter, salt and water. This is mixed in a big bowl and rolled out on the scrubbed kitchen table. A dinner plate is used for cutting out round shapes.

Chopped potato is the first ingredient put on the pastry. On this goes a handful of diced onion. Then a generous handful of finely cubed filet steak. A knob of butter, chopped fresh parsley, a pinch of salt and a sprinkling of fresh ground pepper. The outer rim of the pastry is painted with egg white using a brush. Now closing and crimping. Mum seals the pasties with an even zigzag along the top, neat as a zip. She paints the pasties with milk, pierces the sides with a fork, and puts them on a baking tray. When the tray's full, it's into the hot Belling stove. Thirty minutes, and out they come, golden, fragrant and delicious.

Every Lone Cone Club attender has tasted Mum's pasties, and loves them. They're a miracle of creation. A square meal of meat, vegetables and pastry in one handy package. Smell like heaven, taste even better. They make a welcome change, mean not having to cook. A year after Dad dies, Mr Snel, the Manager, tries one. He's so taken, he insists she choose a Sunday, let everyone know, and make enough for all. The club will pay for ingredients. Mum calculates that if each adult eats two, each child one, they'll need a hundred.

Umali recruits Amina, and the irascible couple spend hours

chopping onions and potatoes. As Mum zips up the pasties and fills the trays, Umali puts them in the oven. The first batch of twenty-five is ready. Umali walks down to the club carrying the cloth-covered tray on his head. He's mobbed by hungry *Wazungu*, most of whom have to wait for the next batch. It's the same next time, and next. The experiment is a great success and a failure. Success because they *love* the pasties. Failure because they love them so much they want more, much more.

Mr Snel calls Mum to the bar for a conference. This can be a nice sideline for her, he says. Becky and Jim need things, and her salary isn't enough. How much does it cost to make a hundred? Thirty shillings. Sold at a shilling each, that's a hundred shillings. The people will be happy to pay that. Now, a hundred pasties went nowhere, did it? Better make two hundred, no two hundred and fifty. Shall we say once a month, every last Sunday?

So begins the Geita pasty factory. Soon, extra labour being required, it won't raise any eyebrows to see, in addition to Umali, diverse and hitherto jungle-bound, ragged, tribesmen sprinting downhill towards the waiting *Wazungu* at Lone Cone Club, trays full of Cornish pasties held aloft, or balanced on their heads.

In 1960 we have an unexpected visitor. Communication out here is still as rudimentary as it was in Von Lettow Vorbeck's days. There's only one unreliable radio-phone at head office. At least Vorbeck had runners for when his telegraph didn't work! I don't know who it is when the stranger knocks on the door. I open it and stand staring for several seconds at a tall man in a white uniform, a funny round hat on his head with writing on: HMS *GAMBIA*. Whatever that means. He knows who I am, and says, 'Hello Jim.' I don't like the familiarity.

'Mum,' I yell, 'there's a *strange* man here!'

'I'm your brother,' says the stranger.

'No you're not!' I say. Mum comes to the door. There's a brief pause, then she throws herself into his arms.

'Fraser,' she gasps. 'Oh Fraser!' She's crying.

'Mum,' he says, kissing her cheek, and hugging her. This is crazy! Who *is* this interloper? I can't bear to hear him call her Mum. She's *my* Mum, not his! I try to slink away in indignation.

'Jimboy,' Mum says, 'come say hello to Fraser.'

'Fraser?' I ask, turning back. The name Mum uses so many times. I have a big brother in the navy. Another one, not Bertrand. Fraser. He went away when I was two. I'm eight now. Can it really be. . ?

'Your brother,' Mum says, seeing my confusion. She takes Fraser by the arm and leads him into the house. He has a long canvas bag-thing hanging from one hand. A navy kit-bag.

'Say hello to your brother properly,' Mum says. I stick out my hand. I'm *not* going to hug him. Okay, he *must* be my brother if she says so. But this is all too quick. Anyway, he'll be just like Bertrand, the other 'brother' who pitched out of nowhere, partied at the club, and buggered off again. Haven't heard from him since. What is it now? Two years or more?

Eighteen

Fraser is intrigued by me. I'm wary of him. I ask him one thing. 'What does HMS *GAMBIA* mean?' *Her Majesty's Ship, Gambia*, he says. The frigate he's serving on in the navy. Named after a West African Country. All navy ships belong to the Queen. *Gambia*'s currently in Gibraltar. Somewhere near Spain. Now I'm informed! Spain's a country, isn't it? Fraser arranges transport to Samina to see Dad's grave. The midges drive us off in short time. He visits the club only briefly, has the mandatory beer with Mr Snel and Dr Weiss, and comes home early. I'm intrigued. He's quieter, *this* big brother, than the other one. He seems more thoughtful, sadder about Dad. Mum says he worshipped him. One morning I watch him sit alone on the tree stump in the front garden. He sees me.

'Come here Jimboy,' he says. I go. 'You're very sad about Dad, aren't you?' I *am*, of course I am! Doesn't *everyone* know that? 'I am too,' he says gently. 'Sit down, I'll tell you about Dad.' Tell me about Dad? What is there to know? He was handsome, brave, strong. I loved him. God killed him. I tried to shoot God. I sit. It's a crude bench of unsanded maninga on two dead tree-stumps. The table is an old cable-drum, painted green.

'Mum told me about Dad's gun,' Fraser says quietly, 'you must be very cross!'

'I am!' I exclaim, bursting into tears, 'he took my Dad, and I *still* want to shoot him. . !'

'I'm your brother. I loved him too. He was also *my* Dad.' I look at him again, through a film of tears. He really does look sad. Maybe he's genuine. He hasn't gone to the club all the time. He doesn't laugh and joke all the time like Bertrand. I step closer. He puts his arms around me and gives me the first masculine hug I've had since Dad died. I feel his chest heave. My big brother's crying! We stay like that a long time. Then he talks.

'I'll tell you about Dad, so you know where you come from, Jimboy,' he says. 'Growing up here in the bush, there's lots of things you'll never know. You come from a good family and you should be proud of that. Especially you should be proud of Dad.' I nod. I *am* proud of Dad, but I want to hear more about him. Fraser, it transpires, is the family historian. He knows everything worth knowing.

'Dad was a Cornishman, born in the family home in Fairmantle Street, Truro. His family were wealthy. His father, Edgar, was a Chief Petty Officer in the Royal Navy, and retired to become harbour master in Truro's still unsilted river port. Sailing ships called there from round the world. Dad's only sibling was his older sister Natalie. They were proud of our surname, which existed in Cornwall way before William the Conquerer won the battle of Hastings in 1066, and our family has a history in Helston going back nine hundred years.'

'Really?' I ask.

'Yup,' says Fraser, 'really. I've studied the family tree. So did Dad's sister, Aunt Natalie.' He continues:

'Edgar's father, our great grandfather, was Joshua. He was born in Helston in 1850. Only a little over five foot tall, with an enormous handlebar moustache, he became one of the richest men in Cornwall, indulging a lifelong hobby and interest in antiques, which several of his descendents inherited. People said he'd "been up and down the Mississippi on paddle steamers, trading antiques, when most *cousin-jacks* hadn't crossed the Tamar to England." He was famed throughout Cornwall for his ostentatious wealth, knockout punch, love of animals, devotion to wife and children, and paradoxical, almost casual, infidelity, which continued into his eighties.

'There was an enduring friendship between Joshua and the mayor of Truro. They were of a type, and, though "pillars of Cornish Victorian society", liked nothing better than to depart from time to time on a stagecoach to London, without telling their wives. Anonymous in the capital, they indulged in wild drinking, gambling and brawling, and many was the public house which suffered serious disruption and damage from their visitations. After a month, or sometimes two, they sheepishly returned to their wives, who forgave them and nursed them back to health. Until next time. They last absconded in their seventies.

'One day Joshua saw a big man whipping a tethered horse. He told him to stop, and the fellow attacked him with a club. Joshua punched him. Sadly, the man hit his head on a lamp-post and died. Fortunately, the presiding judge at the inquest was the mayor.'

'He deserved to die,' I say. 'Anyone who whips a poor horse, or any animal, should be killed!'

'Quite!' Fraser laughs. He finds me funny. I'm glad. He's quite nice, really.

'Joshua's long-suffering wife, Helen, was dedicated. She tried to change him, but it never worked. Once, madly jealous because she suspected he was involved with "the widow Smith", she threatened to "go round and smash her windows", to which he replied "I'll put them in again!" '

'What do you mean by "involved" with the widow Smith?' I ask.

'Well,' Fraser says, blushing. I've never seen a man blush. 'Let's say he *likes* her. . .'

'Are they doing *jigi-jigi*?' I ask.

'Jimboy!' Fraser says, 'You're terrible! Where do you hear these things, who tells you them?'

'Everywhere, everyone,' I say.

'Despite everything, Joshua was popular, wealthy, and the hero of many a widow or single woman, several of whom lived rent-free in his houses in Truro, St Ives and St Austell. Helen and Joshua only had one child, our grandfather Edgar.

'Edgar grew as big as his fierce father was small, and had a temperate, retreating nature. At thirteen, in the year 1890, he went to sea as cabin-boy on a French barque. This annoyed Joshua, because he wanted him to continue the antique business.

'Edgar returned after three years at sea, sixteen years old, six foot tall, broad, suntanned, and worldly-wise. After two months he joined the *Andrew*, or Royal Navy, as boy seaman, Joshua using influence with a captain. From 1893 to 1918 Edgar served in the fleet. He was a pioneering underwater diver, using an experimental helmet fed with compressed air from the surface in Falmouth Harbour. His old helmet is a family heirloom. He served on a battle-cruiser in the battle of Jutland, when Admiral Jellicoe's *Grand Fleet* chased Admiral Scheer's *High Seas Fleet* all the way to its German home ports, never to emerge as a real threat for the rest of the First World War.'

'Wow!' I say. 'Were they *really* big boats?' Grand Fleet sounds, well, *grand*.

'Huge, Jimboy, *ships*, not boats! In 1918, a week after armistice day, Joshua suddenly "gave up the ghost and died".' Sounds like a voluntary thing. 'Edgar attended the funeral, and saw his distraught mother crying out "not he, he not be dead, no, not my Josh!" before trying to jump into his grave. Even in death, the ninety year old rogue commanded love. Three hundred packed the church, many weeping inconsolably. It was rumoured there were several broken-hearted widows among them.

'Edgar was forty when he retired from the navy and returned to Cornwall in 1919. First he lived at home with his mother in Nine Rosewin Row, off Mitchell Hill, which enjoyed a splendid view of the newly built Truro Cathedral. The house had five bedrooms, an indoor bathroom and toilet, and a panelled study where Joshua kept business journals and files. Within a year Edgar met, courted and married Loveday Rowe, a thirty year old spinster with crossed eyes, beaked nose and a sweet nature. They moved into their own home, a two-bedroomed terraced cottage at Thirty-seven Fairmantle Street. Here, our aunt Natalie, and two years later our father, Richard, were born.

'D'you know what's happened to that house?' Fraser says, knowing I don't. 'Number Nine Rosewin Row is still a lovely old terraced house, and you can still see the cathedral. Thirty-seven, eight and nine Fairmantle Street are joined now, and turned into an undertakers. On the other side there's a frozen food shop. They say one side you have chickens, the other side people, both frozen!' *Mzogas.* Can I ever get away from the dead? Before Dad died, I never even thought about them. Then Tembo's puppy, Mr Valari (senior), and all the dead people in my nightmares, like Stroessner, who murdered Mrs Williams, Mum, dead and trying to dig her way to Dad. Fraser continues:

'Richard was sickly, suffered from asthma from an early age, and failed to thrive. Asthma means he had a bad cough. Edgar despaired of his son making adulthood. Loveday doted on him.

'Adding to his Royal Navy Pension, Edgar was well paid as harbour master. Great ships came via the Carrick Roads near Falmouth, bringing cargoes up the Fal and Penryn to the centre of Truro.' [Today the harbour's gone, the river silted up, and where ships used to dock stands a Tesco supermarket. The coming of the railway killed river freight. Truro harbour died of neglect, the river choked on silt.]

'When Richard was three, his grandmother Helen followed Joshua to the grave. She was buried beside him at Kenwyn Cemetery. Edgar and Loveday moved to Nine Rosewin Row. It's not clear if they sold Thirty-seven Fairmantle Street then, or if that was the later work of aunt Natalie. Richard's earliest memories were of Rosewin Row.

'Richard's frail build, his asthma and proneness to pneumonia, worried his parents. "He'll never make old bones," Edgar warned Loveday, but she never gave up, staying up all night nursing him through many illnesses, some he wasn't expected to survive. Richard's health remained precarious throughout his childhood and adolescence. He used that cunningly, allowing his mother and Natalie to cater to every whim. Once when he and Natalie walked past the cathedral *en-route* to school, he threatened to bang his head on the cathedral wall unless she carried his satchel. She did, for several years. He grew up protected by women, and distant from Edgar, who lamented he'd never endure the rigours of a sailor's life. Steeped in maritime history, preferring to walk a deck rather than a road, Edgar suffered in silence.

'Despite his weakly appearance, Richard determined by six years of age that he *would* go to sea. When he said so Edgar laughed. He couldn't see Richard as a sailor. He tried to be gentle, exaggerated the hazards of the sea, the rewards of work ashore.

'By twelve Richard had caught up with other boys his age. He knew Edgar wouldn't use his influence to get him a seagoing berth That hurt, because Joshua helped Edgar.

'It was half way through his thirteenth year he decided to take action. For months he'd watched freighters come up-river from Falmouth to dock at Lemon Quay. One day there was a three masted Norwegian schooner, loading cargo for New York. Her name was *Bergen*.

'Richard persuaded the master to employ him as cabin boy. Without telling his parents or Natalie, he stole away one evening at dusk, taking only clothes tied in a blanket. Within the hour, taking advantage of a high tide and favourable wind, *Bergen* slipped away from Lemon Quay and headed down-river to Malpas, the Fal, the Carrick Roads, then west into the English Channel. By nightfall she'd rounded Lizard Point, and was reaching with a northeasterly wind into the wide Atlantic.'

'Dad *ran away*. . ?' I say. Fraser sees what I'm thinking. Looking for a precedent to justify jumping out the bus at Dodoma. Mum's told him, I heard them talking.

'It was *different*,' Fraser says. 'He went away to make a *living*, not to escape school!'

'But *he* didn't go to boarding school,' I say.

'Enough!' says Fraser, grinning despite trying not to. He continues:

'Richard soon regretted his action, but he was committed now. Seasick and missing home, he tried to learn the duties of cabin boy. He didn't know he had already come under the malign surveillance of the first mate, a bearded giant called Jensen.

'Jensen had reasons for his Anglophobia, but these were never clear. He hated the English so much it was an illness. Someone must have

185

done something bad to him or his family, to so drive him to vengeance and retribution at any opportunity. Jensen was in his thirties when Richard came aboard. Seeing the twelve year old 'English' boy answered a Nordic prayer. His day had come. He didn't know *Cornish* isn't *English*. He bided his time. Vengeance was a dish best eaten cold.'

'We're *Cornish*, not English,' I say. Dad always said that.

'Too right!' Fraser says. At last he agrees with something I say. I warm to him.

'A week into the North Atlantic, Jensen showed his hand. Richard was carrying a tray of crockery to the master's cabin, when he passed the big man. Jensen hissed, "I'm going to get you, English swine!" Richard was startled by the hatred in those pale eyes. His dream cruise had just turned sour.

'The captain was a gentleman, fatherly and kind. He gave Richard small luxuries from his table. Perhaps it was because the captain liked Richard that Jensen waited. But he never missed an opportunity to scowl and whisper threats when alone with him. He made suggestions about Richard's mother, claiming to have known her intimately. This was an error, for certain things were sacrosanct. One was Richard's mother. Jensen would pay, regardless of cost or time.

'The violence began with a slap across the head in a corridor. Then a punch in the face, causing a black eye. There were shoves in the back, bringing falls and broken crockery. A bruising poke in the ribs. The captain noticed the marks and asked questions. For Richard this vendetta wasn't for sharing. He would resolve it on his own. Jensen was his. He wouldn't share him. He lied. He had fallen against a door handle. He'd slipped on the wet deck and struck his ear on a lifeboat. When Jensen saw the boy wasn't telling, he redoubled his efforts.

'One evening, in a wild and pitching sea, he shoved Richard in the back, causing him to fall down the stairs and break his leg. It was a fractured tibia and a splint was made by the carpenter. It was fortunate, because Richard was unable to work the rest of the passage, which kept him from Jensen. The captain commiserated, but Richard didn't say what happened.'

'He should have shot him!' I say.

'You like guns, don't you Jimboy?' Fraser says, grinning again. 'I know all about you.' He continued:

'*Bergen* docked in New York, and the captain sent Richard to convalesce with friends near Manhattan docks. They were a retired sea captain and his wife, whose children had moved away. Richard had a comfortable time. In three months his leg was better, and he began

186

looking for a ship. Despite his experience, he already loved the sea and ships. Maybe it was inherited from Edgar, the father who despaired his son would ever make a sailor.

'He served on several ships for four years, and learned the trade of seaman. He grew in strength and stature. In 1923, three years after he last saw her, while standing in the prow of a ship edging into Hong Kong harbour, he spied a familiar shape. *Bergen*.

'Within an hour of docking, Richard boarded the Norwegian ship and asked for Jensen. He came on deck. He'd been told a man called Penhaligon wanted him. When they met, Jensen was surprised at the change in the cabin-boy. Richard challenged him to a fight. The crew formed a circle. It was one-sided. Jensen won. Richard was carried back to his ship.

'Six months later he spied *Bergen* in Auckland, New Zealand. He went on board. A man called Penhaligon wants you. Jensen came up. The crew formed a circle again. Some took bets. It was more even. They fought until neither could stand, and both were carried away.

'It was a year before Richard saw *Bergen* again. Jensen was slower coming up. Richard knocked him out with a single 'haymaker' punch. He'd been practising it on a ship's coiled-rope fender. There was one more time, when Jensen refused to come on deck. Cowered in his cabin. Richard was prepared. He took a white feather from his pocket and sent it down to the coward. At seventeen Richard had solved the problem. He never saw Jensen again.'

'That'll teach him!' I say. 'But I would have shot him!'

'That's not the kind of man Dad was,' Fraser says. 'You see, Jimboy, he was kind and gentle, but he never, ever, ran away, never let fear get to him. He was a determined, brave man. He didn't need a gun with Jensen. He used big guns in the war, but only to do his duty. That's why he died. Because he did his duty, no matter what!'

'But Jensen was *blurryfucken!*' I say.

'Geita isn't doing anything for your language,' Fraser laughs, before continuing:

'Richard was seventeen when his parents saw him again. Although only five foot seven tall, he'd filled out and gained muscle. When he ran away he was a frail twelve year old. He returned as a sailor and a man, and Edgar and Helen were overjoyed. After two weeks at home in Rosewin Row, Richard was ready to go back to sea. In his last two days he spent time with his father. They went sailing in a Falmouth Bassboat on the Carrick Roads and Falmouth harbour, and drank St Austell's Indian Pale Ale, IPA, at the Heron pub in Malpas. Richard regaled Edgar with things he'd seen and done. He'd been to many countries, and even served eighteen months on *Cutty Sark*, the most famous of clippers. Richard later said those few days with his father were the best they ever had together.

'When he returned to sea in 1924, Richard's qualities were soon noticed and appreciated by officers. He was thought to have the qualities of a bosun. These included quiet disposition, seamanship, respect for authority, and a knockout punch. Those days the bosun had to 'deal with' seamen who disobeyed officers or fought among themselves. In 1927 Richard was persuaded to join the Royal Navy. Soon he came to the attention of an officer with an unusual task. Selecting gifted sailors to loan to the United States navy for an expedition.

'Admiral Jonathan Evelyn Byrd of the United States Navy purchased an elderly Norwegian square-rigged wooden ship called *Samson* in 1927. She was built in 1882, as a whaler with a hull of oak ribs and spruce planking, toughened to resist the crushing ice of the arctic. She was re-fitted, renamed *City of New York*, and sailed from Hoboken on the twenty-fifth of August 1928, bound for the Antarctic at the other end of the world. It was the beginning of Admiral Byrd's first Antarctic expedition, which would last until 1930. Byrd had asked for, and got, experienced sailors from the Royal Navy. One was Richard. It was something he was very proud of.

'Seven years after leaving the Royal Navy, while working as a rigger on a South African gold mine, he rejoined as able seaman in 1938, at the outbreak of hostilities. 'If my country's at war, I'm at war,' he told Mum, who he left standing with three small children on the dock in Cape Town.'

'Which country?' I ask Fraser.

'England,' he says. Right. That's clear. I thought we were *Cornish*. I can't fathom big people. They change what they say all the time.

'Dad served on HMS *Hood,* before being transferred weeks ahead of her fateful battle against *Bismarck.* He was posted to a converted trawler, adapted for convoy escort duty to Murmansk in Russia. When HMS *Turtle* was attacked and sunk by *Dornier* bombers sixty miles off Grimsby in August 1940, he was the last to leave the ship, and single-handedly shot down three enemy aircraft from the listing deck of half a ship. The other half had broken off and sunk. He saved the lives of the captain and a boy seaman. He was one of only eight survivors from a crew of sixty-eight, and spent four hours clinging to a wooden hatch cover in near-freezing water. This caused him to get rheumatic fever, and leaking mitral and tricuspid heart valves. He was awarded the Distinguished Service Medal, or DSM, by Lord Mountbatten, in the

188

company of King George VI, at a decoration ceremony in Portsmouth. Not many of those given out,' Fraser says.

'*Decorate*?' I ask. Images of Christmas trees. Fraser knows what I'm thinking. Funny thing to decorate a man. A tree, perhaps, not a man!

'They just use the same word, nothing to do with Christmas,' he assures me. He grins. He finds me funny. 'Anyhow, because he worked on a gold-mine at Brakpan on the East Rand near Johannesburg before the war, the *Brakpan Times* put Dad on the front page. "Brakpan Man Decorated by King" it said, above a half-page photograph of Dad they got from Mum.'

'Dad was famous?' I say.

'He was, I suppose.' Fraser lights a cigarette, and continues.

'Serving in the Far East Dad sustained a serious head injury. While he was being treated in hospital in Rangoon, he heard from another injured man that his cousin and best friend, Major James Penhaligon, who he knew and loved from small, was killed by the Japanese. It was in April 1945, not long before the end of the war. He was heartbroken. He was also very sick. Dad re-joined the navy in 1939 as an A1 fit man. He was discharged in '46 with leaking heart valves and epilepsy, and a naval health grading of 'E'. He was thirty-seven years old. After a year in hospital for epilepsy, he took a shared job with Mum, running a store in Zululand. That's why you were born in Nongoma.

'Dad had no choice but to come here, to Geita. He couldn't get a job anywhere else,' Fraser says.

'Why?' I ask.

'Because he was sick. Here, in Geita, they didn't examine him before they gave him the job on the ropeway. Anywhere else, he'd have been examined, would have failed the medical.'

A lot falls into place. I've wondered why we live here, in the bush. I love it dearly, of course. Wouldn't want to be anywhere else. . . not that I *know* anywhere else. Apart from Arusha, and I wouldn't want to live *there!*

'Dad was too weak, too damaged in the war, to get better when he got malaria,' Fraser explains. 'So now you know, Jimboy,' he says. 'You can be proud of your name. Of Dad. There weren't many like him. When you grow up, try to be like him.'

'I will!' I say, my chest swelling with pride, 'I will. But *I* would have shot Jensen!' Fraser laughs.

Fraser's been talking for two hours. I've listened. Not been bored. His words are precious. Bring me closer to Dad. Poor Dad. He paid with his life, just so he could be our bread-winner. That's what Mum said. Now I feel love for my thoughtful big brother. He knows so much, takes so much trouble. He also looks, and acts, so much like Dad. I haven't noticed before. It's as if five years haven't happened. Like Dad is talking. Fraser's leaving in a week. A new sadness descends. Can't *anything* be other than sad?

'One thing more you should know,' Fraser says.

'What?'

'Aunty Natalie, Dad's sister.'

'What about her?' I ask.

'She's the reason Dad was poor, why we're all poor.'

'Why?'

'Your dear Aunt Natalie fiddled the old folks out of all their money. She was a bad businesswoman. She kept opening shops, then losing all her money, and every time Granddad Edgar bailed her out. In 1947 he died. By then Grandma had lost it up here. . .' He taps his temple to show what he means. Ah, I think, *Dodoma*, the mad-house on the railway line to Dar.

'Then Natalie really went to town.' I thought she lived in the town. 'She persuaded the old girl to sell Nine Rosewin Row and give her the money. Plus three other houses and a row of shops in Lemon Street. That's in Truro.'

'Why did she?'

'Because she could. An evil woman. She blew all that too. That's why Dad and Mum didn't inherit anything. I told you Joshua made the money. Edgar spent some of it. Natalie blew the rest. That's why Dad took the job here in Geita, why he's dead now!'

'That's not fair,' I say.

'No,' Fraser says. They say it's clogs to clogs in three generations. That's what happened to us!' I feel a surge of resentment towards Aunt Natalie. She killed Dad. It wasn't just God. Mum says I met Natalie when we went to England that time on the Argonaut. It's so long ago now, I can't remember her, try as I do. Mum says Fraser shouldn't say these things about Aunt Natalie. Dad wouldn't like it.

Fraser walks in the garden. Under the acacia tree, he finds Lutoli and me smoking cigarette butts collected at the club. We're nine, seasoned smokers. I try to hide my fag-end in my cupped hand. My smoking is widely known about and condemned in Geita. Mum's given up the fight. I'm a man, I say, and men smoke. Lutoli has no reservations or fear. As Fraser stares he takes another drag, inhales deeply, lets smoke curl from his nose. I can do that too!

'Don't hide that,' Fraser says, 'I saw you from the verandah.' There's a look of amazement on his face. 'How long you been smoking Jimboy?'

'Since Dad died,' I say, 'or I think so.' I drop my burning butt and stamp it into the ground.

'Mum know?'

'Yup.' This is an inquisition. Lutoli's butt has burnt to the end. He extinguishes the end and ambles away. He doesn't know *Kiingereza* or English, but knows when things are getting unpleasant.

'Right,' Fraser suddenly exclaims, 'I've got an idea.' An idea? What idea?

'What are those cheap cigarettes the poor *watu* smoke, you know, the beggar-ones. . ?' he asks. I'm surprised he remembers the cigarettes. I've forgotten he lived in Geita two years before he joined the Navy.

'The *wasikini*?' I say.

'That's them. The poor beggars. What are the cigarettes called?'

'Ten Cents,' I say. He says he remembers them. The awful *Ten Centies*. Known to the *watu* as *Centie Kumis*. Tiny packets of ten thin, filterless cigarettes, filled with dark, vicious tobacco. People say it isn't tobacco at all, but *mavi*, or shit, from lions.

The name's in the price. Ten cents. The original price. When dinosaurs roamed the earth. In 1961 it's eight times that. Infatuation, Dieti said, causes prices to go up. Happens all the time. There's a hundred cents in a shilling. Twenty shillings in a pound. At eighty cents, you can get twenty-two packets of *Centi Kumis* for a pound.

'They're the ones,' he says. He fumbles in his pocket for change. He extracts two ten cent coins. They can't be called *small* change. They're huge, with a big hole in the middle. It's so the rural *watu* can keep them tied up on a string. Wear their money like jewellery. Not the *wasikini*, they hide their money. It'd spoil the image. 'Go to the store and buy me a packet,' Fraser says.

'One or two?' I say.

'Just one, I'm sure it will do,' Fraser says ominously.

Barrat stores sell everything. Food in tins, fresh food such as there is, sweets, alcohol, cloth, shirts, trousers, ammunition. And tobacco. There are no restrictions on who can buy what. Mr Barrat gives me what I ask for, and soon I'm back with Fraser, who's been joined by Becky under the tree. He's asked her if *she* smokes too. Yes, she says, unwilling to be a wimp. At twelve, she can't be seen as inferior to her ten year old brother.

'Okay,' Fraser says, grinning, and tearing open the cheap paper packaging. 'Who's first?' What does he mean, *first*? He sees my bewilderment. 'You're going to smoke this whole packet,' he says to Becky and me, 'five each.'

'Okay,' I say, not realising how bad this really is. I've never smoked a whole *Centi Kumi*. Too strong. Burns the throat and makes you cough. And what if what they say about *simba mavi* is true? Umali swears it is. On the other hand, if Fraser wants me to smoke them, I will. Can't let him think I'm scared. Especially not now, Dad's heroism being so recently discussed. He lights one and passes it to me. I take it as nonchalantly as possible, and puff deeply.

Mistake! The taste and smell is horrible. *Must* be *simba mavi*! The burning in the back of my throat is intense, like I've swallowed petrol. I know, 'cause I've done it. Swigged from a ginger-ale bottle at the garage. Spiro, the mechanic, poured petrol into carburettors from it. Priming, he said, whatever that is. I thought I was going to die. Spiro never stopped apologising. 'You have to be careful,' he said, ' 'cause if you drink petrol you'll be *forked!*' This is similar, but worse. Brother Fraser's waiting.

'Come on,' he says, '*smoke* it!'

'Yes!' Becky says, joining the winning side. Always does that. Crafty. Not crafty enough for Fraser.

'Here's yours,' Fraser says, passing a lit one to her. She's lied about smoking. Apart from a tentative puff or two, after which she choked and went red, she and Gretchen have not continued the habit. She takes her *Ten Centi* gingerly, pretends to draw on it.

'Deeper!' Fraser Commands. She tries, splutters, jumps to her feet and runs indoors, coughing.

'One down,' Fraser says, 'one to go.' His attention turns on me. I take another hateful puff.

'Inhale, Jimboy, *inhale*. . .' he commands. I inhale. The acrid smoke sears the lining of my lungs. I cough and cough. 'Again,' he says. The thin cigarette's almost burnt out now. No problem, he's already lighting another!

By the time I've smoked five *Centi Kumis* I'm green. I'm trying to puff the last of the fifth, when my stomach contracts and I spurt my lunch out on the ground. Only then does Fraser relent. 'Now you know what smoking can do,' he says, 'I'll leave it to you.' He goes inside, his good deed done. I'm as sick as an *umbwa*, or dog, the rest of the day. All I learn is never to smoke *simba mavi*. It's *blurryfucken*, like Lutoli says. Now I know what he means.

Nineteen

I become aware of competition for Fraser's attention and affection, not just from Sandy, hard as she tries. I should have noticed earlier that, ever since he arrived, there's been an unusual, doting presence. I'm nine, and Gretchen Blüger has just turned twelve. She's changed. I haven't thought about it before, but suddenly my jealous eyes see things they never saw before. Gretchen's a tomboy no longer. Gone are the wild hair and scabbed knees of yesterday. Gone the multi-coloured, much-patched dungarees and T-shirts.

Suddenly, clean-scrubbed, wearing fashionable dresses in light colours and whites, and smart shoes instead of battered sandals, and smelling of strange, alluring perfume, is a swan where once there was a chicken.

It's been a long time since Gretchen played naked-water-tree-running with us. Won't now, far too sophisticated. What a pity. I've never thought her pretty before, but now she's beautiful. Her natural blonde hair, framing her aquiline face and perfect nose, her piercing blue eyes. Why haven't I seen it before? Something else. She's changed *shape!* Her legs are no longer sticks. Her waist is narrow. She has *curves.* She isn't flat-chested. Becky says she wears a bra. Like Mum. Alluring and repulsive, all at once. Lacy cup-shaped things with straps, I recall. Crazy, I think. Tits inside. Strange to think of Gretchen with tits.

What impresses and worries me even more are not the physical changes, but something else. Attitude. Behaviour. It's changed completely. I'm used to her running amok with us, climbing trees, throwing stones, abusing the *machula*. Here's something completely new. Here's a smart, curvaceous, beautiful young thing, who overnight is an adult, has space no more for childish things. She isn't spending her days at our house to be with Becky and me. No. It's Fraser. I feel

j

two separate, equally powerful, quite debilitating, streams of resentment and jealousy. It makes my chest feel so full it's going to burst.

I've only just decided to love Fraser. He's my long-lost big brother, and, like me, he's sad about Dad. That's a thought. He's a gunner in the navy. Won first prize in the shooting competition at HMS *St Vincent* in 1954. Wherever that is. Like Dad, he's a crack shot. Where was he when I tried to shoot God? We could've made a proper job of it. Anyway, now I've found him I don't want him to go, ever. He should stay here, with me, in Geita. I want to be like him, walk like him, talk like him. I'm King Louis in *The Jungle Book*, and he's Mowgli. Mum says I want to climb *into* him.

Now here's this girl. I know her, but I don't. She's different. First, she's spotlessly, almost unhealthily, clean. That's not our way in Geita. We're grubby, no matter how often we bathe. We play with so many things. *Kukus*, dogs, wild animals. We dig holes, climb trees, run through elephant grass. Nobody's like this. She's shiny-clean, and has no scratches or scabs on her face. Her hair hasn't got brambles and grass in it. There's something else. Poise. I don't know the word, but I know the impression.

Gretchen's *maridadi*. Beautiful. She's smart, fragrant, un-rough, un-tough, no longer flat-chested. She's quiet, discreet, polite, obviously infatuated. She sits on the verandah, pretending to talk with Becky, but I see where her big, adoring, blue eyes are looking. Fraser's drinking a bottle of beer, oblivious. Gretchen's in love. With *my* big brother. How dare she come here, just when I've found him, and then fall in love with him? How *dare* she stare at him that way?

The other surge is worse. I haven't thought about Gretchen, or any girl, with deep affection. Not *that* deep. Girls are girls. Weaker, less able, less reliable than boys. They're a pain, and handicap too. Not fun, I've thought, trying to outrun a rampant lion if a girl's with you! Not that I've done it. Not yet. Girls are dyspraxic. Don't know where I read the word. They can't throw a stone for toffee! Useless aim. Waste of time. But this is different. She isn't trying to outrun a lion or throw a stone. Nor even climb a tree. Naked-water-tree-running is out of the question. This is new. Completely different. This, I later come to know, is my first experience of bewitchment of man by woman. Not a full, nor a grown one, but, even at this age, a beguiling one.

Suddenly I feel reverse jealousy. It's no longer just anger at *her* attraction to Fraser, who belongs to me. I feel painfully jealous that it's *him,* not me, on whom she's focusing. How dare *he* come here and steal *my* darling? That's new. I've never thought of anyone as 'darling'. From now I'll think of Gretchen no other way.

The last week of Fraser's visit is fraught with emotion. Mum is tearful several times. She's coped better than she could have expected after Dad died. But now she has Fraser home, and he's so like his father it's almost like having him back from the grave. Becky is strangely quiet. I think it's too much for her. She always withdraws into her shell at emotive times, never shows her true feelings.

I ride a roller coaster. Alone with Fraser, I feel a welling of devotion. When I see Gretchen I feel the same for her. When she's talking with him, hanging on his every word, laughing with the voice of an angel, doting on him with her eyes, I feel rage. At both of them. It's a conspiracy. I'm the victim. I have to get away. I escape to the garden, sometimes beyond. Once, after running until out of breath, deeply scratched by thornbushes, I throw myself on the ground, lie hidden by elephant grass, and sob myself to sleep.

When I awake it's dark and safari ants are crawling on my face. That's even more startling than the close-by footfalls and sniffing sounds of a foraging hyena. What shocks me is no one notices I'm gone. Gretchen is still worshipping at Fraser's altar when I come back.

We're all sad when Fraser leaves. Gretchen's the worst. She comes to see him off at the house. She's asked her parents if she can go shopping in Mwanza, so she can be in the Land Rover with him. They've said no, and when she comes her eyes are red from crying. Fraser, who's been amused by the hero-worship until now, is embarrassed to see how heartbroken Gretchen is. My feelings are also intense. Heartbreak and relief, each vying for supremacy.

We fly back to School. It's been decided that's best, although nobody's saying it's because Jimmy jumps through bus windows. I'm airsick before the plane takes off. The smells of pressurisation, plus previous passengers' sickness are enough. Becky makes sure she doesn't sit by me.

I've gone to Arusha since 1958, the year after Dad died. Then it's all European, the colonial government not permitting the admission of black, coloured or Indian students to any school where white pupils attend. By 1960, when I'm nine, Uhuru is close on the horizon. The European-only policy is suddenly reversed. This year several black pupils are admitted to my school. Among them is a young man of eleven, called Robert Matwiga.

Matwiga comes from a rural village, and is very excited at the prospect of attending a European school. The poor chap suffered polio as an infant, and his left leg is withered and as thin as a broomstick. He more than compensates by having a very strong right leg and immensely strong shoulders and arms. In fact, he turns out to be the best sportsman in the school, often beating not only other pupils, but even teachers twice his age at tennis, cricket or any other sport. He has a strange, almost vaulting walk, his thin leg acting as a prop or pole-vault for him to leap forward onto his good leg.

For several weeks after he comes to the school, the children follow him, imitating his walk. When he goes for a stroll there is a single file of suddenly-crippled boys, as many as ten, vaulting behind in gay abandon. The novelty soon dies, fortunately. I don't think the question of cruelty arises.

Matwiga is a courageous chap, replete with wicked humour and intelligence. In his village he has never had a water-closet toilet, or anything resembling a flushing western facility. The first time he goes to the toilet, he comes out glowing with enthusiasm, energy and delight, and exclaims in Swahili, face shining and eyes bright, that his deposit in the bowl resulted in a strange and unique sound, which went '*Tum-Bui!*' To an English ear it would sound like 'Toom-Buwee'. It was accompanied, he says, by an upward splash of fingers of water, like a fountain! After that, 'plop', our old word, is redundant.

Like me, Matwiga speaks better Swahili than English. This disadvantages us in school, but forges a special bond. It also allows us to say funny things about others, without danger. Some refer to us as the 'black and white gigglers'.

Matwiga becomes one of our gang, joining me, Schmedjie, the Finn, and an English boy, David Allen, in an unholy clique. We will embark on several nefarious enterprises together. The thought occurs: Matwiga is a *mutu*. Lutoli is a *mutu*. Matwiga is at school with me. Lutoli is going to school two hours a day, barefoot in a mud and wattle 'school' building near the *boma*. He has to walk three miles along a jungle footpath to get there.

I wonder if Mr Snel, the mine manager, who agreed to pay my fees from mine funds, can be persuaded to pay for Lutoli too. It's only fair. I'll ask him when I get home. Meantime, I'm stuck in Arusha. Colourful Swahili curses come automatically to mind, to describe how I feel about that. *Mapumbu* and *matiti* are in them. Testicles and tits.

Mrs Androupolos is, unsurprisingly, Greek. A teacher, whose subject, of all things, is English. She's short and fat, and very Greek. Her husband is never mentioned, but must have existed, because she has a son, Georgios, same age as me, but, like his mother, short and very fat. It's obvious why. He's always sucking a sweet, and never without a pocketful.

Neither Georgios, nor his mother, speak good, or even much, English, and they do so with strong Greek accents. I can't work out how Mrs Androupolos convinced the school, and particularly the erudite and posh head, Mr Houghton, to employ her as a teacher of English. For the sake of my memories, however, I am very glad she did. If she had failed, my life would have been anecdotally the poorer. Because of her accent, we decide it isn't English she teaches. It's *Greklish*.

Mrs Androupolos is a stickler for discipline. She spends three quarters of a lesson disciplining us and very little time teaching. I think she doesn't know enough English to teach, and practises diversionary tactics to fill the void.

'Good morning cluss!' she says, standing in front of her desk.

'Good morning Mrs Androupolos,' we chorus.

'Good. Nauw, ohpen desks and tak grammahs from eet. Poot on desk and ohpen pudge twenty-foive.' There is rustling and shuffling from the class. Then she finds something.

'Allen, why ees yoor shit bouttons ohpen?'

'Me, miss?' Allen says, fingering his shirt to check his buttons.

'You!' She points at him with her pencil. 'Don' spik mi buck! Kum heere een fraunt!' Allen shuffles to the front. 'Hwy yoo spik?'

'Sorry Miss.'

'Hokay, go buck yoor desk.'

One morning Mrs Androupolos takes the first class of the day, just after breakfast. It's English grammar, and she stands, as usual, hands on hips, facing the class.

'Toddaye we tuk ther grummars,' she announces. 'Nauw feerst ees ther nouns. A noun ees a theeng, saye ufter me, a noun ees a theeng. . .'

'A noun ees a theeng,' we chorus dutifully.

'A noun ees a wud for a theeng!'

'A noun ees a wud for a theeng!' we echo. There's sniggering from Schmedjie and Allan, but I manage to contain myself.

'Hwat ees ther wud for a theeng?' Mrs Androupolos asks, holding her palms upwards.

'Eet ees a noun!' we reply, several more boys fight to control their laughter.

'Hwat ees a noun?'

'A theeng,' we shout as one. Then it happens. Matwiga, who until now has been unusually quiet, stands up beside his desk and fumbles with the flies on his shorts. He pulls his willy out. Holding it between thumb and finger, he raises his other hand in question. A deadly hush descends. Mouths are open. Mrs Androupolos turns blotchy purple, stops walking, talking and gesticulating in mid pace, sentence and gesture.

'Please mees, ees thees *theeng* a noun?' Matwiga asks with angelic face and genuine curiosity. The silence hangs. Not a rustle. The cooling window breeze takes a break. The purple of Mrs Androupolos's face blotches now, white, pink and angry red. She explodes. Spittle flies.

'Poot eet ahwaai, yoo feelthy boy!' she bellows with a quavering voice. The tension breaks, and we burst out laughing. Matwiga prods his offending organ back into his pants. He sits down, grinning hugely. He senses he's rewritten English.

'Hwy yoo luff?' Mrs Androupolos roars at the tittering class. 'Hwat ees so funay?' We lose any remaining control. 'Thees ees no luffeeng theeng!' she yells. We convulse. Mrs Androupolos stalks from the room. The laughter continues. It's beginning to abate when she stalks back.

'Tuk yoor puds,' she shrieks, 'end wraite wun hundred taimes "I weel nort shauw my theeng een cluss!" ' Fresh oxygen. We re-lose control. After a few minutes, Schmedjie begins to write the first of his hundred lines, 'I weel not shauw my theeng in cluss!' He shows us, and, sniggering, we begin to copy his example. We're still giggling when Mrs Androupolos announces, 'Ai am go nauw. You geeve yoor lines for me tomorrow. Robert Matwiga, I report you for Mr Houghton.' She picks up her books and scuttles away.

Apart from teaching *Greklish*, Mrs Androupolos runs the school tuck shop. This is a small affair, and takes place in a classroom next to the quadrangle on Saturday mornings. There is limited choice, and the merchandise is confined to bottles of Coca Cola and Fanta, Sherbet fountains, Rowntree's fruit gums and pastilles, Dominion salted crisps, Kit-Kats, Crunchies, and bars of Nestlé's and Cadbury's chocolate. Sometimes there are also oranges and bananas, but that's rare.

It's soon apparent why Georgios helps his mother in the tuck shop, and why he is so fat. He eats sweets and chocolates all the time. He eats all the profits, or pay, his mother earns from her extra-curricular activity. A change is due, and Schmedjie and Matwiga come up with a plan so brilliant I'm filled with admiration.

'You get caught,' Schmedjie says, 'when you look guilty.' We're sitting on the bank of the river, bored and thinking how we can do something illegal, and get away with it.

'So don' look guilty,' says Matwiga, tossing a pebble into the river. Schmedjie looks thoughtful. Everyone knows he'll come up with an idea when he looks like this.

'Tuck shop,' Schmedjie announces, 'that's what we should do!'

'Do what?' I ask. Matwiga and Schmedjie talk in riddles.

'Rob it,' Schmedjie says, 'we should rob it. . .'

'But don' look guilty,' Matwiga completes.

'Rob the tuck shop. . ?' Allen asks, joining the debate.

'Exactly,' Matwiga confirms.

'But Mrs Androupolos and Georgios are there,' I say.

'That's why this plan is so good, you see?' Matwiga says, turning to me with a grin.

'What plan?' Allen asks, confused.

'This one,' says Schmedjie, getting to his feet. 'Imagine you are Mrs Androupolos and Georgios, and I'm coming into the tuck shop.' He smoothes his blond hair, puts on a stern expression, and paces towards us. When he's six feet away he pretends to scoop up goods from an imaginary shelf, and puts them in a non-existent bag, all the while keeping his eyes fixed on what he's doing, his mouth set in a bored grimace, as if for all the world he'd rather be somewhere else. Having put the 'goods' in the 'bag', he makes eye contact with us, nods condescendingly, turns on his heels and strides, 'bag' in hand, out the 'tuck shop'. It's stirling stuff, leaves us speechless.

'But you didn't *look* like you were stealing,' Allen says.

'Exactly,' says Matwiga. He likes the word.

'Can it really work?' I ask, fear blunting my enthusiasm.

'Did I *look* like a thief?' Schmedjie asks, shaking his head in answer to his own question.

'Who dares wins,' says Allen, catching up, 'they say that in the British army, or something.'

'Of course we win!' laughs Matwiga, clapping his hands. 'Of course we win!'

'They say you should have a, what is it. . ?' I say, struggling for the right word, 'a division!'

'What you mean, exactly?' Matwiga asks, looking serious.

'Something to make them look somewhere else,' I say. 'Then Schmedjie can walk in, take things, and go. . .'

'Who said I'm the one to do it?' Schmedjie says angrily. 'I didn't say I *would!*'

'Straws,' says Allen, breaking elephant grass for the purpose, 'whoever gets the shortest is *it!*' He turns to show a fist clutching four pieces of grass. He proffers them. Reluctantly, we select a piece in turn and pull it out. Schmedjie's is shortest.

'There,' exclaims Allen, 'it's you *anyway!*'

'Shit in buggeration!' swears Schmedjie, who's learnt the term from me, after I heard it from an older boy. Lovely expression.

'You do it?' Matwiga asks, staring into Schmedjie's eyes.

'I don't know if. . .' Schmedjie stammers, for once losing his silver tongue.

'This Saturday!' Allen exclaims, enthusiastic now someone else is *it*.

'Wait a minute,' Schmedjie shouts, 'what about the. . . *division*?'

'That's it,' I say.

'*Diversification!*' says Allen. Clever bugger.

'Yeah, what about that?'

'Easy,' says Matwiga. He stands tall on his good leg, pulls his shoulders back, and limps forward. 'I go in the shop, we all go in, 'cept him, who do it.'

'Why?' asks Allen.

'We keep them busy while Schmedjie does it.'

'What we say?' I ask.

'Hello, Mrs Androupolos, can I have Mars bar, packet Dominion crisps, and Coca Cola, please!' rattles off Matwiga.

'So while she gets them, Schmedjie walks in, takes the stuff and walks out. . .' Allen says in wonderment.

'Exactly,' says Matwiga.

'I'm not sure. . .' Schmedjie begins.

'Can't refuse now,' I say, 'you got the straw.'

'No, you can't,' echo Allen and Matwiga together.

'Okay, if I do it, who's doing it next time?' Schmedjie asks.

'We draw more straws,' Allen says. There's a long silence. Finally we all nod. Our boredom is banished. There's a purpose in life. And danger.

'We better practise,' Allen announces, 'the one doing it must not only not look guilty, but look official too!'

'Official?' I ask.

'Yup, like he's just collecting stuff, routine-like. For a teacher, boring.'

'That right,' says Matwiga.

'Innocent and official,' says Schmedjie, 'it will be hard not to laugh.'

'If you do, we are caught,' growls Matwiga, 'so you better don't.'

The plan is practised over several days. The venue is perfect, because it's our classroom which, on Saturday mornings, becomes the tuck shop. It's never locked. We take turns being Mrs Androupolos, Georgios, and the thief. Allen loans a small cardboard suitcase for the venture. It looks official and non-guilty. We can pack the spoils in it. What thief, after all, would brazenly display a container for his loot? The fourth one of us, not playing thief, Mrs Androupolos, or Georgios, takes the role of diversionary customer, giving Mrs Androupolos a long list of requests. It's so exciting, we can hardly wait for the real thing.

Twenty

Our first raid is planned. It has to be on a Saturday, the only day the tuck shop opens. We've practised our techniques of diversion and official-looking 'taking', which we prefer to stealing. We're only 'liberating' what is rightly ours, Allen says, and Matwiga gleefully agrees. It isn't fair, we concur, that fat Georgios has so many sweets, and we so few. Six days before the raid, on the preceding Sunday, we find to our horror that our nefarious plans are known in a very high place.

Schmedjie, Allen, Matwiga and I sit down on our seats in the front pew of the little church. We have just been singing *Onward Christian Soldiers*. The grey-bearded padre is looking our way as he stands in the pulpit and opens his big leather Bible. He pauses a long time. Then he clears his throat and begins:

'And the Lord spake unto Moses, saying, If a soul sin, and commit a trespass against the Lord, and lie unto his neighbour in that which was delivered to him to keep, or in fellowship, or in a thing taken away by violence, or hath deceived his neighbour; Or hath found that which was lost, and lieth concerning it, and sweareth falsely; in any of all these that a man doth, sinning therein: Then it shall be, because he hath sinned, and is guilty, that he shall restore that which he took violently away, or the thing which he hath deceitfully gotten, or that which was delivered him to keep, or the lost thing which he found. Or all that about which he hath sworn falsely; he shall even restore it in the principal, and shall add the fifth part more thereto, and give it unto him to whom it appertaineth, in the day of his trespass offering. And he shall bring his trespass offering unto the Lord. . .' He closes the Bible, raises his eyes, and stares at us.

'God knows all things,' he bellows unexpectedly, making us jump

in our seats. '*Even that which you may think he does not!*' Schmedjie shifts uncomfortably. '*There is no secret you can keep from his all-knowing eye, no matter how small. . .*' Matwiga's eyes bulge. Deep down, he's very superstitious. His whole village is. He swallows hard. '*All knowing, wise and compassionate, he knows our deepest secrets, our hopes and our dreams.*' The padre's eyes bore into mine. He knows I tried to shoot God. He knows I went to Mlozi to get witchcraft to avoid school. Not that it worked. He knows about our planned tuck shop raid!

'*Yet he allows us, allows us to sin, not because he is weak, but because he is strong. He grants to us free will. He allows us to sin, but hopes we will not. He knows our every weakness and vice. He knows of our temptations, which are of Satan. Yet he does not act to prevent our sins. He watches and waits. He is all-knowing.*' Even Allen has a spooked expression now. Matwiga can no longer meet the accusing gaze. It gets worse.

'*We pray to God for those things we want for ourselves. For the welfare of those we love, for happiness, for the delivery of those in peril. . .*' I feel a sudden tightness in my throat. I do all those things, ask God to protect and look after Mum, Becky, my brothers, Umali, Gretchen, Lutoli, Dieti, Sandy. . . Now the padre's *definitely* staring at me. I avert my eyes guiltily.

After staring at the parquet floor for several seconds, I glance with bowed head at Matwiga, and meet a gaze of naked terror. His eyes protrude frog-like. I feel the same. God knows about our tuck shop plans! We are being warned. The sermon continues, but I can't concentrate. We're in big trouble. With God! The padre's eyes lock on mine. I must be the worst sinner of all! 'Let us pray,' the padre intones, his eyes finally looking down.

'Our Father,' the congregation chorus dutifully, 'Who Art In Heaven. . .'

'Hello, What's Your Name?' Matwiga prays loudly.

'Jesus is his name!' whispers Schmedjie crossly. People are looking at us. Particularly BL Thomas, Vice Principal. This keeps getting worse.

'*Ana jua!*' Matwiga blurts as soon as we're in the fresh air. He knows. His eyes hold superstitious dread.

'*Ndio, najua!*' I agree. Yes, he knows. I share his horror. The preacher knows our plans, he's made that obvious. And if he knows, *God,* his boss, knows! Doom is imminent. What's that stuff. . . brine, that's it, no, it's got a rock in it, no, a stone. *Brimstone*, that's the one. That and. . . *fire!* Fire and brimstone. I don't like the sound of that.

Wonder what kind of stone is a *brim*. Maybe they use them to edge things.

'*Tuwatche!*' Matwiga hisses as we form up to walk back to school. Let's leave it. 'If God knows, and we do it, there will be great *hatari, danger.*'

'*Kabisa!*' I agree. Absolutely! A shudder of dread runs through me. I've had enough trouble with God!

The tuck shop is safe. Our arrangements are like the nuclear standoff between Russia and America – all preparation and no action. Oh yes, then there's the matter of BL Thomas. He looked annoyed when Schmedjie whispered to Matwiga. As if reading my thoughts, Schmedjie turns to Matwiga.

'It's not Our Father, Which Are In Heaven, Hello, *What's* Your Name? It's Hello *is* your name!'

'You mean they call Jesus "*Hello*?" '

'Yup,' says Schmedjie, 'because God is the alpha and he's oh-mega.'

'What?' I ask.

'Mega's big, but he's also the beginning and the end. At the beginning you always say hello. So it's "hello-*is*-your-name".'

'Funny!' says Matwiga. I agree.

Fortune is with us on one thing. BL Thomas seems to have forgotten our disturbance of the Lord's prayer. We do, however, come to his early attention on another matter altogether.

Our minds are ever-seeking. It isn't long after our big fright with the eternal when Schmedjie discovers a hitherto unknown athletic secret. It starts, like most great discoveries, by accident. He's very light-skinned, and rubs sun-cream on before going in the sun. It's too late when he realises he's rubbed toothpaste on his legs. We're outside, and BL tells us to lap round the field. Schmedjie makes his discovery. Toothpaste rubbed on legs makes you fast. He tells us. Soon we, and half the school, are at it. Mint cools the skin. The chilled air feels quick. Even Matwiga tries it on his good leg, and says he walks faster.

The only problem with our speed-enhancer is so many use it, everyone's faster, so the cheating doesn't help! It comes to a head when Schmedjie openly rubs it on his legs on the field and BL asks what's up. There's a strange, minty smell around track events lately, and he's determined to get to the bottom of it.

'Toothpaste!' he declares in his sing-song Welsh accent, 'and why are you putting it on your legs?'

'To go faster,' Schmedjie mumbles.

'Speak up, boy!'

'To go faster!'

'*What?*'

'*Faster. . ?*' BL turns to the rest of us incredulously.

'*Faster*, eh, I suppose you *believe* that?' Putting it this way, it seems silly. Some of us giggle. Even BL struggles to keep his expression stern.

'Showers!' he roars. 'Get it off, and double back. Last one does twenty press-ups, then three laps *without* toothpaste. In future, read the label, it's *tooth*-paste, not *leg*-paste!' In the showers we mock Schmedjie. Stupid Finn! 'Shark-fin,' Allen taunts. What a ridiculous notion, *toothpaste* indeed! Schmedjie doesn't apply for a patent. Or is it a *potent?*

It's Allen who suggests pyjama-leg-cripple-running. It has to wait till after lights-out. We remove our pyjama trousers, and put our bent knees back down the legs. This binds calves tightly to thighs and forces feet against buttocks. Thus shortened, and compelled to walk on knees, we lower ourselves from our high beds, and race each other, on knees, down the aisles between the beds. Excitement comes from the risk element, knowing Miss Baxter can appear, torch in hand, at any time. With self-made handicap, it will be hard, if not impossible, to get away, harder still to get up into bed.

We tell Matwiga he doesn't have to play, but he refuses to be left out. For him the rules are modified. He can climb down from his bed *before* rearranging his pyjamas, and keep his thin leg out of his pyjama-pants. Despite his lopsidedness he's as quick as anyone. The game is compelling. We play nightly. For several days we get away with it. It's Matwiga who cops it.

We've been racing ten minutes. We don't hear a footfall, or the door open. She sneaks up. She's a silent assassin. Suspects something. Some of us, mainly Schmedjie, can't help sniggering while we hobble about. Miss Baxter is expert at not showing suspicion. She comes, waits a bit, seems to go, then comes back. The beam shoots out from nowhere. It lances the darkness in a white, terrifying cone. There's subdued scuffling as we try desperately to avoid the torchlight, which marches determinedly up and down the aisles. I reach my bed, and manage, by herculean effort, to pull myself up. I've just got my legs under the covers when the searchlight finds Matwiga.

He's been desperately trying to squiggle to his bed, but now, like a rabbit in headlights, he's stationary and blinking. His startled face is lit up like a clown, and his expression brings compulsory giggles from several quarters of alleged sleepers.

'What *have* we here?' Miss Baxter says. She's invisible behind the beam. Matwiga neither moves nor speaks. Terror is on his face. He blinks rapidly.

'Speak, *boy!*'

'A game,' Matwiga mumbles.

'*Game*, tying yourself up like a turkey, *crawling* about the floor?'

'Yes Miss.'

'Yes Miss *Baxter!*'

'Yes Miss Baxter.'

'Undo yourself and get back in bed,' she says. She turns to the wall, snaps on the light. We're blinking.

'He's not the only one, *is* he?' she intones menacingly. 'All of you, bedclothes off!' she suddenly yells. There's no escape. We lower the covers. Our legs are doubled up in our pyjama pants.

'Right,' she yells, suddenly more angry, 'undo this nonsense, then all of you to line up here!' She points at the floor. We know what's coming. 'All except you, Master Matwiga. You will write one hundred lines – I will not demean my body.'

'What that mean?' Matwiga says softly.

'It means you find out and write a hundred lines. Before lunch tomorrow!' She reaches in Allen's locker, takes out his plimsole. He's got the biggest feet among us.

Three of the best from Miss Baxter is very sore. We jump back in bed after our turn, backsides on fire.

'I'm fed up with this dormitory,' she announces after the last boy has made an agony-powered leap for his bed. 'I know about the toothpaste, and I'm shocked what you were doing tonight. Let's have no more of it!' She clicks the light off and is gone. My pain is beginning to ebb. Somebody sniggers, then we're all giggling. There's always a funny side.

For a while there's a moratorium on new games.

I get air-letters from Mum three times a month. They're those blue, folded things which double as writing paper and envelope in one. Mum says she'll write every week, but sometimes doesn't quite manage, or else one letter a month goes missing. I look forward to her letters all week. When it's post-time, in the evening after supper, I wait anxiously to see if there's one for me. Miss Baxter takes the letters out of the bag one at a time, and announces who it's for. The lucky ones jump up and grab their letter. Each one which isn't for me is a disappointment. Then it's me, and my heart surges. Other times she finishes, and I'm not a lucky one.

Mum's letters are pretty much the same. Her writing, which she learnt long ago at another boarding school, is a beautiful copperplate script. 'Darling Jimboy, her letters begin, I hope you are well, and that you are happy.' She then says something about home. 'Gooloogooloo is well, but he tried to bite Amina yesterday. Sandy misses you, and I have to let her sleep on my bed while you're away.' Then there's usually something about someone on the mine. 'Rosanna has been very sick, but she's better now,' or 'Higgs broke his ankle when his motor-bike fell over.' There's always a part about Umali and Amina, and sometimes Lutoli too. 'Umali says he misses fishing at the dam with you.' Or 'Amina drank too much again, and got into a fight with the *ayah* who works for Mr Snel.' Her letters round off here, about two thirds of the way down the inside of the air-letter. 'I miss you and love you. You'll be home soon, and I look forward to that. Your ever-loving, Mum. XXXXXXX (hugs and kisses).'

There may never be anything new in her letters, but that's not what I love them for. They are from Mum, from Geita, my home, and they've been there more recently than me. I take my letters reverently to a quiet place where I can read and re-read them over and over. I also smell them, and rub them on my face, because it's the closest thing to home. In my banishment in this alien, far-off place, they evoke a feeling that my real world, that which I love so dearly, still exists, even though it's so far away.

For five weeks in a row I get a letter from Mum every Friday. That's unusual, for two reasons. One is she never manages a letter *every* week. The other is they usually arrive on different days of the week. There's something very unusual going on. I check with Becky, and she's also had a letter every Friday for five weeks. We compare letters. Apart from our names, the contents are almost identical. There's more. The letters are very brief, and the handwriting looks shaky. Not like Mum's usually confident copperplate hand. They're all written in the same pen. We check previous letters and confirm our suspicions. Those were longer, and written with a variety of pens. I go to Miss Baxter and tell her I'm worried about Mum. I think she's written the letters all at the same time. Why would she do that, then date them differently?

'Your mother's fine,' Miss Baxter says. She's telephoned the mine. I don't know how that works. There's only a radio-telephone there, the one in Mr Snel's office at the head office on Top Road. 'They told me she's just fine, so run along and don't worry any more.' I tell Becky, and she says everything must be okay, so we mustn't worry.

206

Twenty-one

At night I lie in bed and think about things which happened here in Tanganyika. Eugen Blüger told Dad about the first time the *Schutztruppe* were bombed from the air. Dad loved to tell me the story. I was only five.

A British biplane first appeared in the colonial war, near the mountains of Oldorobo, in 1915. It came from nowhere, and bombed the *Scutztruppe*'s position. The English had sent tribal spies ahead, to tell the people that the aeroplane was a 'new *Mungu*' (God), and that this *Mungu* would seal their doom. The *Mungu* was hit in the fuel tank by a well-aimed round from an *askari* with a smokey old '71 pattern rifle, and crashed in flames. The pilot ran screaming from the wreck with his trousers alight. His trouser-fire was put out by a German officer with a blanket, but not before his buttocks were thoroughly singed. The *askaris* celebrated, shouting, '*Mungu nyupa si Mungu!*' The new *Mungu* is *not* a God! The plane had done damage. A 50lb bomb had exploded close to the troops. *Oberstleutenant* von Lettow Vorbeck, reconnoitering the battlefield, encountered an injured *Askari* lying in the grass, his left arm blown off from the elbow.

'Don't worry, *Obersti*,' he said, smiling through his pain, 'I have another one, I can still fight!'

An awkward thing has developed with Marais. Ever since his imprisonment under his bed, and being set free by me, he's undergone a complete turnaround where I'm concerned. Whereas he used to glower, he now smiles warmly at me. In place of whispered threats, are offers to help clean my shoes, fetch things for me.

Schmedjie says I've gained a side-kick. Matwiga says a slave. They want me to tell him to do silly things, like put his head in the toilet bowl and pull the chain, or make him abuse Miss Baxter out loud. I won't do that. He may not be a friend, but he's trying to make up for past cruelties. How do I know if the change is genuine, or if it'll last? I don't. Dad had a saying: Give a man a chance. If he lets you down, never give him another. I suppose I never gave Marais a chance. I disliked him from the outset. Being in the next bed, he was a constant reminder of being away from home. His wheezing attacks didn't endear him, especially when they kept me awake. I didn't like his accent, or his thin, gaunt build.

It's four o'clock Friday afternoon. The kids whose families live nearby are going home for the weekend. Those from further afield sit glumly on the grass in front of the circular driveway, where parents collect their darlings. It's not jealousy, we convince ourselves, though we don't talk to Schmedjie at these times, 'cos he's one of 'them', not us. An ancient-looking green long-wheelbase Land Rover with a canvas back pulls up. A huge, muscle-bound, bearded, *Mzungu* in khaki shorts and shirt gets out, and I see him embrace Marais. Must be his farmer-father. They're talking animatedly. Marais points at me, and his father walks my way. For a moment I'm seized with terror. Is this retribution for my part in his kidnap?

'Jan het gesê you kom wid us fore die veek-ent,' he says in pidgeon-English. 'You like eet?' My mouth is dry, my heart pounding. It takes seconds to register. 'Eef you vant eet, ve talk die matron, yes?' This is a very strange accent, almost German, not quite. More important is my relief. Rather than coming to kill me, the huge man is offering me an escape from school, even if just for two days! Marais, who I suppose I should call Jan now, is grinning.

'Yes please!' I say without hesitation. Who'd have thought? I turn to Matwiga. He's not smiling now. I'm breaking the unsaid rule. Like Schmedjie, I'm abandoning my friends.

Twenty minutes later, we're driving out onto the bumpy dirt road out of town. Mr Marais is a man of few words, like his son. The Rover bounces its dusty way to the east, then turns left at a fork, and heads towards a range of distant red hills. The snow-capped peak of Meru is visible to the right behind us. Though there are no clouds, and the sun is bright, there's a cool, refreshing breeze here, unlike the lake-plain of Geita, where even at this time of afternoon it's sweltering. The dirt road deteriorates to a track, formed, I'm sure, simply by the passing of vehicles like this. It winds around obstacles, like giant anthills and rocky outcrops. Without talking, Mr Marais points out herds of wildebeest, kudu, even a pair of grazing rhinos.

The sun comes down to the horizon in the east, a great blood-red disc, bathing the whole world in pink. It's seven o'clock, and nearly three hours since we left Arusha. One moment the sun's there, clinging to the edge of the world, then it plunges and is gone. It's only momentarily dark, for then a paler, golden moon, and myriad stars, suffuse the land in gentle light. We erupt onto a great plain ringed by distant hills, black and mysterious. Then we're stopping. Mr Marais gets out and pushes open a huge wooden gate. He drives us through, then closes it behind. We have reached the boundary of the Marais farm.

The wooden house is half a mile from the gate. We pull up in the drive and get out. I'm stiff all over. The light from the windows is strangely pale, not like in Geita. Jan reads my thoughts.

'*Ons het nie electric nie,*' he says. We have no electric. 'Use die hurricane-lamps.' At the door his mother and two sisters greet us. His mum is a thin, smiling lady, who speaks no English. She says 'velkom' several times, and smiles a lot. One sister is called 'Meisie', which means girl. I don't know if it's a nickname, but find it strange. Meisie's thirteen, and goes to a local 'farm-school'. She's pretty, in a red-haired, freckly way, and she has a ready smile. The other sister is Doreen, which I find also strange out here among these tough people. She's eleven, dark haired, and serious. Maybe it's her name.

'*Julle moet eet!*' Mrs Marais says. She leads us into a warm dimly-lit kitchen. I haven't realised how cold it is outside. It's like that on the high plateau in the evening. Three hurricane-lamps on tables make wheezy blowing sounds, and cast yellow light and shadow around the room. There are rows and rows of copper pots and pans hanging from a beam above an open fire, where orange flames dance around big logs, casting their own flickering light and shadow. We sit on long, heavy wooden benches.

Mrs Marais and Meisie bring a big pot of boiled potatoes, and another with delicious-smelling stew in it. '*Kudu,*' she says, smiling, '*geskiet gister by Pa.*' Shot yesterday by father. After boarding-school fare, it's delicious. Meisie can't keep her eyes off me. I look up several times to find her staring. She grins, but doesn't look away. Jan talks to her in Dutch, then tells me she says I'm handsome. No one's ever said that, except Mum. I say she's pretty too, and we grin at each other like a pair of monkeys. I feel a stab of guilt about Gretchen. But then she doesn't know.

The Marais family go to bed early. I share a room with Jan, which I don't mind anymore. As soon as we're in bed, he snuffs out the whooshing hurricane-lamp. I fall into a dreamless sleep.

They rise early. At six the sun bursts through our un-curtained window, and the farmyard has come to life. It's ice-cold outside. We wash in a small outbuilding. It's simple. There's a handle-powered pump, which you push to and fro until it draws a stream of water from a well, which runs out a tap into a bucket. When the bucket's full, you ladle the ice-cold water over yourself with a small metal jug. Soap all over with the bar of Lifebuoy on the ledge. Rinse off, and you're done. The toilet's in the shed next door. A pit latrine. A bucket of water and a bar of soap are provided to wash hands.

After breakfast of fried *Boerewors*, a long Afrikaans spiced sausage, and eggs, Jan and I go exploring. The plowed earth runs in furrows of deep red-brown, as far as the eye can see. Forty thousand hectares, the Marais farm, Jan says. Too big to contemplate. There are fields with rows and rows of baby maize just beginning to erupt from the soil. Others fields are half-grown, with tiny cobs starting to show. Some places are covered in fresh, peppermint-green grass, grazed by healthy-looking black and brown cattle. They don't have humps, like our scrawny Geita beasts, and they're not troubled by flies either. This is a different world! Everywhere there are sprinklers shooting out revolving jets of water. I can't believe what man can do to the land. It's a miracle.

There's a barn with a massive haystack. Jan, Meisie and I climb the stack and have a midday snooze. Doreen doesn't come. She's playing on her own in the house.

'Did you got a girlfriend?' Meisie asks me.

'Not yet,' I say. Why does she want to know?

The weekend ends too soon. We go back to Arusha, bearing huge packets of *biltong*, dried spiced game-meat, and home-made *beskuit*, an Afrikaner sweet rusk, to dip in tea or coffee. From now on, I don't hate Marais, no, Jan, any more. My friends won't be convinced so easily.

We're only back a week, and I haven't done that convincing, when Jan gets very sick.

It starts with an asthma attack in bed at night, and gets worse and worse, in spite of his inhaler-bottle, until he can hardly breathe at all and his face is blue. In a panic I run and call Miss Baxter. She looks at him for only a second and gets the school doctor out of bed. Jan walks out of the dormitory supported by both of them He's taken by ambulance to hospital. Next day Miss Baxter says it's pneumonia, and he's 'very ill indeed'. He's being treated with penicillin and oxygen.

At lunchtime the grey-bearded school padre who sussed our tuck shop plans comes to hold a special prayer for Jan. Andrew, the English twins Jed and Jack, and I, avoid his gaze. I'm sure he knows we tied Jan up. I feel I betrayed Jan. Not that I liked him then, not that he hadn't been horrible to me for a long time. It's just that I really dislike all three of my co-kidnappers. It was their idea, and I went along with it. I didn't like Jan Marais, and I'd tried to run away from school. I was glad to get involved in anything which would restore my feeling of control. Only it didn't. Then, if not for me these boys would have left him trussed up under his bed for the whole afternoon. They didn't like me untying him. I feel a surge of bitter remorse for my part in the affair.

That night the padre comes back to the school and addresses us in the dining room. Jan Marais died an hour ago.

What is sorrow? What is grief? What is God's plan? What is his message? I go to bed that night, next to Jan's achingly empty bed, which has been stripped of blankets, sheets and pillows. I feel an overwhelming mixture of emotions. Guilt. Sadness. I cry bitter tears, but feel dishonest. He wasn't a *real* friend, was he? I hated him for so long. Yes, he had become much nicer to me, and I've just had a weekend with his family. What about pretty Meisie? How is *she* feeling now?

Maybe Jan Marais would have become a good friend, but I'm still unsure I wanted that. If I say to myself he was going to be my real friend, will I be saying so because he's dead? Did I kill him by hating him so long?

I dream about Dad and Mr Valari (senior), and Tembo's disintegrating puppy. In my dream I talk with Jan, who says death's quite nice, actually, and I should try it. Meisie's standing just behind him, smiling and nodding.

The whole school is in shock. Everyone knew Jan had asthma, but they didn't expect him to die. On Sunday his funeral service is held at the church. The family are Dutch-Reformed, which is really *Much-Deformed*, Andrew used to unkindly say, and there isn't that kind of church in the district. I sit with Schmedjie, Matwiga and Allen, as far away from Andrew and the twins as we can get. I'm never going to mix with them again.

Jan's coffin is made of light wood and has shiny brass handles. It's resting on two trestles in front of the altar. The Marais family are seated next to it. I only see the backs of their heads, except when

Meisie turns her head round during the singing of *Abide With Me*. She stares at me. I don't know if it's accusing or not. She's still pretty, though her eyes are red and tears are streaming down her cheeks. At the end of the service the coffin is carried by six men, including Mr Houghton and BL Thomas, to the Old Marais Land Rover, and pushed in the back. He's going to be buried in the farm graveyard. The family walk stiffly out of the church, looking neither left nor right, and drive away.

The shock lasts weeks, and I feel strangely detached from day-to-day things. I can't believe what's happened, and I keep imagining I see Jan. Once I think I see him in the bathroom, coming out of a shower cubicle. He disappears as I look, and I realise it's just the shower curtain I saw. Another time, just as I'm drifting to sleep, I feel someone touch my shoulder, and Jan's voice says 'hello *Rooinek*, do you miss me?'

I jump upright in bed, but there's nobody there. Only darkness, with a narrow glimmer of dull light from the high window. I start wondering if his ghost is trying to contact me. For days I wander around alone where I think Jan used to spend his time. I know it's silly, but I can't help myself. I'm avoiding all my friends, especially Schmedjie, Matwiga and Allen.

One Saturday afternoon, while the gang are playing down at the river, I'm sitting alone on my bed, staring at the still-unoccupied bed beside mine. I hear a footstep, and Miss Baxter is there. She contemplates me in silence for a long time. Finally she speaks.

'You didn't do it,' she says softly. She's reading my thoughts. I've begun to feel I did. Killed everyone who ever died. Dad, Mr Valari (senior), Tembo's puppy, and now poor Jan. I burst into tears. She sits beside me on my bed and puts her arms around me. I never thought a hug from her would be welcome, but it is. I feel deeply comforted, and understood by another person for the first time since Jan died. After a long time she wipes my face and eyes with a tissue. 'Come to my office,' she says, 'I think a piece of cake and a cup of tea will do you good.'

From this episode I learn two things. You can't hate someone always, and even people who are hard can be gentle and kind. Miss Baxter talks to me about Jan whenever I feel the need. After a month I feel better, if still sad, and, thank heavens, the nightmares have stopped.

Many concepts are posited by us on lazy Saturday afternoons by the river. We muck about with water and pebbles, and dig tunnels deep

212

into the sandbanks. We tire of that, and lie in a group on our backs, enjoying the late afternoon sun. That's when we talk about things.

Petrol explodes in engines. It takes a lot of deliberation and argument to persuade the gang. Matwiga says it's impossible, for two reasons. First, he says, we would hear the explosion. Since the sound of a car, which he can very accurately reproduce, including the sound of gears grating or the car struggling up a hill, sounds nothing like a bomb going off, there can *not* be explosions in the engine. Second, if there *is* an explosion, people will be blown up and killed. Since that is clearly not what is happening to the occupants of that car driving down the school road over there, explosions are out of the question!

Other ideas and hypotheses keep arising. Some are accepted. Like Allan's opinion that it should be possible to drive a car on elephant wee. The thinking goes that elephants are big and very powerful. It's logic that their wee must also be strong. It therefore follows that, being much stronger than any other wee, it will be strong enough to use as car fuel. We agree to look into it sometime. Maybe big money can be made, if nobody else has the idea first.

Allen says there's a thing called a patent, where they write down your invention so no one can steal it. It's a *potent,* I say. Sounds stronger. We'll get a potent, then, we agree. Will we keep elephants at fueling depots, I wonder, or will we just take their wee there? Won't it be a bugger getting an elephant to pee into a car tank just when we want him to?

Our midnight 'feasts' are a lot less grandiose than the title we give them. We scrounge around for things to eat for days beforehand. The obvious, and always first raided stock, is that of grudging Schmedjie himself, who always has a large square tin full of home-baked shortbread biscuits. His mother brings them when she visits, or he returns with them after his frequent weekends at home. His parents live just forty miles away, at Moshi, in the foothills of Mount Kilimanjaro. The rest of us are envious, take vengeance by raiding his biscuit tin.

There is otherwise a sad lack of tasty victuals to take to our midnight feasts. One fairly reliable, and, given the shortages, essential, contribution comes from the grove of lemon trees growing between the football field and library. I have never seen lemons like these. They're a paradox. On the outside, they're the biggest, yellowest lemons. But therein lies the lie. The peel's an inch thick. When removed, the lemons themselves are the size of a plum. The strangest thing is the peel is incredibly sweet, and, we find, very edible.

All that's required to plunder the lemon-source is to amble over that way in the half hour between showers and suppertime. It's essential to wear a baggy jumper, with the bottom tucked into the waistband, to put the pilfered lemons in. Looking strangely and bumpily pregnant, all we have to do is make it back to the dorm and deposit the loot in our bedside lockers. So, pregnant-boy-detection by prefect, Matron or wandering teacher not being all that common, our stock of said item is usually replete. Lemons are available year-round in that climate.

Schmedjie's biscuits and lemons. Not much to feast on. But there's also our 'kitchen hook'.

Woodwork is never my interest, apart from making crude things in Geita. But Schmedjie says we should join woodwork classes, and use the tools and materials to build a 'stealing-hook' he's designed. Schmedjie has, among his collection of artefacts, a key he found on the playground, which, to his amazement and delight, fits the lock on the kitchen door. He's snuck into the kitchen several nights, locking the door behind him. The food's locked away. But, and this is what excites him, there is a large pantry-cabinet in one corner. It's filled with cakes and bread. The cabinet is a wood-framed thing, but the sides are only wire mesh fly-screen. Not only that, but in the far right corner there's a hole three inches wide. Schmedjie takes me on a night-scout of the kitchen. Sure enough, there's the hole. We can get a hand through, but the cakes are three feet out of reach. Have they been put there specially?

Schmedjie shows me his drawing. It's a three foot long carved stick, with a moving appendage at the end. This is a six-inch wooden hook. It's to be attached and pivoted on the end of the long stick. On the top and near the bottom are holes – for string to pull, making the hook swivel up or down. With this masterpiece, he's sure, we can reach and retrieve the cakes in the fly-screen cabinet.

We attend three woodwork 'lessons', in which we are pleased to have little supervision. Schmedjie has carved the hook-bit when the teacher asks what it is. 'Art,' Schmedjie says. The teacher smiles and walks away. He likes art. By the third lesson's end we've completed our work. We smuggle our device to the dormitory and hide it under Schmedjie's bed. We never go to woodwork again.

Our machine works. It fits easily through the hole in the mesh, and the point on the screw-hinged end sticks easily into cakes and bread. Then it's withdraw-to-the-side time. With eager fingers we break the titbit up so the pieces fit the three inch hole, and, bingo – we have something else for our midnight feast.

Our feasts take place after lights-out. The venue is under my bed. The beds are high steel ones, giving three foot of space between floor and springs.

We've burgled the kitchen the night before, and our lockers are full of sweet-skinned pilfered lemons. Schmedjie's mother has just replenished his biscuit tin, and he's got two home-made shortbread biscuits for each of us. I've contributed a packet of *Kool-Aid*, which, mixed with water, makes a very artificial-tasting drink. Robert and Allan have nothing to bring, so it was them who made the lemon run.

That night, as always, lights out in the dormitory is at eight o'clock. We wait half an hour after Miss Baxter clicks off the light. It's difficult to contain our excitement. It always is at times like this. Not that we're going anywhere different, or doing something new. No, it's just the fact that what we're doing is not allowed, and that getting caught will result in more smarting punishment to the backside. Excitement has strange roots.

Schmedjie, who has a luminous Oris watch which glows green in the dark, is our time-keeper. At the agreed time of eight thirty, he rises from his bed, casting eerie shadows on the wall in the moonlight from a high window. 'It's time,' he whispers.

'What you guys doing?' comes the voice of a boy none of us like, and who we've refused entry to our gang of four, which we say can't have a fifth member on account of its name.

'Mind your own business!' growls Matwiga, invisible in the darkness. The questioner shuts up. Matwiga's already punched him once.

The counterpanes and blankets from our beds are draped over the sides of mine. The beds are high, made of strong tubular steel, similar to hospital beds. The springs are hooked all the way round the bed frame, and attached to steel-wire links, which support the mattress. The wire links make a perfect suspension point for a hunter's lantern. Hunter's lanterns are very popular in Tanganyika. Short, square torches, with the lens and bulb on one side, they're ideal to hang under a bed.

We feast. Two of Schmedjie's biscuits, a lot of lemon skin, a bit of sour lemon, four cakes and two stale bread rolls from our kitchen raid, washed down with a mugful of *Kool Aid*. Not much, really, but stolen fruit and cake is very sweet.

It's nearly Christmas, and the dining room and dormitories are decorated with Christmas trees, tinsel and raffia-paper. We rehearse carols for a performance in the assembly room. Boys from the big-boy's dormitory teach us their versions:

While shepherds watched their flocks by night
all seated on the ground
a choir of angels it came down
and glory shone around

becomes

While shitting on the rocks at night
a great big furry hound
a roll of tissue it came down
and bum-hole it was bound

and. . .

Once in royal David's city
stood a lonely cattle shed
where a mother laid her baby
with a manger for his bed

becomes

Oh tell why you are so witty
why such muck is in your head
how you got to be Miss Baxter
with a face like the long-dead

And...

Good King Wenceslas looked out
on the feast of Stephen
when the snow lay round about
deep and crisp and even

....becomes

Wenceslas is just a Kraut
creep and tit and heathen
everyone knows he's a lout
full of farts and piss-en

It's a great introduction to carol singing. We're impressed.
   'What's a lout?' Matwiga asks Schmedjie.
   'A thing that crawls in your hair,' Schmedjie says, 'if you've got
lots they call them louses.'
   '*Lice!*' Allen corrects him.
   'Is that 'cos they's the same size as rice?' Matwiga asks.
   'Course!' I say. It's only logic.

216

Twenty-two

At home Mum makes a confession. Did we suspect anything wrong last term? Well, she's been very sick. Pneumonia and pleurisy, and Dr Weiss was so worried he had her flown to Nairobi, from there on to Johannesburg in South Africa. She spent three weeks in the General Hospital, having oxygen and antibiotics. They said she had a 'tropical infection', whatever that is. Before she went, Mary Miller suggested she write post-dated letters to Becky and me, so we wouldn't know. She lay half-dead, writing six air-letters each. She was so ill, so short of breath, she had to make them brief. Knowing me, she says, she didn't think I'd be fooled. But Mary insisted, and Mum didn't have the strength to resist.

What would have happened if Mum died in Johannesburg? Who would have told us? How would they have explained her letters? They were forgeries, weren't they? If putting a wrong date on, and pretending it's an up-to-date letter is a forgery. For the best possible reasons, Mum has deceived us. This goes to prove the correctness of my most fundamental beliefs. One, you can't trust *Wazungu*. Two, you can't trust grown-ups. Three, I can't even rely on my own mother.

I have nightmares, and Mum dies in all of them. In one I have to bury her next to Dad, on the other side from Mrs Williams, who, disintegrating and smelling like Tembo's exhumed puppy, is sitting on her gravestone, directing my digging. Becky says I'm silly. She doesn't get nightmares at all.

During the long, hot days of the hols, we get so bored we *have* to do something new. Over the years we exhaust many options. Sometimes we go out looking for distraction. Baby birds fall out of nests, and we

217

take them to the girls to nurse. They usually die. We find pythons sleeping in the shade of the big steel pipes carrying the roadside ditches under crossroads. They're only dangerous if they're very big, you're very small, and they can get at you. We're too big and too quick. We throw stones at them, and they slide off into the undergrowth.

The monsoons in northwestern Tanganyika occur in winter and summer, though that close to the equator it's almost impossible to tell which season it is. Most of the time it's hot, cloudless and dry. Suddenly, in a matter of minutes, the sun is cut off and the sky darkens with great pregnant black storm-clouds. Rolling thunder echoes between the hills, ear-piercing lightning bazookas between ground and sky, and the rain comes. In a deluge so dense that it's hard to breathe if you're caught in it. It's as if you're underwater. If you're in a car, you have to stop. Windscreen wipers are useless. You just can't see through the wall of gushing water.

This is when we surf the ditches from Top to Bottom Road. Who cares about pythons? We use small planks like mini-surfboards, held in front as we hurtle down in torrents of brown, muddy water, oblivious to scratches and bruises gained *én route*, from colliding with the sides, or from boulders which, like us, are swept down in the fierce cascade.

Scaring *leguaans*, metre long insect and berry-eating lizards, which look like dragons, and have long, darting tongues, amuses us for a time. They live underground in tunnels, to escape heat and predators. They're seldom seen in the day, coming out to hunt and forage by night. We know how to find the entrances to their tunnels. With us about they experience unexpected shocks while trying to sleep away the day.

Bobejaan bangers, or 'baboon' crackers, are large red explosives, two and a half inches long, and an inch in diameter. They have long white fuses. They're meant for farmers for frightening away crop-stealing baboons. Barrat Stores aren't fussy who they sell to, and at ten for a shilling we find them a bargain. At first we light the fuse and drop one down a hole. Muffled explosion, terrified leguaan dashing out different hole. Dieti refines our technique.

The fuses are three inches long, take half a minute to burn. We bind three or four bangers together, fuses cut different lengths, twirled together. This achieves a series of explosions. Taking our advanced ordinance, we return to the leguaan tunnels. Dull thud underground, frantic scurrying, second thud, more scrabbling, third bang, half a dozen leguaans bolting from holes, blinking in daylight, nostrils twitching, legs pumping in naked terror. Next explosion, they run faster. Anywhere. Leguaan chaos! Weapon breakthrough, atomic bomb class. No lizard can rest in peace!

We cluster-bomb the leguaans a dozen times before this, like everything else, grows mundane and boring. Discussing the problem, we decide to turn our focus on humans. Who else, we think, than the Valaris?

As already stated, the Valaris are a very private Italian family. Worse than the van der Heevers. Mr and Mrs Valari have two children, a fat daughter, Anna, and a son, Gino. When they came to Geita in 1956, they brought Mr Valari's father, Mr Valari (senior). The old man who died in 1957, shortly after Dad, and I saw his *mzoga* in *kifo nyumba*.

Neither Anna, four years older than me, nor Gino, my age, socialise with other children on the mine. They don't go to school, and only speak Italian. I've only seen Gino a few times. It isn't possible to talk with him. Swahili and English draw a blank response. He has the same thin, rangy, look as his father, and the *mzoga* of his late grandfather, Mr Valari (senior). There are no laws about withholding children from school in Geita, or they aren't enforced.

Mr Valari is the only one who leaves the house. Every day he drives his rusty Peugeot to work at the electrician's building on Top Road, and every evening he returns to park in the dusty spot beside his wooden house. Nobody, not even those he works with, know much about him or his family.

There's an uncanny echo of Boo Radley in Harper Lee's *To Kill A Mockingbird*, and the Valaris. The children in that seminal novel try their best to 'make Boo Radley come out'. I haven't read the book then, but the sentiment is similar. We'll make the Valari's come out, whatever it takes. But first we need a quisling. An Italian traitor, who will advise and teach us to abuse our victims in language they understand.

Antonio Barelli is the older of two sons of Marcello and Marula Barelli. Marcello is a gung-ho Italian, in his forties when I'm ten. Unlike the Valaris, who have never socialised in Geita, Marcello does it enthusiastically and energetically. He's known for two things: drinking to excess and singing *O caro mia*. His drinking often leaves him semi-paralysed and incoherent. We imitate that song as '*Oh Kamasutra*', the meaning of which we have no clue, but which delights adult club drinkers, particularly when Marcello, too inebriated to notice our words, sings with us. There's another one of his songs called '*O sole mio,*' which we sing as '*arsehole-meeow*', though why I do not know.

Marcello's also famous for shooting Higgs's night-rider leopard and many innocent elephants, whose feet he turns into gruesome wastepaper bins which he gives to every woman on the mine. The ivory, it's said, he sends to Italy by devious means. Marula, his wife, could easily be a Valari. She's reclusive by nature, and lives somewhere in the shadow of her raucous husband. It's said she doesn't even eat, because she's as 'thin as a rake'. We unkindly say a rattlesnake. It sounds right, although I don't hear her rattle. I've never seen a rattlesnake. They're American, not African. Marcello more than compensates for Marula's non-exuberance.

Antonio is a few months younger than me. His brother Stefano is four years behind him. At six, he's catastrophic. Skinned knees festering to degrees, bruised face due to running collisions, snotty nose sometimes bleeding, and no other language than Italian. A pocket-sized manic accident.

Antonio becomes our quisling. 'Why I shooda do thees?' he asks when we make the suggestion.

'Becos, if you do not, ve kill you!' Dieti growls, confident in our numbers, if not his size.

'Hokay,' Antonio says, seeing the light. He's an affable chap really. He's over a recent bout of chagrin at our mis-sung Italian songs.

Catapults, stones and abuse will be our assault weapons. Dieti suggests adding baboon-bangers to toss at the house and we agree. Can't have too much assault. Abuse, however, is something else. How can we abuse someone who doesn't understand the abuse? Here Antonio makes his invaluable contribution. Becky, Gretchen, Sophia, who, though Italian herself, says she doesn't know bad words, Dieti, Charlie Praze, the Cornish assistant manager's son, and Andrew and George Hunt, the sons of a newly arrived family from Yorkshire, and I, make up the group Antonio will train to swear in Italian. Gretchen has reverted back to tomboy since Fraser left, but I feel different when I'm close to her now. At thirteen her loose jeans and oversize shirt cannot hide the shape of her hips, or that her chest is no longer flat.

'What you thinking?' she asks me one day as I stare and try to visualise her shirt open. Her blue eyes are mocking, and tell me she knows. Teasing me. That makes me angry. I'm diverted by our quisling.

'Sheet,' Antonio says, 'ees *murder.*'

'Vot?' says Dieti.

'Sheet, sheet, sheet!' Antonio explodes, 'eet ees murder, *mur-der!*'

'Vy?' asks Dieti.

'He means the sheet een the toilet, and eet ees murder, spell *M-E-R-D-E!*' quiet Sophia explains, blushing as soon as it's said. Unguarded moment.

'Oh, *m-e-r-d-e*!' I say.

'Yes,' Antonio says.

'Vel, zat iss vun verd,' Dieti sighs.

'Pees ees *Pee-s-ci-a-re. . .* say eet,' Antonio continues patiently. '*P-I-S-C-I-A-R-E,* or say pisa *P-E-E-S-A-H.*'

'*Pisciare,*' we chorus, '*peesah.*'

'Bum ees *culo,* say *KU-LO.*'

'*Culo, ku-lo.*'

'Vagina ees va-geen-ah, spell *V-A-G-I-N-A,* say *Vah-geen-ah.*'

'*Vagina, va-geen-ah!*' I catch Gretchen grinning at me. She finds this funny. If only she knew. I'm falling in love. Find it difficult to breathe when she's near.

'Testicle ees *testicolo, Test-i-colo.*' Gretchen and Becky fall about laughing.

'*Testicolo, Testicolo!*'

'Jigi-jigi ees *Rapporti, Ra-port-ee,*' he says, making the universal finger-in-hole sign. I avoid looking at Gretchen.

'*Rapporti, Ra-port-ee!*'

'Preek ees *pene,* say *peh-neh.*' Becky and Gretchen snigger.

'*Pene,*' we echo, '*peh-neh.*'

'Stop luffing!' Dieti hisses at his sister.

The training goes on for an hour. Then we're ready for the Valaris. It's midday, and Mr Valari and his Peugeot will be at work. That leaves his wife and children alone. At our non-existent mercy.

I wonder what poor Mrs Valari, Anna and Gino think when we launch our assault.

First we hurl and catapult stones onto the tin roof to attract their attention. When they come to the window, they see their little wooden home is completely surrounded. Just like in those Western movies, when the Red Indians surround a homestead. The first to shout abuse is, paradoxically, our quisling Antonio. He assumes he has not only to teach us the invective, but demonstrate its use.

'*Merde,*' he yells, and another hail of stones clang on the roof, to a chorus of '*pisa, culo, vagina, pene, testicolo*' and '*rapporti!*' It's jumbled and punctuated with Sandy's frantic barking, but has the clarity of opera, where, though people sing, talk or stab themselves all at once, everything is heard. Dieti lights a bobejaan-banger, holds it in one hand as the fuse burns down, then hurls it just in time. It arcs towards the window, and explodes. It's like a thunderclap and echoes

221

from the hills. There's an awed silence. Dieti's a great bombardier, or bomber. No wonder the Germans gave us such trouble!

The faces at the window are horrified. The curtains close and they disappear. We shout more Italian abuse, shoot more stones, then withdraw. The first battle of the Valari war is over. It has been a resounding victory. A rout, or is it a *root*?

In a way our raid has a result. Soon, Gino Valari, like Boo Radley, will come out to play, but nobody will want to play with him. So he'll just go back in.

I go home, thinking not of the Valaris, but of Gretchen. That night I dream she says she loves me. That she meant it when she said she'd run away with me that ancient day in water-cave.

'No,' Mr Snel says when I ask if he'll pay for Lutoli to go to Arusha with Becky and me. I've waited for Sunday, when I know he'll drink a lot at the club. Drink makes people more amenable, they say.

'Why not?' I ask stubbornly.

'Because it's ridiculous,' he says, putting his glass of *Whitecap* down on the bar. The two men sitting next to him have fallen silent. No spine, I think. Worms!

'Why's it ridiculous?' I'm standing with my arms crossed now. I always do that when I'm about to abuse a *Mzungu*.

'Take him away,' Mr Snel says, looking over my head. He's high on his barstool. I notice Mum has come up behind me. He's talking to her. I'm dismissed. I draw a big breath. Before I can let rip with what I think of him, and all the *Wazungu* in Geita, I'm forcibly bundled out of the bar, onto the verandah. 'Don't you ever talk like that to Mr Snel!' Mum says when the door is safely closed. 'I'll lose my job, we'll have nowhere to live.'

Lutoli says he told me so. The *Wazungu* will never do something good for him. Why did I ever think they would? It's not in their nature. What about my nature? I ask. That's different, he says, I should know that.

The little black and white *shenzie* dog we captured a year ago, de-ticked, de-flead, bathed in bubble bath, fed on steak, and named 'Dickie', has never forgotten his experience. Life on the outside is tough. He's not able to leave where the miracle happened. We try persuading Mum to let us have him, but she won't budge. One dog's enough. For a while he just hangs around the garden, hoping for a change of fortune.

Before long, he draws Tembo's lonely attention. Ever since his puppy died, for which he unshakably believes me responsible, Tembo has pined for another friend.

Now the *shenzie*-convert, like him outcast, lonely and living on the fringe, draws ever closer to Tembo's cooking fire, gratefully gulping down thrown titbits, coming ever closer to the patient little man, until finally they embrace, and he moves permanently into Tembo's little room. From that day the two are inseparable. I think we've done a good turn.

I come home from fishing with Umali to find I missed Moses, but he's sold Mum a *batamzinga* wife for Gooloogooloo. She's less than half his size, about as big as *Mr Jogoo*, and white all over. A drab affair compared to the groom. Now Gooloogooloo shows his colours. Barely an hour after Mum puts her there, just as Umali and I tiredly reach home, there's a horrible hullabaloo from the *kuku* run. Hysterical cackling of *kukus,* pounding of Gooloogooloo feet on dry earth, thrashing of wings, sharp, triumphant cries, blood-curdling screams from the new bride.

Umali, Mum and I get there together. We're far too late. Gooloogooloo has jumped her all right, but not like *Mr Jogoo*. Tembo, watering the vegetable garden, has seen it all. Gooloogooloo stares at his new wife silently awhile. If he needs conjugal inspiration, *Mr Jogoo* provides it by jumping three *kukus* in fifteen minutes. Gooloogooloo watches and decides what to do.

'*Ari ruka,*' Tembo says, coming towards us. He jumped.

'*Wapi?*' Umali asks. Where?

'*Ju bibi yake,*' Tembo says. On his wife.

'*Arafu?*' And then? Tembo is infuriatingly slow.

'*Ari chinja yeye,*' he says simply, pulling his finger across his throat. He killed her by the throat.

The young turkey-lady lies crushed in the sunshine. Her neck has a gaping wound, and crimson blood spurts, to a diminishing range, from a torn artery. The only other movement is that of her smaller feathers wafting in the hot, dry breeze. Her body quivers briefly. She's dead. We've just registered this when Gooloogooloo leaps, in a single bound, mighty wings flapping, onto the henhouse roof. He steadies himself, fans his spectacular tail, throws back his head, opens his bloodied scimitar-beak, and screams defiance at the world. 'Gooloogooloogooloogooloo. . !' He screeches, then a follow-up 'gooloogooloo' for good measure. Look what I've done, lesser creatures, I've killed the bitch!'

Mr Jogoo, as far from the murder-scene as he can get, tries to make himself small, finds fascination on the ground, scratches at it with rare interest. How the mighty are humbled!

'*Haipende wanawake,*' Umali says. He doesn't like women. Just then Amina emerges from the servant's quarters.

'*Yeye mbaya,*' she says, clucking. He's bad. 'He likes to bite me too.'

Murderous though he obviously is, I find something alluring about this huge and arrogant bird. There's a meeting of souls. I don't give a bugger for rules, and nor, evidently, does he.

'Show me,' I say. Amina grins one-toothedly.

'*Leta kikapu,*' she tells Umali. Bring a basket. A *kikapu* is a large woven grass basket. The *watu* use them for shopping. We keep two in the kitchen. Umali goes, brings one. She places it round her bum and ties the handle-bits together in front with string. Then she opens the gate and steps into the *kuku* run. She's gone just four paces towards the dead turkey-lady, when Gooloogooloo, seeing space behind her, leaps from the henhouse roof and dashes at her. He pecks the *kikapu* viciously, and, though unhurt, Amina screams.

'*Shetani!*' she yells, trying to hit him with her hand. Devil! He ducks his head like a boxer, pecks at the *kikapu* like a left jab.

'*Wanaume?*' I ask Umali. I'm intrigued. Men?

'*Ana penda,*' Umali says, grinning evilly. He likes them.

'*Kweli?*' True?

'*Kweli!*' True!

'Should I try?'

'Try, Jimu, try.'

Amina runs from the *kuku* run, Gooloogooloo pecking at her *kikapu* till she slams the iron gate on him. I wait a second, then open the gate and enter. Gooloogooloo stops in his stride and stares. There's something very like a bull-fight here. Will he start pawing the ground? There's a vicious glint in his dark eyes. Naked terror seizes me. What am I doing in here with this sadistic murderer? I don't even have a *kikapu*. Then, before I can turn and run, Gooloogooloo puts his be-bobbled head on one side, makes a gentle clucking sound with his tongue, and comes towards me. I'm frozen with fright. I can't believe what's happening.

When he's very close, he puts his forehead against my knee and closes his eyes. There's a vibration running through him. Soothing. Almost like a cat's purring. This massive bird loves me. What can I do? I put my hand out carefully. He stays as he is. To applause from Umali and Tembo, I stroke his neck. It's the beginning of my love affair with a psychopathic misogynist.

It's the talk of Geita that we have a woman-hating turkey. Before long, Gooloogooloo's entertaining the populace with his own special cabaret. When they come, expat wives and daughters, to verify the rumour themselves, though they don't really believe it, they're cautious nevertheless. They ask Becky and I to demonstrate. Into the *kuku* run I go, without fear or *kikapu*. Up strolls Gooloogoolooo, long neck stretched out for me to stroke, eyes misty with love. He makes that clucking, purring sound deep in his throat. Out I go.

Becky's debut. In she goes, *kikapu* tied round bum. Gooloogooloo's electrified. A female! Out fan the feathers in his massive tail, out bulge his eyes. He gallops, dust and small stones flying, and furiously assaults her *kikapu*-protected bum. Nobody can doubt his hatred, nor the damage he will inflict on unprotected female buttocks.

By now the females in the audience have to choose: to go in with or without the *kikapu*. None chose without, and all are grateful. He never attacks men, though he doesn't let them stroke his neck like me.

It takes a long time to think of experimenting with Sandy. She's female. Will he attack her, or will she, like the hens, be exempt from his wrath? Sandy isn't keen to find out, and I have to shove her into the run and slam the gate. Gooloogooloo doesn't hesitate. His feathers fan, he paws the ground like a bull, and begins his death-run. I only just let poor, quaking, whimpering Sandy out millimetres from his rapier-sharp, reaching beak. Tembo doesn't like the idea of testing with Dickie. I'm trying to kill his dog again.

I explain Gooloogooloo never attacks males and Tembo relents. Dickie goes in, walks around nonchalantly, nothing happens. Gooloogooloo doesn't even unfurl his tail feathers. He hates all females, except for *kukus*! Snow-White's particularly close. She was the oldest *kuku* here when he came. He's bonded with her. A fifth of his size, she's his adopted mother, and her sisters are his aunts! As we watch, she ambles stiffly up to him, and there's affection in both *Kuku* and turkey eyes. How can this be? Of all females, only *kukus* are exempt from murderous hate?

Umali laughs. When Gooloogooloo came to us he was very young, he says. The *kukus* were kind. Good sisters and mothers. Snow-White especially. He's never forgotten. It's the only explanation. But why the hatred for all other females? His mother abused him, Umali says. What else?

At three years, Sandy has grown into a remarkable little dog. She's almost as low to the ground, and as long, as her *Daschund* ancestors, but her other, chaotically assorted, genes have given her a most unusual appearance. The 'seams' running up her legs and down the middle of her belly are, to Becky and I, proof that, like a teddy-bear, she was stitched together in a factory. She has the nondescript, yet loveable, brown face and stubby black snout of a hyena, which is why Umali teases us by referring to her as *fisi ndogo,* or little hyena. Like that namesake, she is, for her size, extraordinarily strong. Mum says she lifts weights when we aren't looking, because her seamed legs bulge with muscle.

Sandy adores Becky and me. She's never happy unless she's with us. Easy when we're together. When we aren't she has problems. Which *one* should she be with? She can't make up her mind. At night when we go to bed, she splits her time in each room. It becomes part of our soundscape to hear her nails click the wooden floor as she trudges the corridor between us. Arriving in my room, she jumps on my bed, nuzzles me briefly, then lies down beside me. She closes her eyes, and falls asleep instantly. Ten, fifteen minutes later, she opens her eyes, stares at me awhile, then jumps off the bed and clicks her way back to Becky. It goes on all night. It takes a girl's ingenuity to harness this obvious resource.

We have, between us, a sizeable collection of *Illustrated Classics* and other comics, including *Topper*, *Beano* and *War* series. There's no television in Tanganyika. In Geita, too, owing to its remoteness, and, it's said, radio-wave-bending effects of magnetic iron in the ground, there's no radio reception, apart from Radio Congo. This broadcasts a continuum of Swahili love songs or patriotic ditties, interspersed with official announcements.

Leyo ko Stanleyville, Congo, selekali wari sema. . . Today in Stanleyville the police said. . . Who cares what they said? We know the words of all the songs. *Katerina, Katerina, Katerina, mpenzi wangu. . .* Catherine, Catherine, Catherine, my girlfriend. . . *Mwalimu Julius Nyerere ari sema jano ko Dar es Salaam, eti. . .* Teacher Julis Nyerere, soon to be president of an independent Tanganyika, said yesterday in Dar es Salaam that. . . Music. Same tunes over and over. *Malaika, ninakupenda Malaika. . .* Malaika, I love you, Malaika. Joyous guitar and *marimba*, played with energy. Makes you want to dance. In Kenya the Kenya African Democratic Union, or *KADU*, is demanding the unconditional release of its president, Jomo Kenyatta, from permanent internal exile and restriction, after his years of imprisonment by the Imperial British. More music. *Kondukitor, Kondukitor, nyipe tiketi. . .* Conductor, Conductor, give me a ticket. . .

Apart from running wild, there isn't much to do. That's why we get up to so many nefarious things. At night there's Radio Congo, or comics. We read and re-read them constantly. When we get fed up with ours, we swap. Tiresome, dragging ourselves from room to room. That's where Becky gets her brainwave.

'You got *The Count of Monte Cristo*?' I yell from my room one evening.

'Yeah,' she shouts back.

'Can I have it?'

'Okay,' she yells. There's a pause. 'Where's Sandy?' At the sound of her name, Sandy's ears twitch. She's lying on the foot of my bed, watching me.

'Here,' I shout.

'Sandy, Sandy, Sandy,' she calls. Sandy leaps from my bed and scurries to Becky's room. Click click click on the floor. Half a minute passes.

'Call her,' Becky shouts.

'Sandy,' I call. Click click click click. She's beside me. Grinning. She always looks like she's grinning. Rolled up and tucked into her collar is *The Count of Monte Cristo*. Eureka! This is much more exciting than the comic. Carrier pigeon, nothing, here's a *carrier dog!* The radio crackles. There's trouble in the copper-rich Congo province of Katanga. Moise Tshombe is stirring up nationalism. He's only after the copper which makes Kinshasa rich. It's rumoured he's going to secede Katanga from the newly-independent, already bloodstained, Congo. Somebody calling himself *President* Mobutu in Kinshasa has arrested the old President, Patrice Lumumba. He won't stand for Tshombe breaking up the country. Forces are mobilising. Mercenaries are being recruited now in Europe and South Africa. Music break. Malaika. *Nasindwana nakupenda, we, nineku owa Malaika.* I was beaten in love for you Malaika, or I'd have married you. Malaika means angel. Also a name for a girl. I switch the radio off.

'You want something?' I shout.

'*From the Earth to the Moon*,' Becky yells back. I leaf through the pile on my table. Find it, roll it up, shove it through Sandy's collar.

'Call her.'

'Sandy, Sandy. . .' Sandy dashes down the corridor. Clickety click click. 'Got it,' Becky laughs. '*You* want something?'

'Anything.'

'Call her.'

'Sandy. . .' Click click click. She's brought me a *Beano*. I roll up *From the Earth to the Moon*, and as I reach to put it through her collar, she takes it from me with her mouth. I'm dumbstruck as she click-

clicks back down the corridor to Becky. We've invented *Umbwa,* or dog mail. The possibilities are endless. From now on we'll never have to play messenger ourselves.

There's a knock on the front door. I get up wearily and go to see who it is. Oh God, it's Boo Radley! I mean Gino Valari. He's come out. Thin legs like yellow sticks protruding from oversized shorts, pinched face, pale like milk, narrowed eyes blinking in the fierce sunlight.

'Hello,' I say. Nothing. More blinking. He looks exactly like his late grandfather, Mr Valari (senior), or, at least, his *mzoga* or corpse. '*Jambo,*' I say. Perhaps Swahili's better. Still nothing. I smile. He doesn't. Has he come to avenge his family for our attack? Doesn't look like it. He hasn't got a stick.

'I wanna. . . *play!*' he stammers in a low voice.

'Well,' I say, stuck for what to say, 'we're not playing right now.'

'Okay,' he says, obviously relieved. I realise coming here isn't his idea. It's his mother and sister. They've sent him to try and make peace with their attackers. I feel overwhelmed with remorse and shame.

'Would you like some sweets?' I ask, remembering I've just come back from Barrat Stores, and I have a whole roll of Rowntree's fruit gums.

'Yessa pleeza!' There's actually a little smile on his wan face. Everyone loves sweets, even Gino Valari. I reach in my pocket for the gums. I've half a mind to break the roll in half, but I resist, and give him the whole roll. His eyes go wide, and his smile takes over his face. I don't think his parents *ever* buy him sweets. '*Gratsia!*' he says, pocketing the sweets and walking away. It's a strange feeling, pity for your victim, guilt, all that. . ! *And* I never thought I'd give all my sweets away to an enemy. Maybe he's trying to be a friend. What would I call that? A *frenemy.* An *Italo-frenemy.*

Twenty-three

The *fisi* or hyena's Latin name is *Crocuta crocuta*. They superficially resemble dogs, but they're more closely related to cats and mongooses. Adults weigh from 80 to 190 pounds. They are powerfully built, with rough, mottled coats and steeply sloping backs caused by an apparent imbalance between their massive forelegs and short rear quarters. This endows them with a strange, menacing, almost comical, loping gait. Their large ears are erect and constantly scanning, and their muzzles broad and dark. The combination of razor-sharp teeth and the most crushingly powerful jaws in Africa, enable hyenas to sever a deer's limb with a single bite, or break open bones and access the marrow with ease. They are not only scavengers, but fierce hunters who kill and devour wildebeest, zebra, buffalo and other large and small animals. They live and hunt in large groups called clans. The relationship of the hyena with man is very old. In ancient Egypt hyenas were even domesticated and bred for food.

There was always reverse predation of man by wild hyenas, which accounts, at least in part, for the rich African folklore which links this creature with the supernatural and witchcraft. The insane sounding 'giggling' or laughter hyenas make when excited, which they also use to alert other members of their clan of a food source, is enough to send shivers down the spine of any superstitious *mutu*. It's a horrible, secret language of the night, in which they celebrate murder most diabolical. In Sukuma folklore, *fisis* are up to their thick-set necks in the occult.

'If the *mchawi*, sorcerer or witch, wants to kill you,' Amina says on many frightening occasions round the fire, 'he can change into a *fisi*, and tear you to pieces. . . in the morning they find your pitiful remains, that which he has not devoured, on the ground, and there are *fisi* footprints, even droppings, but the *fisi* himself will be long gone, having changed back into the witch-doctor. Sometimes people have followed the *fisi's* tracks all the way to the *mchawi's* hut, where they suddenly end. The evil one has taken pieces of his victim into his hut, and they are still there, but no sign of the *fisi* is seen. This is why you must behave!' I tremble. Will I one day find human parts outside Mlozi's tiny hut? That would be awful! Would Mlozi be inside? One thing's for sure, I'm not going anywhere near his rock at night!

The stories aren't entirely made up. They're based on real beliefs of a deeply superstitious and fearful people. I see Amina and Umali shudder, their eyes go wide, at the sound of the insane cackle of nocturnal hunting *fisis*. That terrifying sound, and the stories about witchcraft and being eaten, is enough to make Becky and me tremble with fright at the mere mention of this dreaded spectre. Our fear is a tool of discipline to Amina, because she only has to mention *fisi* and we obey.

The big bad wolf, or monster, of European fairy-tales may strike fear into children, but the *watu* of Geita fear a reality, not a fairy-tale. Umali and Amina, like most *watu*, have their own *shamba,* or farm, 'in the bush', as the *Wazungu* say. There live elderly relatives, tending a patch of maize, a couple of goats, a flock of scrawny chickens. It's ten miles distant as the *kunguru*-bird flies, but accessed only by a tortuous footpath, not a straight crow-path. When, once a month, Umali and Amina go home, they never lack for company.

So pervasive is *fisi*-fear, that nobody ever walks to their *shamba* after nightfall, unless accompanied by several others, and everyone in the party is armed with a *rungu,* knob-ended fighting stick, or a home-made spear. The *shamba*-goers, up to a dozen, assemble at day's end, usually in the garden of our house, because Umali, being who he is, is a natural organiser. The group talk loudly, like excited children, to show they aren't really afraid of the *fisi* at all. If there's a full moon, their path is lit, and we watch them until they disappear into the bush.

On darker nights, at least one person in the party illuminates the way with a torch, or, if there's an underground mine-worker, he walks in front, carbide-helmet-torch on, yellow finger of light weakly probing the path. They are swallowed by the darkness.

Somewhere a *fisi* giggles. Somewhere else another replies. There's silence. Then the crickets start their din, and the invisible frogs go '*reddit, reddit, reddit.* . .' Becky says frogs are very clever, 'cos they've 'red-a-lot'. It's spooky here in Geita at night, but I love it dearly. The fear outside makes being safe in the house, with electric lights, the cosiest, best feeling in the world.

When they return from their *shamba* odysseys, Amina and Umali have tales to tell, always starring the *fisi*. It's difficult to separate what's genuine, made-up, or imagined in the darkness of the meandering bush footpath, with spine chilling *fisi*-cackles hastening the travellers on their way. All three are probably true.

'Last night we saw a *fisi* who wore the crocodile-tooth necklace of a *mchawi*'. Wide-eyed look of horror. 'This *fisi* sends a message that, unless you behave, he will come for you.'

Mchawi, sorcerer, or witch! Lots of *watu* really think Mlozi's one. So do I. Does he go out at night as a *fisi*? One of Lutoli's friends says he saw a big fisi going into Mlozi's hut late one night. Terrifying. It sends tingling feelings up and down my spine. But If he *really* is a sorcerer, perhaps he can cast a spell for me. He didn't last time, but maybe persistence is needed. Who knows how a *mchawi* thinks? I won't see him in *fisi*-state, I hope, shuddering at the thought. Sunlight destroys *fisi-mchawis*, they say, which is why they only hunt by night. I'll go in the day. Put on a brave face. There must be something he wants. I'll get it. Then, maybe, I won't have to go back to school. I decide I'll talk to Mlozi when the courage is with me.

It's May Day 1960. A Sunday. There's a big celebration at the club. All the children are dressed for the occasion. They've put up a Maypole for us to run round, holding bits of coloured ribbon. Before we do that, there's another ritual. The May-Queen. Becky's been chosen. I don't know why. I think she's ugly, but Mum says I shouldn't say so. Somebody's conspicuously not joining the children. It's Gretchen. She's over twelve, and thinks she's one of the adults. She's standing with the ladies, drinking her Pepsi from a glass. It's even got ice in it. She's wearing a dazzling white dress. Her mum made it specially. Her blonde hair has been permed. That's why, Becky says, it's not hanging all over. She's got lipstick on. Red. She looks like a lady! I hear her talking to Mrs Snel.

'Yes,' she says, sounding oh-so-mature. Then she laughs. It's like crystal glass breaking. I've never thought of a girl's voice being like crystal glass breaking. I'm standing three yards behind her, wishing I was in the group. But I'm just a kid of nine, whereas she's now a lady. As I watch, her slender hand reaches round, and her fingers furiously scratch her bum. That's *my* Gretchen, I think. Can't leave an itchy bum, no matter what. You're still one of us! One day, you're going to be mine. All *mine!* One day I'll marry you, and we'll be so happy! It's nauseating to realise I'm in love. But worse not to think about her.

Gretchen can only act the lady *sometimes*. At heart she hasn't changed. It's a conflict in her. How to play with her friends but be a lady. Sometimes she gives up, reverts to form.

Doctors and nurses. A game with sinister motives. About seeing each other's privates, but pretending there's another *raison d'être*. A child's version of big people's 'coffee' invitation after a party. Medical intervention is no more on the agenda in one than coffee in the other.

We play the game a lot, from when I'm five or younger, because I can't recall the first time. Indeed, supporting this notion is the undoubted fact that the suggestion to play the game never shocks or surprises us. It's as normal to suggest it as hide and seek. It's something we're used to. It's almost humdrum.

There's no point trying to detail more than one particular game of doctors and nurses, because there's so many. One of the last stands out particularly.

I'm nearly ten and the gang are in Mum's bedroom, on the bed and floor, feeling bored. There's Becky, twelve, Gretchen, thirteen, Dieter, ten, Antonio Barelli, ten and his baby brother, Stefano, six. Including me that's seven of us. Gretchen's more-or-less back to her old self today. I don't know who suggests we play doctors and nurses, but suspect it's Gretchen. She looks like she's reverted to her former rough and ready appearance and ways since Fraser went back to the navy, and she played the lady at the May-Day party. Even so, there's something more adult about her than the rest of us. It isn't just her breasts. Today she's got on a loose denim shirt over her swimming costume, so they're not obvious now. Everyone agrees it's a good idea. With Gretchen playing, I think it's a *very* good idea. I can't even dare to think what I might see.

There's only one 'doctor' in a game, and everyone else is patient or nurse. There can only be one nurse, so, barring doctor and nurse, five of us will be patients.

It's a blistering hot day and we've been down to the pool at the club, and swum for hours in the tepid water. None of us has changed back into our clothes, so everyone's in a costume. Only Gretchen's wearing a shirt. It's an old one of her dad's. We've walked like that to Barratt stores to buy sweets. Sweets are an important component of the game of doctors and nurses. Probably having then spawned the idea.

Gretchen announces she's been a patient too many times, so she's doctor today. I vaguely recall being the doctor who examined her last year, or was it the year before? She cheated. Said, 'One-Two-Three, Quick-Look,' and whatever she flashed was gone before I could focus.

I'd like a longer look, but can't say so. I give in. Maybe we'll play a second round, and I'll be doctor again!

Stefano's excited. He's only six, and it's his first game. He wants to be first patient. Becky announces she's today's nurse. She doesn't like being examined, or is it that being examined by another girl is meaningless? I'm not sure.

Doctor Gretchen and nurse Becky go into the consulting room, which is the bathroom off Mum's bedroom. Stefano's jumping up and down by the closed door, impatient to go in and be the patient.

'Next!' comes the nurse's stern command from within. The door opens, and I briefly see doctor Gretchen sitting on the toilet, Becky's standing beside her. Stefano enters and the door closes. There's a hush in the bedroom. Everyone's straining to hear what's happening.

'Now, what's wrong with you?' we hear Gretchen ask Stefano sweetly.

'Nuffink. . .' we hear Stefano whisper, overawed. He hasn't expected this.

'There *must* be something!' Becky says.

'Eet eesa my feenger!' we hear Stefano propose.

'Well, take off your costume,' we hear Gretchen order.

'My. . ?' Stefano says in a strangled voice.

'Pants,' Gretchen finishes for him.

'Off,' orders Becky.

'Now!' says Gretchen. There's a long silence.

'Take two of these,' we hear Gretchen say. The door opens, and out walks Stefano, naked, carrying his bathing shorts in one hand and two Smarties in the other. He looks bewildered.

'Next!' Becky bellows through the door. Nobody moves. The consultations are frightening today.

'Jim, *you* come in,' Becky shouts, 'it's your turn.' What the hell, I think, why not? Do as must do! Maybe it'll set them an example for later.

'And what's the problem with you today?' Gretchen smiles sweetly from the toilet seat. Her denim shirt's unbuttoned from the midriff up, and I can see her costume. It's a white one, contrasting strongly with her suntan. This is no accident. She was buttoned up when she went in.

'It's me dick!' I sigh, knowing it'll come to that anyway.

'Take off your costume,' Gretchen says. I knew she was going to. I take them down. She has Becky's ruler in her hand. What kind of medical instrument is *that?* She prods my willy with it, and says, 'that doesn't look good at all!' I stand there, waiting for the prescription. 'Take two of these,' Gretchen says, handing me two Smarties.

233

The others go in and show their wares. All get the same medicine. Then the girls announce the game's over. There will be no second round. I'm crushed. They're laughing to kill themselves. We've been fooled again!

Donald Coutts, the bachelor Scotsman, competes with Eugen Blüger's timber business, but unlike Eugen, who has ten lorries, he has only three, and they're older and smaller. He doesn't need much. A single man with frugal tastes, he has no one to support. How much does it cost to stay sozzled on *Johnny Walker Black Label*? He earns enough.

At the club, Donald becomes expansive, and ever more Scottish, when he's had a few '*wee drams*'. He's heard from one of his *tunny-boys* that I want a holiday job. The *watu* always know everything I'm thinking.

'Jimmeh,' he says, 'whad ye like ta wurk fur mae?'

'Yes please,' I say. I'm ten, and it's time I earned some money.

'D'ya know what you have to do, as *tunny-boy, loon*?' I thought that meant lunatic, but I'm reassured it's 'heeland' for lad. Of course I know what I have to do. There are six *tunny-boys* on the back of a lorry. They get the name because they lift *tuns* and *tuns* of wood.

'Load wood,' I say.

'Reeght then, I'll pay ye the saime as the uthers. That's two shilling a day. Start tomorrow. Thae lorry leaves at seven.' He turns back to his drinking friends. I'm dismissed. But I've got a job!

Mum is worried. I'm far too small. The *tunny-boys* are young men, not little boys! Don't wreck my career, I tell her. Dad would have wanted me to earn for the family, and I'm going to do it. Becky says I won't last the day. Dieti says I should have asked his dad, and I can't trust Donald Coutts. He doesn't like *Scotch* people. Who can like someone who drinks themselves?

The morning breaks. The sun's shining through where I left the curtains parted last night. Couldn't risk not waking in time. I'm up, dressed in old clothes, and ready to go when the old Bedford lorry creaks into our drive. The driver and young men on the back all know me. '*Kuja*, Jimu,' one shouts. Come, Jimu. I'm helped up onto the back. It's a tipper, has a sloping floor.

The gears grate, and we trundle down the hill, turn left by the club, and rumble along Bottom Road past *kifo nyumba*, the little church and African hospital. Half a mile and we turn off onto an overgrown bush path, created not by bulldozer or road-machine, but by trucks forcing their way between trees. The lorry bucks and undulates over scrubby ground, and we *tunny-boys* bend and duck as branches sweep inches above our heads. Sometimes we're too late, get hit and scratched. The boys are teenagers, and, despite ragged clothes, are a happy lot. We talk and joke in Swahili.

'You want money?' one asks me, smiling.

'*Ndio,*' I nod.

'To help your mother?' asks another.

'Of course.' They all laugh.

'*Jimu's* small, but he's a *real* man!' says the first. I'm happy with that. I like my new workmates.

The lorry bundles through low-hanging bush. Then we emerge onto a man-made waste-ground. This is where they have been harvesting trees for years, and they've created a clearing several miles wide. Only short dead stumps interrupt the barren landscape, and even small bushes don't seem to be succeeding here.

'Everything's in the trees,' says Obani, the friendliest tunny-boy. 'Everything here is of the trees. When they take them, they kill everything.' It certainly does look that way. The cleared ground is bone-dry, and dust rises up from the tyres to choke us. Man making desert out of paradise. We drive over the uneven ground and park next to the edge where the forest still stands, tall trees cowering in anticipation of their fate. The bush is eerily quiet. Not even a *njiwa*-bird makes its call. It's as if they know what's coming.

The tunny-boys and I decamp. There are three two-handed saws. Six men get sawing down three tall maninga trees. They've got incredible strength and energy. I'm left sitting on a stump, watching. The driver has instructions I'm not to touch the saws. There are some left-over logs lying about, and he says I can load those. The first one's three foot long, and a foot in diameter. I'm shocked by its weight. Several tunny boys stop sawing to watch me, and laugh at how I struggle. It's almost impossible to lift. I strain, make a huge effort, and heft it up to my belly, where I cradle it in both arms. It's so heavy I can feel the rough bark scratching me through my cotton shirt. I struggle towards the lorry.

The driver helpfully engages the tipping mechanism and brings the back down to my height. I'm being watched by seven pairs of eyes. I can't drop it. I'm a man, I have to prove it! I get to the lorry, brace my log against it, then heave up with all my might. It moves only slowly, and I feel it tearing the skin on my stomach. It reaches the lip and I make a final effort. It rolls down and clangs against the steel floor of the tipper. The *tunny-boys* and driver applaud. I'm breathless, sweating, and my stomach is burning like fire. I look down. My shirt is torn to rags, and there's a big bloodstain on it.

Obani and the driver are concerned. '*Hi ni ngumu,*' says Obani. This is hard. 'Sit a little, then take logs small-small!' I sit gratefully on the stump of what was once a giant tree. The sawing continues. The sun is like a furnace-blast. I know furnaces, because I stood near the smelter on Top Road once and they opened it. I thought I was cooked through! Now the sun's burning my neck. That, and the stinging on my stomach, and I decide I don't like this job. I look gingerly inside my ragged, bloody shirt front. The scratches are several, long and deep, and burn like petrol.

I force myself to my feet and look for smaller logs. Even two-foot ones are heavy, though more manageable. By the time the first tree cracks and groans, begins to fall, then crashes to earth with a heavy impact, I've loaded twenty, and they look like a fair pile in the lorry. A tunny-boy pulls on a whipcord to start a petrol-powered saw. It's one they leave out here, covered with canvas. It's on big wheel-barrow type wheels, and has a circular toothed blade two foot wide. They push it up against the tree trunks. It cuts through them with a grating, shrieking noise, and hurls wet sawdust and wood fragments in all directions.

The three trees are cut down and sawed into logs. The lorry's fully loaded. I've been carrying more small logs. We've been here five hours. It's after one pm, I can tell by the sun, which is pulsating white heat onto my burning face and neck. It's time to go. We clamber onto the timber pile and find a seat in any low point. This trip will be more precarious than before. We can't duck for cover. The driver knows, and goes very slowly. Even so, we're almost swept off by some low-hanging branches. After a long time we reach Bottom Road and turn left towards the mine. I'm beginning to feel sick and I've got a pounding headache. It's those sword-fighters in my head again!

By the time we reach the weigh-bridge, I'm no longer able to concentrate. Obani's really worried about me. '*Pole Jimu,*' he says. Take it easy *Jimu*. 'You'll be home soon.' I faint, and fall against his shoulder.

To Mum it's cerebral malaria again and she and Umali put me to bed, and dab my forehead with cool damp cloths. Amina goes for Dr Weiss. 'Sunstroke,' he says, looking at my tomato-red face. 'He vill niffer learn, und vot a mozza you are!' It takes me days to recover. I never work as tunny-boy again. Worse, I'm never paid for my day's work! I should have heeded Dieti. Whisky-swilling Donald Coutts can't be trusted, and I'm not built for hard labour in the tropical sun.

Twenty-four

In 1960 the talk is of *uhuru,* freedom, for Tanganyika Territory. The British government is grooming Africans to take over from the colonial administration. *Mwalimu*, Teacher, Julius Nyerere is leader of the Tanganyika African National Union, or *TANU*, and is tipped to be president. In Geita, because of its remoteness, plus the absence of television or radio reception, news comes late, and in incomplete or garbled form. The most reliable information comes from English newspapers posted by sea and rail, two months old, and not much concerned with affairs in this insignificant corner of empire. Tanganyika never makes front page, and articles about its future are limited to short, telegrammatic, columns on pages three or four.

The bush telegraph is more effective. Just as the call of '*nyoka*', snake, lights a bush-fire, magically assembling *watu* to chop it to pieces, the call of '*uhuru*' from Dar-es-Salaam reaches across salient, plain, mountain, forest and lake, to every corner, every village, every hut and every person. Groups of *totos*, or children, from toddlers who can barely walk, to young adults, brandishing paper flags with green, yellow and black stripes, begin to assemble at the workplaces and homes of foreigners, there to dance and sing over and over a new song.

'*Oh-Oh-TANU, wa jenga nchi!*' goes the opening line. Oh-Oh-TANU, of nation building!'

'*TANU,*' a solo voice sings.

'*Wa jenga nchi!*' chorus the others. Of nation building.

'*TANU.*'

'*Wa jenga nchi!*' When the singing and dancing ends, it becomes customary for the group's leader to abuse and threaten the foreign *Wazungu*, or, at different places, *Wahindi*, Indians, or *Wachina*, Chinese.

'This our country, you go from here! Go back home! We will seize your house!' Not our house, I muse, the *mine's!*

One day Lutoli is with a group of twenty dancing, singing *totos* outside our house. I don't blame him. I know he wants *uhuru*. The song is the same. TANU of nation building. Mum is at work. Umali, Becky and I sit on the front steps to watch the performance. When the song and dance end, after many repetitions of the chorus, a *toto* of twelve steps forward to demand we leave the country.

'*Apana!*' Lutoli exclaims at last. No! 'This is *Jimu*, our friend of long time. Not like the other *Wazungu!*' Poor Lutoli. I know him well. He's a patriot, and wants Tanganyika to be free, like he wanted for our country *Kichoncho*. He can't let these demonstrations go on without him. Then he encounters this – the nearest thing he's got to a brother, me, bearing the brunt.

'*Ni kweli,* it's true,' the lad who has begun to harass us says. Lutoli visibly relaxes. Everyone knows *Jimu*. When they're gone, Umali turns to me with a worried expression.

'What will your mother do after *uhuru*?' he asks.

'*Sijui,*' I say. I don't know. 'I think we'll stay.'

'God will help!' he says, '*Mungu ata saidia!*' Will he, I wonder. I've had an on-off relationship with God!

'*Allah hafiz,*' I add out of respect for Islam. God willing. Do they have a different God?

In December 1960 Tanganyika is plunging headlong towards *uhuru* within a year. The British government in Whitehall can't wait to sever their links with this unprofitable colony. *Mwalimu* Julius Nyerere is touring every region to make speeches to local branches of TANU, the Tanganyika African National Union. His title is based on him being a teacher before he went into politics. He flies with a small delegation to the mine airfield in Geita in a *de Havilland Dragon Rapide* biplane of *Caspair* Air Charter Services.

Mr Snel has arranged a welcoming committee. The mine works have closed early, and nearly all the Europeans on the mine are lined up next to the dry grass runway as the beautiful old-fashioned-looking, high-nosed, double-winged, twin-engined aeroplane taxis to a very noisy halt in a cloud of dust and bits of flying grass stubble, just yards from us. It looks like an antique from the First World War. On the side in bold red letters are the words:

CASPAIR CHARTERS – DAR ES SALAAM

Mr Snel and a smartly dressed Adrian Venter escort the entourage of five from the plane. The *Wazungu* are dressed in shorts and shirts. The visitors are wearing bright tribal gowns and skins. We've had a lecture about being polite to important guests, even though they're black. I find that very rich, coming from people who usually talk about animals better than black people.

Mwalimu Nyerere is a dapper man, only six inches taller than me at nine. He's got grey hair and a friendly manner. He walks along the line of assembled *Wazungu*, fly whisk in hand, and shakes hands with each man, woman and child. He's got a very broad smile and even, shiny white teeth. Then he gets into a police Land Rover which has come to fetch him from the boma, and they roar off in another cloud of dust. Our moment of excitement is over. Everyone removes to the club.

There's a nine hole golf course beside the club. The first tee-off is next to the bar, and the ninth hole is just across the way. Golfers start and end their game next to the venue of their real interest – drinking. Almost all the *Wazungu* men, and several of the women, take up golf. This is in no small part because everyone knows promotions, favours, perks and permissions to go on leave are agreed with John Snel, the mine manager, on the golf course, or in the bar, known as the tenth, or the nineteenth, hole, depending if you go round once or twice.

Geita mine is up on the hillside along Top Road. From there the three parallel connecting roads run down. The club's on Bottom road, where the flat land begins. The golf course is there. Because the area is semi-arid and very hot, it's not possible to cultivate grass which can be mown and rolled to make the surface of a green. The solution is 'browns'. Stones are sieved from the sand, and raked to make a smooth surface. After each game a *bibi,* or 'wife', drags a log around on two ropes to remove shoe-prints and ball-tracks.

The fairways are created by removing trees and cutting the wild grass with a tractor-drawn mower. On the edges of the fairway the bush remains as it has ever been, and continues for many miles in all directions. The bush next to the golf course is dense with trees and thornbushes, and inhabited by every kind of beast, bird and insect. As the sun goes down in the evenings, golf-stragglers are subjected to a cacophony of wild African sounds, including the screech of crickets, the distant giggle of hyenas, the grunt of wild pig, the croaking of frogs from invisible waterholes, and, just occasionally, the bone-jarring roar of a lion. There is tangible relief on their faces when the players finally reach the bar.

The caddies are African boys aged eight to eighteen. I know them all by name, and some are friends from before I can walk. They're paid

239

a pittance to caddy, but take revenge by failing to find balls in the rough, and 'discovering' them later. These they sell back to the club. Some balls change hands more often than they're hit by a club.

The caddies also play golf. They have no clubs, but make their own in a variety of ways. One common design is to take a piece of steel concrete reinforcing and make a bend where it hits the ball. To give it weight a stone is bound on with string, then sealed with sticky sap from the blue gum tree. The handle is a wrapping of rag. It's amazing how these urchins, using their home-made clubs, are able to hit a ball. In 1961, when I'm ten, Mr Snel decides, for fun, to invite the caddies to choose a team to play against him and four of his *Wazungu*.

The caddies wipe the floor with them. Embarrassment. Grown white men, posh equipment and clothing, thoroughly beaten by ragged, illiterate child-caddies with homemade clubs. The caddy who beat Mr Snel is Lutoli's cousin. He's twelve. The invitation is never repeated. 'Tell your little black friends that's the last time they play!' says a scowling Mr Snel to me. I'm with four white kids, but he singles me out. He wasn't this way about black people when *Mwalimu* Nyerere came to visit. The caddies say his attitude just proves he's *blurryfucken*.

With my *rafikis*, friends, I'm a *mutu*, just like them. With the *Wazungu*, I'm a *Mzungu* kid. Different things are expected of me. I can't be half-and-half. I'm complete in each role. My mind, loyalties, ways and speech are identical to my *rafikis*, then I have to snap into *Mzungu*-role with my white friends. The roles have to be separate. There can be no *enosis*, or union, no blending, because there *is* no middle ground. Except when very young, and even then in a limited way, African and white children don't play together here. African children don't speak English. White children don't speak anything beyond kitchen-Swahili.

I am unable to use one set of thought and language in the other setting. I'm constantly at risk of 'too much blackness' or 'too much whiteness', depending who I'm with. It won't do to moderate, because that'll mean being less adroit in either. The trouble is I also share both groups' ideas and prejudices. As a Swahili, I despise *Wazungu*. If I don't, I'm a sellout. As a *Mzungu* I despise *watu*. If I don't, I'm a 'savage'.

I'm becoming not just a hypocrite, but the very embodiment of the idea. Both my peer groups are constantly amazed at what a chameleon or *kinyonga* I am. 'I don't know how you do it!' Lutoli says. 'One second, ours, next second theirs!' – '*Jimu*,' he says another day, 'I think you're a black person in the skin of a white!' Multiple personality, here I come!

The *Wazungu* kids play golf, to varying degrees. There aren't so many choices of things to do, so it helps relieve boredom. On the golf course too, we discover, during the day when the big people are at work, is a sense of tranquillity and freedom which is entrancing. We don't have to play golf. We can play tab, or hide and seek, which involves skulking in bushes next to the fairways, or else just walk and talk, feeling in that wide place we are the only people on the planet.

One day I'm walking with Lutoli, George Hunt and Sandy on the freeway of the third hole. George's nine, like me. His parents have come out to Geita with him and his older brother Percy a year ago. From York. He's a rogue, always up to mischief. Unlike me, he has a fierce father to protect him. It's always easier to blame Jimmy. Since Percy and George came I've been blamed for more things than ever. The Hunt family speak in a thick Yorkshire accent which is difficult to understand.

We come to a dense copse of trees where the real bush begins. Sandy stops dead, like a midget Pointer, with her nose in one direction and her tail straight out in the other. Who knows what she's inherited in her *Shenzi* lineage? From deep in her throat comes a low, grumbling growl. As we stare we see a remarkable sight.

He's a little man, only four foot tall, and he has snow-white hair and beard, contrasting starkly with his wrinkled mahogany skin. He's dressed only in animal skins. Above his waist, and up to his chin, he wears a zebra skin, the black and white stripes reflecting the patterns of sunlit ground and shadow all around. Below his waist he wears only a small furry leather *moochi*, attached by a leather thong between his legs and round his waist. It doesn't bear looking too closely, because, as George puts it, 'ya can see 'is whole loonch-box from t' side.' In one hand he holds a *gabori*, flintlock rifle, taller than himself. Over his shoulder is slung an animal horn which contains gunpowder.

Gabori is the Swahili name for a muzzle-loading gun. The tribes round Lake Victoria made copies of Arab *jazails*, brought to the region by slave traders in the eighteenth century. They even carved some of the Arabic designs on the stocks, though they had no clue what they meant. By now, such guns have almost disappeared. But there are people who still make and hunt with them. The mysterious 'pygmy' tribes who live in the jungle. They hold a great mystique for their larger, village-living brethren, who believe the small people have powerful witchcraft, and can cast devastating *dua*, or spells, on anyone who troubles them.

'It's alright, Sandy,' I say to my growling canine companion. She

241

I

stops and wags her tail. Sandy has a lovely nature. If it's okay with me, it's okay with her.

The little man speaks no Swahili, and we have no idea what language he does speak. But he doesn't seem afraid of us, and doesn't run away when we approach him. We have to communicate with smiles and hand signs. He seems pleased to meet us, and soon catches on to the signing. In a strange, convoluted way, he tells us he has been hunting all day, but has not been fortunate. It's a long way to his home, deep in the bush, and he will be setting out to go back now. He points to the south with his *gabori*. Somewhere Bushirondo way, to us the great unknown territory. European explorers used to have a habit of disappearing in that area years ago. I ask if I can examine his gun, by pointing at it and grinning. He hands it to me.

The *gabori* is an amazing work of art and cunning. The barrel is made from a length of one inch water pipe. Where he found that, I have no clue. The end is sealed by being bent and beaten over a fire, thus welded closed. The stock is carved of *maninga* wood, which has been smoothed by rubbing with powdered stone, similar to pumice. There are three modern steel hosepipe-clips holding the barrel in place. On the side of the barrel next to the stock is a depression, with a small hole in it. The flintlock mechanism has been formed from beaten six and four inch nails, and there is even a special bend, at the end of a small hook-shape, where a fragment of white flint is bound with thin rawhide.

I return the *gabori* to the pygmy, and make gestures of shooting. I *have* to see if this thing works. He grins hugely, and unslings the buck-horn from his shoulder. He shows us its contents by removing a wooden stopper. It's a dark grey powder with the gunpowder smell of an exploded firework. Umali later tells me the pygmies make their gunpowder from ingredients they find in the bush.

The little man pours a measure of powder into the end of the *gabori's* barrel. Then he inserts a wad of dry leaves, and rams it in with a long, thin stick. He produces a leather pouch, much like his immodest moochi, and unties a thong at the top. He withdraws a steel ball bearing almost an inch in size. Where he got those I can't fathom. He drops it into the barrel, and follows it with another wad. He carefully prods the barrel again. Then he holds the *gabori* in one hand and pulls back the 'hammer' which holds the flint. He trickles powder into the depression, then puts the horn back over his shoulder. He points at a baby tree thirty yards away, and motions for George and I to stand behind him. We do. He sights his *gabori*.

There's a loud click, a brief pause, then an ear-piercing blast, and the little man almost disappears in a cloud of acrid black smoke. Before the smoke has cleared we run to the target-tree, except Sandy, who, much alarmed, bolts headlong into the bush. The tree is small, about five foot high and two inches wide. It's cut in half! When we turn to congratulate the shooter, he's gone. Sandy emerges sheepishly from her refuge.

Twenty-five

A month later George steals a box of a hundred 0.22 bullets from his father.

'Won't he find out?' I ask. The box is labelled 'BSA 0.22 calibre'. The bullets inside have shiny brass cartridges.

' 'Ee don't nauw owt,' George says, ' 'ees allus too droonk!' George is never complimentary about his dad. He isn't wrong, though. I've seen old man Hunt staggering out the club. Mrs Hunt too.

'What we going to do with them?' I say.

'Mak a goon,' George says, 'an' shoot summat wi' it, *ka-boom!*' He makes a pistol of thumb and index finger, and grins. A gun. A good idea. But how? Bullets go off when they're hit on the back of the cartridge by a firing pin. Everyone knows that. The bullets have a little red dot in the middle of the cartridge base where they have to be hit. First, though, we'll have a bit of sport. Fire will set off a bullet, won't it?

We find a fire easily. The *watu* always burn the *majani*, or grass, before planting. Distant smoke tells us where they're burning today. It's on the left side of Compound Hill, where the slope is gentle, and the *watu* grow *mahogo*, cassava to the English. We creep up on the burning hillside, careful not to be seen by several ragged fire-tenders, who surround and beat out the flames with bundles of green twigs and leaves if they threaten to go the wrong way and burn the compound. From a hiding place behind a big thornbush, we each hurl a handful of live bullets into the flames. Nothing happens. For about half a minute. Then, suddenly, we're in the middle of a shooting gallery, with bullets popping off and whizzing everywhere, including our way. One, George swears, parts his hair! We, in one direction, and the fire-tenders in another, bolt for our lives, us shocked by what we've done, them certain the *djinns* of the fire have awoken, and are out to kill them.

At home, we decide to use our ammunition more conventionally. We have to make a gun.

'Let's start with the barrel,' I say.

'Okay. What'll weh use?'

'Water-pipe,' I say, remembering our pygmy's *gabori*. 'We need one the same diameter.'

'Diam – a *what?*' Sometimes George seems a sniff short of a cold.

'Thickness,' I say enigmatically. He nods.

'Whah'll wa get woon?' he asks.

'Engineering works,' I say. That's where they do everything, and it's where the outdoor dump is, the one where we got the helmets. They throw all their scrap out there. There are piles of off-cuts, including water pipe. Nobody ever fusses if we take something.

We poke around in a huge pile of rusting iron. 'What 'boot this woon?' he asks, pulling out a piece of pipe with a two-inch diameter. The bullets are only a quarter inch. Poor George. . . has he *any* idea at all?

'This would be better,' I say, finding a thinner piece. Quarter inch. I drop a bullet into the end. It stops at the rim. Perfect. Just then Jaswan Singh comes out the workshop. A friendly old *Singa-Singa*, or Sikh, who always wears an immaculately wrapped maroon turban. Anand Singh's uncle. He's a fitter and turner in the workshop. He's often helped me choose things from the scrap pile.

'What you looking for?' he asks in Swahili. One thing about Geita *Singa-Singas* – they're all fluent. Unlike most Europeans.

'*Chuma*,' I say. Iron.

'*Hio?*' That one? He points at the pipe in my hand.

'*Ndio.*' Yes. I decide to press my luck. 'Please cut it for me.'

'*Wapi?*' he asks, taking the pipe. Where?

'What youse sayin'?' George asks.

'Shurrup!' I say.

'*Hapa*,' I tell Jaswan. Here. The pipe is three foot long. Needs a foot off.

'*Nta Kata*, I'll cut it,' Jaswan says, turning and going back into the workshop. '*Kuja*,' he adds over his shoulder. Come. We follow. He puts the pipe in a vice, and saws it with practised ease. The unwanted end falls off in seconds.

'*Sasa?*' Jaswan asks. Now?

'Please cut here too,' I ask, pressing my advantage. This is very labour-saving. I show him where I want a slot cut out, four inches from one end. For the chamber, where the bullet goes.

'What you making?' Jaswan asks, his smile tinged with suspicion. '*Bunduki, labda?*' A gun, maybe?

245

'*Apana,*' I say. No. 'A thing to play only.' Lying is so easy when there's a higher purpose. He sets to cutting the slot with a jigsaw and a grin. This bit of cutting is complicated. Two parallel cuts halfway through the pipe, then a longer cut joining those, to remove half the diameter. We could never have done this part without Jaswan.

'*Chukua,*' he says at last. Take it. 'Don't shoot anyone,' he adds. He shakes his head. Of course we're making a gun. He knows. He really is *such* a nice old man.

'*Asante sana,*' I say, taking the pipe. Thanks a lot. Jaswan has done the hardest part for us. We walk back to the camp.

'Ya spehk Uffricun real gud,' George says.

'An' you don't,' I reply.

'Ah don' wanna spehk blurry Uffricun,' he spits, 'it's munkeh-talk!' I stop and grab his shirt collar. I pull his face close. He pales.

'Don't ever say that again,' I breathe.

'Okeh, keep yoor blurry hair on,' he stammers. I let go his collar. We walk in silence. Why do English people, even those new from Yorkshire, think so badly of the natives? A constant problem for me. I'm between both. Neither European nor African. I don't want to hate either.

'Come to my place tomorrow,' I growl when we come to where our paths fork, 'we can start work.'

'Yoor plehse?' He looks relieved we're still in business.

'Yup. I've got other things we need.'

'Okay. I'll cum t' yoor plehse,' he says.

At home Umali is curious about the piece of iron pipe. 'What are you making, *Jimu*?' he asks.

'We're just playing,' I reply. Last thing I want is Umali to twig.

'This is not for playing,' he says, clicking his tongue. 'You are building a gun!' He's holding the barrel up, squinting through it. There's *nothing* for it. I have to admit the truth, persuade him not to tell Mum.

'*Ndio,*' I say. 'Yes, yes, it's a gun. Please don't tell Mama.'

'*Wewe!*' Umali says, shaking his head. You! 'You are not afraid of the danger of a gun. You think bullets will just turn to water?'

'*Maji?*' I ask. Water? What's he talking about?

'The *Maji-Maji* water-water rebellion against the Germans long ago.'

I remember something about it. It was before the First World War. Between 1905 and 1907. I ask Umali, and he tells me. A spirit medium called Kinjikitile Ngwale claimed he was possessed by a snake-spirit called Hongo. He changed his name to Bokero, and announced to the people that, by the use of *maji,* water, mixed with castor oil and millet seeds, the bullets of the German occupiers would be magically turned into water.

Confident this would happen, Bokero's followers, known as the *Maji-Maji*, hurled themselves at the Germans, who mowed them down in great numbers. Altogether hundreds of Germans and close to three hundred thousand *watu* were killed, before the cry of '*Maji-Maji ni wongo!*' the *Maji-Maji* is a lie, spread through the country. The rebellion was over.

'No,' I say. 'I don't think this way!'

'*Pole pole, Jimu,*' he says, smiling wearily. Slowly-slowly, *Jimu.* This means be careful. 'I haven't forgotten your father's gun. . !' When I shot God. He'll never forget. But he's smiling. He won't snitch to Mum.

Next Day George is there nice and early. I place our gun barrel on the kitchen table.

'Hoo'll weh fire it?' George asks.

'With a nail,' I say.

'A *nayle*?' he asks, bewildered.

'Yup, but first we have to make a stock.'

'A *fookin* stock, whah's 'at?'

'The wood part,' I say. I've found a plank under the house. No clue how it got there. I put it beside the barrel, and draw the outline of a rifle butt and stock. 'Here,' I say, giving him a saw. 'Cut this out along the pencil mark.'

'Okeh,' he says, pleased to have *summat* to do. I leave him to it, and go in search of hosepipe clips. The ones used to hold a water-hose on a tap. I've seen some rusty ones on the rubbish outside the mill. By the time I return, two clips in hand, George has finished cutting. A reasonable job.

'Now,' I say, 'we make a groove for the barrel.' After two hours working with a small, rusty chisel and hammer, we've formed a long hollow on the top of the stock. We sandpaper it smooth. With the hosepipe clips, we secure our barrel into the slot. It looks like a gun already.

'What nayle we gonna use?' George asks.

'This one,' I say, producing my work of the previous evening. It's a six inch nail bent at ninety degrees, two inches from the head. I've also

247

filed the end to a fine point. Bolt and hammer in one piece. I slot the long pointed end into the back of our barrel. When in as far as it will go, the point is just beyond where the back of the cartridge will be.

'How'd we mak it gaw?' George asks.

'With rubber,' I say, 'inner tube rubber and a nail.'

'Anoother fookin nayle?' George exclaims.

'Like this,' I say, driving a two inch nail into the front side of the stock. I retrieve a strip of tube rubber from my pocket. Left over bicycle tube rubber from catapult making. I attach one end to the hammer-nail, the other to the little nail on the stock. I pull the hammer-nail back, then release it. It springs forward. It'll strike the cartridge hard. I cut a groove in the stock, where the hammer-nail, under tension, can recess. This is the trigger mechanism. A flick of the thumb releases it for firing.

We're in our front garden, standing six yards from the big tree. I'm holding our gun, aiming at the broadest part of the tree trunk. This isn't an accuracy test, that can come later. Beside me, wildly excited, is George, who lost the coin toss to be the first shooter. On my other side is Sandy. Behind us, excited too, but filled with trepidation, are Becky, Gretchen, Dieti and Lutoli. Is our home-made gun going to work?

I prise the bent-nail bolt slowly upwards in its deep notch. Nothing happens. I increase the force of my bent thumb. It moves a bit more. I apply more pressure, and suddenly it's free, and jerking forward on its stretched rubber spring. There's a sharp crack as the point strikes the back of the bullet, and smoke pours out of the chamber and barrel. Sandy yelps and runs away. Everybody dashes to the tree to see the damage.

Our little 0.22 bullet has wobbled about in the oversized and smooth-bored water-pipe barrel, and on emerging has turned completely sideways. It's hit the tree horizontally, side-on, instead of with its end, or point. All it's done is half-bury itself in the bark, and I easily dig it out with a penknife. The hard, white wood under the bark is unmarked. I feel crushing disappointment. All this effort, and we can't even penetrate a tree!

We try twice more, with the same result. It also becomes apparent that our gun is wildly inaccurate. Aiming at one tree from ten yards, I hit another two yards to its side. Our *bunduki,* or gun, project is a singular and humiliating failure. Disaster is complete when, hearing the shots, George's father, who just happens to be in earshot, comes and confiscates our invention, at the same time getting most of his box of bullets back. We've thrown twelve in the fire and fired only three from our gun. He's suspected George was the thief, and leads him off by the ear.

Umali is relieved. He hasn't told Mum what George and I were making, but he's been tormented with anxiety. '*Siku lala usiku mingi,*' he says, beaming happily, despite my grumpiness. I didn't sleep many nights. '*Risasi si maji, Jimu!*' Bullets are not water, Jimu. May as well have been, I muse angrily, the way that stupid bullet turned side-on to the tree! In a curious way I am forever linked to Bokero and his *Maji-Maji* warriors.

Twenty-six

Ninth of December 1961. *Uhuru* day. At precisely midnight, Tanganyika Territory will gain independence and be just Tanganyika. Far away in Dar-es-Salaam Sir Richard Turnbull, the last British Governor, is preparing for a formal handover of power to the new Government under TANU and *Mwalimu* Julius Nyerere. The symbolic guard for the hauling down of the Union Jack will be provided by a contingent of sailors from HMS *Belfast*, World War Two heavy cruiser of the Royal Navy. It'll be a brief ceremony, then Sir Richard, carrying the folded flag, will board *Belfast*, and sail away forever. The newest member of the United Nations will be born. In a dozen places across the huge country, smaller ceremonies are about to commence.

In Geita we assemble at eleven pm on the edge of the dusty parade ground at the *boma*. A detachment of two hundred *King's African Rifles*, complete with military band, marches up and down, rifles sloped and gleaming bayonets fixed. The *askaris* wear khaki shorts and shirts, brown leather belts and boots, tightly-wound puttees and red fezzes. They look very smart, and they're perfectly in step.

Contrasting with the khaki uniforms of their men, the four white British officers are dressed in full-length regimental whites, complete with corded revolvers in holsters and glistening white pith-helmets. The European expatriates look on glumly. The minute hand on the big clock moves inexorably towards that which they dread.

The Union Jack on the flagpole flutters in the light breeze. The marching band has come to a halt, but the *askaris* are wheeling round at the far end of the parade ground, a white officer strutting peacock-like in front. On the small wooden platform next to the flagpole another white officer stares fixedly at the flag. To his right is the retiring District Commissioner. To his left is a small African man with

250

white hair. Not unlike Nyerere himself. New District Commissioner. Just behind these notables are wives and children, black and white, all dressed for the occasion. Standing at attention beside the flag-pole are two immaculately turned out *askaris*.

The minute hand on the clock approaches its zenith. The bandmaster brandishes his stick, and the band begins to play *God Save The Queen*. Not *Gorde Sieve Our Greasious Quinn*, I now know. Suddenly there's a crackling sound, followed by ear-shattering bangs as fireworks erupt in riotous colour into the sky. It's midnight.

The sky is lit by catherine-wheels and rockets, trailing pink, orange and red light. The band breaks into a different tune. *Mungu Ibariki Afrika*. God Bless Africa. The two *askaris* by the flagpole are lowering the Union Jack. In its place they raise a new flag. It's got two broad green stripes at top and bottom. In the middle is a black stripe, separated from the green by two thin gold, or yellow, ones. Green represents land, black the people, and gold the country's mineral resources.

The *askaris* fold the Union Jack into a tight triangular shape. They must have rehearsed this over and over. A very tall one takes it and marches stiffly to the podium. He continues up the three steps, comes to a halt in front of the white officer, stamps his foot mightily, and hands the triangle to the *Muzungu*. The officer takes it and salutes. The *askari* salutes, about turns, and marches back to stand beside the flagpole. It's over. Tanganyika is British no more.

Tribal dancers erupt onto the ground, the shrill ululating of women drowning out the second verse of the anthem, *Mungu Ibariki Tanganyika*. Several European women are weeping openly. On the podium the *ex* and *new* District Commissioners are shaking hands. From this minute the *askaris* and their officers are no longer *King's African Rifles*. Now they are in the Tanganyika army. They're standing at attention. The officer in front has his pith-helmet in his hand. He's raising it and shouting something, but we can't hear what. Must be 'Hip-Hip-Hooray!' The *askaris* take their fezzes off as one, and raise them in salute. They've practised this too.

Funny, I think. Tribal warriors, then *Schutztruppe* in the First World War, then *KAR*, fighting for Britain, far from their own country, now Tanganyika army. How many different things they've had to learn! I wonder how long the white officers will be allowed to stay.

This is it, then, I muse. I'm ten and a half, and I no longer live in a British colony. What is going to happen to us now? I look at the gleeful, whirling dancers, then at the sad faces of the *Wazungu*, my *Wazungu*, because I'm white like them. I've heard several say they

251

won't stay. Can't live under 'them'. Am I the same? Do I want to go away too? I look at the dancing *watu* , the beaming faces of the *askaris*.

I think of Umali and Amina, who are not here. Lutoli. No! I don't want to go. I *belong* here. These *watu* are *my watu*. I know them better than I know the *Wazungu*. I've had more kindness, more happiness with them. The *Wazungu* don't even speak their language. How can they expect to understand, or like, people if they don't even know their language? I'll stay. I won't go.

It's strange how even momentous historical events come and go, leaving little trace on me. For a few days there's nothing else than *uhuru* on everyone's mind. Then the reality of hot, sweltering days, the burning sun, the relief of evening coolness, and everything which was before, reinstates itself, is once again most important, and life moves on. Geita never felt governed by the British, and it doesn't suddenly feel governed by the new rulers in Dar.

We children have to entertain ourselves, because there's no TV, no English-language radio, no newspapers or magazines less than several months old, and a very limited supply of fly-blown torn comics, which do the rounds many times before they disintegrate. Nothing has changed in the months since *uhuru,* except the sign outside Lone Cone Club. It used to say 'Whites Only'. Now it says 'Members Only'. I believe they've made the new District Commissioner and his wife members. Where does that put Higgs's *bibi*? Nobody's saying.

We continue our efforts to escape boredom. When we don't feel like getting really dirty and 'running wild' with our African friends, we're stuck with each other, and there's nothing to do. At such times we have to use our imaginations. Of course, there's always the big swimming pool at the club, and the weather is always hot. But there's a limit to how much you can swim, or play in a pool. There are reptiles and birds to tease, but even that has its limits.

New ideas are always being looked for. Some actually end up as plans to do something, such as building a go-cart out of an old pram, or making bows and arrows from small tree branches, and hunting anything that moves. Some ideas are just that, ideas, and not acted on. We can think of something, discuss it, and develop from it a whole mythology.

The international collection of *jambas* is an example. It's one of those monsoon days when the rain comes down in drops the size of pomegranates and the corrugated-iron roof resounds to the torrential impact with deafening noise.

How many nationalities are there on the mine? Italians, Germans, English, French, Jewish, Cornish, Scots, Indians, Africans. . . All, we decide, must have something particular and related to race in the gas they emit from their backsides. We should, we decide, attempt to creep up behind individuals who look like they're going to emit, and 'catch' it in a paper bag. '*Jamba*' is Swahili for fart. The words 'international' and 'chase' speak for themselves.

We hypothesise on the subject at great length and in considerable detail. German *jambas*, we feel, will have something sharp, acrid and toxic about them, Germans being, by consent of Dieti and Gretchen, military people who can make explosives very well. Italians, being cowards to a man (or woman) will have softer, more fragrant, perhaps tomato-sauce-tinged, *jambas*. Scots *jambas* will be mean, short, sharp, and lacking in body. English ones have to be honest, roast-beef flavoured, and loudly delivered. Indians' will smell of curry and chillies, and come out wailing, like their music. We aren't too sure about the others. However, careful catching, sniffing and comparison will shed light.

In the future, confusion, even anger, occurs among some adult attendees of Lone Cone Club, when certain children invade their rear-body space, holding open paper bags pointedly close to their backsides.

It's 1962, and Geita is invaded by cowboys. There's a company based in Nairobi called *Airspray Limited*. They spray insecticide on crops from specially adapted aeroplanes, all over East Africa. The gigantic cotton plantations to the west and south of Geita, some which measure their land in tens of square miles, have decided the future of pest-control in their fields is from the air. Airspray send out a team.

A ground-crew with two long-wheelbase Land Rovers, towing trailers, leaves Nairobi and heads for north-western Tanganyika. On board are support workers, including an engineer and pest-expert. There are stores of dry chemicals to be mixed with water for spraying. They also have spare parts for the plane and the Rovers, because there aren't any out here. It takes the ground-crew three days to reach Geita. In the whole district there's only one club, or large group of expats, and that's our mine. Everyone's delighted when the travellers roar out of the bush and announce they'll be camping by the club for a week. Visitors are scarce and very welcome.

Sven Edmündsen is engineer and crew-boss. A huge, powerfully built, red-haired, wild-bearded, man in his forties, he's Sweden's answer to the great macho white man of Africa. In Nairobi he has a grand house, a pretty Italian wife, two children in expensive private schools, and a white gull-wing Mercedes sports car. In the bush he's a heavy-drinking, rabble-rousing, dictator over crew and pilot. Provided he's obeyed, he's got an uproarious sense of humour, and is a man others like to be around.

They set up camp on open ground near the club. They pitch a huge bell tent for stores and three smaller ones for quarters. Their two *Kikuyu* labourers share one, Sven has one, and the pilot and pest-fundi share the third. On his shortwave radio he contacts base in Nairobi and tells his pilot to come.

What took the terrestrial crew three days takes the pilot four hours. Suddenly overhead from out of the heat-shimmered sky is the reverberating throb of a 235 horsepower *Lycoming*, flat four, 0-540 six cylinder aerial engine. Until then I haven't encountered such raw aeroplane engine-power. The noise bounces off the surrounding hills and echoes down the valley, until there's nothing else in the world.

Everyone stops to stare at the bellowing midget in the sky. This is the *Piper Pawnee* the ground-crew told us is coming from Nairobi. Piper name all their planes after North American Indian tribes. The pilot is Eric Butler, a young befreckled Rhodesian from 'Down South'. He's every bit as wild as his boss, Sven, but *he*'s got the controls of the plane, and he's determined to show us.

'Get your fat arse down here!' Sven yells into the microphone.

'In due course,' Eric's voice crackles from Sven's speaker, as the *Pawnee* rockets past, just ten feet from the ground, before turning on its tail and shooting skywards, corkscrewing as it climbs. It's so powerful it stands on its tail, defying gravity! He levels out at five hundred feet, roars round the very edge of Compound hill, an angry insect with a deafening voice. Geita has been woken.

Eventually the *Pawnee* lands. By then we've run the half-mile to the landing strip. Sven and Eric have a good-humoured row, and everyone repairs to the bar of Lone Cone Club. There's serious business at hand. The business of drinking.

When the visitors and their hosts are quite merry, Eric decides the time has come to take the children for a ride in the *Pawnee*. He's a good flier when sober, he says, but better when 'oiled'. It's throttle *after* bottle for him! We're queuing up, and I'm at the front. Behind me are Dieti, Andrew, Antonio, Becky, Sophia and Gretchen. To no avail. Eric calls the big girls first. Gretchen, Becky and Sophia.

The *Pawnee i*s a unique aircraft. It's small, but immensely strong, built to withstand rough treatment, collisions with small trees, bumpy landings, short runways, any weather. Her cockpit is a little, upright, glass enclosure, halfway down the fuselage, designed to give the pilot all-round visibility in the air. The huge *Lycoming* engine gives the plane a power-to-weight ratio no other commercially built aircraft can match.

On the ground the *Pawnee* stands with her nose pointing skywards. The runway in front can't be seen from the cockpit until the tail comes up on the take-off run. Till then the pilot steers by looking out one side, staying parallel to the runway edge. There's only a single seat, so we have to go one at a time, half-standing, half-sitting on the radio beside Eric. This is particularly difficult for the big girls, but Eric doesn't mind. I do. I don't like Gretchen sitting so close to him, with her legs bent over his knees. He starts the engine, and without ado opens the throttle. The hugely powerful engine hurls the plane round in its own length, throwing up an impenetrable cloud of dust, to stand facing upwind. Then it's hurtling across the flattened scrubland, and seconds later shooting impossibly into the sky. I'm glad to see Gretchen still alive after they land.

Eventually it's my turn. The raw power of the plane is like riding on the back of a buffalo gone berserk, the g-force tugging at cheeks, neck and back. There's hardly time for fright. We're rocketing across the sky towards the hillside. Through the blur of the hurtling propeller I make out individual trees and rocks. Unless we turn, we're going in. At the last moment Eric tugs the stick to his left and stabs the opposite rudder. The *Pawnee* yaws, banks and turns, the hillside slipping past inches from our wingtip. Eric's laughing like a maniac. '*Like* that?' he yells above the crescendo of the engine.

'Yes,' I lie. Will I ever get back on the ground alive is all I'm thinking. Soon, miraculously, I do. I watch as others take their joyride. There's a common factor. Each is paler after their flip with Eric. Even Lutoli. He's terrified, and it takes a lot of persuasion getting him into the cockpit. When he gets out, he is violently ill. '*Siwezi ku kwenda ju tena!*' he exclaims when he's stopped vomiting. I won't go up again! Later he tells me that, whereas before he always believed hell and damnation was deep underground, he now realises it's in the sky, and *Shetani*, the Devil, is a freckled *Mzungu* pilot. He doesn't like him. He's *blurryfucken!*

I, on the other hand, have huge respect for Eric. He goes out spraying cotton every day, after drinking all night. He flies out at sun-up to land on strips of dirt road where the crew have flattened grass and bush on the sides, fills up with chemicals, takes off, sprays cotton, lands, refills, takes off six or more times, before heading back to the airstrip just ahead of sunset. He constantly jokes about his job. 'Watch thine airspeed,' he laughs, 'for the earth shall rise up and smite thee!' It's an old saying from WWI Royal Flying Corps days, but he faces danger daily, and it never fazes him. Sometimes he spots victims on the golf course, and, being Eric, 'buzzes' them. This includes charging straight at them at full throttle, six feet off the ground, turning through ninety degrees to pass between trees, levelling, causing the golfers to hurl themselves flat and pray. He roars overhead, in touching range, then rockets skyward, barrel-rolling on the way.

When he lands, the crew extract parts of cotton-plants from spray-pipes on the trailing edge of the wings. They say spray-pilots in East Africa have died flying into concrete-hard anthills. The ants here build mounds four, even five, feet high. They can't be seen for vegetation. Meeting one at a hundred miles an hour is a hell of a way to find it. Eric lives a charmed life.

The *Selekali* Land Rover screams into the club drive and brakes in a shower of small stones and a cloud of red dust. The government police from the *boma* always arrive like that nowadays. The Rover has hardly stopped when the passenger door flies open and a tall young *askari* in khaki uniform and bright epaulettes jumps down. He stalks to where Kaizer and I sit on the low wall.

'*Wapi Kenya Mzungu ya ndege?*' he commands, addressing Kaizer, who until then was enjoying an icy *Whitecap* while watching red ants carry potato-crisp fragments up a crack in the cement wall. How should *he* know where the Kenya *Mzungu* of the bird is? And he doesn't like the look, or tone, of this *askari*, three, even four, decades his junior. It's Sunday afternoon, and he's enjoying sitting here, not being harassed. Maybe the pilot from Kenya is in the bar. Probably is.

'*Ndani,*' he says laconically, and as disrespectfully as possible. Inside.The *askari* snorts derisively, then strides round the back of the Rover. He opens the door. Two very drunk and sheepish *Kikuyu*s get out, looking scared. They are the Airspray Ltd labourers.

'*Ngoja!*' the *askari* shouts, before heading into the club. We don't have long to wait. Two minutes later he emerges with a bemused Sven Edmündsen and Eric in tow.

'These *Kikuyus*,' the *askari* announces in broken English, 'is *your!*' The *Kikuyus* look apprehensive. I notice one has a big lump and a cut on his forehead.

'Yes. . .' says Sven.

'Drink *moshi* making by criminal!' says the *askari*.

'*Solly Bwana!*' the injured man whispers.

'This time, this time. . . they go. Not allow Kenya *Kikuyus* running here wild!' admonishes the *askari*. Sven and Eric nod. They're getting off lightly. Through the side window of the Land Rover I see there's someone else in the back. I get up and walk around. The door's still open.

Sitting on the raised mudguard, with handcuffs on and a huge steel dustbin-still between his knees, is someone I recognise at once. It's Moses' brother, Iwe. He stares at me ruefully.

'*Jambo* Iwe,' I say. He looks very sorry for himself.

'I didn't got the line-sense,' he explains.

There's another, more regular, but equally dashing, visitor to the mine. Otto Müller has a good-looking, blue-eyed, blond son called Werner. Gretchen's cousin. In 1962 he's fifteen, and already six foot tall. He's at school in Mwanza, and goes there by boat every weekday morning. The hard-working ferry-boat *Lotanga*, which Dad, Umali and Wait sailed from Kampala in Uganda all those years ago. On weekends Werner helps Otto with his farming business. One of the tasks Otto gives him is to drive to Geita mine and sell farm produce to the employees.

There had once been an elderly Volkswagen Beetle on the farm, I was told, but Werner, while learning to drive on a winding dirt road near Lotanga, rolled it down the side of a minor precipice. The body was trashed, but the chassis, engine, gearbox and wheels survived. Otto and Werner cut the bodywork away, in front leaving an exposed driver's seat, gear-lever, clutch, accelerator and brake-pedal. Behind that they built a raised wooden-sided back to load goods.

Every Friday, early in the evening, Werner roars into town in his ramshackle vehicle. He goes straight to the club, where his arrival is heralded by his engine's noise, and everyone comes dashing out to seize a share of the fresh, high-quality produce of Lotanga. Legs of pork and lamb, home-cured bacon, cartons of fresh frozen milk, still cold after sixty miles of hot road, bunches of carrots, cabbages, runner-beans, onions in netting, and other things not otherwise seen in Geita. Lotanga is much more fertile, has more water, and is run by a proper farmer. The prices are high, but nobody cares.

When his load is sold, which only takes minutes, Werner goes in to the club with his customers. He's only fifteen, but this is Geita, Tanganyika. When a boy is big enough, he's big enough. Nobody minds, except perhaps his father, who is far away in Lotanga, that he drinks some of the profits in beer. Werner is popular and always surrounded by adult club members, who ask after his parents, Lotanga, and how things are going in Mwanza. After all, although everyone gets trips with Fritz, they don't see Mwanza more than once in three to four months.

There are two others who show great interest in the dashing young man-in-a-go-cart. Gretchen, his second cousin, and Becky, my sister, are both fourteen, and it's apparent they like him. To my relief, and proving his lack of taste, Werner prefers Becky to Gretchen, and I'm able to breathe again. But it isn't all rosy for me. Mum is protective of her daughter's virtue, and I'm given the task of shadowing Becky if she goes anywhere with Werner. There follow boring hours of sitting outside the club, near the pool, watching them hold hands and sometimes kiss. Werner sleeps over at the Blüger's house, and Becky is forbidden to go there during those times. I see to it she doesn't sneak away when nobody's looking. I don't endear myself to the young sweethearts, but Mum is pleased with my surveillance work. I will have more of this to come.

Before Becky and Werner can get too serious, long leave to England beckons.

I don't want to go because I want to be with Gretchen. I know I'm in love with her because I can't get her out of my mind, and when she's close I feel so full in my chest, like it's going to burst. At night in bed I've stopped imagining I'm in my little enclosed canoe on the wild ocean.

Inspired by movies where the hero dies slowly and in agony while a beautiful woman laments at his bedside, I nightly live and relive a tragic and drawn-out scene of my own death, after fighting bravely to save Gretchen and suffering a terrible wound. Gretchen, who too-late realises she loves only me, is weeping and sobbing by my side, but still looks ethereal and beautiful. Sometimes she wears a T-shirt and jeans, sometimes a dress, but she's always Gretchen, my one and only love. My love is pure, and I don't demean it by letting a kiss, let alone other things, enter the script.

'Please don't die!' she whispers in my ear, her hand gently brushing my forehead. But it's too late. There's nothing anyone can do. I feel the death-rattle in my throat. Like those cowboys who wait till their lady is there before they expire.

'I love you,' I manage to gasp with my last breath.

'I know you do,' she says. 'I love you too. . !' Death has always been around me. Now I'm in love with dying, just so long as Gretchen is there.

Twenty-seven

Six times there are man-eating lion scares. Lions don't usually prey on humans. Men and their weapons are far too dangerous. Like many wild, but sentient and intelligent creatures, lions avoid the noise, smoke, guns and artificial night-time light of man. They have, however, an unforgiving social order, and when an elderly member of the pride, or one with an injury, is unable to play a full and active role, he is excluded and has to fend for himself. Lacking the speed and agility essential to the hunt, and the help of comrades, the outcast seeks out slower, easier prey than before. Hunger overcomes natural phobia, and the outcast is inevitably drawn to the vicinity of humankind.

Victims of a 'rogue' lion at Geita are the most vulnerable people, selected as least-risky choice. The compound has no electric light, and none of the *watu* have guns. Even so, the lion is careful to choose someone who wanders away from the settlement. Being old, or injured, he relies more on stealth and concealment than speed.

The history of lion attacks on *watu* is the stuff of folklore. One man is pulled from his bicycle and dragged three hundred yards from the path in 1956. The remains of his body are found three days later, flattened, bloodied grass pointing the way. His lower belly and genitals, and soft neck-flesh, have been consumed. The lion is saving the rest for later. The remains are his grisly larder. Then, in '59 a woman walking from one of the latrines of *machula* fame is attacked. Her baby is torn from her arms and taken off into the bush. No part of it is ever found.

When a lion attack happens, Geita panics. Mr Snel orders everyone to stay indoors, especially at night. If you go somewhere it must be in a car. These are to be parked close to the front door. Outside lights are to be left on – lions don't like it. On leaving the house, you dash to the

259

car and lock yourself in. Makes me think lions can open cars unless locked from inside.

During a 1960 scare Mum doesn't obey the rules. 'It's a *man*-eating lion,' she tells a chiding Mr Snel, 'not a *woman*-eating one!'

I'm eleven in 1962, and Geita is again under siege when we return from Arusha. There have been four known lion killings of *watu* in three weeks. Some say there's more than a single rogue at large, because, while one victim is taken from a footpath near the mine, three are attacked *inside* the compound. The latter behaviour, seeking prey *inside* a human encampment, is unusual even for a rogue.

We've lived too many years with this on-off danger. After a week of obeying the rules, Dieti and I decide to ignore the curfew about walking in the bush. It's far too hot and boring to stay indoors. Besides, we've been away in Arusha three whole months, and there's fun out there in the scrub and jungle. We've never been attacked by a lion, and we're confident we won't be now.

'Let's go to Tarzan-Swings,' Dieti says. His German accent has almost disappeared, except when he's excited, which is sad because it used to be amusing. He's spent the night with us because he's not allowed to walk home in the dark. It's a dashing idea. The girls say we're crazy, and they don't want to end up a lion's lunch. We say we're not scared of any lion, and, besides, we'll take big sticks.

'If you go, I'll tell *Vati!*' Gretchen warns her brother.

'Okay, we won't go,' Dieti says, but his foot nudges mine under the kitchen table.

'Let's read comics,' I say in my best 'defeated' voice.

'Okay,' Dieti says in his. And we shuffle off to my bedroom. We burst out laughing after we close the door.

'We better wait a bit,' Dieti cautions. Good idea. The girls will be suspicious a while. Maybe we gave in too quick. We read old *Classics*. Mine is falling apart, and even the sellotape has turned yellow and is peeling. After an age we hear the girls leave the house. In the circumstances they'll walk directly, and quickly, to the Blüger place. Good, we're on our own! There's only one person to elude now – Umali. That should be easy.

We're out the house, running helter-skelter downhill towards the club on Bottom Road. We've got *rungus*. They're inch-thick sticks, four foot long, with three-inch solid balls of wood at the end. Made by selecting the right small tree and digging it up. The ball is the root-bit. The *rungu* is cut to length, stripped of bark, and dried in the sun. A natural weapon. More than equal to a lion should we meet one!

Turning right on Bottom Road, we carry on to where the road

curves to the left, and the settled area ends. Here the natural vegetation begins again. We plunge off the road onto a footpath which winds into the bush. We know this area well. After three minutes we come to one of our favourite places. 'Tarzan-Swings' is what we call it. There's a natural clearing in the bush. In the middle is a gulley four yards wide, and at the bottom a fast-running stream.

On the banks are great weeping willows, their down-hanging branches and tendrils reaching tentacle-like towards the ground. Selecting and grasping one, we make Tarzan-like whoops, and swing over the gulley and stream. It's exhilarating. Sometimes in the past my 'rope' has broken and I've fallen into the water. I'm better at choosing ropes now.

We swing several times, then decide to go home. We've proven our point – no man-eating lion can scare *us!* But even we know staying here too long is chancing our arm. We start on our way back. It's strangely quiet. Eerily so. Not even a *njiwa*-bird cooes.

We are just approaching where the path joins Bottom Road, when Dieti digs me painfully in the side. I turn instinctively to complain, and freeze. We're stopped, staring back up the path.

He's huge. Massive. *Gargantuan!* I've never seen a lion so close, and I didn't imagine they could be so big. He's only yards away. I smell his fetid, rotten breath. At eleven I'm four foot tall. The lion's higher. He's got a great head and magnificent mane. His mouth is half-open, and we see his yellow fangs and hear rasping breath. One of his ears is shorter than the other, like the top's been bitten, or ripped, off. He's just fifteen yards away. He and we are stationary, staring at each other. His eyes are cloudy yellow and bloodshot. He doesn't blink.

Dieti, several inches shorter and a lot thinner than me, is white as chalk. His lower lip trembles, his eyes are saucer-wide. I can't think what to do. What *should* you do? My heart beats hard and fast in my chest. I can even feel it in my neck. '*Huyu na ngoja ana potea*' comes to mind. Umali says it. He who waits (hesitates) is lost. Is that the advice I need? I've got to do something! Before I can decide, it's taken out of my hands.

The lion takes a step towards us. Instinctively, we take a step backwards. He takes another. So do we. He starts strolling, we turn and walk. He follows, his breathing loud and rattly. We turn onto Bottom Road. When we're eight yards from the path, the lion joins the road behind us. 'Don't run!' I whisper through clenched teeth.

Dieti's in a daze, like an automaton. He's just coming along, doing as I do. He's still very white. I count our steps. One, the lion takes one too. Two, three, four, he keeps in step. We've covered a hundred yards of Bottom Road. The lion is walking a bit quicker now. He's no longer in step. We walk faster, try not to run.

The gap is down to twelve yards. My self-discipline dissolves and I break into a run, pulling Dieti with me. Looking over my shoulder, I see the lion look confused. He isn't running. He's stopped now, just staring after us. We reach the bend in the road, then he's out of view. We keep running all the way home.

I tell Umali what happened. In minutes he's got a posse of *rungu*, panga and spear-wielding, excited *watu,* who head off to find our strolling lion. He must be *mzee,* old, Umali says, or sick. Otherwise he'd have had us. I think that's what gives Umali the courage to go after him. After nearly an hour they return, disappointed. They can't find the *simba.* At the club that night, Dieti and I are celebrities. For someone speechless with terror, Dieti has undergone a metamorphosis.

'I wanted to throw stones at him,' he says to Mr Snel, 'only Jim wouldn't let me!' I listen to this in amazement. 'I think we could have killed it. . .' Dieti confides, his courage immense now the lion's not about.

The rogue-lion hunt is redirected to south of Bottom Road. Next day two hundred spear-wielding tribesmen, plus six *selekali*, or police, *askaris* with rifles, sweep the bush. But it isn't them who get the credit this time.

Two miles further south, next to his shamba, a Gallua tribesman sets a lion-trap. He tethers a kid-goat to a stick in the ground. This is the bait. If a lion grabs the kid, that'll move the stick. Just six yards away, balanced on two tall forked sticks, is an ancient Arabian muzzle-loading *jazail* loaded with powder and ball. The flint-bearing hammer is cocked, the trigger connected by fishing line to the goat-stick. He checks his trap carefully, gives the kid a dish of water, and retires to bed in his hut.

He's woken by a loud retort, and agonised lion-roaring. He runs outside with a spear for protection. He doesn't need it. The *jazail*-ball has struck the lion in the chest, penetrated his heart. He's lying on the ground in the moonlight, his lifeblood gushing from his wound. The kid, unhurt, is bleating pitifully.

Next day the *simba* is displayed outside the mine store. The tribesman has sold it to Marcello Barelli, who wants the skin. He's huge, seven foot long, plus a tail of four foot. It's the same lion which walked after Dieti and me. He's got the mane, and the half-torn or bitten-off ear. He's also got a septic foot and three claws missing. 'Thees,' says Mr Barelli, 'eesa why he no catcha you, Jeemy!' I've a lot to be grateful for. Even sepsis.

*　　*　　*　　*

Meantime, the English language gains no favours from me, or those I know. Umali's 'come quigelly', my 'muttony on the bounty', Jackson's 'Greasious Quinn', Antonio's 'Inglish in the pinglish', Iwe's 'line-sense', Choudhry's 'ledger shits' and many *watu*'s '*blurryfuckens*' are just examples of how the King's English is murdered in Geita.

I grow up believing snakes are bad tempered, because Ursula Blüger, Gretchen and Dieti's mother, is always alluding to it being so. 'I voss cross like-a-snake!' she exclaims to anyone who cares to hear. 'Gretchen vos cheeky, und I vos like-a-snake-cross!' Ursula continues to be cross like a snake, on and off for years. When Gretchen's twelve she 'vos kissing vis a boy', which made Ursula 'cross-like-vun-big-snake'. It made me cross like a *bigger* snake, though I never knew if it was true, or which boy it was.

Also abusing the language is the mine motor mechanic, Spiro. He's of mixed Greek and African blood, and has an accent midway between the two. I think cars are powered by a person under the bonnet when I'm young, because it's always the 'injun' who's 'forked'. It seems unnecessarily cruel to me. The back of a car is clearly a tiresome thing too, because sticking out there is the 'exhausting pipe'. I can never work out if 'rainwipers' are there to clean the air or the windscreen.

One day Antonio manages to 'borrow' a pair of walkie-talkie radios from his dad's Land Rover. They're ideal, he says, for planning and co-ordinating a *machula* attack. We decide to try them on a practice run. We'll pretend we're ambushing the machula and use the walkie-talkies to communicate. There's no *machula* coming that day – we know his timetable. We'll pretend. Antonio will 'see' the *machula* and radio an alert to me. We separate and crawl through the undergrowth. After a few yards I stop. The radio crackles into life.

'The *machula* is-a-coming,' it says, 'are-a-you-a-ready to attack-a-heem?'

'Roger!' I reply, pressing the 'send' button. That's how soldiers speak on radios.

'Eesa-not-a-Roger, ees-a-Antonio!' comes the furious reply. Walkie-talkies will never work in Geita. Not with Antonio!

I begin to take notice of the signposts in Geita. The signwriter's an elderly Sikh who, when not writing signs, works for Adrian Venter in the reduction works. **'Mane Rod'** says the sign at the top of the hill. For a time I think it's to do with a male lion who was shot nearby. **'Mwanza-85 mils'**, says the one where the road leaves the mine.

'Petrouelem-Dangres', says the big red and black sign at the filling station. Barat Stores has a very special sign. It's neatly done in black, with paint on cardboard:

NO AKS ME CREDIT

MABE YOU NO PAY
ME GIV CREDIT, MABE ME CRY
ME NO GIV, MABE YOU CRY
...BETTER YOU CRY!

All the signs are beautifully painted, but nobody bothers with spelling. Makes it ridiculous to learn it at Arusha. What's the point of perfect spelling? We understand, don't we?

I'm so bored with other kids. Mum says I've been a little old man from when I could walk. One Sunday at the club I go outside looking for Kaizer, my old friend. The *Wazungu* in the bar are already well-oiled on *Whitecap* and whisky. The kids are mindlessly eating crisps and drinking Pepsis. Kaizer is much more interesting. I ask Ishmael, the barman, if he'll sell me a bottle of *Whitecap* for the *askari,* and he agrees, as long as he delivers it to him personally, because Mr Snel, the manager, has strong words about selling *pombe* to *watoto*. I resent that. I'm not a child!

'*Asante sana!*' Kaizer says when he gets the beer. Thanks a lot. '*Ni moto leyo.*' It's hot today. Ishmael leaves us.

'Tell me about the Japanese,' I say.

'*Hawa,*' he says, 'them'. He takes an appreciative swig from the bottle, wipes the back of his hand across his mouth. His stories of fighting in the jungles of Burma are the most entertaining tales in Geita. I can imagine myself crawling through the undergrowth, a *Lee-Enfield* rifle with fixed bayonet in one hand, my ears pricked for the sound of enemy movement, a twig breaking, the sudden flight of startled birds. When Kaizer speaks, I'm *there*.

'*Hawa,*' he says again, 'a treacherous people. They fought like tigers, didn't mind if they died, but did worse than that!'

'How?' I ask, keen to hear how bad they were.

'One day in the great Kabaw valley, we came to a wooden Japanese fort on top of a hill. They'd been under attack by an Indian division for three days. They'd killed lots of Indians.' Just like John Wayne, I snigger. But these are not red-Indians. They were *Indian* Indians. I

264

suppress my humour. 'There were dead Indians everywhere. But the Japanese had losses too.

'Their commander decided to withdraw his remaining men because he could no longer defend the perimeter. He left six badly injured soldiers behind, with pistols and hand-grenades, and ordered them to kill as many enemy as possible before dying.' Kaizer takes an exaggeratedly appreciative swig of *Whitecap*. It's very hot and close today. It'll rain later, I can tell.

'You like my stories, don't you?' he says.

'I do, *mzee,* old man, they are tales of a brave man,' I say.

'You, child, will charm the whole world, one day!' Kaizer laughs. He drinks more beer, then continues.

'We crept through the bushes towards the log fort. We knew what the Japanese could do. They could be completely quiet one minute, then suddenly the whole world may go mad with bullets and explosions. They were so sly, so prepared, so dangerous!'

Kaizer stares at me. Suddenly he looks very old. His hair, short and curly, has always been shot-through with grey, but now it's white. He looks smaller, too, than the Kaizer I know.

'We came,' he says, 'in range. They *must* start shooting. Nothing. We waited, not to expose ourselves by leaving the undergrowth and bushes. Nothing. Then Samuel, an *askari* from Uganda, drew the pin on a hand grenade and threw it over the rampart. We lay low. There was an explosion. We waited for shooting, a machine-gun. Nothing!' Kaizer sits silent on the wall for half a minute. He shakes his head.

'The platoon commander, a *bwana* called Lieutenant Harris, who none of us liked, mainly because he spoke bad Swahili and looked down on Africans, gave the order to advance. He shouted, "Let's go boys!" We weren't his "boys", but this was the army, and we had Japanese to fight. Maybe when this war was over we'd fight the *Wazungu*. Who are *they* to rule us?' He smiles enigmatically. I'm a *Mzungu*, after all. He sips his beer, looks into the dark distance.

'We jumped out of our hiding places, rifles with bayonets fixed, and made a mad dash over open ground to the fort. We ran like madmen. We knew these people were clever. They could wait, let you think you're safe, get you in the open, then shoot at you with two, three, or more of those terrible machine-guns. I'd seen men cut to pieces, just when they thought they were safe!

'We got to the wooden poles. They were young trees, a foot wide, pointed on top, tied by rope in a stockade. One *askari* threw a grenade over, and it went off. Then we were climbing, standing on other's shoulders to reach the top. As the *Mzungu* Harris put his head over the

m

parapet, he was hit between the eyes. He fell back, eyes wide open, brains hanging out the back of his neck. *Wazungu*, you see, can also be killed!' Kaizer pats me gently on the shoulder, 'even you, Jimu!'

'*Na jua*,' I say. I know. Dad died, after all.

'Others got over. I was fourth or fifth in line,' Kaiser says. 'We couldn't see where the shot came from before there was another, and the Ugandan Samuel fell to the ground with a bullet through his throat, gurgling, blood pumping from a huge hole in his neck. We saw who shot him. A Japanese soldier, perhaps eighteen years old, who looked only twelve, with no legs, tied to a small tree, his stumps stuck in the earth. I looked at him, and he pointed a long pistol at me. His eyes were wild, like a cornered *fisi*. I brought my Lee-Enfield up and fired at the same time. My bullet hit him in the forehead, blew half of it away. He collapsed against his ropes, brains dripping onto his lap. It was very close.' Kaizer puts down his empty *Whitecap*.

'Meantime the others found there was only one Japanese still alive. He'd lost an eye and half his jaw. One of our hand grenades. He was lying there, moaning. Bayonet thrust through heart and he was quiet. We'd won the fort.'

'Very brave,' I say. I don't find it strange that, at age ten, I hear the most gruesome details of war. The Swahili, unlike the English, don't dress things up for children.

'What happened then,' says Kaizer, 'was terrible.'

'What?' I ask. What can be even more terrible than I've heard?

'*Makopo*,' Kaizer says, tins. 'Food, labelled in Japanese, with pictures on, of the contents. They were among the kit of the dead Japanese soldiers, in small rucksacks. We hadn't eaten fruit a long time. Our rations were bully beef and biscuits. Some *askaris* grabbed the tins, opened them with pocket knives or bayonets, and started to eat. Within seconds the first one staggered, tried to scream, fell to the ground and was dead before he got there!'

'Poison?' I ask.

'Cyanide,' Kaizer answers. 'Kills quicker than any other poison. Three men died in minutes. The others stopped before they were poisoned too. The Japanese didn't care *how* they killed us, even if they did it after they themselves were dead!' Suddenly this war-stuff feels ugly to me. I thought soldiers were men with *heshima*, honour. This is something else, alien. Cowardly, even. I shudder at the thought of being killed with poison by an enemy who is already dead. Such behaviour is not only without *heshima*, it's downright *hovyo*, or completely without manners. *Majinga* behaviour, loutish and immoral.

Cyanide! That's what they use in the 'reduction works' on Top

266

Road. Part of the process of refining gold. By the time they've got pure gold out, there's a grey mud-like residue called 'slime'. This is dumped to form a 'slime-dam' a mile west of the mine. Over the years they've made three slime-dams. They're over a hundred yards long, forty wide, and thirty foot high. They've dried to a brick-like grey consistency, except on the top of the one still being used, where the surface remains runny. There's a noxious, acrid, sour, choking smell there, which never goes. We children are forbidden to approach the slime-dams. Some of us, particularly Dieti, Lutoli and I, ignore that, and go there anyway.

It's strange, climbing the steep path up the sides, walking on the grey lunar surface, trying not to breathe deeply, feeling we're getting away with murder. It can't be *that* poison, or we'd be dead long ago. I should be. Last week Lutoli jumped in one of the stagnant pools on top of a dam and pungent grey water splashed in all directions. I got some in my mouth. It tasted like nothing I knew, horrid. Like biting a raw pawpaw, only worse. I spat it out, and spat some more. Couldn't get rid of the taste for hours.

'*Mina jua*,' Kaizer says, reading my thoughts. I know. '*Wena chesa huko.*' You play there. Are there no secrets at all in Geita?

Cyanide. . . I file away a thought for the future. If anything ever happens to Gretchen, I'll want to die. The cyanide is there. I wonder how much grey slime I'll have to eat to do the job.

267

Twenty-eight

In June 1963 we go on long leave. Mum's contract is renewed every two years. Within that time there are two periods of leave. After one year, we have two weeks 'local' leave, spent anywhere within the East African Community of Tanganyika, Kenya and Uganda, all expenses paid by the company. After a further year, it's 'long' or 'overseas' leave for four whole months, fully paid, anywhere in the world. The generous leave allowance, and payment by the mine of boarding school fees, are the reason most expats stay so long in their jobs.

The day before we leave I pay a visit to Mlozi, the *mchawi*. He appraises me without expression, sitting cross-legged on his *mwamba*-rock. I tell him we're going far away across the sea.

'Further than Bagamoyo?' he asks. That's forty miles.

'Much further, and over a bigger lake than the great one at Nungwe!' He stoops and crawls into his crude hut, and emerges with a small piece of still-furry animal skin, tied with thong into a little bag. I think it's from a goat.

'This will bring you safely back,' he says, giving the golf ball sized bag to me, 'only you must not open it, or look inside. It has strong *dawa*, but must stay closed.' I take it from him. This is the first time he's wanted to help me. I tremble at the power of the medicine in my hand. I won't tell Mum, or she'll make me get rid of it. Anyway, I believe in the power of the *mchawi*, and the *hirizi*, or charm. I will take the *dawa* to England. Who knows, I might need it there. I'm staring at Mlozi. He gives me a very rare half-grin, before turning away and recommencing his strange and incomprehensible monologue with the sky.

Our long journey begins with the drive to Mwanza. There we catch the *gari-moshi* to Dar. Two days and nights. Much excitement. Becky

268

and I are able to appreciate the scenery, not being blinded by the misery of going back to Arusha. Even so, I'll miss Gretchen, whom I love from afar, though I pretend not to. Hot, dry plains, herds of grazing wildebeest, water holes, small groups of elephants, patches of verdant green, isolated villages, ramshackle stations, running, laughing totos, wizened hawkers of fruit, elephant-hair bangles, carved wooden rhinos, elephants, lions, Masai warriors, replete with spears and beads.

Beyond Dodoma, where we're delighted not to alight, the locomotive struggles up into the cooler heights of central Tanganyika.

A hand-rung bell calls us for meals in the dining car, a splendid Victorian statement of art, craftsmanship and excess. In sumptuous luxury, several courses are brought on silver trays by waiters in white, badged *EAR & H* uniforms, and red fezzes. Between meals, we watch the country glide by, consume *EAR & H* chewy peppermint sweets, drink Coca Cola ice-cold like the advertisements tell us to, and re-read *Illustrated Classics*.

The heat of the hinterland, having returned on the descent to the coastal plateau, begins to abate again as the train races towards the sea. The acacias, the flat-topped African trees, and stunted, thorny ones of the plains allow an occasional palm tree to share their space. The palms grow more numerous, until they're in the majority. Soon the red soil changes to a lighter, sandier colour, and only palms grow. It's at this part of the journey we begin to smell the sea.

The *Agip* motel in Dar is a notable institution in more ways than one. It's in the middle of town, half a mile up a straight and potholed tarmac road from the beach. *Agip* is an Italian company whose main business is petroleum. Their premium petrol, advertised on huge billboards in Dar, is called *Super-Corte-magiori!* This has to be said with an Italian accent. Their other business is motels. The best I've seen.

The motel, which I can't distinguish from a hotel, is an oasis. The temperature outside far exceeds forty Celsius, and the air sweats with humidity. Stepping through the glass doors, we enter a refrigerated paradise. There's a lounge, with iced drinks in tall glasses, a dining room where cool, unbothered, smiling waiters in white uniforms and red fezzes bring platters of cold meats, bread and salads to our table. The manager, a jovial middle-aged Italian lady, stands nearby, checking fastidiously on our comfort and satisfaction.

We've eaten lunch, checked into our room. It's even cooler here than downstairs. Mum and Becky are sharing a double bed. I've got a single next to them. We've got our own bathroom. The big window looks down the street to the beach, and the deep-blue sea beyond.

Can't believe it's so hot outside. We couldn't have stood it much longer. We open the window and look out. It's like colliding with a sheet of corrugated iron. It's so hot it takes our breath away, and our cheeks are burnt. This is a crisis. We've got to get to the beach and swim in that blue water. But how, with that furnace outside, are we to get there?

Becky provides the answer. With the window hurriedly closed, she stares through the glass and makes a brilliant observation.

'Chemists!' she says.

'Chemists?' I say. What's she talking about?

'Chemist shops have air-conditioning,' she says. She's a genius. We can see two chemist's signs, equally spaced between here and the beach. Hurriedly we change into costumes and T-shirts.

'Mum, Becky and I exit the Agip into the dazzling furnace, and dash for the first sign. The string-pulled bell sounds as we enter the shop. We let the door close and stand just inside, savouring the 'coolth', as Becky calls it. The young Indian lady behind the long wooden counter smiles. She must be used to heat-refugees coming in and not buying. After three minutes we're ready for the next hundred yards. We're standing by the door of the second chemist, bracing ourselves for the final dash to the sea. That'll be even better than air-conditioning.

Becky and I peel off our T-shirts on the run, and continue straight into the water. It's tepidly warm, but once we're in over our shoulders it's refreshing anyway. It's beautifully blue, like one of those holiday postcards on a stand in the last chemist. And smooth as a breathless pond. We look back at the beach.

The sand shines brilliantly white in the sun. Every ten yards there's a coconut palm leaning crazily over the water's edge. Pulled up on the beach between the trees are half a dozen *jahazis*, open sailing *dhows*, each with a single outrigger on one side, in the curious manner of the Tanganyika coast. White *kanzu*-clad *Warabu,* or Arabs, fishermen, their faces mahogany brown, are sitting in the shade of the palms. A few are mending nets, others playing a strange game. The objective seems to be to flick a pebble with a thumb, so that it strikes another and drives it into a small hole in the ground. I don't know what they call it, but it's causing a lot of excitement and laughter.

This is paradise. The beach runs along a narrow channel leading to the harbour. It's sheltered from the Indian Ocean by the headland, which is why the water is so calm. A cargo ship comes down the channel, heading into harbour. As it passes, a hundred yards away, its wake creates waves which spill towards us. By the time they get here they're over six foot high, and it's great fun jumping into or over them.

Mum's more cautious than us. She can't swim. She's lying in six inches of water at the edge, being assaulted and rolled over by the wake-waves as they run to the beach. It's great to see her laughing and enjoying herself.

Two more ships provide entertainment. Then we spot another ship on the horizon. As she approaches, we see she's much bigger than the others. She's tall and lavender-mauve coloured, and has a wide vermillion funnel. The colours of Union Castle line, Mum shouts from the water's edge. This is the Mail ship we're sailing on to England, the MS *Kenya Castle*. Our excitement and happiness can hardly be contained. What could there be better than this? The glorious beach, the warm sea, the *dhows*, palm trees, and there, steaming closer every minute is a great ship, which just tomorrow will carry us over the waves to England. Sometimes good things overwhelm me.

Kenya Castle displaces seventeen thousand tons, and is 576 feet long. That's what it says under the big picture at the reception desk, where, having climbed the gangplank from the baking heat outside, we are, again, relieved by the coolness of air-conditioning. She takes up to five hundred and twenty-six passengers. She's a mail ship, and carries, in addition to passengers, mail and assorted cargo between South and East Africa, and England. Fore and aft are covered holds and cargo cranes. She's a handsome ship. Our cabin has a porthole and three bunks, two on the floor, one above. I dabs the top bunk. The bathroom is along the passage, and has six toilets and four showers.

Becky and I run around exploring the ship. There's a lovely little swimming pool on the after deck, closed, emptied and netted over in harbour. There's a grand dance floor in one of the big rooms and a massive dining room too. There are bars in several places, and a library. Downstairs, along from reception, are several glass-fronted shops selling all kinds of things. Plus a ladies' hairdressers. Becky likes the look of that. My eyes fall immediately on very large yellow packets of cigarettes in a shop window. They're called *Matinee Filters,* and they're two bob for fifty. It's duty-free!

An hour after we board, the ship's speaker system announces we will be sailing in half an hour. 'All ashore that's going ashore,' the man says. Some people are kissing and hugging. Some are crying. Not us. We're just wildly excited.

The ship's horn bellows, a long deep sound, followed by three shorter, sharper blasts. Stragglers head down the gangplank, and no sooner has the last one stepped onto the wharf, than the crew begin to wind the gangplank up into the ship. Men are running up and down the quay, loosening great ropes from huge steel bollards set in concrete. There's vibration underfoot. The engines are coming alive. The hooter sounds again. Suddenly there's a narrow gap between the ship's side and the wharf.

The water boils as the propellers thrust it down the length of the ship. The gap widens rapidly. On the other side two tiny tugs are pulling us away. The vibration changes, and increases, and the *Kenya Castle* starts to glide forward. The tugs release their hawsers and back away. We gain speed, and now the wharf is off to our right, and drawing away. A yellow and black pilot-boat bobs in our wake, waiting to take the pilot off.

Music starts playing on the afterdeck next to the pool. They're giving away cold drinks and ice-cream cups. Becky and I join the throng of other children, trying to get as many ice-creams as possible. They're very generous, or stupid, because it's help-yourself, and there are boxes and boxes full. We're gorging ourselves as the ship sails past the Inn By The Sea, and the beach where we swam just this morning. There are people in the water, jumping over the waves like we did. Mum finds us. It's six thirty, and the first sitting for dinner is at seven. There's just time, if we hurry, to shower and dress.

Supper is formal. We're shown to our table by a white-uniformed maître d', who pulls a chair out for Mum and Becky, but not me. I don't care. Who wants his chair pulled out? The table is round, and has six places. Two old ladies and an old man sit down. Mum makes polite conversation. Geita, now where on earth is that? Posh accents. They come from Nairobi, in Kenya. The old man is an engineer. His wife's a teacher, the other old lady her sister. The bread rolls are fresh, warm and delicious with melted butter. Better than Umali's *sconsies*. I won't tell him. The soup is tomato, very good. I choose roast chicken as main course. Mum and Becky go for steak pie. We finish off with ice-cream. Someone says the shops are open after supper. I check my money. I know what I'm buying.

Half an hour later I'm sitting on the deck in front of a covered hatch, smoking the first of my newly-purchased *Matinee* cigarettes, inhaling deeply like I've learnt. This is bliss. No one can see me here, and I've got more cigarettes that I ever thought I'd have. I'll be spending lots of time out here. It's getting dark. The sun is an orange orb on the horizon one minute, then it's gone.

Sleeping in a bunk in a ship at sea is special. It's almost, but not quite, the same feeling I get when I imagine myself cocooned in my canoe. There's the gentle fore-to-aft pitch, the left-to-right roll, the constant vibration of the engines, the creaking of the whole ship as it weathers the sea. From the porthole, directed from an attached scoop, is a fresh stream of sea-air. This is as near as possible to paradise, I think. In the neverland between waking and sleep, I imagine Gretchen comes to sit on my bunk. She's smiling. 'I love you,' she whispers in my ear.

Our course is north, first port of call Mombassa, Kenya, where we dock next evening. There's loading and offloading of cargo, passengers leaving and others joining. Then we're back at sea, heading north in the Indian Ocean, towards the Red Sea. We have five days at sea. Hours of swimming and sunbathing, making friends who smoke with me in the hiding place on the far side of the hatch, sleeping, or just staring in wonder at the ever-changing hue and colour of the sea. At the neck of the Indian Ocean we enter the Red Sea. For a day we're close to the African shore, and see bleak red cliffs and rocky outcrops. An officer says we're actually five miles off, which I find hard to believe. It looks close enough to swim.

Aden is a very Arabian town. Mum's nervous about Becky. She remembers the trader in Benghazi who wanted to buy her for six camels, the one who said he'd 'look her good'. The ship doesn't dock here, but anchors outside the harbour. We're taken ashore in wooden motorboats which are not as well built as *Lotanga*. We have two hours in the bazaars, and Mum buys a camel saddle-seat, made of leather-covered wood. Soon we're back on board, sailing for Suez, Egypt. It's a day's voyage, then we're at the entrance to the Suez canal.

The canal is close to a hundred miles long. It heads due north from Suez to enter the Little Bitter Lake, which connects to the Great Bitter Lake. From there it runs a short way to Lake Timsah, then it's a ruler-straight northern course all the way to Port Said on the Mediterranean. There's not much to see, except sand and desert, the occasional camel, and a very infrequent Arab on a camel. There is one thing I see which I'll never forget. Cleopatra's needle, an officer tells me. A tall, impressive stone monument in the desert, close to the canal. I particularly note this structure because we're gliding past it as I cut my birthday cake.

The ship's chef and confectioner is a proper Yorkshireman, who Mum talked to about my forthcoming twelfth birthday, due during our traverse of the Red Sea. He responds by making a huge light blue birthday cake, with the words 'Jimmy' and 'Twelve' written in white icing. I am surrounded by twenty children of different ages, singing 'Happy Birthday', as I make my first tentative cut in the cake. That's when I spot Cleopatra's needle. I don't see anything else worth remembering. After sixteen hours we enter the Med at Port Said.

That night at dinner the old engineer from Nairobi drinks two whole bottles of South African wine, and becomes even more talkative than his usual raucous self. At the next table the steward, Dennis, is being very gracious to the ladies. One of them, whose name is Mrs Johnston, seems very happy to have his attention. She has a loud, irritating voice. The old engineer says she's flirting with the steward. Her husband, a grumpy man with a grey beard, doesn't seem to mind, or notice. The engineer says to his wife 'she's mutton dressed as lamb.' I ask Mum what that means. She tells me it's big-people's talk.

We stop at Genoa in Italy. Here Mum depresses Becky and me by dragging us to see a 'famous' cemetery, where they first bury people for a few years, then dig them up, collect the bones, put them in little boxes, and plant them in a 'memorial wall' with photographs of the deceased on the front. I manage to persuade Mum to buy me a very realistic toy cap-gun. It fires special, very loud caps. It'll make me famous in Geita, because nobody's ever seen, or heard, a toy gun like this.

I've got more adventurous where I smoke, and now I've taken to lighting up on the boat deck. It's ten at night, and the ship is chunneling along to the west into the teeth of a blustering, salty wind. The moon is full, and there's a broad, shimmering golden highway of moonlight on the sea, all the way to the horizon. Suddenly the lifeboat beside me comes to life. I nearly choke on my cigarette.

There's somebody, or something, *in* the boat! A corner of tarpaulin lifts and out pops a man's head. In the moonlight I recognise him. It's the dining-room steward, Dennis. He doesn't see me. I'm in the shadow of the boat. I hear him whisper something. There's more rumbling, then a lady's head joins his. Her voice is clear, as is her anxiety.

'Are you sure there's no one?' she says. Who could miss that raspy voice? It's the lady with the angry bearded husband at the table next to ours. Mrs Johnston, that's it. The *very* irritating voice. She, labelled 'mutton dressed as lamb' by the old engineer.

What's she doing in a lifeboat, at night, with a steward? If they wanted to talk there'd be no need to climb in there. They've been up to something, and I know what it is. I wish Umali was here. I could tell him I've caught *Wazungu* doing secret *jigi-jigi* in a lifeboat. I stay in the shadows as they climb awkwardly down. He's first, then he turns to help her. She's standing with one foot in the boat, the other on his cupped hands. She slips, and they fall together on the deck. She cries out, but it's hushed. Her pain isn't enough to overcome her fear. They struggle to their feet, briefly kiss, and go off in separate directions.

274

Marseilles, a brief stop. Then Barcelona. The Rambla, a long, wide boulevard crowded with shops and people. Not my scene. Far too busy. Gibraltar, now that's better. A slower pace, very British. The passage is coming to an end. Leaving Gib, the ship turns north up the Atlantic, towards our harbour of destination. Thirty-one days after embarking in Dar es Salaam, we disembark in King George VI Docks, London.

We travel by train to Plymouth in Devon. My eldest brother, Bertrand, who is still in the navy, has married, and he, his wife and two year old daughter, live in a large caravan in a park at Plymstock. My brother Fraser, also still in the navy, has rented a chalet in the park.

Becky and I are resentful of our brothers. They talk with Mum about things we don't know, and times we weren't there. There are other unpleasantnesses. Bertrand decides to discipline me and orders me around. I don't like the food they eat. It generally comes out of a tin, and it's usually things I've never seen before, like 'spam', a foul concoction of cooked tinned meat. They don't have fresh fruit.

Bertrand's got an old bicycle which he grudgingly lets me ride. Cycling around a footpath in the park, I come across three older boys. I'm twelve, and they're at least thirteen or fourteen. I stop and talk with them. They ask me where I got my funny accent, and I tell them. They start calling me 'wog' and 'nigger'. Strange, I think. These Wazungu are just like those in Geita, though so far apart. In Geita they've always said 'Jimmy's run wild, like a native!' Here, in green and pleasant England, I'm being called wog and nigger. Do they have some kind of extrasensory communication with Geita bigots? I don't know. But I'm not going to let them get away with this.

I remember my vows to myself. I said, long ago, I am my own father. I meant there is no man to fight for me, so I must do my own fighting. Also, in my pocket I have Mlozi's little leather bag of dawa. These fools know nothing of the power of a mchawi. I'll teach them to treat me like this! I dismount, take two steps towards the nearest boy, and punch him with all my strength on the earhole. The impact is so hard a harsh vibration travels all the way up my arm. He falls on the ground and rolls about in agony, crying like a lady opera singer. I take two steps towards the second boy, but he runs off. The third has retreated beyond range. I look down at the squirming one on the ground. There's blood pouring out his ear. 'That's how we niggers fight!' I say, remounting my bike. At last Mlozi has given me the hirizi. With that I cannot fail. It's about time he really helped me. He may be strange, and all, but he's my Swahili brother in the end! Later my big brothers have to placate the boy's father, who says I 'attacked for no reason.' His innocent son has a burst eardrum and needs an operation.

'Apologise!' Bertrand says when he drags me to the caravan door.

'I won't!' I say through clenched teeth.

'You will!' he says, twisting my arm behind my back.

'Okay,' I say, seeing there's no way out, unless I attack my own brother, here in front of the boy's father.

'That'll do,' the man says, surprising me by his lenience. When I look where his eyes are focused, I realise why he's being so nice. Fraser has just stood up and is glowering. I find out he knows Fraser. Two months ago he drank more than he should have and began to randomly abuse women in the King George. Fraser thrashed him and threw him out in the rain. This, he must think, is a violent family.

We travel down to Cornwall by train. It's half an hour to the Tamar River, which marks the border between England and Cornwall. The railway bridge was designed by a famous engineer called Isambard Brunel, in eighteen ninety or something. What kind of name is *Isambard?* Sounds like a Muslim singer. Who cares, anyway? It's a strange-looking thing, the bridge, like huge elongated oil-drum-sized pipes looping into the sky. I don't know why they think it's great. Mum's got a special mission. We're going to St Day, to see Dad's sister, Natalie. The one Fraser told me about that day in Geita. She's the one who spent the family money. Why Dad died in Tanganyika. It's on the train Mum tells us the real agenda of our visit.

The mine has fallen on hard times. The government in Dar es Salaam is taxing it to death. They believe foreign-owned companies should pay the entire cost of developing the country. They're killing the goose which lays the golden egg. Geita Gold Mine's days are numbered. Mum hasn't told us before, because she didn't want to ruin our holiday. Even more pressing than the state of the mine is our education. Becky has outgrown Arusha, and has to go to secondary school. I'll be in that position next year too. If the mine's going to close, it's best our education should continue in Britain. Next week Mum's going back to Tanganyika. We won't be going with her. Becky and I look at each other and burst into tears. We didn't expect this.

Aunt Natalie lives in a terraced cottage in St Day, near Redruth. It's just like her; small, old, and seen better days. I don't like her, or her house. I remember what Fraser told me in Geita. She's spent all the family's money. She's why we're poor. Becky's going to live with her in a place called Elstree in Hertfordshire. That's near London. Aunt Natalie's got a job looking after a rich old woman there. How much older can that lady be than Aunt Natalie? *She* looks a hundred to me.

276

Natalie and Becky will live in the very-old lady's house, and Becky will go to a local day-school. As these plans are unveiled in the low-ceilinged, damp-smelling cottage, Becky sits weeping silently, accepting her horrible fate. I'm still waiting to discover mine. Something tells me I won't respond passively like my victim-sister.

'You, Jimboy, will be staying with your cousin Mable in Redruth,' Mum says.

'No I won't!' I'm not even going to begin this discussion.

'You have to. You can't come back with me. . .' She's trying to be gently persuasive. Poor Mum. I know she means well, but I won't let her go back alone. If I do, I'm sure I'll never see her again. I've got to stand firm, regardless of what she says. It's for her own good.

'Remember Dodoma?' I ask. Where I jumped out the bus. I know this question will put her mind in the right way. It means I'm deadly serious.

'Why?' Mum asks, sounding alarmed. I know she thinks I'm not only emotionally brittle but half-mad too. I've done enough to deserve that. Shooting God, killing Tembo's puppy, spying on Mr Valari's corpse, abusing Alice and Mrs Snel, swearing at adults, jumping through the back window of a moving bus. . . Add to that being stung by a scorpion, narrowly escaping a black mamba, being chased by a lion, throwing live bullets on a fire, manufacturing a firearm, and my latest coup, the near-killing of the English boy in Plymstock caravan park, and her concerns are clearly well founded.

It's a long, hard process wearing Mum down. I see a chink in her determination when she says I'll have to go to boarding school in Nairobi, Kenya, if I don't stay here. I'm due to move on to high school from Arusha next year. I agree readily. At least Kenya's not so far. By the time we get to cousin Mable's house, the odds are even. Her house is even smaller than Natalie's. She's enormous, and her husband is thin and short. Nothing fits. No way will I stay here, in this country, with these people!

I can't bear to be so far from Geita, or, I suddenly realise with a jolt deep in my chest, Gretchen. I've been missing her terribly. Am I in love? Must be, or I'd be able to stop thinking about her for a bit. I want to go back, marry her. I know I'm a bit young, but there must be exceptions. Some twelve year olds must marry, surely? I wonder what she'll say. I make the most important speech of my life.

'I'm not staying here, no matter what you say!' I say in front of Mum and Mable. 'If you try to force me, I'll run away. You can't watch me all the time, and I'll go as soon as you don't!' There are expressions of surprise and anger. Mable plays right into my hands.

'I'll take you in hand,' she says in a strong Cornish accent, 'if I have to whip your behind till it's black and blue!' Thank you Mable.

'You will not!' says Mum. The battle is won.

A week later Mum and I stand at the rail on the British India Steam Navigation Company ship, *BI Uganda*, as she eases away from the dock in Southampton. There's a waving crowd on the wharf. In it, at the front, are Becky and Aunt Natalie. Natalie's wearing a black fur coat. Becky's holding a small white Maltese Poodle. Mum bought it to cheer her up. Becky looks very sad. She cried when she had to go ashore. Natalie gruffly told her not to be so silly. I know Mum would change her mind about her too, if it wasn't too late.

We retrace our journey from Dar. Gibraltar, Barcelona, Marseilles, Genoa. I refuse to visit the cemetery again, though Mum's keen. What is it with her and this Italian Cemetery? Then Port Said and the canal. I see Cleopatra's needle again, from the starboard side. Last time it was port. Suez, and the Red Sea. I can't wait to get home. I'm missing everyone. Not just Gretchen, but Umali, Amina, Lutoli. Not to leave out Sandy, or even old Gooloogooloo, and several of the chickens.

The two days on the *gari-moshi* are a forced delay. It can't pass quickly enough. At last we're at Mwanza station, and there's Fritz, standing teutonically erect and looking, as always, stern.

'Velkom beck,' he says, taking Mum's suitcase unsmilingly. In the Land Rover he tells us the news. Dr Weiss telegrammed from Switzerland to say he was coming back early from leave. I hadn't realised he *was* on leave. Gretchen is at home with her family in Geita. I'll be seeing her again. I've begun to forget what she looks like, and she's even stopped visiting me in my dreams. Fritz has no more news for us, lapses into his usual silence.

Twenty-nine

At Lone Cone Club Mr Snel, the manager, is perturbed by the sniggering behaviour of Dieter Blüger, aged twelve. Mr Snel has had several *Whitecaps*, and, as usual, has become expansive to his sycophantic audience of Gordon Praze, assistant manager, Harold Norris, explosives storeman, Dr Josef Weiss, Eugen Blüger, Dieti's father, and close personal friend, plus several mine wives.

As he sits on his barstool, he occasionally, and surreptitiously, shifts his backside slightly, to allow a small passage of flatus. Beer, in excess, does that. He continues his monologue, about the pioneering days when there were no wooden houses at Geita and he and his colleagues lived in tents. His attention is interrupted. Dieti, standing on the bar rail, because he's small, is not only sniggering, but rattling something. What an annoyance kids can be, Mr Snel thinks. I can tell by his expression.

Gretchen, Sophia and I are sitting at a table near the door on the verandah, watching Dieti. He lost the draw, and he's on a mission on all our behalves. To catch Mr Snel's *jamba* in a paper bag. It's difficult keeping straight faces, not bursting into laughter. Poor Dieti. By losing the draw, which was done with straws, he's got to not only catch it, but *smell* it too. That's the rules.

Mr Snel purposefully ignores Dieti. But his body-language tells another story. We can tell he has a strong urge to fart again. To hell, he must think, shifting his bum, and letting go. This one is different to the previous ones, which were sly, surreptitious affairs. Unexpectedly, there's a squeak and a loud roar from his backside. This is what Dieti's waiting for. He has the paper bag open and in position. Mr Snel is just turning to see what he's doing, when Dieti folds the bag closed, jumps down, and, forgetting himself in excitement, shouts 'I haff it!'

279

Everyone is taken aback to see Dieti fleeing gleefully to the door onto the verandah, again shouting, 'I haff von, an Afrikaner von in ze bag!' We convulse, but try to pretend we're uninvolved.

Mr Snel is a fast thinker. He's sussed what's going on, but decides to ignore it. Outside the club, in the shelter of the hibiscus plants, Dieti sniffs the contents of the bag.

'It smells uff beer!' he says. We fall about.

BL Thomas, Deputy Head and Sports-Master leads an 'assault' on Mount Meru annually. There's a big board on the wall in the assembly hall, and on it, in golden letters, are listed the years and names of pupils who 'conquered' the mountain. Becky's name is there under last year, nineteen sixty-two. This year it's my turn. Anyone who has been to Arusha knows how the Mountain dominates the town which lies in its shadow. Every aspect of Arusha life is determined by Meru. The clear drinking water flows from its streams, the cool and temperate climate is due to its snow and ice-clad heights.

At some time or other, everyone who knows Arusha feels driven to climb Meru, whose Masai name means 'the one who does not make a noise', for the ancient volcano has slept since its last eruption in 1877. That, or an earlier eruption, tore a huge chunk out of the crater's side, leaving a razor-edged ridge upwards to the summit. Meru is not an easy mountain to climb. Far more have climbed Kilimanjaro, which, although higher, has a gentler slope, and easier route to the top. That's why BL Thomas loves Meru. He's tough, and wants Arusha pupils to be tough too.

We go by bus to Momella Gate in the Arusha National Park. There's four teachers, including BL Thomas, and fourteen pupils, including Schmedjie and me. We begin hiking over a great expanse of open grassland, lead by a *wa-Arusha* park ranger and ten porters. We see warthogs, several different types of buck, and a solitary, furious-looking, terrifyingly large African buffalo. The worst-tempered animal in Africa, someone says.

Someone else says we shouldn't worry, because the *most* dangerous animal in Africa is a monkey with a machine-gun. We laugh. The buffalo stares with renewed malevolence through dark, hooded eyes, his tail swishing like a pendulum. Even the ranger looks anxious. Schmedjie goes even paler than usual. Just when we think it's all over for us, the beast backs away, making grunting noises, into a copse of small trees and bamboo. We go on up the slope, relieved at our escape.

Schmedjie's face is pink from exertion. There's a giant fig-tree arch, where we stop and eat a lunch of bread and butter with hard-boiled eggs, washed down with sweet tea made on a primus. Then we continue upwards into a forest of alpine trees. White and black colobus monkeys stare languidly down at us, like they've seen it all before, while hornbills and other screeching birds of several kinds and colours erupt from the canopy in panic at our passing. I never thought I was scary before.

We emerge from the forest. There are tall cliffs ahead in the distance. Now we're in a grassy glade. The afternoon sun is hurtling in a ball of bright orange towards the western horizon. We can see plains far below, in gaps between the clouds. Clouds below us! I've never seen that before, except from the Argonaut on the way to England, and the trusty old Dakota.

Between here and big-brother-mountain Kilimanjaro is a seemingly endless plain of green, criss-crossed with shadows from the peaks of Meru and other mountains. Kili's peak is shrouded in mist. Somewhere between here and Kili, Schmedjie says, is his family home. I must come home with him soon, he says. Here, now, in the middle of the glade, we reach Miriakamba Hut. We're 8100 feet above sea level, and it's getting cold. We've been walking six hours, and are glad to be able to stop. We spend the night, eat hot tomato soup and bread, and talk excitedly about tomorrow until we fall asleep.

It's steeper next day. Since we left Miriakamba the slope's got worse with almost every step. We enter the dense Montane forest. It's lush with ferns, lilies and flowers, and criss-crossed by icy mountain streams. It's one tired step after another. This is getting difficult. There always seems to be a huge tree, a stream, or waterfall gushing over moss-covered rock, in our way, and our course, already hard due to steepness and slippery mulch underfoot, winds tortuously.

My foot slips in muddy water and my shoe comes off. I'm not so sure this climb is such a good idea. Nor is Schmedjie. 'Shit,' he says, 'I wish we were on top!' So do I. I struggle back into my icy, wet shoe. An ordinary school-shoe. Bata, lace up. Andrew Miller's cast-offs. Someone said buy hiking boots, but where's the money? BL Thomas has stopped with the forward-crew, and is resting and waiting for us by a great fallen tree. We're the stragglers. It's only a ten minute respite, then we continue.

After five hours we reach Saddle Hut, 11480 feet above sea level. The air is thin and cold. This is the last 'base-camp' before the 'assault' on the summit. We've been climbing up 'Elephant Ridge'. I never see an elephant, and doubt anyone ever does. 'Too bloomin' steep for such big things.' Schmedjie agrees.

281

The hut's not for sleeping in. Here the mountain slope is even steeper, and there are no longer trees. The ground is grey ash and volcanic stone. Left from ancient eruptions, BL says. My feet sink four inches deep with each step and ash sucks at my wet shoes. The summit ridge is starkly visible from here, with the lesser peak of Little Meru before it.

The main peak, half-hidden by wafting cloud, is a tall, wide, grey cone, draped with snow, which glitters in the afternoon sunshine. Forbidding, lunar, other-worldly. Looks close, yet far. The porters light a fire against the biting cold, and burn big tree-branches they've cut in the forest. We sit round the fire and sing hymns, lead by BL in a soprano voice. He's Welsh and loves to sing.

After two hours, and a meal of hot sausages in baked beans, we lay our sleeping bags on the ash slope. It's only seven o'clock, but we're getting up at one in the morning. Lying zipped up in my bag, I let my fingers dig in the ash. It's ice-cold. No wonder I feel cold under my body. I put my head into my bag and breathe inside to get warm.

'Not much fun here,' Schmedjie whispers.

'Nope,' I whisper back.

'It's cold,' he says, and I can hear his teeth chattering.

'Go to sleep, you two!' a lady teacher hisses from nearby. The cross one who teaches French.

We lie there on our backs, heads up the slope, feet pointing down, staring up at the sky which is suddenly dark and pinpricked with a thousand winking stars. The milky way is up there. It's so cold I'll never be able to sleep. My feet, in two pairs of socks, still in my shoes inside my sleeping bag, feel like solid lumps of ice. There's only one thing I can do to make me feel better.

Think about Gretchen. How should I think about her? I've died a hundred ways already, with her, beautiful but distraught, weeping inconsolably by my bedside, touching my brow, kissing me gently on the lips as I expire. Tonight, on the stark volcanic ash of Meru, I imagine her alone in a house somewhere. There's a war, and I've gone off bravely to fight for liberty. I've been killed. Yes. The Japanese. We all live somewhere they invade.

Where did Kaizer, my *askari* friend, fight the Japs? Malaya, that's it. The Kabaw valley. An ambush. I've walked into it and died bravely fighting to protect my pinned-down comrades. After a long battle they kill the treacherous Japs, then carry my body through the bush to Gretchen, who's waiting in the house. It's so darn sad when she sees my broken, bloodied corpse, I find myself sobbing into my sleeping bag. I've mastered the art of thinking myself into deep misery.

282

Somehow I must have slept, because I'm woken by BL Thomas bashing an empty bean-tin with a rock. It's a 'wonk' sound, not at all like a bell.

'Rise and shine,' he's shouting as he beats the empty baked-beans *kopo*. Schmedjie groans and looks at his luminous Oris watch. It's one in the morning. The porters have already revived last night's fire, and one is making porridge in a huge *sufuria*. We roll up our sleeping bags. They're staying here. We're not taking anything we don't need for the final assault on the summit. We eat our hot oats with milk and sugar.

We assemble for a final talk by BL. Nobody to be alone between here and the summit. Watch your footing. Try to keep up. If you do get left behind, and feel you can't continue, stay close to the route the others took and wait for them on their way down. Time is important. The weather can change suddenly up there, bringing strong winds and icy conditions. When we reach the summit we'll stay only briefly, before going back down the way we came.

It's dark, and fiercely cold, as we set out on the last leg of the climb. It's two in the morning, and even at this height the sun won't wink on us before four-thirty or five. For a while it's almost straight up, a blind ascent, one climber behind another, BL in front. After ascending for two and a half calf-and-foot painful, and hard-breathing, hours, the sun's first rays suddenly pierce the dark from behind a rocky escarpment, and in minutes the world is bright and sparkling with light.

We're negotiating an undulating ridge of rock and ash, which sweeps away in a curve to our right. It seems like forever, one foot threatening to slip over the edge, the other trying to maintain purchase. Ahead, the others are drawing away from us. Schmedjie's limping, and I don't feel that good either.

I don't know how, but suddenly we're at Cobra point, and the dreadful ash-ridge is below and behind. The views are stunning. We can see the rim of Meru's crater. Away to the west, the bold grey rock and glittering snow of Kilimanjaro's peak floats above the clouds. Far, far below, in the direction where the pale blue sky is unbroken by cotton wool cloud, the great Rift Valley of East Africa is laid out like an artist's impression. Is this what artists call inspiration, I wonder, or is that breathing-in, which is getting more and more difficult?

Miss Moss, the French teacher, has attached herself to Schmedjie and me. Maybe it's because we're stragglers. Truth is, Schmedjie has blisters. Big, bloody ones, on both his ankles. His Mum bought him special climbing boots, and they're a worse disaster than my *Bata*

283

shoes. Schmedjie stops and pulls his boots off. Then he tries to pull off his two pairs of socks. The back ends don't want to come off because they're stuck with blood and stuff to his heels. He says he's in a lot of pain.

There's still an hour to go to Socialist Peak, the new name for Meru's summit. I persuade Schmedjie not to rip his socks off. He puts his boots back on and we carry on upwards, Schmedjie limping ever more painfully, Miss Moss wheezing almost as bad as Marais used to, and me just wishing all this could end.

Nearly an hour of agony. We reach a place where the rock is covered with slippery ice, and very steep. We can't see any of the others. Miss Moss finds a flat rock to sit on. It's right on the edge of the crater, and we can see a gigantic cone of ash at the bottom, like the remnants of a giant's barbecue. Socialist Peak is just above. Just one more big boulder, can't be more than a hundred yards, and in a clear patch of air we briefly see some of the expedition going up a path on one side. It's unmistakably BL leading them. An icy wind is whistling, almost howling, through dark clefts in the rocks. Cloud and mist whirl about, and the view of Socialist Peak is whited out.

'Far enough,' Miss Moss wheezes, 'we've conquered the mountain, we don't need to go up on that rock.'

'That's right!' Schmedjie exclaims, tugging one of his boots off. I'm tired. I'm scared. I've never been in a place like this. All I want is the warm cosiness of the dorm at Arusha. Why did I come on this stupid thing anyway? I subside onto the rock beside Schmedjie. We've conquered the mountain.

The others start to stream down from Socialist Peak. We join them in the descent.

'No, you didn't conquer Meru!' Mr Houghton says. We're dumbfounded. 'You got to the crater-rim, but you didn't go up Socialist Peak and sign the book, so that's not a success, is it?'

Schmedjie and I are in tears. This isn't what Miss Moss said. She told us we didn't need to climb that little rock, that we'd already conquered Meru. One more failure to add to my list. How can I *ever* trust these cheating *Wazungu*? I wish I was home with my honest *watu* in Geita. *They* wouldn't deceive me like this. 'English sheets!' Schmedjie says. I agree. He's white, but he's a *mutu* too! I think it's the English I hate, not all *Wazungu*.

That night in bed Gretchen weeps beside my deathbed as I lie dying. I'm a brave mountaineer who never made it to the top, but did his best and saved the lives of others. It's so sad. I fall asleep weeping for our lost love. My last thought is how pretty she looks when she cries. She's wearing the same sparkling-white dress she wore that May Day at the club, when Becky was May-Queen. That's when Gretchen suddenly scratched her bum.

Schmedjie invites me to spend the long weekend with his family, and I eagerly accept. Usually I watch the lucky ones whose families live within range leave on Friday afternoon, knowing I'll have nothing to do for four days and have to sleep in an empty dorm, which is very spooky. I get so scared that I hide a thick two foot stick under my mattress, and after lights out move it under my pillow. If any spooks try to get me, they'll have to fight first.

The Schmedjies arrive in a black Citroen DX, like the ones in films about French police. There's Mr and Mrs Schmedjie, and Ulla, Schmedjie's sister, who is twelve and pretty, in a pixie-way. The whole family are blonder even than Gretchen, and pale-skinned. They talk to each other in a language even more guttural than German. Finnish. Last week in a row Matwiga called him *Mulisha*, or finished. When did they *start,* I wonder.

The road to Moshi is untarred, stony and potholed, and the Citroen undulates on its hydraulic suspension like a boat on the sea. I get seasick. They have to stop twice and I vomit on the side of the road. Fortunately it's only forty miles to their house. I go to bed early, because the smell of stew in the kitchen makes me feel worse.

Early on Saturday morning everyone is up and ready for the day's adventure, a trip to Kibo Hotel, halfway up Mount Kilimanjaro. It's at the very end of the road up the mountain, the highest point accessed by car. From there on up it's walking and climbing. I still don't feel very well and I don't have breakfast.

The car journey up the mountain is awful. I try to sleep, but the nausea won't let me. Nor will the popping in my ears. After two hours of winding round hairpin bends and precipitous passes, where the world is far below in miniature, seen in gaps in the clouds which waft by like shredded cotton wool, we emerge onto an alpine plain, and there, in a clearing, is the hotel. When we get out the car it's very cold, even though the sun is shining.

We're sitting in a large dining room and food is about to be served. I'm terribly cold. I excuse myself and go out into the sunshine. There's a bench in front of the hotel and I sit down. It feels a bit warmer in the sun, but still my teeth chatter, and I'm shivering all over. After ten minutes Mr Schmedjie comes out to check on me.

'Are you okay?' he asks.

'Cold,' I manage to say. He puts his hand on my forehead, and looks surprised.

'But you are very hot, Jimmy,' he says.

'Cold,' I say.

'Have you had malaria before?' he asks.

'Yes,' I say.

'You've got it again!' Now I begin to feel nauseous and I vomit on the ground, my stomach heaving even though it's empty, and all that comes up is horrid, bitter yellow stuff. 'We'd better get you back to the school,' Mr Schmedjie says.

Their long weekend and visit to Kibo ruined, they drive me back to Arusha. I'm so ill now, so cold, even though they wrap me in a blanket, I don't even notice the journey. By the time we reach school I'm unconscious.

I lie in my sick-bay bed hour after hour. There is something I can do to entertain myself. I feel that one of my top molar teeth is made of a hard green crystal. When I close my jaw firmly, the sharp point comes up against the lower molar. If I really increase the pressure, the green crystal penetrates the substance of the lower tooth. Strangely, it's a pleasant sensation, not easy to describe, like biting on hard liquorice, feeling it give way and divide at the force of the bite.

Why is it pleasant? The entire thing is false. I don't have a green crystal for a tooth. It cannot penetrate another tooth. But the sensation is real, and re-experienced at will. It banishes other things. I tell the doctor. He says there may be 'an organic cause'. Malaria can do that. Something about *somatic hallucinations*. Whatever that means. Why teeth and the sensation of one being penetrated by another made of crystal? The psyche, he says, is beyond analysis.

Sick-bay is a haven of peace. Being there means no lessons, lying in a comfortable bed with good counterpanes and pillows, and sharing the room with only four others. The food is better than the muck we normally eat at school. Because we're sick we have perks, such as a never-ending supply of classic comics to read. They're the ones confiscated from the dorms for reading by torchlight after lights-out. There's a pretty nurse with red hair who walks around and checks on us by day and night. Everyone's in love with her. Except me. I'm only in love with Gretchen. I think about her every time the lights are out. One day I'll marry her. I wonder if she knows.

It's because it's so nice in sick-bay that nobody wants to get better. We claim to feel worse than we really are, because that's how to prolong paradise. Here we feel valued, important and privileged. The risk is the check-up by the visiting doctor. We live in fear and dread that he'll say we've recovered enough to go back. Tactics evolve.

Another boy in sick-bay shares a secret. Eating toothpaste makes you vomit and gives you a temperature. The first part is true. I get violently sick. Temperature. . ? No, it doesn't do that. Old faithful is needed. Go to the bathroom when doctor's approaching. Run hot tap till very hot, drink as much as possible. Take a mouthful, hold, limp as if very ill back to bed. Only swallow hot water when doctor produces thermometer. Reading is up by at least one and a half degrees. Doctor checks carefully, says you've got to stay another day. *Yahoo*, but don't show jubilation.

We constantly discuss how to stay longer. One chap decides to fall off the garden wall and hurt himself. He's allowed out there because he's re-something. *Re-suppurating*, someone says. *Re-coperating* someone else says. Anyway, he falls, and breaks his leg. He's been told he's well enough to go back to his dorm next day and is determined not to. With a broken tibia, he's taken to the General Hospital, where a plaster cast is applied. Next day, despite his heroics, he's back on his dormitory, back to classes, with plastered leg and walking-stick. Garden-wall-jumping doesn't work.

Thirty

Anand Singh is a fine figure of a man. He's a Sikh. There's a saying – *all Sikhs are Singhs, but not all Singhs are Sikhs.* Anand is. He was Dad's second-in-command on Geita ropeway, and proved a loyal friend to Mum after Dad died. 'Anythings you are wanting,' he says, 'you are telling me pliss, I am getting!' He's a big man, with an impressive beard, and he always wears a perfectly-wound turban, bright crimson, deep blue or striking orange. He served with the Indian Brigade in Burma during the war, and distinguished himself in combat against the Japanese. Mentioned in dispatches, Higgs says. Knew his commanding officer in the Irrawaddy delta. I've seen Anand talking with Kaizer. Different battles, same war, same country – Burma. They like and respect each other. '*Mahindi mzuri,*' Kaizer says. Good Indian. 'First-class fellow, you know!' Anand says.

Anand came to Tanganyika with a group of Sikh volunteers, all ex-Indian Brigade, who sought their fortunes in the African bush. He managed, a few years later, to bring his wife from Punjab, and soon they had three bouncing children. They're a happy family. Anand works hard, his wife looks after the home and children, and the family prospers.

After Dad died in February '57, Anand was a stricken man. He loved Dad, like an older brother. Dad was like that. He took the unfamiliar, the foreign, and particularly the weak or unfortunate, under his wing, and supported them any way he could. He showed this penchant for unconditional regard and kindness many times in his life, an example being his homemade advocaat for the injured Eugen Blüger.

After Dad's death, Anand moved into the number one position on the ropeway, with loyal Wait as number two. He took over MZ202, Dad's faithful open short-wheelbase Land Rover. It's such a paradox.

Here is this fine, trustworthy, and obviously promotable man, in a senior position on the mine, who has never done anything to discredit himself, is never unfaithful to his wife, and is widely respected, yet, because he is not white, he cannot become a member of the Lone Cone Club. Not that this matters a great deal to Anand. He's teetotal and wouldn't enjoy the drunken talk of the *Mzungu* hierarchy.

Anand constantly reminds Mum that, if ever she needs anything at all, she must call on him. Over the years he's as good as his word.

But Anand assumes extreme fame for something completely different. Ridge-Eight, known as 'Ridgate', is where the ropeway to Geita mine begins, seventeen miles away across hill, valley and sweltering, fetid bush. The evolution of the gold diggings at Ridgate is one involving tragedy, failure, and sudden success when someone realises that, although a stand-alone mine can't pay, due to the low pennyweight-per-ton of gold ore there, reducing costs by adding the ore to the harvest of Geita mine, and milling it together, means a profit can be made. By the time we arrive in Geita, Ridgate is a subsidiary gold-bearing-ore-source, not a mine.

The tunnels dug into the hillside by the early nineteen-twenties miners are crude. Narrow, shored up with logs hewn from the hillside, and only five foot high, they lead into darkness, and curve where the old diggers followed the yellow seam. The tunnels are abandoned in favour of open cast mining now. The gold-bearing rock is only sixty to a hundred feet deep, and the zigzags of the seams makes it sensible not to laboriously follow them in a tunnel, much easier to blast the top of the hill to kingdom-come, or to *blurryfucken* as some of the workers say, collect the good stuff in open air, and shovel it onto waiting ropeway buckets.

The disused tunnels provide the sweating, labouring men with something they cherish, even in the bush at forty degrees, with midges biting, snakes always near. This is privacy for intimate bodily functions. They have become bush-toilets.

In 1963, working at Ridgate, trying to fix a problem on a suspended bucket, which has a tendency to get stuck and hold up the works, Anand feels the urge to relieve himself. He enters an abandoned tunnel, shining his torch ahead. He comes to a fork and finds a convenient spot. He undoes his belt and the buttons on his trousers, and squats down. When he hears the growl, he thinks his bowels are in a worse state than he anticipated. Then he sees the eyes. Bright yellow eyes, big as teacups, staring at him from the dark just yards away. The next growl is louder and the eyes advance.

Anand tells the story for years to come. He runs, without bothering

289

to pull up his trousers, constrained at the ankles to short steps, just five yards ahead of the growling beast. He erupts into bright sunlight, 'and am exposing my most hidden secrets to everyone!'

Wait hears the leopard before he sees it. On the back of the Land Rover is Dad's old Czech *Brno* twelve-bore over-and-under double barrel shotgun, which Mum gave to Anand. It's loaded with two rounds of buckshot. Wait grabs it and whirls, just as Anand reaches the car and the leopard erupts from the tunnel only feet behind. He pulls both triggers and the beast collects the impact from both barrels. It slides to a halt, dead, with its blood-spattered nose against the back wheel. Isn't it strange? Dad loved Anand, and, though he's long-dead, it's Dad's old shotgun that saved Anand on this day!

I'm ten when I see the dead leopard. Anand drives MZ202 to the mine store, as part of a tour to show the beast to everyone. The bush telegraph has already done its work. '*Chui na jaribu ku kula Singa-Singa!*' Leopard tries to eat Sikh. That's around the mine-store workers long before the triumphant Anand and Wait roll into the compound.

The leopard is laid lengthways on the back of the short-wheelbase Land Rover. His neck is bent, and his head upright against the back window of the cab. His hind quarters and tail extend four feet beyond the open tailgate, to which it's tied with rope. The tip of his tail brushes the ground. He's at least six foot long if he's an inch. His nose and eyes are peppered with shot, and the side of his throat is torn open by the shotgun blast.

Wait stands atop his kill, waving Anand's shotgun. There's applause from the *wanaume*, or men, and a very grateful Anand Singh. Embarrassed, but smiling, Anand knows he's escaped by a whisker. He owes his life to Wait. And, he tells Mum, to 'your gracious late husband.'

At Lone Cone Club there's a peril more dangerous than Anand's, or any other, leopard. Harold Norris. He's a Sussex man, who always seems sixty years old. He's got a chin which juts so far his bottom teeth protrude beyond his top ones. This, and a strange nasal twang, give him a distinctive, very odd voice. He has a general-factotum type of job, nobody knows exactly what, including Harold. He loves to stand at the bar and tell long-winded stories of reminiscence about the 'early days' of Geita mine. Everyone knows they lived in tents, and lions walked in at night. His stories always start by defining precisely *which year* he's talking about. Subject hasn't come up yet. There's a detailed analysis of daughter Carol's age, and what wife Hilda was doing at the time.

'It was in 1949. . . Carol was three. Yup!' Pause. 'Carol was three, and Hilda was learning to drive. . . No, it was in 1948. Carol was two, and Hilda first came to Geita.' Pause, scratching of prominent chin. 'No, it was in 1947. . . Carol was one, and, and. . . And *then* again, maybe it was in 1949. . .' Big accentuation of word 'then'. Thoughtful expression. More chin-scratching.

'No, it was 1946!' Harold looks pleased with himself, takes a mouthful of beer. Now, his victim thinks, after several minutes of trying, he's pinned down the year, can get on with the story. Harold looks thoughtful again. His chin gets even juttier. 'Now let me see. . . it was in 1947. Carol was one, and Hilda. . .' The victim despairs and looks desperately for rescue. Nobody has ever heard a story from Harold. He's never sorted out *when* it was. There's only one person who was bold enough to say he wouldn't listen to this.

It was 1956, and Dad was having a quiet beer. Harold sidled up and stood beside him. 'Hello Dick,' he said, bottom teeth glinting.

'Harold,' Dad said, many times exasperated by endless stories which didn't start, 'why don't you go where you're wanted?' Harold was taken aback, and never started another story with Dad. Mum said Dad was cruel. Dad said it was either that or shoot the bugger!

In '63 Harold's still at the bar most nights, waiting Venus-Fly-Trap-like for another victim to regale with how old Carol was and what Hilda was doing. Sometimes, not able to trap an adult, he comes out the bar to regale us kids with his never-starting stories. If we see him coming, we dash for cover.

My relationship with Mrs Snel has been fatally jaundiced, at best, since that long-ago day I told her to 'Speak Swahili, Dammit!' then carried on decapitating her precious flowers. That, and the things I said about her private parts, of which, though she didn't understand, she got the gist. To me she's the epitome of *Mzungu* oppression. To her I'm the devil himself. It's not on purpose that I add fuel to the incinerator of her distaste. I'm cogent of what Mum said so many times about keeping on the right side of the dreaded *Wazungu*. If I can I'll avoid the old harridan. But fate keeps stepping in.

It starts in a small, dense wood down a narrow valley near the caravan park at Plympton in Devon. We're on holiday and it's 1962. Fraser decides I've lived with two women too long. It's about time I become a man. He'll toughen me up by getting me to kill something. He has a small four-ten shotgun and a box of cartridges. He takes me into the wood, points out a little brown bird in a tree, and tells me to shoot it. This isn't the first time I've shot at a bird, but up to now it's only been with a catapult, and I usually miss. Now I point the gun, determined not to be 'soft'. I pull the trigger. The gun barks, the little bird disintegrates, and Fraser pats me on the back. 'Well done!' he says. I'm bewildered. I've killed again. Like Tembo's puppy. But was it fair? Did the bird have any chance at all? When she hears about the killing, Mum says there's a bird-widow somewhere, and poor little baby-birds with no father. I'm sad and tearful, which Fraser says proves the ineptness of women to bring up a boy.

Back in Geita I wrestle with my confusion. Am I really a *softie*, a 'mummy's boy', like Fraser says? If not, why was I upset after I shot the little brown bird? Maybe killing is something I have to get *used* to, to stop it upsetting me. It says that in war-comics. Maybe if I kill more I'll get over this pity-thing, this awful feeling when I do it. Just then the pellet-gun appears in the camp. Charlie Praze has one and boasts he shoots lots of birds. He feels nothing at all, he says. I nag Mum till she gives in and buys me a used *Gekado* 1.77 airgun from a shop in Mwanza. It's made in Germany, like the old *Mauser* rifles. I take target practice, shooting empty cans and poisonous blue-headed lizards high on tree-trunks. Charlie says pigeons are good to eat. I shoot a couple. Umali roasts them. They taste rancid and there's hardly any meat. Is this God's punishment? He can't like the idea of me with a gun. Not that the range is enough to get him!

It's an ordinary, boring afternoon. I've had the gun a month and I don't know what to shoot any more. The sun is scorching the bush. I'm walking up a narrow footpath which winds from our house to Top Road. It's very still, quiet as the graves at Samina. The air shimmers in the heat, and there isn't a breath of a breeze. I wonder where the *njiwa*-birds are today. Just to hear a friendly *ooh-oor-oor* would make me feel less lonely. Have they fled because they think I'll shoot them? I won't do that. They're my *rafikis*, friends! There isn't even a *Mwewe* bird soaring high on the thermals from the burning land. Are they, too, departed? I approach a tall acacia tree through the elephant-grass beside the path. Suddenly the silence is broken by a loud, almost human, and very eery sound. '*Haa-daa-daa*', it goes, '*haaa-daa-daa*'. There's a drumming sound of big wings beating the air, and a most curious creature alights on a branch high in the acacia.

The *hadeda* ibis is a very strange creature. It's a guinea-fowl-sized, long-legged wading bird, with a scimitar-shaped, downward curved, beak, half as long as its body, which it fishes with in the shallows. Its light grey body is relieved by orange on the front of its bill, and bluish-green on its tail and the tips of its wings. It has staring yellow buttons for eyes. I've seen *hadedas* before, but not often. Geita's a bit far from Lake Victoria. I remember, long ago, Umali talked about this bird. Witchcraft, like the *fisi*, and long life. *Kagogo* is a Swahili name. *Wazee*, or old people, are often called *kagogo*.

Sitting on a high branch in the acacia, oblivious to danger, this strange bird contemplates me beadily. It's spooky. After loudly announcing its arrival, it's quiet, perching and analysing me with those evil buttons. No surprise ancient Egyptians mummified ibises, and entombed them with their dead. Not just *watu* are superstitious. I feel dread run up my spine. I'm being challenged by God. He hasn't forgotten me, and now he's disguised as a bird. Something else. I've only seen *hadedas* in the air or on the ground. Why is he perching in a tree? It proves that this is a challenge. I bring the airgun to my shoulder and take aim.

As puzzled as me, scientifically, not superstitiously, is Mrs Snel, who, unseen and unsuspected by me, is also watching the *hadeda* from the other side of the tree. She's known for her interest in ornithology and the *hadeda* has been intriguing her for weeks. Today she's lucky. She's just arrived when he makes his loud call and perches. She focuses her Zeiss camera.

My pellet hits him square in the head. There's a brief flurry of wing and tail, and the heavy bird plunges, stone dead, at Mrs Snel's feet. She's dumbstruck. Then she yells in fury. 'Who did that, *who* shot the bird?' I can't see, but I hear the familiar voice. The grass rustles as she stalks round the tree. Only one escape. Oblivious to scratches and pokes of thorn and twig, I plunge into deep elephant grass and throw myself flat. Mrs Snel goes round and round the tree, ever more breathless. She passes me by feet, while I hold my breath and try to still my pounding heart. She returns to the *hadeda*-corpse, then, at long last, goes away.

Next day is Sunday. At the club Mrs Snel strides purposefully my way. She stops feet away and my heart pounds again. 'Did you shoot my ibis bird?' she says.

'Me?' I say, 'what ibis bird?'

It's Saturday the twenty third of November '63. It's ten in the morning. Gretchen, Sophia, Antonio, Stefano and I are playing near the weighbridge on top road. We like watching the trucks full of wood drive onto the metal platform to be weighed. We hear Dieti shouting from far off. He's running our way. 'Kilt,' we hear him shout, but the other words are indistinct. He runs up, out of breath, and stops.

'President Kennedy,' he wheezes, 'kilt in Dallas!'

'What?' I ask. The president of America?

'*Vati* heard it on hiss shortwave radio. Kennedy vos shot, in Dallas, yesterday!' The girls start crying. I can't understand them. They don't even know the president. Or America. Antonio and Stefano agree with me. We go off to play our own, boys-only game. Who's Kennedy anyway? Where's Dallas? Gretchen looks so pretty when she's crying. I wish I could hug her.

For Christmas '63 Mum gives me a second hand bicycle. It's red, and a girl's one, but I neither know nor care. It's my first bike and I discover the freedom of the road, or, at least, the dirt tracks and footpaths of Geita. My bike has a cable-driven speedometer on the handlebar and that spurs me to reach speeds which astound me. Downhill, pedalling furiously, I'm often able to do more than fifty miles an hour. This, on sandy surfaces strewn with stone, wearing no helmet, nor any protective gear.

Charlie Praze, the assistant manager's son, has always had a bicycle. It's another thing that separates and divides us. Just like I have no father, and he does, I have no bike, and he does. Now I have one, he cycles to my house often, then we ride off somewhere together.

Charlie is a year older than me and has always been taller and stronger. From when he was nine, his parents, who can afford it, have sent him to boarding school 'at home' in England. Where Becky is now. To us in the colonies, that's the height of posh. School at 'home' is a 'good thing', because it stops children 'going native'. That's what Charlie's mother tells Mum, knowing she can't afford to send Becky and me to a private boarding school in England.

One day Charlie arrives at my house and asks me to ride out with him to a village ten miles away. On the way we come across three ragged *totos* aged between six and seven. They're very frightened of us, which I don't understand. Charlie jumps off his bike and leans it against a tree. Then he breaks a twig off a tree, holds it like a gun, and points it at the terrified *totos*. In Swahili he says, 'Give me all your money!'

The *totos* burst into tears and plead, saying they have no money, but please don't kill them. I watch in horror. The poor kids think the stick in Charlie's hand is a gun! White people, or *Wazungu*, have strong magic. Even though they've watched him break the twig from a tree, they believe he can shoot them with it. When the smallest of the three, a little girl, produces two ten-cent coins and offers them to Charlie, who is laughing delightedly, I break my silence.

'Stop it,' I say.

'What?' Charlie says, turning to me, surprised.

'Stop making them cry,' I say.

'Why should I?'

' 'Cos it's cruel,' I answer.

294

'You're a girl,' he says. Seeing their chance, the three *totos* disappear into the undergrowth beside the path. Charlie looks around. 'You've let them go,' he snarls.

'I'm going home,' I say, turning my bicycle.

'I don't like you anyway,' Charlie shouts after me. I don't care. I have already decided I don't like Charlie Praze either. 'Oh yeah,' he shouts, 'and I'm going to *have* your little Gretchen!' He makes the sign of one index finger through the loop of another with a thumb. I stop and let my bicycle clatter on the road.

'You what?' I say, my hands balling into fists, my throat constricting. I take two steps towards him, but he laughs and rides off.

'I'll get you!' he shouts as he pedals away. I have exactly the same thought, but it's *me* who'll get *him!*

I'm pedalling the bike uphill towards our house when I have my first attack. It starts with an urge to cough, but when I do I need to cough again, and harder. It gets worse and worse, until eventually, after dropping the bike onto the ground, and kneeling on all fours in the dirt, I vomit. Then the coughing starts again and I fight for my breath. After a long time I recover, but I'm not strong enough to pedal my bike. I push it the rest of the way. I don't know why I've had the coughing fit and I don't mention it to anybody.

At home I tell Umali about Charlie. He says he's a bad *Mzungu,* and I did right to confront him.

Two days later, lying on my bed reading a comic, I have another attack. This time it's so severe that, trying to dash to the bathroom to vomit in the toilet, I faint from exertion and lack of oxygen. I strike the side of my face on the big brass door-knob. When I come to, my face is burning, and there's a pool of blood on the floor. Sandy is licking me desperately, whimpering. Umali hears the thump, and he's there, hoisting me to my feet. He's amazingly strong for someone with pin-legs.

'What is it?' he asks in Swahili, 'what is making you fall, Jimu, are you sick?' He looks anxious. His eyes are wide and there's sweat on his brow.

'*Nine kohoa,*' I begin. I was coughing. I can't continue because the coughing starts again. Umali helps me to my bed, but I cough so hard I vomit all over the counterpane before I can lie down.

'Jimu, Jimu, you are really sick,' he says. He uses the word *ugonjwa,* which conveys seriousness. Dad was *ngonjwa* just before he died. I regain my breath at last, but now I feel a new emotion. Panic. The *watu* who are *ngonjwa* always die. I'm going to die. I tell Umali.

'You won't die Jimu,' Umali says soothingly, '*pole*', peace, but his words belie his expression. I'm sweating profusely and feel exhausted. Umali fetches a damp cloth and wipes my face. He rolls up the counterpane I vomited on, pulls it from under me.

'*Lala Jimu*, sleep, I'll tell *Mama* you are *ngonjwa*, and she'll call *Bwana Muganga*.' The doctor. He draws the curtains on the bright sunlight. I'm so sleepy. Umali gently wipes the graze on my cheek with a cool damp cloth. Then he leaves, closing the door behind him. I notice a large *sufuria* on the floor. For me to vomit in, just in case. I didn't see him bring it in.

I awake to find Mum and Josef Weiss standing beside my bed. 'Vot iss wrong?' he asks.

I start to speak, but start coughing again. I cough so hard I think my lungs will burst, and I vomit on the floor, missing Umali's *sufuria* by a foot.

'It's serious,' I dimly hear Josef say to Mum. I notice Umali's worried face behind them.

'He play with the *totos*, so vot you expect?' Josef says to Mum.

'What do you mean, Doctor?' Mum asks.

'He hass Tuberculosis, TB, is vot I mean,' Josef replies. 'Bring him to hospital in der der morning, und I do zer chest X-ray.'

Next morning Mum drives me to the hospital. In Geita there's really only one hospital, if wards, operating theatre, dispensary and doctor's office make a hospital. I have another coughing fit on the way, which makes Mum drive poor Maisy far too fast for the dirt road. The hospital is known to us as the 'African hospital', because only Africans are admitted there. If Europeans, or *Wazungu,* need to be in hospital, they're admitted to that little bungalow known as the 'European Hospital'. Where Dad died, where Stroessner blew his brains out. If a *Mzungu* needs surgery or an x-ray, that's done in the African Hospital, then they're brought back.

Maisie skids to a halt with locked wheels in a cloud of dust on the stony ground beside the hospital. We walk past the big mango tree out front. It's one of the places Lutoli and I often sneak at sunset, when nobody can see us, to throw big sticks and knock mangoes loose. Soon they'll be ripe enough again. At this time of day the tree is the hospital waiting-room. Sitting on the ground at its base are twenty *watu*, all waiting to be seen by a nurse or the doctor. They'll wait for hours and hours, trying to escape the fierce sun in the tree's shade.

'*Jimu!*' I am hailed as we go past. It's Lutoli. I stop. He looks thin.

'*Nini unafanya hapa?*' I ask him in surprise. What you doing here?

'*Nina kohowa*,' he answers. I am coughing. He gives a short cough to demonstrate.

'*Mimi vilevile,*' I say. Me too.

'Come on,' Mum says, waiting.

'I won't go in unless Lutoli comes too,' I say defiantly. Mum stares at Lutoli, at me. Her face breaks into a smile. She's known Lutoli since his infancy.

'Come, Lutoli,' she says, 'I don't care what the doctor says!' The three of us walk into the hospital. Josef is waiting.

'Vot iss *ziss?*' he exclaims when he sees us, 'der United Nations, *TANU,* or vott?'

'He's my friend,' I say.

'Your friend, eh?' he says, cocking his head.

'*Mna ugonjwa?*' he asks Lutoli, who's trying to hide behind Mum. Are you ill?

'*Ndio, Bwana Mukubwa,*' Lutoli whispers, his voice hoarse with terror. Yes, Big Master.

'*Una kohoa?*' Josef asks. Are you coughing?

'*Ndio,*' Lutoli manages.

'Dass ist ein plague,' Josef retorts to Mum. 'Der TB iss all arount!'

'Can you see both boys?' Mum asks.

'Vell, vot a mudder you are,' Josef mutters, grinning despite himself. 'Die mudder to der naughtiest boy uff Geita, und now also to hiss black freund!' If it was up to Josef, he wouldn't separate the races anyway. Saw enough racial hatred in Germany. But unwritten colonial rules have to be obeyed. Not now. 'Come in, all uff you!' he says, his gruff voice breaking into a laugh. 'Vott can zey do anyvay?'

X-rays show we both have 'spots on der lungs', which means tuberculosis. We are lucky to live in our time, Josef says, because just twenty years ago there was no effective drug treatment. Josef starts us on Streptomycin. It's the antibiotic which kills the TB bug, which he says is *mycobacterium tuberculosis*.

Streptomycin is given by injection into the bum. The syringe is made of glass, and very big. The needle is thick, because the preparation is viscous, or is that *vicious?* The pain when Josef plunges the needle into the upper outer part of my buttock is bad. When he presses the plunger it's unbearable. After the injection my whole cheek is numb and achey. We have to have another injection twice a week for six weeks.

Walking to the hospital for my third torture I think I can't go through with it. Mum's persuaded me I must because I'll die if I don't. My feet carry me unwillingly closer to the hospital. I'm in two minds. My heart's beating hard with two kinds of fear – death fear and vicious-injection fear. My mouth is dry, and I feel sick. I'm terrified of

297

the next needle. There's a debate going on in my head. I can't face this injection. My bum still aches from the last one. I'll refuse to have it. I'll go in to the hospital, then refuse. That's more manly than just not going. That's stating my case.

Lutoli and I are truly *wadugu*, brothers. He's waiting for me under the mango tree, and he's made the identical decision to me. '*Sitaki!*' he says. I don't want.

'*Mimi vilevile!*' I reply, relieved I'm not alone.

'*Kuja!*' shouts the male orderly in white shorts and shirt, standing in the open doorway. Come! Josef only gave the first injections, then the orderlies did it. Lutoli and I look at each other. Should we run for it? There's a wordless conversation between us. It's ridiculous. If we didn't want the injection, why have we come? We've got this *blurry ugonjwa*, sickness, and we'll die without treatment.

Lutoli's eyes say he's beaten. Reluctantly, he walks into the torture chamber. I'm just behind. He undoes the top of his shorts and lies face-down on the couch. A grinning orderly appears, holding the huge glass syringe needle-upwards. He's actually enjoying this! It's the last straw. Even as the needle pierces Lutoli's skin, I'm turning to run. Too late, there are two more beefy orderlies between me and the door. There's no escape. How have they anticipated me like this? Later, Josef tells me, 'I know you, Jimmy, I know you vill try to run vun day, so I tell zem votch you, und zey do!' It's a choice. Impossible wrestling match and injection, or injection only. I submit in terror and futility.

For six weeks I have to rest at home. Sandy is with me all the time. Finally I'm allowed to ride my bike again, and hang around with Lutoli and my friends. The TB is cured, Josef says, looking at the latest X-ray. Certainly I'm feeling better, and that horrible cough has gone. Lutoli says he's better too, and it was all worth it. I'm still cross about the injections. You should be grateful, Mum says. I am, but why did it have to hurt so much? Something to do with a saying I heard. What was it? Oh yes – 'gaining pain', or is it 'paining gain' – sounds stupid either way.

Thirty-one

I've been enchanted by Red Indian kayaks ever since I remember cowboy films. They're so cleverly made, of sticks bound with rawhide and animal skins stretched tight over the frame, making a robust, waterproof and portable vessel. What a thing to have, I think. With one of those, I can get someone to take me to Nungwe Bay on Lake Victoria, just fifteen miles from the camp. There I can paddle out in my own boat! Maybe I can even fit a sail. I have images of my canoe gliding along on open water, leaving a long straight wake behind. Perhaps, even, it'll turn into the long-range canoe of my endless imaginings.

Three times in the last two years I've gone into the bush with Umali's panga and cut long sticks from trees. I've laboured long to bend and tie them into a canoe-shape with self-made sisal string. I've stretched and nailed old bed-sheets over the outside, and painted them with left-over house-paint for waterproofing. Three unmitigated disasters. Everything wrong. Paint not waterproof, comes off in the rain. The twigs of the frame change shape with drying out, and my canoes end up like bent sausages. Tembo mercifully notices my humiliation and burns the evidence on the fire outside his hut. I'm grateful.

One day I have a *Eureka* moment. If you can't do it, I think, find someone who can! Jaswan Singh, the old Sikh who helped with the gun, is the obvious choice. Sure, he's a fitter and turner, not a carpenter, but wood, steel, what's the difference? I need a plan for my canoe, something I can show the old man. I sit with a pencil and paper and draw my very first boat-plan. It's got two long, bent side-poles of wood and these are joined to a single bottom, or keel-piece, by a dozen ribs. After rubbing out and re-drawing several times, I'm ready to take my plan to the engineering works. This is what it looks like:

JIMU'S PLAN:

'Dis vun vill be capsizing!' Jaswan says, scatching his beard. He met Dad lots of times in the early days, in the company of his cousin Anand. He told Mum, just like Anand, that he'd always help the Penhaligon family. I know he meant it. It doesn't strike me that I'm taking advantage of an old man's promise. He's staring from under his big glasses. 'This boat, Jimu, cannot be staying up on thin bottom like this,' he says. He takes a pencil from behind his ear and draws next to my plan:

JASWAN'S PLAN:

'Now,' he says, with wider bottom, there is chance.' He smiles. 'If you want building, I help. But *you* do working, yes?'

'Yes,' I say eagerly, 'thank you.'

'Well, first you must be deciding what wood you are using. For top-pieces, I t'ink two inch by one. We have plenty.' He points to a pile of thin-cut timber on the floor. 'How big you are wanting boat?'

'Dunno,' I say.

'Vel, say nine feet long, then you are needing eleven foot for allow bending, yes?'

'Yes,' I say. Jaswan is very clever.

'So, you are selecting two pieces, and cutting to eleven foot. You know how use saw?'

'Yes, I know.' He smiles.

'Using this,' he says, handing me a roll-tape measure, 'marking eleven feet. Then you are needing two shorter ones, ten feet, to go lower, under top ones, yes?'

'Yes,' I say, feeling a bit out of depth.

'Well, start now. I am having work to do. When you have cutting these woods, calling me!'

'Thank you, *asante*,' I say. He smiles.

'You are reminding me much your father,' he says, and leaves me to it. I pick up his tape measure and walk over to the pile of timber. It's the beginning of my first real construction project.

It's the day after I start my boat-building when Dieti comes to my house just after I've returned from the engineering works. He's found a remarkable thing on Top Road, on his way to our place. He's never seen anything like it before.

'Look at zis!' he says excitedly when he arrives. The excitement's brought back his German accent. I've also never seen anything like it. It's a glossy magazine. On the front cover is a photograph of a topless lady. She's got big tits, very pale in comparison to the rest of her, which is deeply tanned. She's smiling. Doesn't look ashamed at all. The magazine is called *Playboy*. Odd, what's a play-boy, or any kind of boy, got to do with tits? What does *play* mean?

'Gretchen has titses like dese,' he says, 'I haff seen zem!'

'Really?' I say, suddenly more interested.

'Zere's more inside,' Dieti says, 'look!' He turns a page, and there's a lady, completely naked, lying on a beach. Her breasts are huge and only a raised knee hides her privates.

'Where did this come from?' I ask.

'On der road, somevun must haff dropped it,' he says. He turns more pages. More naked ladies. It makes me feel strange all over.

'What you going to do with it?' I ask him.

'You keep it!' he says.

'Thanks,' I say. 'That'll be nice.' What else is there to say? Where will I hide it? Just then there's footsteps in the passage, and Dieti shoves the magazine under my pillow. It's Umali. He wants to know if we want *chai*, tea. No thanks we say. He leaves, and out comes the magazine. This needs serious study.

The boat-building is slow. I select pieces of wood, measure them, mark the desired length with a pencil, then saw off the excess. Jaswan sets up a trestle-table for me, and begins to assemble the pieces. The two eleven foot lengths are screwed together at the ends, then separated in the middle by a two-foot-six plank. This, Jaswan says, will be a

301

'thwart', or seat. The two ten-foot lengths are similarly attached at the ends, but separated in the middle by a shorter plank of twenty inches. Thus the bottom, though flat, will be narrower than the top of the canoe.

Next Jaswan sets me cutting sixteen two-foot lengths of one-by-one inch timber, to make ribs which will join the top and bottom of the frame. When they're all cut, Jaswan marks each one with a notch, top and bottom, and gives me a jigsaw to cut the notches out. These will help attach the ribs at each end. When it's done, he drills them all with a big drill, and screws them into place. It's been three days work, and the frame is beginning to look canoe-like.

'I have canvas you can using for outer-skin,' Jaswan announces on the fourth day. He holds up a roll of thick white canvas. It looks perfect. 'You can be using small nails,' he says, producing a jam-jar full of one inch nails with very big heads. I spend the whole day cutting and nailing the canvas to the ribs of the canoe. Jaswan intercedes often, to help me pull the fabric tighter. By the time the workshop closes, there's a very definite canoe on the trestle table.

'Tomorrow,' Jaswan says, 'you can be painting. I have tin thick oil paint not needed – green.'

'Thank you, green's great,' I say. What a kind man Jaswan is!

One afternoon when I'm at home because I have to wait two days for the first coat of green oil-paint to dry before applying a second coat, Dieti arrives in an excited state. When he's like this he always blinks furiously and his head nods repeatedly. Charlie Praze once called him 'Noddy', but the title hasn't stuck, because Dieti's a more meaningful name – we all know him as a very funny little chap. At twelve he's still the size of a nine year old, and his mother is often heard to lament that 'Dieter vill chust not grow!'

Dieti is so excited he has difficulty telling me why. Between the violent blinking and nodding, and his other habit of stammering when aroused, it's almost impossible to understand what he's trying to say.

'Come,' he says. 'Qvick, she is. . . zere. . . in ze bass, nakkit!'

'Who?' I asked.

'Gretchen. . .'

'Und?' I say, despite myself.

'Und, und,' he nods, whether in agreement or in habit I cannot tell. I think it must be habit because there's nothing to agree with.

'Und Gretchen, in ze bass, und, und. . . she iss nakkit!'

'Ze bass?' I ask incredulously, wondering how Gretchen could be in a fish, naked.

'In mein haus,' Dieti adds, nodding and blinking simultaneously. A fish in the house, with Gretchen in it, naked? No, suddenly I understand. She's in the *bath*, at Dieti's house! He sees comprehension on my face. Gretchen! At fifteen she's blossomed into a beauty. So perfect, so poised, so fragrant, so. . . *artistically created.* How can the same God who invented scorpions, killed Dad and sent me to Arusha, make someone like Gretchen? When I'm near her I feel I'm with an angel. She can see how I feel, and I know she's amused. I'd love to see more of her. Her body, I mean.

'Ve go, yes, ve spy from der upstairs. . ?'

'Yes,' I shout, his excitement mine too, 've go now!' His accent is catchy. Ve, I mean we, run the winding footpath to Dieti's place, arriving there breathless, but wildly motivated. We dash past the framed picture of Eugen Blüger with *Generalveldmarschall* Erwin Rommel, in the lounge, me avoiding Rommel's steely gaze. He wouldn't approve of this venture.

'Up zere,' he says breathlessly as we approach the bathroom door. There is, when I look up, a hatch in the ceiling. Dieti holds a finger to his lips. There are splashing sounds coming from the bathroom. 'Ze table,' Dieti whispers, pointing at a wall table in the passage. I take the glass vase off and place it carefully on the floor. Then we lift the table and carry it to below the hatch. Dieti stands on the table and pushes it open. It's very dark up there. He pulls himself up and his short legs disappear.

'Are you komink?' comes a whisper from above. I climb on the table and grab the edge of the opening. Then I haul myself up. It's pitch dark. After a while my eyes grow accustomed and I can make out Dieti's silhouette. There are a few paper-thin slivers of light coming through where the corrugated iron sheets of the roof are joined. The overlaps between the sheets are waterproof, but light has a way of getting through.

I look and feel my way. The ceiling is built of raw sections of sawn timbers, which threaten to splinter my fingers at each touch. The planks are in big squares 4 foot across. Between the spaces is ceiling board. It's used in all the houses here. Three quarters of an inch thick, it's made of compressed wood fibre, sawdust and glue. It's very soft, and not made to bear weight.

'Zat vay!' Dieti whispers, trying to control his breathing. I look and see a small round hole, half an inch wide, five yards from where I sit on the rough wood. From the hole a yellow beam shines, making a large bright patch of light on the corrugated iron roof.

'You go first,' I say, suddenly seeing something very funny in this.

It reminds me of the name of a mythical book called 'Jumping Off Mountains,' by Yugo First. I fight to suppress a giggle.

'Okay,' Dieti whispers, and he starts crawling towards the light. I stifle my ill-timed chortle and follow. It's very difficult feeling my way along the supports, and I have several splinters in my hands and knees.

Dieti reaches the light. I feel a surge of jealousy. He's going to get the first look. Gretchen. . . I want to be first to look through the peephole. I wish Dieti would, well, I wish he wasn't up here with me. God has a strange way of giving you what you wish for.

I'm just behind Dieti, one of his feet no more than six inches from my nose, when, distracted by the prospect of peeping through the hole, he makes a fatal error. He puts his weight on the board between the wooden supports. With a tearing sound the board gives way, and Dieti plummets, with a loud crash, into the bathroom below.

There's a rent in the ceiling three foot by two. In the brief millisecond before hell breaks loose, I see the top half of Gretchen, wet blonde hair hanging limply, at one end of the bath, and a stunned Dieti half-kneeling in front of her, with one arm at a crazy angle over the side of the bath. Gretchen's arms are just coming up to cover her chest.

Dieti was right. In that briefest glimpse I see they're just like the ones on the lady in *Playboy*. Only better. Gretchen's mouth is opening to scream, and she's jumping up, concealing her groin with a facecloth. I've seen enough, though in better times I'd like to see more, and I'm furiously retracing my crawl back to the hatch. The screams burst about me. Gretchen, shocked, indignant, angry. Dieti in agony.

I get to the hatch and climb down. No point closing it. The game is up. I flee down the corridor. As I near the kitchen I collide with Dieti's mum. Mrs Blüger was in the garden. She's hurrying to investigate the commotion.

'Vot is it?' she shouts, grabbing me by the arm and pulling me down the corridor. The sound from the bathroom has changed. Gretchen has stopped screaming, but Dieti is howling like a hyena. As we reach the bathroom the door flies open. Gretchen has a towel around her. Dieti is still in the bath, his arm over the side. His face is contorted in agony and he's sobbing. There's blood on his lips. He's hit his mouth on something.

'They were spying on me!' Gretchen yells furiously. She throws the door open and points at the devastated ceiling. Of all the Blüger family, only Gretchen has no trace of a German accent.

'You fell from zere?' Mrs Blüger asks Dieti. He subdues his anguished sounds to a whimper.

'*Mein arm, mein schulter*!' he gasps, trying to hold his arm and

304

shoulder at once, spittle and blood coming from the corner of his mouth.

'Vot you sink you are doink?' Mrs Blüger demands. 'Vait ven *vati* hears about zis!'

'You too, Jim!' she adds. 'Your mudder vill know uff zis!'

'Sorry,' I say lamely.

'You *vill* be,' says Mrs Blüger, letting go my arm and going to examine Dieter. I'm free. I run pursued by demons.

At home I lock my bedroom door, get into bed, and cover my head with the blanket.

I get off very lightly for my part in the botched venture. Not so, Dieti. He hits the side of the bath with his left arm, breaks both radius and ulna. His mouth-bleed is from catching his lip on the broken ceiling-board. He has to wear a plaster cast on his arm for two months. Fortunately, after the shock of what happened, Mr and Mrs Blüger, and even Mum, see the funny side. 'Boys vill be boys,' Eugen says to Mum. Gretchen decides it was quite funny, really. . !

How am I going to face Gretchen? It's obvious I wanted to see her naked. But it was Dieti's idea. If she was amused by me doting on her before, she'll be laughing to *tapika* now. Vomit. But Gretchen is a strange girl.

I'm lying on my bed reading a comic. It's a hot afternoon, just for a change. Gretchen doesn't come round often now Becky's in England. I could go over to the Blüger's house, but I don't know if I can face her. My shame is too keen. It's only three days since our disgrace.

'Hello.' A melodic female voice. Gretchen, standing by my bedroom door. She's come over, even though Becky's not here! She's wearing blue dungarees and a bright yellow shirt. Her blonde hair is cut short. She looks radiant.

'Hi,' I say, sitting up on my bed, trying to keep my voice even.

'May I come in?' A half-smile plays at her lips. What's she up to?

'Yeah,' I grunt, my voice squeaky, my heart racing. She comes in. She has something in her hand. A rolled-up magazine. My heart pounds. I know what it is.

'Can I sit?' she asks. There *is* nowhere except my bed. This would be so great, if I hadn't spied on her. She doesn't wait for my answer. She's sitting on the edge of my bed, smelling of wild flowers, looking like a nordic goddess. She unrolls the magazine. It *is* the *Playboy* Dieti found on Top Road! How did she get it?

'Do you think my tits are like these?' she says.

305

'Dunno,' I say, my thoughts reeling. Is she here to tease me? There's a smile tugging at the corner of her mouth. I decide to play her game.

'Maybe they are,' I say, trying to sound nonchalant.

'You had a good look, didn't you?' she says.

'Maybe, maybe not. . .'

'Come on, I saw you up there, staring at me.'

'Yes,' I reply truthfully. Why isn't she angry? Why does she think this is funny?

'You like me, Jim?' she asks, looking serious.

'Yup.' What else can I say?

'I know you do,' she says. 'Do you think I'm as pretty as the girls in this magazine?' She's watching me closely, her face only inches from mine.

'Of course you are,' I say. 'Prettier!'

'Was it you or Dieter who thought of spying on me?' She's using her brother's formal name. What does that mean? Now here's a conundrum. If I say it was me, I'll be a filthy beast. If I say him, I'm selling out on Dieti.

'It was me,' I say.

'No it wasn't. Dieter told me it was his idea. You know, I wish you were older. You're a brave little man!' I like the *man* bit, not the *little*. She's getting up to go. There's something I need to know.

'Where did you get the *Playboy*?' I ask.

'Under Dieti's bed, when I helped Mum turn the mattress.' Thank goodness, she's saying Dieti, not Dieter. Must be softening. 'As soon as I saw it,' she continues, 'I knew it was connected to you boys spying on me.' I remain silent.

'Bye,' she says sweetly as she leaves my room. I lie there, my senses reeling again.

My canoe is built, painted, ready for launching on Lake Victoria. I've named her HMS *Geita*. She really looks the business. Everyone's jealous of me. Jaswan is delighted with the result. He's even made me two laminated wooden oars, and fashioned and fitted swivelling iron rowlocks. All from scrap on the dump. Then the bomb strikes. No way am I allowed to launch it on the lake. Mum's spoken to Mr Snel, who says I'll be eaten by a crocodile, or drown, so that's it. No lake! The club swimming pool is as far as HMS *Geita* will ever go.

I decide to bide my time, do sea-trials on the pool, and work on Mum and Mr Snel later. HMS *Geita* is launched on the pool, and soon becomes a source of great fun to all the *Wazungu* children. Now there's more than just swimming to be had.

The pool is huge, Olympic size, which makes it fifty metres long. Kids crowd into the canoe, as many as six at a time, paddle about, rock and capsize her, squealing and falling in the water. They turn her upright, clamber back in and carry on. The green oil paint never dries. I don't know why, but it leaves green streaks all over the sides of the pool from scraping by.

I take lots of passengers for rides in my canoe. Principal among these is Sandy, who stands in the prow like an old sea-dog, and won't get off even when I put the bow up against the side. When nobody's there HMS *Geita* floats forlornly, upright or capsized, at one end of the pool or the other, depending on the breeze. My canoe has become a fixture in Lone Cone Club pool.

Becky has been writing heart-rending letters about how unhappy she is in England. Aunt Natalie's a real witch to her, she says. She begs Mum to bring her back home to Geita. She can continue her studies through a correspondence course. I can tell Mum's weakening. I'd love to have Becky back, so I add my powers of persuasion to hers.

Meantime light entertainment comes again to Lone Cone Club. Dieti and I are walking past the half-open door to the room behind the bar, the one where glasses and ashtrays are washed, and crates of beer and cold drinks stored. Mrs Snel's in there with the cleaning maids and there's a hullabaloo going on. The maids are screaming in laughter, and she's shouting at them. 'What,' she yells in broken and nasal Swahili, 'has got into you?' This ignites fresh paroxysms of laughter. 'I only wanted a Swahili *kisimi*. . !' Fresh gales of uncontrolled mirth. Dieti and I fall about. Mrs Snel is asking for a Swahili saying, or lesson, but saying *kisimi* instead of *kisimo*. The 'i' in place of the 'o' is critical. She's asking for a Swahili clitoris!

Thirty-two

On the twelfth of January 1964 African rebels led by a Ugandan revolutionary, self-styled 'Field Marshal' John Okello, seize power from the Arabs in Zanzibar. The Sultan, Jamshid-bin-Adbullah, scion of the ancient Albusaid dynasty, whose influence once stretched from Muscat in Oman in the north, to the coasts of Tanganyika and Kenya, the islands of Zanzibar and Lamu, and across the Indian Ocean to the shores of India and modern Pakistan, is deposed. He and his family are plucked from certain doom by the Royal Marines, and taken to England on the carrier HMS *Centaur*.

In a frenzy of hate-driven killing, seventeen thousand Arab men, women and children are driven into the sea and shot by the victorious revolutionaries. For many days the straits of Zanzibar, between the Island and the little Tanganyikan port of Bagamoyo, is littered with bloated corpses. Some float up onto the beaches north and south of Bagamoyo, where hyenas feast on the unexpected bounty. Many more are consumed by frenzied sharks driven wild by the bonanza of carrion.

On holiday with relatives in Bagamoyo is Amil Mistree, a clerk who works with Mum at the mine store. Amil is a small, trim man, who wears large, thick, glasses. He's extremely nervous, and reminds me, perhaps because of the magnification of his eyes by his spectacle lenses, of a rabbit caught in bright torchlight. He tends to panic when the sums on his 'leger shits' don't add up, and he's always asking Mum 'to be helping me pleeze.'

At Bagamoyo, Amil and his relatives are woken in the small hours by the sound of explosions and gunfire. The coast of Zanzibar is only four miles away. They are alarmed. Later that morning, towards noon, the first bodies float up onto the beach below his cousin's home. Many have big holes where chunks have been bitten off by sharks. Flies, always abundant here, are carpeting the rest. Panic-stricken, Amil takes his wife and children and flees the coast. Three days later, exhausted, dusty and terrified, he arrives back at the mine, having travelled by bus and not had any sleep. The first thing he does is seek out Mum at the mine store.

Amil brings the first news of the massacre to Geita. Until then all that's known is that the 'corrupt' sultan has been overthrown by the 'valiant forces of freedom' on the island of Zanzibar. 'I am shaking,' he says, 'it is terrible. They are keeling everybody. I want to go to Kenya!' Suddenly all the Indian clerks want to go to Kenya. Aziz says he can't live in a country with *blurryfucken* murder going on. Even the Indians have got this word now. '*What* kind of murder?' Mum asks.

'Any fucken kind!' he says.

There are too many eye-witnesses to what happened, Mistree being just one, for the government to keep it secret long. All over Tanganyika, and outside (for many have fled), people are describing the horrors they witnessed. After a week, the government-run news agency admits there have been 'limited' casualties during the coup. It will be years before the figure of seventeen thousand dead can be openly spoken of. The offspring of former slaves have exacted an awful vengeance from their Arab overlords.

The leader of the Afro-Shirazi party, the revolutionary regime on Zanzibar, is Sheik Abeid Karume. John Okello, who leads the revolution, is soon seen as a threat to Karume and has to flee the island. Within days *Mwalimu* Julius Nyerere, president of Tanganyika, meets Karume and his associates in Dar-es-Salaam. On the twenty-sixth of April 1964 they announce to a waiting public at home, and the hastily-assembled international media, that Tanganyika and Zanzibar are merging forthwith into a single republic, to be called Tanzania.

I'm in Arusha when Tanzania is born. The president of the new state is Julius Nyerere, the vice president Abeid Karume. We are in class when the local TANU 'chief' goes from one classroom to another, giving each group of children a talk about the corruption of the ex-sultan of Zanzibar, the courage and wisdom of President Nyerere and Vice-President Karume, and detailed instruction on how 'Tanzania' is to be pronounced. It is *TUN-ZUN-EE-AH, not* to be said the way of the 'English Colonists', rhyming with 'Tasmania'. After the dignitary has departed, Matwiga is jubilant. 'Our country is powerful,' he says, 'even more powerful than Kenya, or England!'

'Kenya is more powerful,' growls Dobson Muwengi, a Kenyan who came to Arusha school the previous year. He's fifteen, the rest of us only twelve or thirteen. He's a foot taller than us, and twice as strong. He's also been made prefect by Mr Houghton, and he loves to throw his considerable weight around. There's murmured discussion at what he says, and we agree, without reservation, that Kenya is the most powerful. It's amazing how we switch from how to pronounce Tanzania to the power of Kenya.

Dobson Muwengi is proving to be a blight on our collective happiness. Not only does he push us all around, but he also snitches to Miss Baxter, or the teachers, if we do anything that's not allowed. He needs to be taught a lesson, but how?

'We could ambush him and beat him up,' Matwiga suggests. Schmedjie, Allen and I are not so sure. Muwengi's very strong. Anyway, even if we do, he'll just tell on us, like he always does.

'Let's think of something more subtle,' Schmedjie says.

'I don't know what you mean,' I say.

'Secret, more secret,' Schmedjie says.

'Why you don't say so, instead of that sub-tull stuff?' Matwiga snorts.

'Well, we're only twelve,' I say, 'and Muwengi's fifteen.'

'So?' Matwiga asks.

'We have to be careful. . .'

'Subtle,' says Schmedjie.

'Oh no!' snorts Matwiga.

'No, look,' says Schmedjie, I have a plan.

'What?' Matwiga and I ask together.

'We hate Dobson Muwengi and we ought to do something about it. Trouble is he's much bigger, and older, than us, so we decide discretion is called for and valour can wait for another day.'

'*Dis-kre-shun, val-oor, sub-tull?*' Matwiga says, 'you mean we be *sneaky?*' That's a word he understands. Me too. Anyway, Schmedjie is our thinker, so we turn to him for a plan. Without hesitation, he suggests a stink-bomb, which he thinks will 'stink the bugger out'. It sounds brilliant and we eagerly agree. Only none of us know anything about chemistry and we haven't a clue how to proceed.

'Listen,' says Schmedjie, 'we can make a very easy stink-bomb!'

'How?' asks Matwiga.

'Hydrogen Sulfide!' says Schmedjie.

'Hide-my-what?' Matwiga says, crossing his eyes. It makes him look really curious.

'Fool!' says Schmedjie. 'It's a chemical, stinks very bad.'

'Like what?' says Matwiga, more interested.

'Like a bad fart.'

'That's what we need!' pipes up Allen, left out till now.

'But,' intercedes Matwiga, 'where we get this. . . *hide-beside*?'

'Eggs,' says Schmedjie, 'rotten eggs.'

'Why you not say so? Why all this fancy-stuff?' Matwiga exclaims. Schmedje ignores him.

'All we do is get a couple of raw eggs. We make a little hole in the shells, then leave them in a sunny place a few days. *Boof* – hydrogen sulphide!'

'And?' I ask, feeling even further out of the discussion than Allen.

'Put them in a Marmite jar which we can seal, then unseal and put under Dobson's bed when he's sleeping!' Schmedjie has an evil grin.

We can only speculate on the nightmares that Dobson Muwengi experiences over the next weeks. Every night after lights out, we wait to hear him snore. Once he begins, the Marmite bottle comes out, the top comes off, and the bottle is put under his bed. Pretty soon his snores change, and he begins to toss and turn in his sleep. He never wakes, but his sleep is inhabited by unimaginable demons. There's collateral damage too, because his closest cronies have their beds next to his, and they too are restless in their slumbers.

In the early hours, before the first light creeps through the dormitory windows, one of us holds his breath, retrieves the bomb, shuts the top, and replaces it in a locker. Sometimes, on getting up, Dobson looks tired and confused. We love it. This we call 'Secret Revenge, Codename: *Stink-you-Out*'. Whether it's caused by our hydrogen-sulfide bomb or not, Dobson Muwengi mellows towards us, and we agree the problem is solved. The Marmite bottle is ceremonially buried.

Thirty-three

In July 1964 Becky wins the battle with Mum and comes home to Geita. It's fabulous seeing her. She's fifteen, and quite the young lady. She's got a woman's shape and talks with an English accent. She's even forgotten much of her Swahili. She's brought the first part of her correspondence coursework with her. Mrs Day, the accountant's wife and ex-teacher, is going to supervise her two hours a day. The gang re-unites – Gretchen and Becky, Sophia Fortuna, Antonio, Dieti and me. I haven't seen Lutoli in months. He's gone off somewhere with his fat aunt. Anyway, it's a joyous time, and we eagerly listen to Becky's English adventures. Then, like everything, we adapt to Becky being home, and go back to our normal activities.

One afternoon, at about four pm, I'm alone down by Tarzan-Swings, where the creepers hang from the trees over the stream and where we were chased by the old lion with the septic paw. Suddenly there's a sharp retort from somewhere to my left, invisible through the dense bush. It's still echoing from the treetops as I run to investigate. Through bush and bramble, tearing reaching creepers from arms and face, I find the source of the sound.

Bending over the still-quivering body of a Thomson's gazelle is a black man in smart, pressed khaki shirt and shorts. He turns at my approach. It's Fritz, the stern driver with the German accent, the former *schutztruppe* with von Lettow Vorbeck in the First World War.

'Hallo,' he says, clearly uncomfortable like I've never seen him before, 'I vos chust shooting!' My eyes go to the gun he's holding. He sees my stare. 'Zis iss mein old gun, from der vore.'

'You kept it all these years?' I say, impressed. It's 1963. That war ended in 1918. That's forty-five years. Suddenly I realise Fritz is very

312

old. He must be seventy, at least. I notice for the first time his short hair is completely white.

'You vonte tell zem?' he says, for the first time I've seen him not scowling. 'Zey don't like blacks to haff ein gun. . .' This man, despite his gruffness, is an old soldier and a distinguished elder, and he's having to plead with me, a mere child, not to tell on him. In an *independent* Tanzania!

'Of course not!' I say. No point speaking Swahili to Fritz, he doesn't like it.

'You *vonte?*'

'I won't. Can I see your gun?'

'Here, der iss no bullets in.' He hands it to me. It's a beautifully made thing. The wooden stock is smooth with age and polish. The barrel and metal parts are jet-black. This gun has been lovingly kept. It's got a bolt, like Dad's Wesley Richards 375 Magnum, the gun I shot God with. Engraved on the side of the chamber is '*Gew.98 Mauser*'. Gew is short for *gewehr,* or gun, in German. Under that, in small letters it says 7.92. Fritz sees where I'm looking.

'Vos design 1898,' he says, 'und der bullets iss 7.92 millimetre.' He smiles shallowly. 'Vos replacing der *Mauser model '71,* vot vos smoking too much, und giff avay der position.'

It's beautiful. What a treasure! 'You keep it at home?' I ask.

'Yes, but iss hided. You vonte tell zem?'

'I vonte, *nein,*' I say, despite myself. 'Your secret is safe with me.'

'Sanks,' he says, slinging his lovely old rifle, and turning to the dead Tommy. He's drawn a big knife. He'll butcher it here. Lots of meat for his family. His gun is a great asset to him.

I'm walking away between the thornbushes when my attention is caught by a mound on the ground with rocks arranged round it. At one end is a three foot high stone. It's a *ziara,* someone's grave, out here in the bush. It looks like its been tended, because there's no elephant grass growing on it. I turn back to Fritz.

'*Nani hi?*' I ask. I want to know who was buried here. He stands up from his task.

'*Mein bruder*, Hans,' he says. His brother Hans? I didn't know he had a brother. He stares at me speculatively, as if trying to decide something. Then he says it.

'Your fadder iss buried at Samina, yes?'

'Yes.' What's Dad got to do with *this* grave?

'Next to hiss grave iss ein odder grave, von a vite voman, vun Mrs Villiams,' he says.

'Yes,' I say. I know that. But what's the connection.

313

'Mrs Villiams vos shot und kilt by Mr Stroessner in 1951,' Fritz says. I know that too. Dad read about it in a newspaper in Johannesburg. Mum never stopped telling us about that, or how strange it was he ended up buried beside her.

'Vell der driver vos also kilt by Mr Stroessner. . .'

'Yes, I know, '

'Hans, *mein bruder*, he vos der driver!' Suddenly it makes sense. Here in this patch of forsaken ground is buried the other victim of that night's awful work by the madman Stroessner. A few miles out, off a fork in the Boma road, Dad lies dead beside poor Mrs Williams. Here lies the poor driver who was taking her so trustingly to Mwanza that fateful morning.

'You look after his grave,' I say.

'He vos goot man. Vos by me ven ve fought vid *Obersti* von Lettow Vorbeck in der *schutztruppe,* in der first vore.' He's finished speaking, returns to his butchering.

Fritz is a strange old man. He never says very much about himself, which is why I'm so surprised to hear about him from Kaizer.

It turns out that in this year, 1964, the legendary Paul von Lettow Vorbeck has died, more than half a century after he first took up his post in *Deutsch Ost Afrika*. In the national commemoration of his life, the West German *Bundestag* votes to fund back-pay for any of his still-living *askaris* from the World War I *Schutztruppe*. A temporary cashier's office is set up in Mwanza, and 350 old men gather to make their claims. That's all, out of a total of thousands of *askaris* in the *schutztruppe* during the 14-18 war. Very few produce the certificates given them by Vorbeck in 1918. Some offer fragments of their old uniforms as proof of service. Suddenly the German banker in Mwanza, who's got the money, comes up with a brilliant idea. Lead into a room one at a time, each claimant is given a broom, and ordered in German to perform the manual of arms. Not one man fails the test. Not a single one was 'trying it on'. Among the old men is Fritz. But he's a quiet person.

Coincidence can be a strange thing. I've just been enamoured by Fritz's old GEW.98, German-built Mauser rifle, when I become aware of another Mauser rifle. This one's a .22 Mauser bolt-action rifle of much more recent vintage. It's one of the assistants at the mine store who find the box. A *baruti*, or dynamite box, which has been put on a deep shelf years ago, then lost to memory when other things are put in front of it. It contains the 'personal effects' of Stroessner, the German

314

who shot Mrs Thomas and Fritz's brother that early morning in 1951. When he's told about the discovery, Mr Snel decides to open the box and dispose of the contents. There, among several mouldy shirts, shoes and trousers, is the rifle. Why it wasn't destroyed after the murders, nobody knows. The pistol he shot himself with was thrown in the lake.

'Can I have it, Mum?' I ask when she tells me about it.

'No, Jimboy, you can't. Who'd want a murderer's gun, anyway?'

'I do,' I say, 'it's not the gun's fault!'

'No,' she says with finality. 'Mr Snel is handing it in to the police, and they'll destroy it.' It's final. No Mauser.22 for me. I never understand this thing about destroying guns which have killed someone. They're made to do that, aren't they? I'll have to destroy this fridge,' someone might say, 'it made its contents *cold* you see!'

'Anyway,' Mum says, 'you're dangerous enough with that airgun!'

Mlozi's hut has long settled into the corner of Top Road and Compound Hill, and the banana-thatch roof is completely overgrown with thornbush. Useful, keeps lots of animals at bay. There are other plants growing around the hut. Some I recognise, some I don't. Chillies, wild garlic, a spiky dark-green leafed plant. *Bhangi,* Lutoli says. Cannabis.

In just six or seven years Mlozi's gone from a fresh-faced, if dirty and oddly attired teenager, to a fat man who looks forty. His long braids are brown and streaked with gray, and have more coloured ribbons than ever. He's lost all his front teeth. There are long raised scars on his forehead and cheeks, where he's scratched himself with a shard of glass. There are now hundreds of small bones tied to his ankles.

It's a long time since I first saw him. Or since he was saved from stoning by the *n'gombe*-rich *mzee*. I tried telling him his *dawa* worked for me in my fight with those boys in England, but he just spoke to the sky. Anyway, the *watu* have finally accepted his presence here, and as the years pass some begin to doubt he's mad, or possessed by *djinn* or *jinni*. The numbers of doubters grows. There are those who believe he is *mchawi*, witch, who has powers which can heal their illnesses, or relieve their poverty. They bring him *ugali* and fish, *mboga* and flying ants. He doesn't always acknowledge the gifts.

The *wasikini* consider Mlozi more than just *mchawi,* but indeed a prophet. They come to him for advice, and forecasts of their futures. In return, they share the spoils of their begging with him. He's particularly keen on brightly coloured cloth, which he tears into

315

ribbons. Mlozi doesn't talk. He mumbles in a high-pitched voice. It takes practice to understand what he says. 'Go to the tall *Mzungu* woman in the house of the water tank, and you will be rewarded!' Mlozi tells a squatting one-eyed *masikini*. He's talking about Mrs Barelli. Two hours later the *masikini* is back. He's been given an old ball-dress. It has lots of coloured ribbons. Mlozi's eyes widen with excitement. Two prizes in one – the *masikini* has a dress, and Mzlozi's got more ribbons. His reputation as *mchawi* is enhanced.

Thirty-four

Heath Fotherington is a late-middle-aged, home counties, Oxbridge-sounding man. He came to Geita, people say, as a 'remittance man' from Hampshire. Remittance men are common in Tanganyika, and probably everywhere where the sun never set on the British Empire. They are, it is said, from powerful and wealthy origins, but so disgraced their families that they were paid annual stipends to go abroad and stay there. A condition was that, if they ever returned to England, they would be cut off from further emoluments, and, in all likelihood, end up in the gutter.

If Fotherington is an aristocrat, he doesn't say so. But he speaks and acts like one. He was appointed as mine store manager in Geita by 'friends' at the *Rhodesia-Katanga Mining Company* Head Office in Chelsea, which, it's rumoured, was arranged by the Colonial office. Talk about smoke and fires – he's a remittance man!

He arrived in 1955, to take command at the mine store. He had a military past, everyone thought, because of his bearing and speech, and the way he stuck his rolled-up newspaper under his arm, like a baton. He also marched everywhere. He never said anything about that, which spawned speculation that he disgraced himself, or worse, in the service of HM forces, and left under a cloud. We never know for certain. But he *does* look like a comic version of a pale-skinned, plump, desk-bound military type.

Fotherington has no doubts about himself. He's 'happily single', and has brought with him his only companion, a Maltese poodle, given to him as a parting gift by his aged mother. He and the poodle become a common sight on the footpath between his house and the mine store. He dresses in brilliant white safari suits and a cream Panama hat, 'to keep the sun off'. There's something very Noel Coward and *Mad Dogs and Englishmen* about him.

Of the business of the mine store, Fotherington never claims to have any knowledge. That, he says, is the 'province of Number Two', to know, and to do. He, he says, is 'Number One', which means he doesn't need to 'get his hands dirty', or 'bother with detail'.

'Number Two' is Mum. She left school at fourteen, not because she wanted to, and despite achieving the highest marks in her class. She had to work with her mother and sister to bring up four younger siblings. They did sewing for a factory, and delivered the finished items miles away on foot. At eighteen she met the man of her dreams, the 'stranger from far who is very close', as prophesied by the fortune-teller at the Johannesburg fair. They were married in 1934. By '39 the world was at war, and Dad was in it. 'If my country is at war, so am I.' He left her in South Africa, with three children. Bertrand, born in '36, Fraser in '38, and Rose, my mentally handicapped, deaf sister, who was born in '39. She was three months old when Dad sailed from Cape Town to join the war.

Mum suffered Dad's illnesses and injuries after the war. She helped him run the concession store in Nongoma, Zululand, where she did most of the work. The fire on the day I was born ended any future in Zululand. In South West Africa, now Namibia, she had me christened in the Swakopmund Lutheran church. Then in late 1951 we came to Geita.

Despite her early departure from school, Mum is an intelligent and able person. She has handwriting which everyone admires. She calls it 'copperplate' and explains it was taught by nuns at Marist Brothers boarding school in Natal, where she spent six years.

When she starts at the mine store in '52, her appointment is a favour by Mr Snel to Dad. She proves not only an invaluable worker, but a guide and mentor to other staff. They value her precision, her handwriting, and her organisational skills. The mine store, previously chaotic, becomes a beacon of efficiency.

Apart from Mum, the clerical staff comprises six Indian men and an Italian woman. In one corner of the room, cut-off, not by a wall, but by his reclusive character, is Mr Hessler. No one ever understands his job, but it's something to do with ordering special machinery for the ore-mill. He keeps his own files and his own counsel. Between his desk and Mum's is Mr Fotherington's. When, infrequently, he's in the office, he reads old English newspapers, and leaves Number Two, and lesser numbers, to do the work.

Mum is a chameleon and has an ability to adapt according to who she's with. She doesn't talk down to anyone, no matter how incompetent or foolish they are. It makes people comfortable with her.

Though she sets high standards for herself, she never complains if others don't meet them.

Among the staff are diverse characters. Aziz is an effeminate, slim, fair-skinned young man from Pakistan, which recently split from India. The *watu* say he's *mfeba*, or homosexual. Chavda is a dark Bengali, forty-something, solidly built, short and bearded, with very formal, strongly accented, Victorian English. He's perpetually on the verge of leaving his wife because she's 'not playing game!' Nehru, who the others joke is a son of India's President, is a round faced, smiling, retreating young man, whose parents are from Bangalore and have a tailoring business in Mwanza. Amil Mistree, who brings news of the Zanzibar massacre, has two significant roles – nervous wreck and thick-spectacle wearer. His anxiety prevents him doing much, and he's constantly blinking. The *watu* call him *bundi ogopa*, or frightened owl.

Rosanna Barucci, the Italian lady, is the only European assistant. Her English is atrocious and difficult to understand, and her writing's worse. But she's young and pretty, and has an infectious sense of humour. Sometimes this gets her into trouble, such as when Mum tells her we're stopping in Italy *en-route* to England.

'Be careful,' she says conspiratorily, 'when-a-you-go-a-my-country!'

'Why?' Mum asks.

'You are-a-weedow, no?' Rosanna says, hands on hips.

'I'm a widow, yes. . .'

'Well-a, we throwa stones ata weedows eena Italy!' It doesn't go down well. Mum recounts Rosanna's warning many times over succeeding years. It badly affects her opinion of Italy. For years she says Italians are 'so cruel, they stone widows, you know!'

Mum's desk is in the centre of the office. There's always a queue waiting to consult her. Aziz stands waiting patiently while she completes an entry in a thick black ledger. When she looks up he grimaces and says 'thees ledger shit is *sheet!*'

'Let me see the sheet,' she says.

'The shit is wrong, all figures wrong, I am wanting balance, but I am not getting. . !'

'Calm yourself Mister Aziz,' Mum says, taking the document from him. 'This problem is not so bad. . . what you have done is add the last two figures, when you should have subtracted them. . .'

'Oh, thank you Mrs Penhaligon!' He shuffles away, relieved. Nehru is next. 'Thees ledger shit is completely wrong, and I am not getting what I am wanting. . .'

After Nehru is Chavda. Then Rosanna. Waiting behind her, twitching and blinking furiously, clutching a huge ledger to his chest, is Mistree.

'I canta understan theesa theeng!' says Rosanna.

All morning Mum deals with her own work and that of the other clerks.

Mum entertains her colleagues. Swahili, Indian and European are always asking her to perform '*cabaret*', as soon as the onerous presences of Hessler and Fotherington are out of the office. Hessler is bald, and nick-named '*Kiwanja ya ndege*'. Landing place of the bird, or aerodrome. Some call him *Embakazi,* the airport in Nairobi.

'*Fanya Bwana Norris!*' an Indian clerk says. Do Harold Norris. Him of the jutting jaw, nasal accent and never-ending search for when it is he wants to talk about. A circle of clerks quickly forms round Mum. African workers from the warehouse join. Bush telegraph, or is it mine-store telegraph? Everyone's grinning in anticipation. Mum puts down her pen, and strikes a Harold Norris pose. She can jut her jaw just like him. She puts on his faraway look.

'It was 1959,' she intones nasally. The chuckles begin. Her audience is spellbound. 'Carol was two, and Hilda was pregnant, no, Hilda was two and Carol was pregnant. Now let me see. . . no, it was 1854. Hilda wasn't born, and Carol was nowhere!' Roars of laughter. People are clutching their sides. Mum should be on the stage.

'And then again. . .' Mum intones, jaw sticking out ridiculously. There's shuffling and stifling of giggles. Mum goes on. 'No, it was 1525, and Hilda. . .' Something is wrong. The audience is trying to look busy, reaching for files, putting on serious expressions.

'Very nice!' says *Embakazi*, who's come back early from lunch. 'I vish zer vos *so* much enthusiasm für der verk!'

When he goes out again, it's '*Fanya Embakazi!*' Do *Embakazi*.

'Vell,' says Mum, putting a book on her head to create a smooth landing-strip, and assuming an angry expression, 'der verk iss nussink für you, you only play der fool!' There's a riot. One time Embakazi sneaks back and sees himself portrayed. Instead of being furious, he laughs as loudly as everyone. Mum has a way about her.

'You are vasted here,' *Embakazi* says, 'you shood be on der stage!'

Mum is a joker and entertainer. It's her personality, and I know its source. It's because she doesn't want anyone to be sad. She's had more than her fair share of that in her life, seen enough. She wants to cheer people up, make fun and laughter. She's a polished comedian. People who don't know would never imagine the tragedies she's endured. She's a natural choice in amateur plays, specially comedies. In Geita she becomes a central player in the stage performances at Lone Cone Club.

320

In 1964 the performance committee, of which Mum is secretary, meets over cocktails to discuss staging a play. Someone has suggested *Aladdin and his Magic Lamp*. Mum thinks that a bit stilted, and suggests it be set it in China instead of Arabia, and called *Aluvadin* (for 'hell-of-a-din') *and his Magical Gamp*. It's agreed. Here begins the saga of the ***Untoward fake Chinese Writings.***

The play has reached the stage of final dress-rehearsals, the costumes have been designed, cut and stitched by volunteers. Mum looks hysterical in her long black cloak, pointy scarlet collar, black mascara make-up and false beard, and she evokes a convincing and sinister wicked uncle to Aluvadin, played by Rosanna Barucci, of *widows-will-be-stoned-in-Italy* fame. There are only four days till the performance.

Mum decorates the edge of the stage with Chinese-looking inscriptions, painted in black on pieces of hardboard. Geita's Chinese carpenters have been recruited to construct the stage props, so they're witness to the new signs. Ah Wong, the Chinese boss-man, objects vociferously. 'Why-ah-you a-wite-ah-dis?' he enquires of Mum. She doesn't know what he means. He turns to his countrymen and gives a short, high-pitched speech. As one, they look outraged, and lay down tools. They march off to the Chinese single quarters.

It takes Mr Snel hours of diplomacy to intercede and make peace. Mum's accidental writings have *allegedly* foully and wickedly abused the Chinese carpenters, with vulgar sexual suggestions, and foul aspersions on their parentage. In the peace deal, the signs are turned round and rewritten on the back by the Chinese. We discover the meaning of the new signs after the play is over. Wide-eyed white people are illiterate monkeys, they proclaim. For all that, the pantomime is a resounding success, and popular demand results in three performances.

Late in '64 Heath Fotherington goes to England on long leave. After he's been gone a month, Mr Snel asks Mum to see him at his office on Top Road.

'Any problems at the mine store?' he asks.

'Nothing I can't cope with,' Mum replies.

'Good. Then I'll send a message to Mr Fotherington, saying we don't require his services any more!' Thus, from long distance, Heath was fired. His salary was sixty-five pounds a month, compared to Mum's thirty pounds. Mum took over his duties and they gave her a five pound raise. It wasn't much, she said, but he'd never done any work anyway.

Thirty-five

By mid-1964 Charlie, with whom I'm struggling along after the stick-gun threats to the *watoto* and his abuse about Gretchen, Dieti, Antonio and I, all thirteen, are keenly interested in female anatomy. The problem is there are only four *Wazungu* girls on the mine. The culture in Geita, and all Tanzania, precludes even the notion of thinking about tribal girls. One only has to see what happened to Higginson! It's two-way too. Young *wanawake* aren't remotely interested in *Wazungu* boys. The only *Wazungu* girls are Dieti's sister, Gretchen, who I've loved for years, Becky, Sophia Fortuna, and a newcomer, a Cornish girl called Megan Hewlett. Her family came to Geita last year. Her Dad's an engineer, and both her mum and dad are keen Lone Cone clubbers. Megan's also fourteen, like Gretchen and Sophia. She's slim, and prettier than Sophia, who we think is fat, but she's not a patch on Gretchen. Becky is pretty, everyone thinks, except me. These girls will be the focus of our study of female anatomy.

It's Dieti, as always, who comes up with a plan. He overheard Gretchen talking to Sophia and Megan, and gained the impression they were discussing nude swimming. There's only one place on the mine they can do that – the swimming pool at the club. Suddenly a lot of things make sense. We already know the girls like to go swimming on their own.

We've often wondered about the giggling and secrecy we've observed in recent weeks. This is it. They're swimming nude in the pool! All we have to do is find a way to spy on them, without them finding out. We consider the possibilities. The main problem is there are no plants or bushes close enough to the pool to afford good spying positions.

It's Charlie who suggests the upside-down boat idea. He's been

322

more friendly lately, and hasn't talked about Gretchen again. My wood and canvas canoe has remained floating on the pool for many months. It's become an accepted fixture. People play with it. They row it around, dive off it, don't mind it being there at all. It's often capsized, left floating upside down on the surface. Sadly, the design is better suited to upside-downess than right-way-up. So much for old Jaswan Singh's careful drawing. Perhaps HMS *Geita* should have been a submarine. There's a foot of air inside when it's upside down. . . an ideal place to hide if we know the girls are coming.

The boat is unlikely to attract attention because it's always there. With goggles and flippers, we can skulk underneath. When we hear the girls splashing we can swim out on underwater sorties, and feast our eyes on close-up naked female bodies. We can swim back under the boat for more air, then venture out again. It's a cunning plan, we agree unanimously.

Three days after we confirm our plan, an opportunity arises. It's nine in the morning, another cloudless day with an already blazing sun. The big people are at work.

Dieti comes running through the bush, along the path through eight foot elephant grass and thornbush, to our garden. He's wearing his swimming costume, and has flippers and goggles clutched in his hands. Excitement always brings back his stammer and German accent. 'Zey are goink!' he shouts breathlessly, 'zey are on ze vay!' Charlie and I are sitting outside with our catapults, taking target practice at a blue-headed lizard high on a gum tree. We leap into action. We dash through the grass to the club. We can't afford to be seen or our game will be up.

When we reach the pool there's nobody there. We're relieved. Dieti stands on the bench in the men's changing room to keep watch. For once the boat is upright. Charlie and I swim out and capsize it. We check the air pocket underneath. There's at least a foot. Suddenly Dieti dives into the pool, shouting 'zey're here!' We submerge together, and come up under the canoe. Our breathing sounds so loud I fear we'll be heard.

After an eternity we hear girly laughter and splashing. D-Day! This is what we're waiting for!

How does love begin? What is it that lights the fire of emotion in a young boy's heart? How does what was ordinary yesterday suddenly become everything? What drives young boys to want to die, let alone live, for the sake of their beloved? I don't know.

At fifteen, Gretchen is a beauty. She's tall and lithe, blonde and blue eyed. She has a pretty face, charmingly freckled, she's shapely but slim, inquisitive and mischievous, all at once. Her figure is of an older girl. Thin waist, long legs, prominent breasts. Although she's exceptionally intelligent, humorous and friendly, I don't think she's any idea of the effect she has on me.

They're out there somewhere, not far from where we cling to the thwarts of the capsized canoe. Our goggles and flippers are on. All we have to do is hold our breath and swim out, and the wonders and mysteries will be revealed, magnified by goggles, air and water.

Antonio and Charlie waste no time. They're off. Dieti inhales hugely, and plunges. He wants to study Megan. I don't blame him, but she's not a patch on his sister. *That's* who I want to examine. Strangely, I hope she'll be different, all over, including *down there,* to other girls. She has to be. She *is* different, in all ways! I can hardly contemplate Gretchen having the same bits as other girls. Surely an angel like her doesn't *pee?* Other excretory functions don't enter the equation. She's too perfect, too beautiful, too ethereal and angelic, to indulge in basic human functions. But there's that paradoxical and fervent hope she *is* like other girls, that she does pee and other things, so she'll be human, not an angel, after all, like me, so I'll have a chance with her. I'll forgive her all these things, and love, protect and cherish her all my life.

Her breasts I've seen before, scantily covered in a bikini top, leaving little to speculate on, especially when I got an aerial view that day in her bathroom. But down there, under the water, though I've seen her in bikini tops *and* bottoms – it's going to be different. I've always averted my gaze, for fear of discovery by those sky-blue, mocking eyes. This time she won't know of my presence!

Transparent green water, dulled girlish laughter, splashing, bubbles ascending to the surface, a shiny film three feet above. Clear view for ten feet, then the green of pumped lake water closes off further vision. Holding breath, swim towards the yelps and giggles and wanton splashing. Kicking flippers, heading forward, where *are* they? Breath running out. Have to breathe. Won't make it. *Have* to breathe. Breath bursting to come out. Turn, swim, back, stay deep, kick, kick, kick. Hands out. Where's that darned boat?

Suddenly the side looms, under, come up in the foot of trapped air. Exhale explosively. Take deep breaths. Heart pounding. Where *are* they? Must be somewhere else. Get breath first, let pounding in chest

324

and ears subside. Breathe. Regain composure. Ready to try again. This time different direction. I'm about to swim out when Dieti comes back. He says he blew his first sortie because his goggles were full of water.

'But I've seen zem,' he gasps, drawing air into his lungs. 'Zey are nakkit, *oochi!*'

'Where?' I whisper breathlessly.

'Becky's over zere,' he says, pointing to one side. I'm not interested in my sister.

'Gretchen?' I ask, cutting him off.

'Next to her, or Sophia. . .' I'm off again, deep breath, mouth closed, head down, kicking, going deep. . . back into the green opacity, dull girly shrieks and splashing reverberating in my head. Then I see a foot. A female foot. As soon as I see it, it convulses in a kick and disappears in an explosion of bubbles. My breath is getting short again. Time to retreat.

I turn and kick out for the boat. And don't find it. I swim and swim and swim. Right into the concrete side of the swimming pool. I don't see it coming, because the only thing that matters is getting away out of sight before letting go my breath. The impact knocks my goggles off.

I surface involuntarily. It's funny what guilt and fear can do. I'm convinced every living person and thing is on to me, watching and waiting. As my face meets air I know the game's up. Nobody notices.

Sophia, Becky, Megan and Gretchen are ten yards away, in the middle of the pool, so taken up with their own antics they don't spot the surfaced spy. They're oblivious to other pale shapes gliding beneath them. Antonio, Charlie and Dieti, moving shark-like through the shallows.

I become brazen. I breathe easily, let oxygen revive me. Then, with the patience of the unnoticed, I check out the range and direction of my target. Gretchen's long wet blonde hair marks her out. She's a little away from the others. Her laughter really does sound like breaking crystal, pure and melodious. My breath comes harder when I see, just an inch under the water, the soft whiteness of her breasts.

I take a huge breath and submerge. I kick off from the side in the direction of Gretchen. Slim, moving legs, hard to see for bubbles. I can't get too close, or I may get kicked, leading to instant discovery. What to do? Suddenly the question is redundant. Gretchen, on reaching the other side, turns and stops swimming. Now she treads water, her legs moving only gently. She's looking in the direction of the other girls. If she looks nearer, just below her, I'm there, a stationary white whale. This isn't right! This is someone I *love!* What am I doing here, spying on her? She's only five feet away. I close my eyes inside my goggles. It can't be like this. When, if ever, I see this, it'll be because she wants me to, not a sordid, stolen thing. It's all out there, on the other hand, just feet away through the water. All I have to do is open my eyes, and feast. No, that's disgusting, wrong, beastly, because anything hurtful to Gretchen is hateful to me. I don't want her humiliated, or sad. I have an urge to produce a magical towel and reach out to her with it, eyes closed, so she can cover her nakedness.

Reluctantly I force myself deeper and head back in the direction of the canoe. My breath comes out in an explosion, and it takes me a minute to breathe normally. The air under here is warm and stagnant. Charlie has come back. He's breathing like a locomotive. 'I saw Sophia's fanny!' he gasps. It's crude. I won't be talking about Gretchen or what I've seen. 'I'll look at Gretchen now,' Charlie says.

'Too late!' I exclaim, determined he will not. 'They've spotted us...' I have never forgiven him for what he said he was going to do to Gretchen that day on our bicycle ride.

'Have they?' he says, surprised.

'They have now,' I say, using both arms to flip the canoe over into its upright position. The girls scream in unison. The game is up. But they don't *know* we were spying. No, we just happened to be doing one of our crazy experiments under the canoe, when they decided to go skinny-dipping. They've reached the side and pulled their costumes on underwater. At that range there's nothing to see.

'What you doing down here?' Becky shouts.

'Swimming,' I shout back, 'you?'

That night in bed I think only of Gretchen. She's unmistakable. Becky is shorter and has darker hair. Sophia is dumpy, with black hair. Gretchen is the sun-kissed Aryan blonde, with golden skin, long golden hair, and legs and arms of a swimmer or ballerina. In my dreams I'm back in the water, and there's no one else in the pool except Gretchen and me. She swims breaststroke, just two feet above me. She knows I'm watching and doesn't mind. Her arms and legs flex and straighten in breast-stroke. My interest is all of her.

Her flat, golden stomach, punctuated by her belly-button, meets her rib cage, and higher up her breasts thrust forward with each stroke. Her flat belly ripples with muscle as the ship of her lithe body powers through the water. She rolls onto her back and continues swimming. Now I see the taut shape of her buttocks. If I could surface I'd love to see the view up there. It's my first erotic dream. In the morning I'm ashamed. I've let myself, and Gretchen, down. I pray to God to return me to the way I used to think about her. This carnal stuff is dishonest and scary, and what will Gretchen think if she ever knows my thoughts?

326

Thirty-six

In late '64, aged thirteen, I come home from Arusha for the last time. Primary school is over. There's a quota for non-African children at the two respected high schools in Tanzania, in Mbeya and Iringa. Only twenty of the brightest are allowed, which rules me out. My grades, and those of my friends, are shocking. Mr Houghton is interviewed in the East African Standard about why so few of his pupils make the grade. 'If you start with poor material,' he says, 'what do you expect?' He goes on to say half the children at Arusha school couldn't even speak English when they started. Describes me well, I think. Schmedjie, Allen and Matwiga also feel well portrayed, and we're all rather proud of ourselves. We say goodbye with the casualness of young people who don't stop to think this is the end of our friendships.

Now, at home, surely, Mum will relent. I've singularly, or as part of a plurality, if I count the others, failed at school. She'll see sense at last, and arrange an underground job for me on the mine. I know I failed as *tunny-boy*, but that was the sun. There's no sun in the tunnels or stopes, so I can be a miner. Can't be that much to it!

'No,' she says in a tone that brooks no argument, 'you are *not* going underground!'

'Well, *what* am I going to do then?' I'm exhausted by her persistence. Can't she see school and I don't get on?

'You are going to St Mary's in Nairobi.' Nairobi's in Kenya. I've never been there. St Mary's doesn't sound too good.

'What's that?' I ask.

'A Catholic boarding school. You're very lucky, because Mr Snel has arranged for the mine to pay your fees, and it's very expensive.'

'But I don't want to go,' I say, despair seizing me again.

'I'm going with you,' she says.

'What?'

'You've got three weeks holiday, then I'm taking you to Nairobi, and we'll have a nice time there. We'll stay in a hotel and visit your new school. Please, Jimboy, don't make this any harder than it has to be!' I try to argue, but it doesn't have any effect. I decide to play for time, await developments. Surely, life being what it is, something will come up. Perhaps a full-frontal assault on the idea of Nairobi is ill thought out. Maybe an opportunity to change my destiny will arise. Unfortunately, something dreadful happens, which puts my little problem into terrible perspective.

It's Amina who breaks it to me. It's the middle of the day, and I'm bored reading the same old *Classics*. I'll have to get another proper book from Higgs, or Mr Hessler. Hammond Innes, or Desmond Bagley. Or Alistair MacLean. Good adventures, those. I must be the best-read *Mzungu* kid in Geita, and it's all due to Higgs and Hessler. It's improved my English no-end. I've caught up with boys my age at school. I learnt more here, in the bush, than in any school! I get off my bed, where I've been lying for an hour, intermittently reading and trying to think of a way to avoid Nairobi. Sandy jumps down and follows me into the yard. It's awfully hot and bright, and I have to shade my eyes.

Something's going on. Umali and Amina are sitting outside their quarters. Tembo's with them. Nothing odd about that. But I *know* something's wrong, badly wrong. You don't grow up with people without becoming sensitive to everything about them. They aren't just sitting there, they're sharing bad news, awful news. Terror grips me, and I almost fight my footsteps towards them. My heart is pounding, my mouth dry. What is it? What can be so bad? As I reach them and look down, Amina turns her head to me, and I see she's crying. Tears are streaming down her cheeks and her face is contorted in anguish. Umali looks up. He's also weeping.

'Jimu,' Amina croaks, swallowing hard, '*kaa, mtoto, kaa.*' Sit, child, sit. She pats the log beside her.

'*Nini?*' I gasp. What can it be?

'Lutoli,' she says in a whisper, '*Lutoli na kufwa!*' My head spins. *No,* Lutoli can't be dead!

I feel a thump in my chest. I sink onto the seat beside her. '*Nini?*' I say.

'He was killed, Jimu, by the cotton-lorry, it fell on him when it rolled in the road!' I can't believe what I'm hearing. I play for time. The conversation can't end, because then it will be true. . .

328

'*Wapi*?' I say. Where?

'Between the cotton-gin and Mwanza,' she sobs, 'last night.' She sniffs loudly, wiping her eyes on the back of her hand.

'*Alakini. . .*' I interject. '*But. . .*' Amina puts her scrawny arm around me.

'*Pole toto, pole!*' she murmurs. Peace, child, peace!

'S*ababu?*'

'We don't know, child, it's a matter of God. . .'

'But?' I whimper, '*Alakini. . ?*' My eyes fill with tears, masking my vision. '*Why* did the lorry fall on him?'

This time it's Umali who speaks. His voice is strangled, and he's weeping shamelessly. He looks very thin, very old. 'Lutoli was travelling to Mwanza on top of the lorry.'

'*Sababu?*' I ask.

'His mother sent him to buy medicine, medicine for her back.' Amina whispers, 'He was on top of the lorry when it overturned.' She sobs loudly. 'The poor boy was crushed!' I can't believe I'm hearing this. Not Lutoli, not my oldest, best friend in the world! But why are they saying this if it isn't true? It's this detail which does it. It's this that brings it home. Something so trivial, so normal. Going to buy medicine for your mother. Then, out of nowhere, sudden, violent death. It isn't expected. Not in the script.

I see Lutoli standing there, smiling his big smile, his eyes twinkling with mischief. Only he's not there. He's *dead!* I'm never going to see him again. Never hear his voice, never share a joke, we're never going to lie in the sun together again, and plan the future of the world. The first dreadful, hopeless, painful sob erupts from deep inside and I can hardly breathe. Amina wraps her arms round me. Umali stands and puts his hand on my head. Our little family has been shattered, and grief has flown to us on dark wings.

How do I deal with this bereavement? Do I know how to? I don't know. All I know is God is, yet again, targetting me. He won't let me be happy. That's why he took Dad, sent me to boarding school, ensured I was always in trouble, and now, finding me still resilient, he's taken my best friend. Lutoli, *Lutoli!* I can't believe he's dead. A *mzoga*. A corpse. Like Tembo's puppy, and Mr Valari (senior). How can someone so young and handsome and alive suddenly turn into a *mzoga?*

'Lutoli is only thirteen!' I say to the sky, to God. 'Why can't you leave him alone?' There is no answer. There never is. I recall how I felt when I dragged Dad's gun out and tried to shoot God all those years ago. If there's no answers, you have to shake things up. Maybe

329

shooting God doesn't work, but what else is there? If God made us, if he exists, then he needs to look in my heart. He'll find hate, pure, black hate, like I'm sure he never intended. Hate for him being unkind. For being a torturer. For being unfair. And, most of all, for not caring! So much for religion, for God, and for all the things the priests say. Even while they do so, there's murder afoot, and 'God' is the perpetrator.

Lutoli's *maziko*, or funeral, is on his mother's *shamba*. There's no road there, just a footpath winding six miles through the bush. Mum has no choice but to let me go with Umali and Amina. One of the Chinese carpenters kindly makes up a crude coffin. It has four rope handles. Umali and Amina collect it from the carpentry works and take it to Lutoli's aunt's hut, where Lutoli's *mzoga* is lying. The *selekali,* or police, brought it there from Mwanza mortuary. It's sewn up in a canvas bag, and Umali tells me it's soaked with blood, which has clotted and dried.

Umali won't let me go when they deliver the body. I know what he thinks. I'll want to see the *mzoga*. I won't, really. That phase of my life is past. I don't want to see Lutoli's crushed, bloodied *mzoga*.

The *watu* transport Lutoli's coffin on a low cart made from plywood and two pairs of pram-wheels. They pull it with a rope, others holding the back to prevent it going sideways, through six miles of tortuous jungle path. Leading the procession are two weeping, wailing women, his mother and his fat aunt, who, to my mind, was more like a mother. His mother hadn't had that much to do with him of late. Yet *she* it was who sent him on his errand of death!

We reach the *shamba* after more than two hot, sweaty hours, itching and burning from insect-bites, thorn-scratches, perspiration and plain old heat. The fresh pile of red earth directs us to the grave. More than a hundred *watu* have come, only a few I recognise. Most are wearing tribal gowns and *kanzus*.

'*Tunahuzunika!*' wails an old woman with red clay marks on her face. She's even fatter than Lutoli's aunt, who's too overcome to speak. 'We are grieved!'

'*Ghamu!*' chorus a hundred others. A word for collective sadness and grief. The surrounding forest resounds with crying voices, male and female.

The fat woman wails loudly. 'Our child Lutoli, he who we loved, travelled only thirteen years.' She opens her ample arms to the sky, then she continues, 'The day before yesterday, he was crushed by a lorry. . .' Standing beside me, Amina grips my arm. She's crying

330

shamelessly. Right now, I don't know what's wrong with me. My eyes are dry. I *can't* cry!

'This is not the meaning of his life,' preacher-lady says. '*Apana!*' No! '*Mungu,*' . . .there's that word again, God! 'God called him home – *Mungu ali ita yeye nyumbani!*' Yes, I think. God does that. It's his style. Only it's not home at all! Just before they start filling the grave, Amina asks me to say something.

'Lutoli and I walked together all the years we had on earth,' I say in a strangled voice. 'He was my friend, my brother. . .' Then the tears come. I can say no more. Umali and Amina both reach for me, and pull me to them. Our bitter tears flow. I reach into the *kikapu* I brought. It contains just two things. A goodbye *barua*, or letter I've written to Lutoli, wrapped in a piece of leather I cured myself. The hide of a mole I caught, skinned, salted, soaked, dried and scraped, like Lutoli and I did together so many, many times. The letter says, in Swahili, that even though you are gone, you will be with me all my life, and we shall meet again, wherever it is people meet. I didn't know what else to write, so I didn't. The other thing is my beloved Chevrolet steering wheel, the one Lutoli and I cherished for ten years, ever since I found it on the beach at the Inn By The Sea in Dar-es-Salaam.

I'm standing, trembling with grief, blinded by tears, holding the wheel in one hand, the leather-parcelled *barua* in the other. Amina takes pity on me. Gently, she takes them from me, and hands them to Umali, who lies down beside the grave, and gently drops them onto Lutoli's coffin. The two *wanaume* with the shovels start putting soil into the grave.

Three young women and an old man are standing a little apart from the others. They're better dressed than the other *watu*. Amina tells me they come from the Lutheran mission near Biharlomoulo. The old man makes a signal, and they begin a hymn I've heard many, many times. It's a Swahili version of an old German hymn – *Gott ist die liebe*, God is love. Taught to the *watu* in the time of *Deutsch Ost Afrika*, the establishment of Lutheran missions, and von Lettow Vorbeck's brave *schutztruppe*. You just can't escape that history! I've even heard old Kaizer humming the tune outside the club. Told me they used to sing it in the Burma bush when they buried their dead. One of the young women sings very high, the other two a little lower. The old man harmonises in a deep base. Without backing, they sound like the very angels. It's exactly the same hymn the *wanaume* sang when they filled in Dad's grave all those years ago. I know, because Mum talked about their beautiful voices for years, and never forgot the tune. Can it be fate? Dad, Lutoli, both so loved by me, the same hymn, in the same language, so many years apart?

Mungu ni pendo
Apenda watu
Mungu ni pendo anipenda
Sikilizeni furaha yangu
Mungu ni penda
Anipenda

God is Love
Loves his people
God is love, he loves
Listen my friends
God is Love
He loves you

There is no doubting the serene beauty of the voices, nor the sincerity or emotion of the singing, but I've just about had enough with God. If he loves us, why does he keep killing us? Why is Lutoli now lying broken in a hole in the ground? Grave – pah! It's just a posh word for a hole! And me, I never got that thing right, how to bring back dead people!

'*Iko ko mbinguni*,' Amina says, pulling me to her. Can she be right? Is he really in heaven? I'm not sure.

Next day my feet carry me up the steep rocky hillside to the site of Lutoli and our country, Kichoncho. I sit on a *mwamba,* or flat rock, in the clearing where we made our declaration of independence all those years ago. It's midday. I haven't eaten breakfast, felt too sick. The sun is high in the shimmering pale blue sky. A lonely *njiwa*-bird coo-cooes, a haunting, mournful sound. Does he know what has happened? That Lutoli is dead? There are no *mwewes*, or hawks navigating the high airwaves today. Is that out of respect for my departed friend?

I can see Lutoli standing here, beside this rock, smiling. We're making up our list of constitutional rules for our republic. I've just suggested 'no bad *Mzungus*'. He counters, laughing, half his face hidden by a rusty army helmet, his brilliant white teeth flashing, with 'no bad *anybodys*'. The image is so strong, I can almost reach out and touch him. Hot tears run down my cheeks. I weep inconsolably for the loss of my best friend. Then I weep for Dad, poor Jan Marais, Mr Valari (senior), and even Tembo's puppy. Then for life itself.

332

Thirty-seven

It's only a week after Lutoli's funeral when I reluctantly travel with Mum to Kenya. If there's anything positive about going to Nairobi, it's that Gretchen is at school there, in Loretta convent, the girl-equivalent of St Mary's. I don't know if I'll get to see her, though. We fly direct, but bumpily, from Mwanza to Nairobi in an aged East African Airways DC3, or *Dakota*.

Brunner's hotel is less salubrious than the New Stanley, which is famed throughout East Africa. There, even film stars on location in Kenya or Tanzania are photographed sipping pink gins in the Thorntree bar. Brunners is old-fashioned, respectable and affordable. Mum and I book in and are shown to our room. A bit strange, at thirteen, to share with Mum, but there it is. We're famished, and go down for lunch as soon as we've freshened up. There are only three other diners, all at different tables, when we sit down. We're next to the window. We order, then talk about the school. I still hope I can wear Mum down.

'St Mary's is a very good school,' she says, 'I'm sure you'll like it.'

'I won't!' I say.

'Someone mention St Mary's?' says an old gentleman who was sitting at the next table, but's now standing by ours.

'Yes,' Mum says, 'my son, James,' she smiles at me, 'is going to be a boarder there.'

'Really!' says the old man, pulling a chair and sitting down stiffly. One leg sticks straight out, like there's no knee. What a cheek, I think, scowling. 'And where are you from?' He's got an accent. I've heard it somewhere. London. Cockney, that's it. Those war films, the London blitz. The firefighters talk like that. Flames everywhere, men in tin helmets trying to put them out. 'Stawn va crauws, might, vis is a bloomin shau, innit?'

'Tanzania, near Mwanza,' Mum says. No point saying Geita, no one's heard of it.

'Tanganyika, eh?' he says, shaking his head as if he doesn't believe it. 'Name's Lopey Perkins, 'cos I *lope* 'stead of walk. Got the *Lopey* bit in Tanganyika, only when it was German East Africa, or *Deutsch Ost Afrika*!' He laughs. 'Mind if I join you?' he belatedly asks.

'Not at all,' Mum says, to my annoyance. Lopey. How sad to be called that! He's had his meal and orders coffee. It's obvious he wants company, is keen to talk.

Lopey is seventy-four. He first came to Kenya from London, to manage a farm in the northern highlands. That was in 1910, when he was twenty. The job wasn't to his liking, so he went to Nairobi to seek his fortune. He did 'vis and vat', before joining another Londoner in a newsagency-cum-tobacconist-cum-gambling-shop-cum-illegal-liquor-outlet and clandestine pub, which thrived in the happy-go-lucky pre-war settler town.

'May I smoke?' he asks, lighting his pipe with a match before he gets an answer. We don't mind. The tobacco smells like Dad's. He rests his stiff leg on the other one. It looks funny, one leg sticking out like a pikestaff. He puffs his pipe contentedly, and continues.

In August 1914, *Oberstleutnant,* or Lieutenant-Colonel, Paul von Lettow Vorbeck, acting against the express orders of hapless *Deutsch Ost Afrika* Governor von Schnee, forbidding offensive operations, brought the First World War dramatically to East Africa. Realising he was outnumbered and outgunned many times by the British, he launched an audacious pre-emptive attack against the railway over the *Deutsch Ost Afrika*-Kenya border. It was down that line the British would bring an invading army, and Vorbeck knew it.

The attack, though only causing minor damage and little loss of life, galvanised this sleepy outpost of British empire, until now obsessed by fears of the looming European battles to be fought by their kith and kin against the rampant Germans under the terrifying plan of their nefarious war strategist, Feldmarchal Graf Alfred von Schlieffen. The slaughter at Passchendaele, Verdun and many further battles would exceed their worst fears. Now bellicose farmers and white hunters, bearing arms, flooded into Nairobi, demanding uniforms and a mission. Some formed their own units with made-up names. Lopey, on a rush of patriotism, sold out to his partner, bought a Lee-Metford rifle, and joined a rabble of farmers calling themselves the 'Kenya Avengers'. They ran around a field to get fit, and practised shooting at crows. Then they were ordered to grow up, join a proper unit, or go back to their farms.

Seventeen companies of King's African Rifles were hastily augmented by settlers and two brigades of Indian and British troops fresh from India. Recruited as lieutenant into the KAR, Lopey took part in the disastrous amphibious assault against Tanga on the second of November 1914. Some said General Aitken was more suited in appearance and style to colonial campaigns of the eighteen hundreds, than fighting a quality foe like Vorbeck. Aitken's ineptness was exceeded only by that of his polyglot army.

Vorbeck allowed the landing by withdrawing his *schutztruppe* inland. The allied forces followed, thinking this was a pushover. They ran into a murderous machine-gun and rifle-fire ambush. Three hundred were killed in minutes, mostly officers and NCOs. There was a lull. From the German positions the *Schutztruppe askaris* hurled abuse at the terrified Rajput and Punjabi soldiers lying prone on the ground. '*Wahindi ni madudu!*' – Indians are insects, they shouted. A Punjabi's rifle went off by accident, and a hundred Rajputs fled all the way back to the beach and into the water.

Lopey led a KAR platoon across a field where hollow logs contained hives of ferocious African bees. Roused by the noise of battle, the bees attacked. One man was stung three hundred times. Hundreds of Indian and KAR troops fled towards the safety of the sea, pursued by dive-bombing bees. High in the leaves of a palm tree a *Schutztruppe askari* sniper spotted a KAR officer trying to stem the retreat. It was easy to tell an officer – he was white, and he wore a pith-helmet. The *askari* had one of the best rifles ever to come out of Germany. The Mauser Gew 98 (*Gewehr*, or rifle, 1898) had largely replaced the old, smoky, model 71, and it had never been bettered. It was a bolt-action carbine, firing a 7.92 calibre round of which it held five in a box-magazine.

This is amazing. Lopey's describing the same type of gun Geita's driver, Fritz, has in his hut. I tell Lopey I've seen one. Not who's got it, 'cos that was a promise. Yes, those guns must still be around, he says. There were thousands, and, provided they were cleaned and oiled, there's no reason they shouldn't last forever.

The *askari* was a good shot, and his *Schutztruppe* officer had issued him with this state-of-the-art rifle, fitted with a Zeiss telescopic sight. He had modern *spitzer* bullets, with pointed tips, and superior long-range ballistics. He worked the bolt, ejecting a spent cartridge, and inserting another *spitzer* in the chamber. Leaning with his back against the high Baobab trunk, he took careful aim. It was a long shot, just over four hundred yards. He held his cheek firm against the oiled stock, inhaled deeply, held his breath, like he'd been trained by

335

Vorbeck himself, slowly steadied the wavering of the sight across the target, and gently squeezed the trigger.

'If it 'adn't 'it bone,' Lopey says, 'it would have gone straight frew, and I wouldn't be called *Lopey!*' The pointed bullet struck the top of his right tibia, just below the kneecap, and shattered the bone. How he got off the battlefield, later famed for the '*Battle of the Bees*', is a saga of agony and crawling, and rolling into a ditch where he lay till the shooting stopped.

It was a rout. The British suffered eight hundred dead, five hundred wounded, two hundred and fifty missing, against the Germans who lost fifteen Europeans, and fifty-four *askaris* dead or wounded. Vorbeck, ever a gentleman, was magnanimous in victory, allowing the British to collect their dead, and retreat in orderly fashion to the beach. He ordered enemy wounded to be treated in Tanga hospital, alongside his own men. Outnumbered eight to one, Vorbeck had bloodied the British Bulldog's nose. He'd also captured sixteen machine-guns, hundreds of rifles, and six hundred thousand rounds of ammunition. It would supply his *schutztruppe* for a year.

'I 'eard vem singin', the German *askaris*,' Lopey says. 'Got ter give it to vem, vey've got good voices! It was while I wuz beein' carried off on a stretcher, dauwn to va beach. Vey must've been five 'undred yards away, but we 'eard em. Vey was singin ver marchin song. It went like vis. . .' And the old man actually begins to sing! In Swahili!

Tuna-kwenda, tuna-shinda
Tuna-fuata Bwano Obersti
Askari wana-endesha
Askari wana-endesha
Tuna-kwenda, tuna shinda

We go, we win
We follow Bwana Obersti
The askaris drive on
The askaris drive on
We go, we win

Incensed at the ignominious defeat of his massively superior force, Aitken ordered a bombardment of Tanga town. The first naval shell hit the hospital, crammed with British and Indian casualties. Others hit the retreating allied lines. In ten minutes the British losses were doubled. The bombardment ceased. Aitken went to pieces. His career was over, his reputation destroyed.

336

'It were only va shelling wot stopped vem singing,' Lopey says.

Lopey was taken on board the cruiser HMS *Fox*, part of the navy's Tanga blockade. The ship's surgeon removed the bullet. It was he who told Lopey it was a *spitzer*. He'd extracted many, was an expert on bullet wounds. He gave Lopey two choices. 'Wired straight, or off,' he said. Lopey chose wire. His knee never bent again. His nickname was born. I wonder if Fritz, our surly German-African driver, shot him. Could it have been with that same old Mauser *gewehr* he showed me down by Tarzan-Swings? In deference to my oath to Fritz, I'm not saying anything. But I never seem to be able to get away from the old war in Tanganyika, do I?

'Vat Vorbeck,' Lopey muses, 'hell of a soldier. Know what 'e said when he was asked why the bloomin' bees attacked us, and not his men?' He's asking me.

'No.'

'*Gott mitt uns, und die bienen auch!*'

'What's that mean?' I say.

'God wif us, and the bees too!' Lopey smiles in reminiscence. 'Cheeky devil, but 'ad a point, he did. As if 'e didn't capture enough guns and ammo from us at Tanga, just a few months later, in April 1915, *Gott* was wif 'im again!'

'What happened?' I ask. I love talking about the *Schutztruppe* and von Lettow Vorbeck. It's connected to Geita. There's Fritz, the driver, who was in the *Schutztruppe*, as were several old *askaris*. Though Kaizer himself wasn't, his father was.

'A ship called SS *Rubens*,' he says, knocking tobacco out of his pipe by hitting it in his palm. 'British ship, captured by va Germans in va North Sea, re-named wif a neutral Norwegian name, vey loaded her in Emden, wif munitions and supplies for Vorbeck, ven sent 'er round the Cape of Good Hope to run va British blockade. When she got off Tanga, she made a run for it, chased by a whole bleedin' flotilla of Royal Navy ships. HMS *Hyacinth* shelled her, set her ablaze, but her Captain steered for va beach, ran her aground. She didn't sink. Next day va fire was out, and the supplies were fine. The Germans and ver *askaris* waded out and retrieved the cargo, 'appy as Larry! And,' Lopey says, tamping dark tobacco into his pipe bowl, 'there was nuffink ve could do to stop it!'

'Guns?'

'Hundreds, half a million bullets, *Spandau* machine-guns, small field-guns, shells, new uniforms, cases of whisky, cigarettes. . .' Lopey shakes his head. 'Vorbeck was a good soldier, also *lucky!* Vat's what yer've got to be in life, young man, *lucky!*'

What an interesting man Lopey Perkins is! I know a lot about the East Africa campaign, but always like to hear more. It's funny, living where the *Schutztruppe* fought, being British myself, then meeting someone who fought on *our* side! But is it *my* side? I don't know which side I'm on. I like Germans, and I like the Swahili people. I think I'd have been in the *Schutztruppe* myself, though not during the *Maji-Maji* revolt. That was murder.

Lopey is lonely. His wife died long ago. Typhoid, he says, an epidemic which killed indiscriminately. His two grown-up sons are no longer in East Africa. They only write when they want money, he says. He insists on showing Mum and me Nairobi, drives us all over the town in his two-tone brown and beige Ford Prefect. Everywhere we go people recognise and wave at Lopey. He's very well known.

After the first war, with his wired-up leg, he decided to make money, and started his own match factory in the Ngong Hills near Nairobi. They were called Lopey's matches and sold all over Kenya. In five years he was a millionaire. 'Lived the life of Riley,' he says, grinning with his pipe clenched in his teeth. Then he lost his money. Unfair competition, he says. He worked as a letting agent and debt-collector from then until he retired, a year ago, at the age of seventy-three.

Lopey takes us out to Woodlands, the Nairobi suburb where St Mary's school is. It's six miles out of town and has lush, leafy roads and great mansions. The school is on a huge piece of land. There are manicured lawns, cricket pitches, rugby and football fields, and an eighteen-hole golf course, of professional standard, Lopey says.

The school building is a huge double-storey horseshoe. On one side, both floors are given over to classrooms. On the other it's dormitories. The joining bit of the U is dining room and kitchen downstairs, and bedrooms for the Catholic Fathers upstairs. The open part of the U leads down a broad flight of stone steps to an Olympic-size swimming pool.

There's not much time to look, because Mum and I have an appointment with the Headmaster. Mum's made me dress up in beige trousers and a white shirt, and she's bought me new brown shoes. I think it's my first pair of new shoes ever. Lopey waits on a bench looking out over the quadrangle in the middle of the horseshoe.

Father O'Leary is a big and very old man. His study is huge and panelled in wood. There are thousands of books on the floor-to-ceiling bookcases. In one corner there's a tall, wide earthenware vase, and protruding from it are several long thin canes. I don't like the look of them.

'Pleased to meet you,' he says with an Irish accent, rising from behind his desk. He shakes hands with Mum, not with me. He motions us to sit. 'So this,' he says, staring at me over the top of his half-spectacles, 'is young Francis!' Here we go again! Just like Miss Baxter in Arusha. Enemies call me that. Unless they call me Jimu, or at least Jim, I know times are going to be hard.

'We're a proud school,' he says, and Mum nods to show she appreciates that. 'There is strict discipline, a strong work ethic, and the highest grades of any school in Kenya.' Mum's nodding again. 'Our boys excel in all the sports, so they do! Did you see the playing-fields, golf-course, the swimming pool? Yes? We have other sports. For example, all boys do boxing, and there are *no* exceptions!' He's staring fixedly at me from under hedge-like eyebrows.

'What think you of sports, Francis?' he asks. His eyes are icy-blue and bore unblinkingly into mine.

'I like games,' I say weakly.

'Games, so! Here you will learn to play sports, become good at it, like all the boys!'

'Do I *have* to box?' I ask in a small voice. His face breaks into a grin.

'To be sure! There are *no* exceptions. You'll be learning to love it. It'll toughen you up, build character.' Mum's looking strained now, and I know her smile is forced. Father O'Leary changes the subject. 'We need to talk about the subjects you'll study.'

Mum and Lopey leave me at St Mary's, and he drives her to *Embakazi* airport for her return flight to Geita. I'm shown to my dormitory by a particularly sullen senior who doesn't even address me by my name, calling me only 'you'. It's upstairs from the classrooms, and leads off from an outside passage overlooking the quadrangle. The unsmiling lout hands me unceremoniously to the dorm prefect. 'He's for you!' he says, then leaves.

'I'm dormitory prefect,' the red-haired boy announces, 'but *God* to you. Do I make myself clear?' He's got dandruff in his red hair and his teeth are yellow. There's a sniggering knot of six boys round him, here for the entertainment.

'What's your name?' I ask, perhaps foolishly.

'Clever, eh?' says the prefect in an exaggerated nasal tone, taking my forelock in his fingers and beginning to twist.

'Stop dat!' comes a barking, oriental-accented voice from behind the others. The prefect lets go my hair. A short, broad-faced Asian boy with very wide shoulders steps forward. He faces up to the redhead. 'You wan' tlouble, Loper, you come Kim!' he spits. Must be *Roper*. So that's the prefect's name, not God after all. He looks far too shaken and pale to be God. In fact he's positively quaking.

'Look, Kim. . .' he begins, but Kim cuts him off.

'No *you* look,' he says. 'You bully, that all!' He turns to the other five. One's already gone. 'Wan tlouble with Kim?' he asks. As a body they turn and find more interesting things elsewhere. When they're all gone, including Roper, who scuttles away in the distraction, he turns to me.

'Me name Kim Dong. Jus' like *ding-dong*. I come Kolea. My fadder, he ambassador. We be flen, yes?' He smiles, transforming his face. 'Dey all lubbish!'

'I'd *like* to be your friend,' I say, feeling intense gratitude to my benefactor.

'I have plesent for you,' he says, 'come with me!' He walks to the row of steel lockers against the far wall of the dormitory. I realise there's no one else in the dorm. They've scuppered. Kim's got quite an effect. He opens his locker and takes out something wrapped in a cloth. 'Dis for you!' he says, handing it to me. I take it pensively. It's heavy. What can this strange little chap be giving me, so soon after meeting? He's watching me intently. I unwrap the package. Inside is the most beautiful hand-axe. It's got a handle like a sheath-knife, and a shiny, razor-sharp three-inch-wide axe-head in place of a knife-blade. I don't know what to say.

'If me not lound, you chop-chop bastas, yes?' I smile weakly.

'By way, what name?' Kim says.

'Jim,' I say.

'Jim and Kim, dat sound good,' he says. 'Loper give you tlouble, you call Kim. Or use axe. Unastan?' And before I can answer, or thank him for the gift, he's gone. I cradle the axe in my hand. Will I chop-chop the other boys if they 'give me trouble'? What would Father O'Leary say?

It isn't long before it's apparent that St Mary's and Loretta convent have little interaction. I'm unlikely to see much, or any, of Gretchen. I miss her so much! All I can look forward to is seeing her in my dreams. Will she, just in a dream, kiss me with her perfect lips?

Thirty-eight

The 'new boys' are weighed on a Saturday morning. Father Cox, Dean of Studies, operates the scales. Strange thing for a 'studies' dean to do. It's decided by weight who will box who in the preliminary bouts of the Kenya Secondary School Boxing Championships. There's no choice. Everyone boxes, at least till they're 'eliminated'. I don't like the sound of that.

I'm a pragmatist. I'll fight if I have to, but running away seems wiser. Maybe it's growing up with the lions and *fisis* in Geita. Doesn't pay to go toe-to-toe with one of them! 'When you see one, run like the dusty-wind!' Umali says. I agree. Now, willingly, and for no possible benefit, I have to stand and fight someone who, just for pleasure, wants to kill me. It's crazy.

On Monday the fight-lists are posted on the noticeboard. I can't believe what's there. Penhaligon–Roper. Right at the top of the list. Bantam-weight. Bryan Roper. Prefect. Redhead bully, who's only left me alone because of my Kung-Fu bodyguard, Kim Dong. It hasn't stopped him sneering from a distance, or whispering that 'he won't be here always, then I'm gonna *eat* you!'

Worst of all, Roper's last year's all-Kenya schools bantam-weight boxing champion. He may have red hair and freckles, but he's built like a weight-lifter. I've seen him in the showers, and I know he's going to smash me in the ring. I'm walking back to my dining table, feeling nauseous, when Roper sidles past, grinning. 'Can't bring Kim into the ring, Jimbo,' he whispers, 'I'll have you to myself!'

'Wat dat one say?' asks Kim, who's become my shadow. He's even swapped places with another boy to sit next to me for meals.

'He's gonna get me,' I say miserably, 'in the ring.'

'You fight Loper?' Kim asks.

'That's what it says.'

'You know box?'

'Nope.'

'No wolly, I teach you Kung-Fu!'

'No time, it's next week,' I say.

'Ah, so, I teach you one-punch. Special punch. All you need.'

'Thanks Kim,' I say, 'but I think I need more than that.'

'You win, sure you win, Jim!' My little companion is beaming. His confidence in me is flattering, but misplaced.

Compared to Roper, I'm a gawky no-hoper. He's a ruddy tiger, and I'm for it, big-time! In Geita I could go off and get my catapult, and shoot him in the forehead with a good pebble. Or I could make a bow and shoot him in the chest with a bamboo arrow tipped with a five inch nail, its point flattened with a hammer and filed to razor-sharpness on granite. Not, alas, here!

'You're very good to me,' I tell Kim. 'I had a friend before, a very good friend. . .'

'You *had* good flen?' he asks.

'He died,' I say. I tell him about how we grew up together, learnt to talk under the big baobab tree. I tell him about the Republic of *Chichoncho* on Compound Hill, the tuberculosis we had together, the trust we shared. And how he died under a ginnery-lorry. By the time I'm done we're both crying.

'You good fella,' Kim says, wiping his eyes with a handkerchief. 'I know when I see you!'

There's talk round the school. Roper's going to smash up Penhaligon. What good luck, having me to himself in the ring, where my yellow friend can't save me! I should have known better than to cheek Roper. After all, his family are famous sugar farmers, very rich and respected in Kenya. Who am I, from the bush in Tanzania, who doesn't even have a father, to insult Roper? He's last year's champ, and he's going to give me a well-deserved pasting. They're all going to be there for the show.

Lopey Perkins comes to visit in his two-tone Ford Prefect. He promised Mum he would, and he's as good as his word. He finds me sitting on a bench in the quadrangle. As always, he's dressed in grey flannels and a tweed sports-jacket. He sits down beside me, his kneeless leg projecting like he's going to hang clothes on it.

'Why so glum?' he asks, tamping tobacco into his curved Meerschaum pipe.

'I've got to box a boy called Roper on Saturday,' I say miserably. He strikes a match on the side on the bench, holds it to his pipe, and draws deeply. He lets the fragrant smoke curl from his nose.

'Bryan Roper?' he asks, 'last year's champ?'

'Yup.' How does Lopey know?

'Nairobi's a small place,' he says, reading my thoughts.

'What am I going to *do?*' I plead. He takes a deep puff from his pipe, and looks thoughtful.

'Only fing you *can* do, Jim, is *win,* vat's what!' he says at length.

'How am I going to beat Roper?' I ask. 'He's stronger than me. . .'

'First fing you do is stop saying vat,' Lopey says. 'You can beat 'im if you want.'

'How?'

'Well, I'm no boxing fundi, but I've been in a fight or two, and I know a few fings,' Lopey says.

'What?'

'Well, he'll be dancing round, being fancy, trying to hit you wif his left and right hand.'

'And?'

'You 'aven't time to train as a boxer, like him, so you just go in vere as a *fighter!*'

'How do I do that?' I ask. Just then Kim comes along.

'Hello,' he greets Lopey, 'you Jim flen?'

'I am,' Lopey smiles, 'you too?'

'Me him *good* flen,' Kim agrees.

'He says I mustn't try to box Roper, but fight him,' I say.

'One-punch, hard one face, dat all,' Kim says. 'I teach!'

'Now, Jim, see, you 'ave more friends van you fought,' Lopey says. 'Tell you what, you let vis friend of yours shauw you 'ow to frow one big punch. Vat's all you'll need. No fancy footwork, nuffink, just vat punch, and you'll end it vere and ven.' He turns to Kim. '*Kung-Fu,* aye?'

'Flom velly small,' Kim says. 'Only five.' How does Lopey know these things?

'You teach 'im the punch,' Lopey says. He stands, tapping his pipe on his hand. 'I'll be 'ere to watch va fight, Jim. You learn vat punch from your friend.' He turns to leave, then turns back again. In his hand is a five shilling note. 'For you,' he says, 'buy some sweets and colas.' He vaults away on his straight leg.

'You come with me,' Kim says. 'We go plivate place, me teach you one-punch. Den ve have smoke, yes?'

Saturday afternoon, it's half-past four. I should be down at the gymnasium, getting ready for my fight with Roper. Three rounds of two minutes. How am I going to even walk there, let alone survive? I'm terrified and feel queasy. I've practised Kim's punch as best I can.

343

The trick is making a tight fist, holding the elbow close to the body, turning the fist as far outwards as it'll go, till the bent fingers are facing up. Then, after taking in a deep breath, begin to slowly exhale, at the same time bringing the bunched fist arcing up from low down, rotating inwards, so the bent fingers will face exactly downwards at impact. It has to be done at short range, so as not to waste energy before hitting the target. Even more important, Kim tells me, you have to drive every other thought, every other impulse, every ambition, every emotion out of your soul. When you do this, it needs purity, no pollution by anything else, which will weaken the effect. I'm doubtful I'll get the chance to use 'one-punch'. Not with Roper dancing around like a demented marionette, poking his fists out with lightning speed.

'We go now,' Kim says. There's sympathy in his voice, but insistence too. I feel ridiculous. I'm sitting on the edge of my bed. I've got my PT shorts and T-shirt on, and a pair of plimsoles with short white socks. I don't look like a boxer. I've seen Roper and his partners on their way to the gym. They call it sparring, or something. They wear fancy stuff, matching black shorts and singlets, fancy red shoes with treads like a tyre. And they look confident. Especially Roper. When he sees me he ripples the muscles on his shoulders, and grins like a *fisi*. He mouths 'gonna getcha!' I'm sure he will. I remember something from the Bible. The old priest in the church in Arusha. 'A time to live. . . a time for something-to-do-with-stones, and a time to die.' My time to die is near.

'Betta go now!' Kim repeats.

'Okay,' I sigh, standing up.

'Old man, you flen, he waiting,' Kim says. Lopey. How does Kim know he's here? We leave the dormitory and start the long walk to the gym.

It seems the whole school has turned out for the boxing. I scan the faces for Gretchen, but she isn't there. A forlorn hope. If she was here, and I got killed, at least she'd hear my last whisper that I've always loved her. There's another fight on. A boy in red shorts is being pounded mercilessly by another in black shorts, who's bigger than him. I don't trust this fight-by-weight thing. Those two are never the same weight.

I see Lopey. He's got a ringside seat, and his straight leg is sticking out sideways. His Meerschaum pipe is clenched firmly in his teeth. He's sitting next to Father O'Sullivan, dean of discipline. They're talking and laughing like old friends. How do they know each other? He sees me and waves. Even Father O'Sullivan nods my way and smiles. It's an evil smile.

344

Suddenly the boy in the red shorts lands a huge blow on the forehead of the one in black, who falls straight on his back with a loud wallop. The referee, Father O'Donaghue, stands over him, counting. . . 'seven, eight, nine, ten!' He waves his arms, fight over by knockout. The fallen boy sits up, looking confused. He's led from the ring. Father O'Donaghue walks to a corner and looks at a list. 'Next bout,' he shouts, 'Penhaligon versus Roper.' Bryan Roper, standing by the ropes, pulls two apart and jumps into the ring. He dances around, flicking punches into thin air. A blast of applause rises from his acolytes.

'Get him!' one yells.

'King Roper!' shouts another. Yet another makes loud chicken-noises. For me. Saying I'm frightened. Laughter ripples through the crowd of more than two hundred.

Kim helps with the gloves. They're old school ones, brown and cracked, not like Roper's, which are his own, red and shiny-new. Kim does up the long laces. He punches me affectionately on the shoulder 'Lememba,' he whispers, 'one-punch. Loper, he fall down!' I climb warily into the ring. Father O'Donaghue points to a corner, where there's a stool. Lopey's left his seat and is standing just outside the ring. I put him down as my 'second'. Kim joins him. When I sit down, Lopey leans forward and talks in my ear. He almost has to shout because of the noise.

'Vis is your chance,' Lopey says, 'vis is vere you shauw vat lout wot you're made of. Do' ya hear me?' He grabs my chin and turns my face to his. There's a determined glint in his eye.

'Yes,' I say softly. Doesn't seem to be anything else to say. My heart is pounding so hard – it feels like it's going to exit my chest. There's a bitter, burning sensation in my throat. Like bile after vomiting.

'Good. Daun't worry if 'e 'its you.' Is he stark-raving *mad*? That's *exactly* what I *am* worried about! Kim winks, smiles encouragement. Okay for him too!

'Seconds out, Round One!' Ref O'Donaghue shouts. Lopey doesn't have to get out. He already is. A bearded man with red hair climbs down from Roper's corner. His father. They look the same. The ref motions us to approach and touch gloves. Roper's got a murderous look in his pale blue eyes. Wild-animal like. He's said he'll knock me out in round one. After, that is, he's 'played with me a bit'. We go back to our corners. A boy in school uniform rings a bell, and Roper leaps across the canvas towards me.

The first jab stings beyond stinging. It's on the side of my face, and I don't see it coming. Nor do I see the second, which is straight on the nose, and makes my eyes water. Everything swims. There's a fast-moving, blurred image of Roper dancing about, every now and then coming closer, then I feel pain. I put my gloves up to protect my face.

He hits me in the stomach, completely winding me. I feel like vomiting. I put my gloves lower, he hits me in the mouth. Funny, the blows don't hurt as much now. I'm aware of them, but they sting less. I try punching back when he gets close, but he ducks to one side and wallops me on the temple. I go dizzy, then the bell rings. I've never had two minutes so slow. Or so horrible. Why do they do this? Why make people fight? The audience are a bunch of hyenas, baying for blood, even now, between rounds.

I'm sitting on my stool. Lopey's wiping my face with a wet cloth. Blood pours from my nose. He produces a thick tissue, tells me to blow. I try, but it hurts too much. I'm breathing through my mouth, like an uphill locomotive.

'You did well,' Lopey shouts. ''E's using up energy. He 'asn't knocked you dauwn. . .' That's comforting, I think. Not yet, he hasn't. There's all the time in the world for that, and meantime he'll torture me. The wet cloth makes my face sting again.

'Seconds out, Round Two!' the ref shouts, and the uniformed boy rings the bell. Roper's out from his corner like he's jet-propelled.

'One-punch!' Kim shouts as I get to my feet. Roper hits me twice in rapid succession, on the nose again, and my other cheek. My head rocks. Suddenly I feel different. I can't explain it. I'm not frightened now. I feel angry. Very angry. He hits me again, on the forehead, knocking my head back. Now I'm furious.

I have a rage I've never known. It's bursting in my chest and pounding in my temples. Life just isn't worth this! One-punch, I think, one-punch. Might as well do the only thing there is. My right arm is moving down my side, bending at the elbow, my fist turning into an iron-hard ball inside my glove, my wrist straining as it rotates outwards.

Roper hits me on the nose. I hardly feel it, though blood spurts onto the canvas. I don't care. He can hit me as much as he likes, but I'm going to unload a punch like he's never felt before. It's for Mum, for Dad, for Lutoli, for Umali, for Becky, for Gretchen, for Sandy, for Geita, for me, for life, for death, for everything. I breathe in as deep as my lungs can draw breath, bend my left knee, begin to exhale, turn to my right, and uncoil my loaded fist. It's this or nothing. Remember England, I think. I need a shot just like that one, only better. Then I had Mlozi's leather pouch with its *hirizi*, or magic. I haven't now. My anger will have to do.

My fist comes up in an arc, twisting through ninety degrees, every muscle in my body convulsed in one supreme effort. It smashes into Roper's face just as he darts forward. I hear a bark like a dog from my own throat and feel the impact judder down the length of my arm, in my shoulder, into my spine. There's a harsh crunch on my knuckles. Like breaking ice.

Roper stops. Completely. For a moment he stands there, shock and incredulity on his face. Then he topples and falls backwards. He hits the canvas like a load of logs. Silence breaks out. The shrieking support for Roper chokes off, like the power's cut. Ref runs to inspect Roper, who lies stretched out in the middle of the ring. His red-bearded father jumps in frantically. Ref counts, and Roper doesn't move. He's out. I've won. Kim jumps into the ring and raises my hand. So ends the unbroken list of wins of the Kenya-Bloody-champ!

I climb down. My face is a mess. Lopey and Kim put my dressing-gown on me. Then they lead me out. Lopey's brought cakes and a flask of hot, sweet tea. We sit on a bench. 'You done it!' Lopey says.

'Did I?' I say. I still can't see straight.

'You did,' Lopey says.

'One-punch, see, it work, Loper, he *KO'd!*' Kim laughs. We eat cake and drink tea. There is never a sweeter tea-break.

'You fix him good!' Kim exclaims.

'Did I?'

'Bryan Roper's got a broken jaw,' Lopey says. Suddenly I feel very satisfied. Maybe, even, this has all been worthwhile. Does this make me Kenya champion? I ask Lopey. No, that'll take more fights. No thanks, I say.

It takes weeks before the bruises have gone, my nose is back to its original shape, and I can breathe through it. Roper's away for two weeks, then comes back with a wired-up jaw. He doesn't tease me now. Nor do his friends. He doesn't look half as cocky. I strut around school as equal partner to my good friend Kim. Some boys come to us for advice, even protection. We never turn them away.

Thirty-nine

Kim and I are addicted smokers. We discover we started at the same age, five. This gets us into serious trouble at St Mary's.

There's a dense copse of bushes next to one of the playing fields. Kim and I find a way into a thicket with a tiny clearing in the middle. This becomes our den and smoking-place. Kim's got a source of cigarettes on the 'outside', and we're never short of *Sportsman* filters and matches. We keep them here, in our den, protected by a biscuit tin. We come at least once a day, more if we can, and light up in safety. For a while. Then we're seen entering the bush by one of Roper's gang. Lacking the courage to attack us himself, the coward waits till we're gone, then investigates. He finds our biscuit tin and takes it to Father O'Sullivan. At least that's how we think the dean of discipline gets it.

It's Friday night. I'm lying half asleep in the dormitory. Suddenly there's a sharp, stabbing pain in the back of my neck. I'm physically pulled up into a sitting position. Despite the darkness, I can see it's Father O'Sullivan standing at the foot of my bed. He's wearing a white cassock, and holding the end of a shepherd's crook. The handle is round my neck.

'Up, boy!' he growls. I get out of bed. I'm aware of the invisible eyes of other boys watching in terror. O'Sullivan makes these night-raids frequently, and we live in dread.

'To my office!' he says. I follow him lamely out the dormitory to his office. The door's open, the light on. He sits behind his desk. The clock on the wall says ten o'clock. There's a biscuit tin on the desk. It's open. There's a packet of *Sportsman* cigarettes and a box of matches in it. It's Kim's and my secret smoking-tin. Not secret anymore. I stand in front of the desk, blinking in the bright light, feet together, hands at my

348

sides. This is how we're supposed to stand when seeing the dean of discipline. One boy got flogged for shifting from foot to foot.

'Well, boy,' he says, pushing the tin towards me, 'what have you to say?'

'Nothing,' I mumble. There's no point saying anything. He's got the evidence. There's no getting away with this. Smoking is strictly prohibited. If I say anything, he'll just want me to say more. If he doesn't know Kim's been smoking too, I'm not going to tell him. If he does know, it won't be through me.

'Nothing?' he asks in a deceptively soft voice, 'did you say *nothing?*'

'Yes,' I whisper, my throat dry.

'Well then,' he says, we'll be needing to jog your memory, won't we?' I know what that means. He stands and walks round the desk. In the corner is the three foot high earthenware vase, and sticking out of the top are a selection of long Malacca canes. He selects one and takes it out. 'Bend, boy, hands on desk!' he says. I bend forward, splay my fingers on the smooth wood. He flexes the cane in two hands, feeling its springiness. 'Three of the best,' he says, 'just to help your memory!' He steps back and raises the cane in the air, up almost to the ceiling. Then it flashes down.

The pain is indescribable. It's worse than anything I've ever felt. It's almost beyond endurance. The upper part of my buttocks explode in agony. We're not allowed to straighten up when the blow lands. My fingers ball into fists, I involuntarily bite my lip, and I stay in the same position. The second blow hits. If anything, it's worse. It's exactly on the same place. This time I almost jerk upright, but manage not to by supreme effort. Third. It's beyond belief. Nothing can describe it. Somehow I remain bent over the desk. He's putting the cane back now, walking round behind his desk. He sits.

'You may stand upright,' he says softly. How can someone who causes such pain talk so gently? I straighten up. He's staring at me with a look that's almost compassionate. 'Now,' he says, 'I hope you've recovered your memory. I ask you again, what have you to say?' He taps the side of the smoking-tin with an index finger.

I want to blurt out it's a tin with cigarettes and matches, and it belongs to Kim and me, and we've been smoking in the bushes, and we're very sorry. . . But I know I can't. I mustn't say anything. If I do, it'll get Kim into trouble too, and it won't help me either. The dean knows what he knows. I've started by saying nothing. I've got to continue. No matter what. I stare back, hands at sides, feet together.

'Well?'

'Nothing,' I say, even though it comes out as a sob. I'm disgusted with myself. But my bum's on fire. It's burning, and it feels like there's a lion gnashing it.

'Recalcitrant?' he asks, almost sweetly. 'Brave?' He shakes his head. 'It's not brave,' he says, 'it's foolish!'

'I know nothing!' I say.

'Have you taken leave of your senses?' he asks in a silky voice, 'do you know what trouble you are in?' He's standing again, walking to the canes. He reaches for a different one. It's longer.

'Bend!' he intones like he's giving communion. I lean over the desk again and splay my fingers. Somehow I don't scream or jerk upright. It's over again. Another three. I don't think the last one hurt as much. He's sitting again. I'm standing upright.

'Memory any better?' he asks solicitously. '*Regained* your senses perhaps?'

'No,' I whisper. He stares at me a long time. I stare back.

'A hero, eh?' he asks, 'suffering to protect your friends?' Now I'm vindicated. *Friends,* not friend. He's just fishing. He doesn't know Kim's involved, or he wouldn't use the plural. Also, if he already knows about Kim, he wouldn't be trying to find out from me. He knows I'm guilty, that's why I'm here. But he doesn't know about Kim. The coward who's told on me hasn't said anything about Kim. Either he doesn't know, or he's frightened Kim will find out who told and get him. But I haven't told. And right now I know the dean can give me a thousand of his 'best', and I still won't tell.

'Not going to talk, *are* you?' he says, shaking his head and looking sad. 'A pity you aren't as single-minded with your studies!' He stares again, trying to decide what to do with me. His eyes go briefly to the pot of canes. Then he seems to change his mind. 'This unpleasant matter is not closed,' he says, but you may now return to your shameful bed.' I turn and leave with as much dignity as I can muster with my bum on fire. What's 'shameful' about my bed, you nasty old bigot? I think.

'What happen?' Kim whispers from his bed, next to mine.

'He's got our tin,' I whisper back.

'I hear, he flog you,' Kim says.

'Yup.'

'What he ask?'

'Who else.'

'You tell?'

'No.'

350

'He flog thlee time, twice!'
'I know.'
'You no tell him me smoke?'
'No.'
'You *velly* good flen!'
'Thanks.' There's silence for a minute. Then he talks again.
'How he find tin?'
'Someone told him.'
'Who you think?'
'Dunno.'
'Tomollow me fine out. Den me fix him.'

'Good, Kim,' I say. If he can find out, Kim will definitely fix him. But how can he find out? Cowards tend to be very careful. Cover their tracks. The pain in my bum has been replaced by a dull throbbing. It takes a long time to go to sleep.

We rise at six every morning, shower, dress, and assemble in the school church for mass. It's cold in Nairobi at that time, and there's never enough hot water for everyone. So, freezing after a cold shower, we shiver in the unheated stone church, and say over and over:

'Hail Mary, full of grace.
The Lord is with thee.
Blessed art thou amongst women,
and blessed is the fruit of thy womb, Jesus.

'Holy Mary,
Mother of God,
pray for us sinners,
now and in the hour of our death. Amen.'

Our version is different:

'Hail St Mary's, full of crap.
The fathers are with thee.
Cursed art thou amongst everyone,
and painful the bruises on our bums, by Jesus.
Bloody St Mary's,
Mother of pain,
do us a favour,
piss off now and forever. Amen.'

351

To avoid the cold and drudge of morning mass, we take turns locking each other into our tall wall-lockers. When it's our turn, we sit it out in the dark, cramped space, but it's preferable to going to church. We've got tiny spy-holes in the doors of our lockers, so, holding our breath, we can watch Father O'Sullivan do his dormitory inspection. Sometimes it's difficult not to burst out laughing.

In the showers I see my backside in the big mirror. There are horizontal bruises across the top of my buttocks. They're deep purple, with bright red edges. Nearly all the boys have welts on their bums. Bright purple and red new ones, brown and yellowing old ones. Many have both. It's a uniform under the clothes.

It isn't just the dean of discipline who flogs us. There's also the dean of studies. Father Crab is a short, stout man with a monk's haircut, bald on top, ringed with a thick roll of hair. He's got a points-system. There are 'plus' and 'minus' points in the classrooms. If you pass a test, you get a plus. If you fail, it's a minus. If you talk in class, or are caught reading a comic, or chewing gum, or a hundred other things, you may be given one, two or even three minus points, at the discretion of the teacher or power-crazed prefect.

Just before lunch on Mondays, Father Crab makes a tour of the classrooms. The class prefect gives him a list of all the plus and minus points. Anyone with plus-five is given a 'big plus', which goes towards his term report. That means he won't carry any plus points forward, and will begin the next week with zero. Anyone with minus-five has to leave the class and queue up outside Father Crab's office. They wait for ages, until he completes his classroom tour. Then he comes and flogs each boy in turn, in the order he sent them. The others, waiting terrified in the queue, hear the loud whacks, and shuffle forward, as, one by one, their jet-propelled classmates hurtle past, faces contorted, hands caressing buttocks.

The psychological pain of the points system is even worse than the physical. On Fridays the best you can have is plus-four. Too few to have them taken away on Monday, enough to ensure you won't be flogged. It's rare to be in that position. More usually it's minus four. Too few for flogging, but dangerously close. When it's like that, it's rare you get through Monday morning without gaining the fateful extra minus. Or two if you're at minus three. The prefects just can't help themselves.

*   *   *   *

There are other developments. Someone wants to curry favour with Kim. He knows who told Father O'Sullivan about our smoking. Kim's a strange chap. He won't tell me who the informant is. Something to do with honour, an agreement he made. But the traitor is someone we both know. Roper. He was seen going into O'Sullivan's office, our smoking-tin in his hand! I actually feel sorry for him. Unable to beat me in the boxing ring, he's resorted to filching on me to the dean.

'What me do?' Kim asks. 'You wan keel?'

'No,' I say, 'leave him to himself. I'd hate to be him.'

'Okay, but I talk him. He know I know, he scare!'

'Okay,' I say. After that Roper's even more retiring than before. I wonder if he knows it's only me preventing Kim from knocking him into next week.

There are few distractions, apart from treachery and floggings. Many boys are convinced there's a tunnel from St Mary's to nearby Loretta convent. For the fathers to get at the nuns. Fathers and nuns, everyone says, are always doing *jigi-jigi*.

Sven Edmündsen, the airspray engineer, comes to take me to his home for the day. He arrives in a white gull-wing-door Mercedes Benz sports-car, and we hurtle through Nairobi with the wind blasting our hair. Sven's on leave, but his crew, including mad Eric, the Rhodesian pilot, are spraying crops somewhere near Geita. This makes me homesick. We arrive at Sven's sprawling house. His wife and two young sons are waiting for us. Sven's told them all about Geita. What's it like growing up in the bush, they ask. I tell them it's nice. We eat Norwegian food. I don't like it much.

Sven knows Lopey. Everyone in Nairobi knows Lopey. In fact, he's coming here this afternoon. Lopey arrives in his Ford Prefect. Parked next to Svens's Merc, it looks very drab. We sit and drink tea and eat cake on the patio. Lopey tells them about my great victory against the Kenya Champion. Sven's sons are impressed. So is Sven. I feel inches taller. Lopey drives me back to school. Just a week later the term comes at last to an end. I'm more grateful than ever I was at Arusha. Boarding school hasn't got easier with time. It's got worse. Or is it just that St Mary's is worse? I wish I could see Gretchen. That would cheer this place up.

Forty

My maddest escapade begins mundanely, if starting in the bush, travelling over untamed territory by Land Rover, then catching a steamer on Lake Victoria is mundane. Normal for me. I've been travelling to St Mary's boarding school this way for over a year. It's 1965 and I'm fourteen years old. I've always hated going to boarding school, and spent much energy pondering how to avoid it. Trouble is, and always has been, what on earth will I do, and where will I go if I actually succeed in running away? This perennial question has nagged me constantly since I was six, and answers have never been forthcoming.

In my imagination I build myself a primitive mud and grass hut on the shore of Lake Victoria, and for this journey I plunder as many ideas as possible from *Robinson Crusoe* and *Swiss Family Robinson*. After all, I'll never be able to show myself again to a *Mzungu,* or I'll simply be caught and returned whence I have flown.

My daydreams and night-time imaginings on this topic invariably lead me into mental anguish. Perhaps I'll succeed in establishing a bush hideaway and manage to feed myself. But won't I become lonely? Can I persuade another boy to run away with me? Oh, how I miss Lutoli! There are no other boys I think of I'll get on with. Of course, there's Kim, but I know he wouldn't run away. Even if that isn't the problem, will I ever see Mum again? If I do, I'll be caught. If I don't, what am I running away for? After all, it's missing *her* I hate most about boarding school. The whole idea is crazy. Anyway, how will I protect myself from lions, leopards, snakes. . ? I'm good at making and shooting a catapult, but what will that do against a charging rhino? Can I steal a gun somewhere? Where? My wish to escape is purely emotional. Logic? None, not a trace.

But the thoughts won't leave me. What if I build that *proper* canoe?

A really watertight one, covered with animal skins, unsinkable? I can put food in, and store water in *kalabashes*, then seal myself in. If it's on the sea, the wind and tide will carry me where they choose, and I'll be safe and snug inside. But how will I see out, know where I am? A periscope, perhaps. No, it'll never work. And again, I'll not see Mum. Self-defeating. But a nice, cosy idea to fall asleep with, knowing I'm not committed to do it because it's only thoughts.

How many nights I have lain in my dormitory bed at Arusha and Nairobi, exploring these ideas and notions I cannot say, except that they were in the many thousands, probably every single night for over eight years. I also did it every time the holidays were drawing to an end. It was a distraction from the horrible truth that I was going back where I hated it so much.

In the last few days of every holiday at home in Geita I stayed in bed, avoiding contact with anyone. My daydreams about escape, my hapless scheming and plotting about a hut by the lake, or a sealed-in canoe, were better than seeing people and places I'd soon be missing. Paradoxical, avoiding what I wanted not to leave? When all else failed my imaginings gave me comfort.

My mind has been playing these games since I was six, when I first arrived in Arusha. Now I'm fourteen, have been at St Mary's a year. The Easter holiday has galloped to an end. I've done my usual thing of these times, and withdrawn to my bed and musings. The dreaded morning comes. Five am, and the Land Rover blows its horn in the drive.

We drive to Mwanza, arrive at eleven. The sun's high already, searing white. We're dropped off at Mwanza Hotel. Fritz is going to the bank on mine business. After that he'll find a shady alleyway between the adobe buildings by the lake to eat his lunch, cool down and pass the hours. Later he'll collect us and drive down to the docks. MV *Victoria* is scheduled to dock at five, sail at six.

Mum has befriended the first officer on *Victoria*. Jack's a nice man. He's bearded, pipe-smoking, middle-aged and suntanned, and he cuts a dashing figure in his white tropical uniform. His wife and children live in Port Bell, Kampala, from where he sails on *Victoria*. After each tour he has a fortnight at home. He's a former Pacific & Orient Officer, and sailed on 'real ships and real oceans' for years. Now he's satisfied to be in the sun, well paid, and never have more than two weeks away from home.

Jack meets us on the gangplank. 'Back to torture?' he asks sympathetically. He smiles wryly. Unknown to Mum, the minute the boat sails from Mwanza he'll give me a cold bottle of *Whitecap* beer and a whole packet of *Crownbird* cigarettes. That's what I love about Jack. A real gent !

Sometimes I seem to have a loosely-formed idea that something different, significant, even exciting, is going to happen, but I can't say precisely what. It happens to me many times. Now I feel it again. Big-time. I've endured a whole year at St Mary's. For the whole holiday I've tried, like in previous years, to persuade Mum not to send me back.

My efforts are futile, and there's no chance my pleas, pestering, threats or blackmail can succeed. Even so, pride, and hatred of boarding school, make it impossible not to join a losing battle with all the energy and cunning I can muster. Deep down, at the beginning of the first term in 1965, I have a vague, delicious, anticipatory feeling – *this* time there will be more than just tearful pleas, threats to change love for hate, bribes of undying devotion, or even promises, despite my tender years, to don a miner's helmet and lamp and go down the mine to wrestle a living from the gold-bearing quartz and granite.

Mum is unmoveable. She, poor lady, pleads, cajoles and bribes in turn, pointing out I need an education, can't grow up 'wild' like my little black friends, who, despite their cunning, their knowledge of nature and their ability to survive, and even thrive, on very little, can't read or write, do arithmetic, or quote the date of any historical event, apart from recounting fireside stories handed down from equally 'illiterate and innumerate' elders and ancestors.

Mum and I both know, as always, that our daily arguments, tears and remonstrations are a screenplay we have written for ourselves, and nothing will come of them. The last day of the holiday will arrive, my cases will be packed, and early the next morning, while the African sky is still black, cool and breathless, Fritz will pull into the driveway in his Land Rover, the tyres squeaking on the gravel. There's a grim inevitability about it that no amount of scheming or arguing can change.

This time, despite the well-rehearsed drama, I have that feeling of something different pending. *This* time there's going to be a difference. Something will present itself. An opportunity unthought of and unexpected. It's going to declare itself suddenly and dramatically. And if it means not going back to school I'm going to seize the chance. Is it just the product of wishful thinking, or desperation? One, the other, both? Is it a remnant of my childish way of avoiding a bleak future, by magical thinking?

I have a feeling of anticipation, a knowledge that it's going to be different this time. I'll show them that *Jimu* won't accept boarding school forever. The opportunity, whatever it is, will show itself, and I'll take it. It's only this that lets me carry on with the fruitless, hopeless, pleading and begging. I go through the motions, inch by inch giving in to the inevitable, but with an exciting secret speeding my pulse. I get in the Land Rover that morning, bear the trip to Mwanza, and, as the sun presents its farewell orange orb over the lake's horizon, I board MV *Victoria*.

Ten minutes after the tearful farewell with Mum, I watch her fading into the amorphous shapes of receding people on Mwanza quay. Shortly afterwards, while I can still taste the salt of tears, and feel a choking lump in my throat, I take my first sip of ice-cold *Whitecap* beer from a clucking Uncle Jack. Off the port side, just fifty yards away, bucking like a wild colt on the white wash and waves of our wake is an unmistakable shape.

Lotanga! Her paintwork's faded. She's loaded to the gunwales with laughing *watu* and cargo. Bunches of bananas, live chickens hanging upside-down on string, black goats, brown sheep. Grey smoke curls from her thin funnel. She's going to Mwanza, perhaps for the tenth time today. The half-naked skipper smiles and waves. Big white teeth. I wave back. Strange to think Dad, Umali and Wait brought her all the way from Uganda.

Lake Victoria is an enormous body of water. The indomitable explorer John Speke, in his tireless quest for the source of the Nile, found himself on the shore of Lake Victoria late in 1858. Staring at the vast body of water from a high vantage point, he declared it to be 'The great blue pearl of Africa'. He wasn't wrong. It's roughly rectangular, aligned North to South. Between the most southern point at Mwanza in Tanzania, to the northern shore at Jinja in Uganda, is 400 miles of open water. From Bukoba on the Tanzanian west shore to Kisumu on the eastern shore in Kenya is three hundred miles. The total area covered by the lake is sixty thousand square miles. By comparison England covers less than forty thousand, and the whole British Isles only slightly exceeds the size of Lake Victoria.

There are ports on all sides of the lake, and vessels ranging from sailing canoes with outriggers, to large *dhows* of ancient Arabian design and traditional build, ply the waters as in centuries past. They carry goods and human cargoes, legitimate and smuggled, in the time-honoured tradition of an ancient water-highway connecting three huge countries which, between them, cover an area as big as all Europe. In the shallows by the lake's edge, fishermen cast out nets just like those of their forefathers, and pull in rich harvests of fish for sale in village markets.

For me the greatest spectacle on that beautiful inland sea is the passage of a steamer. The first steam powered vessels were introduced at the beginning of the century by the Germans in *Deutsch Ost Africa*. When World War One ended, Britain, already the colonial power in Kenya colony and the Uganda Protectorate, took power in Tanganyika Territory, their name for *Deutsch Ost Africa*. Now they controlled every port on the great lake. A few German steamers not sunk in action by the British were recruited into service, and others were added.

I don't know the number, nor the names, of all the steamships carrying commerce on the lake in the nineteen sixties, but there are at least ten. Most are rusting hulks, conveying produce from one lake port to another, plus a few fee-paying tribesmen travelling *al fresco* on deck, some with goats, sheep and chickens, some with only personal possessions tied up in cloth or bundled into broken suitcases, and yet others with nothing at all. Some steamers and *dhows* with similar cargoes can be smelt for miles downwind. However, even these hulks, seen underway from a distance, with foaming bow-waves in front, set against the crimson of a rising or setting sun, are things of extraordinary beauty.

There are two special steamers on the lake, princesses of the water. The older is SS *Usoga*. She is, I know, a very old ship of between two and three thousand tonnes. Built more than half a century ago, she has gracious lines, a tall black funnel, and a row of solid brass portholes along the sides. On board, the decks are laid in teak, and the guardrails are mahogany. She has twenty double cabins, immaculately fitted out in teak and brass, a dining room for fifty, a bar, and a magnificent Victorian lounge overlooking the stern. She's a gracious old lady.

The other special ship is newer, built on the Clyde in Scotland in the late nineteen fifties in a 'CKD', or Completely-Knocked-Down form, transported to Mombasa on the Indian Ocean coast of Kenya, railed to Port Bell, Kampala, in Uganda, welded together, and launched as flagship of the East African Railways and Harbours fleet. She isn't built as solidly as the *Usoga*, but at three and a half thousand tonnes is bigger, lighter, faster, more airy and more reliable than poor old *Usoga*, whose coal-fed steam engines have seen better days. *Victoria*'s not a steamship like *Usoga,* but a diesel-turbine powered vessel, hence she's called MV, for Motor Vessel, *Victoria*.

I've sailed to school before on both *Usoga* and *Victoria*. I love them both. Particularly on the homeward run.

Victoria has a cruising speed of ten knots, so she could make passage from Mwanza in Tanzania, on the southern shore, to Kisumu in Kenya, in fifteen or sixteen hours, if not for the time wasted loading

358

and offloading passengers and freight at the small Tanzanian port of Musoma, thirty-five miles south of the Kenya border on the north-east shore.

Victoria departs Mwanza dock at six on Sunday evening. She makes her way effortlessly through the calm lake waters. There's a spectacular sunset over the lake, and a cool, relieving breeze borne of evening and movement. Underfoot is the comforting deep throb of the great diesel engine. I've had a whole bottle of *Whitecap*, and smoked two *Crownbird* cigarettes, and I feel less bereft and homesick now.

I still have a sense of anticipation. It's occurred before at times like this, but never with such a feeling of certainty. I know this time something is going to occur. It will happen because I'm fed-up with it not happening.

It's slavery, I think, when *where* you are, *what* you do, *who* you do it with, is decided by others, without consultation. I've begged Mum to arrange home tuition for me. Why do I have to go away? The impossibility of arranging, or affording, a home tutor deep in the African bush never occurs to me. Grown ups are all powerful, omnipotent to my mind. It's them who make me go to boarding school, isn't it? They're the only ones with money, cars, power. If they wanted me to have a home tutor, it would happen. I've made an alternative offer too. I'll give up this 'education' thing. I don't need it. I'll work on the mine. Why can't they accept a fourteen-year-old? Too small? That's an excuse. They're just against me. They punish me by sending me away. I'll show them!

It's cosy in my cabin. Almost as nice as my imaginary canoe. I'm in my bunk and half-asleep when we dock in Musoma at ten. I hear rattling and banging as the crew go about their business. It's strangely comforting. I'm fast asleep before *Victoria* returns to the open water on the last leg north to Kisumu, Kenya, a hundred and twenty miles away.

I wake at six in the morning. The ship is powering its way through flat, calm water. There's no land anywhere. The freshness of the breeze is invigorating and strangely exciting. Today's the day. An outline of a plan is forming in my head. I knew it would. I go for breakfast in the dining room at the stern. It's a feast. Bacon, eggs, tomatoes, toast and marmalade, coffee.

Standing on the deck, leaning on the taffrail, watching the ship's wake and smoking a *Crownbird* cigarette, I feel a sense of well-being and optimism like never before. Jack stands beside me, smoking his pipe. What a nice man! I wonder if he senses what I'm thinking.

The morning draws on, *Victoria* chugs northwards, and by eight we're in sight of three Kenyan islands. The sun is a vicious white circle of unbearable brightness and heat, and shade on deck is difficult to find. The water reflects the sunlight like molten metal. Small *mtumbwi*s, dug-out canoes paddled by half-naked tribesmen, appear, the occupants vigorously wielding oars towards destinations only they know, their bodies shining and canoes shimmering in the wavering, light-bending, heat. In the distance a larger vessel, a *mashua,* with a dirty yellow patch of sail fluttering in the breeze, makes its way to somewhere else. Lake birds soar and dive after invisible fish.

At ten we see land-proper. The Kenya coast of Lake Victoria. The ship closes with the torpid town of Kisumu surprisingly soon. The rusting cranes and barges moored to the shore drift into view. So do the glinting, unpainted corrugated iron roofs of many town buildings. Some are, blissfully, painted. They're red, green, and a kaleidoscope of colours, mainly weathered and rust-tinged. But the raw steel roofs mirror the blazing sun, bedazzle the view, and send laser-like, blinding, rays straight to the eye, causing screwing up of eyelids and shielding with a hand.

The engine groans in reverse. The water boils astern, and the ship slows as if tugged backwards by a giant hand. She glides slowly, gracefully, alongside the berth of concrete piles, wood and iron. Ropes fly, yells resound in Swahili, men in tattered clothes run to secure mooring ropes. It's midday, and we've arrived.

I've done this trip many times. I know the routine. The train to Nairobi leaves at six this evening and arrives early tomorrow morning in the Kenyan capital. There, a Father from St Mary's will be waiting on the platform to take me to the school in his car. I have six hours to kill, in the hottest, worst town on lake Victoria. I call it the 'blinding headache town'. It's the sun reflecting from the iron roofs which blinds me, and I have to walk around with my head bent, looking at my feet. I get the fiercest headaches, like the top of my skull is going to explode and leave my brain exposed to be completely fried by the sun.

Six hours, supposedly, with nowhere to go, except to hang around. I'm a lone European boy, with a huge suitcase to lug about, a hundred shillings in my pocket to last three months as pocket money, never enough for that time, and a train ticket to Nairobi in the top pocket of my jacket. This jacket is equally gruesome to carry or to wear in this hellhole.

Things won't go according to the plans of others today. I've had enough of that, my life dictated by strangers. Mum colludes with them, but it isn't what she really wants. How can she *really* want me so far away? Dad's been dead nine years. She lives alone. She's always frightened alone. I know, because she says. Sometimes a misled but well-meaning mother needs positive action to make a proper decision.

360

To hell with Mr Snel, the manager, to hell with the bosses, to hell with those who make laws about children going to school, to hell with Father Cox, Father O'Sullivan, and all the fathers. They're misguided, stupid, evil, or all of those. They'll learn today that, Jim can, will, outsmart them. They'll be amazed and awed by my courage, vision and resourcefulness. They'll have no choice but to meet at a table of negotiation. This will be my future with big people. Negotiation as equals, not *diktat!*

When you're going to do something unexpected or illegal, or contrary to instructions, you should have an alibi, a plausible excuse, or a damn good explanation. I'm not out to be an obvious rebel, palpably ignoring rules and expectations. No, I'm going to craftily manipulate events, with every angle, every argument, every question, addressed by cogent, intelligent and reasonable argument. I'm the victim of circumstance, not the author. I will occupy the high moral ground.

Last night, walking on deck, I meet a sailor of mixed Arab-African race. He stands beside me, staring at the moon rising above the horizon as *Victoria* thunders northward. Behind us is a phosphorescent wake.

'*Una enda wapi?*' he asks. Where you going?

'Nairobi,' I answer, though I'm determined not to.

'*Gari moshi?*' he asks.

'Yes, the train. How else?'

'What time does it go?'

'*Sa kumi na mbili,*' I say, twelve hours. In East Africa the day is measured from when the sun comes up. So seven in the morning to Europeans is one o'clock to the *watu.* Twelve hours means six pm.

'*Apana!*' He says,

'No, you say what?'

'They've changed it. It goes every day at seven am now!' This is exactly what I want to hear. It turns out not to be true, but who cares about truth? Here's my excuse, legitimate and not self-invented. I've been told to catch the six o'clock train. There isn't one. So I can't catch it, and I can't be blamed for that!

I am now, I convince myself, abandoned, in a hellhole, and my clear and irrefutable duty is to go home. I can't do that by simply staying on the *Victoria* for the return trip to Mwanza. Jack will find a 'solution', and make it possible for me to continue to Nairobi. He'll use contacts, find a lorry driver going that way, or insist I stay overnight at his house, then catch the train tomorrow. He's dangerously sensible, too resourceful, too kind. I can't risk him.

First thing to do is get away from Europeans. They're too nosy, too

361

q

interested, too interfering, to let me execute my plan. I carry my case slowly from the harbour, down a side road leading from the European-type buildings at the waterfront, from the shops, out towards shanty-town Kisumu. When I get there, with aching arms from my heavy bundle, which I've changed from hand to hand several times, there are no white faces. Instead, the dusty streets, bounded by wood and iron shacks in stages of decay and rust, are thronged with black people of several tribes, laughing, yelling and talking at once in Swahili. It's not only *my* first language, but the common tongue of the lake.

I walk among these bustling people, safe and relaxed. They, I know, will understand and sympathise with my plan. Just like me, they can't comprehend the workings of white men's minds.

A fat *mama* is selling *karanga*, or peanuts, on an upturned tea chest, measuring them out with a small tin which once contained baked beans. I like the look of her. She has a kind face, and I think she'll help. I approach, my case pulling painfully at my aching arm. '*Jambo Mama*,' I begin, using the polite greeting for an older woman.

'*Jambo Mzungu ndogo*,' she replies, beaming. Hello small white person.

'I want to catch a bus to Tanzania,' I say. Her smile fades and she cocks her head to one side.

' Tanzania, child, why Tanzania?'

'My home, my mother,' I manage to say, suddenly overcome with emotion and longing. Some for Mum and Becky, some for Gretchen. Some to be home in Geita. Tears pour down my cheeks in a totally unplanned, but genuine, display of sadness. She's around her makeshift table of upturned tea chests in a second, putting her great fat arms around me, and hugging me to her breast so tight I can hardly breathe.

'*Pole, ndogo, pole, usi lia. . .* Quiet small one, quiet, don't cry. . .' she croons, stroking the top of my head with one hand and forcing my face between her huge breasts with the other. 'God will help. God will help.' In my dejected misery a little flame is lit. I have found an ally to help me in my plan.

'Come home with me,' she says. 'We will talk, and if you want to go to your mother, we will make it so!'

She orders a young female assistant to continue selling *karanga*, takes my heavy case in one hand, my hand in her other, and leads me down a succession of more and more confusing alleyways, until we come to a hovel which is her home.

'*Mimi ni Ngina*,' she says, I am Ngina. She places a rough-hewn wooden stool on the ground outside for me to sit on, then fetches

362

another for herself. 'Now tell me everything, *white-man-small*. Does your mother send you away when she must know you are not happy?'

'She is forced by *Mzungu* bosses.'

'But you are a *Mzungu*, little one, she chuckles,' her great belly wobbling.

'Yes, but not like them!'

'I can see that,' she says, shaking her head and smiling. 'You are a *Mzungu Ki-Afrika-Kabisa!*'

'*Asante sana*,' I say.

'You must home go at once, tell your Mama you can, together, stand against the bad *Mzungus* who separate you from her. They are evil, unkind, and you, my small African *Mzungu*, will win.' She smiles again, and squeezes my shoulder.

'My brother Kalebu is *lori-busi* driver. He leave tonight, not to Tanzania, but a place call Narok, a hundred and ten miles from here. You get off there. You will find another bus to take you Narok to Ikoma, from there another to Mwanza. With God's help you will come, at last, to your home and your Mama.' I relax. This is what I was praying for. 'Kalebu will be here in an hour. Meantime, rest. There is a *kitanda* inside you can lie on. Leave your case, it will be safe. Sleep a while, small *Mzungu*. Everything will come to pass. You will be back with your Mama, and she will rejoice.'

Forty-one

The bed is made of crude wooden planks, and its legs are placed in *kopos*, or cans of water. That's to stop the *kijitu*, or evil dwarfs, from climbing up. They're repelled by water. I lie on the hard grass mattress. I'm exhausted and soon fall asleep. I dream of Gretchen. She's wearing a white dress, and grinning over her shoulder at me, while hugging another boy. He's got his arms around her narrow waist. They're muscular and hairy, and they're pulling her so close that he's bending her body. I can't see who he is, but murderous feelings rear in my breast. Gretchen winks prettily, and disappears, leaving me in a long, dark tunnel, like one of the hill-shafts at Geita mine.

Ngina's brother arrives at four pm. They take a peep at me and decide I need to sleep. They leave me till quarter to seven. Ngina and Kalebu discuss their novel visitor, who's so desperate to go home to his *Mama*. When they wake me, they've decided I'll go with him on his bus as far as Ikoma.

We'll drive forty miles to Kericho, forty more to Sotik, thirty to Narok. There we'll cross the border into Tanzania, go through the village of Lambayala, and drive a hundred miles to Ikoma. There he'll introduce me to a Tanzanian driver he knows. He'll take me on, south and east, past a village called Manyanya, which means tomatoes, the hundred and twenty miles to Mwanza. I'm looking forward to a nominal three hundred and thirty miles of dirt road and ancient bus.

I've been on bus trips nearly as long before. But there are many stops along this road, at least seven or eight, and they take an hour each, Kalebu says. He and his passengers have to relieve themselves, eat, drink, load and unload their heavy *mzigo*, or luggage. I calculate. Say the average speed's thirty. The roads are awful. That'll be eleven hours. Add seven or eight hours for stops, that makes eighteen or nineteen. *If* we don't break down or have an accident. From Mwanza, Kalebu says, I can make my own arrangements.

We leave from a bus-stop, the only evidence of which is the existence of a hand-painted, fading yellow and black sign nailed to a very unhappy looking tree. It's seven in the evening. Early twilight. Kalebu is wearing a rakish but very tatty red cap, on which 'KTTC' is just discernible in yellow letters. Kenya-Tanzania-Transport Company. On the bus, in large red letters, is the legend 'Lands-Rokett'. This bus makes the Dodoma-Arusha transport look modern. It's out of a museum where they don't look after things.

It's a Bedford, or what's left of one. At least thirty years old, if not more, and wearing poorly. It's blue and red, or was originally. Like the Dodoma bus, it's covered with added artwork everywhere a brush can reach. There's a few stencilled, fading coloured advertisements. 'Drink Coca Cola, ice cold.' Difficult if you've got no fridge, and hardly any *watu* have one. 'Smoke *Sportsman*, Kenya's favourite filter cigarette.' Red packet. '*Crownbird* gives you smoking satisfaction.' They've got no filters. Yellow packet. What's best, filter or no filter, favourite or satisfaction? Hardly anyone here speaks English, let alone *reads* it. The driver's door is missing. No matter, who needs a door? The bonnet is bent and rusty. Old accident, never repaired.

If I thought it was tight on the Dodoma bus, I have a new experience of what 'squeeze' means! The bus has seats for forty. At least seventy are determined to board. There's no queue, just a gathering. *Watu* of all ages, tribes, sexes and sizes. Some in groups, some alone, all with *mzigo*, or luggage, at least their own size. Several *mzigos* are alive. Squawking and bleating. *Kukus* hang upside-down, legs bound. Goats bleat; small ones carried, big ones tugged on ropes. A *batamzinga*, or turkey, just like Gooloogooloo. A fat calf. Pretty and confused. A *karamu*, or feast, is planned, in a village somewhere between here and someone-knows-where. A wedding, perhaps.

There's a pungent odour of dung and urine, frightened animal, unwashed humanity. Kalebu is ordering the boarding. Trying to. It's chaos. His assistant is a boy no older than me, but a lot thinner. In fact he looks sick, very sick. Belying his size and appearance, he's hefting the non-living *mzigo*, and some *kukus* in grass cages, onto the rusty roof rack which covers the whole roof. When they're parted from their *mzigo*, or not if it's *too* alive, the struggling *watu* surge forward to jam the doorway, the living *mzigo* exerting itself to new heights of squawk and baleful bleating.

'*Kuja, Mzungu!*' Kalebu says, grabbing my elbow and pulling me through the knot of struggling *watu*. He tugs me up the aisle, to three

365

seats. One is occupied by a grey-bearded *mzee*, or elder, in worn-out trousers and shirt of indiscriminate colour, the other two by an enormously fat *mwanamuke*, or woman, dressed in a floral *kanzu* or loincloth, with tribal scars on her cheeks. Kikuyu marks. She's got massive breasts. Though covered by the *kanzu*, I can see they're as big as pressure-cookers.

'Malaika, *hi ni rafiki yangu, Jimu*,' he says. Malaika, this is my friend, Jimu. Jimu, Malaika will care for you.' The huge woman's face creases in a smile, showing she has only bottom teeth. On her lap is a young billy-goat. There's at least six chickens in the woven basket at her feet. She clenches herself, and manages to move her buttock a foot to one side. She's still occupying a seat and two thirds. I have no choice. I let myself subside into the sliver of space, and find myself hard against a bony *mzee* on one side, enveloped in pungent soft flesh on the other. The baby goat on Malaika's lap puts his head on my knee. She strokes his neck. The *mzee*, luckily, has only one piece of *mzigo*. A very small, battered cardboard suitcase. I wonder where he's going, and why.

'*Jambo Mzungu ndogo*,' She says. Hello little *Mzungu*. She's very friendly. 'Ngina told me your business.' She smiles even more broadly. 'Don't be afraid, I look after you always, *Jimu!*' Looking into her eyes, I know it's true. She will. That's how it is. *Watu* tell the truth. They love children, I know that from all my memories. I've never felt let down. Different with *Wazungus*, or Europeans. With the *watu*, even their *dishonesty* is somehow honest. I understand them. I feel a welling of warmth for fat Malaika. How *did* she get the name? The love song about someone with that name wasn't about a woman as fat as this! Or *was* it? *Malaika, ninakupenda Malaika*. Malaika, I love you Malaika. It's a lovely song.

The diesel engine rattles into life, shaking the bus in a metallic jingle. The floor plate under my feet vibrates unrhythmically. It's not been tuned, I think, grinning to myself. It's un-musical. That's a worry. I hope it doesn't mean it won't manage the trip.

Why do I analyse everything? Why does my brain import all this into a simple thing like a vibrating engine? Mum took me to Dr Weiss last year. Told him I worry too much, make 'mountains out of molehills'. Josef says she's lucky I didn't die of the cerebral malaria when I was five.

'I haff niffer heard uff a young vun vot didn't die in a coma like zat. So vat, he iss a leetle emotional und obsessive, ja? Ve can't know vot brain-damages he iss having.' He smiles. 'Jimmy iss vun devil, ja? But iss not his fault.' I look at Mum to see if she's clocked the point. *Not* my fault. He removes his glasses, takes a fountain pen from his pocket.

He draws the outline of a brain in a continuous stroke. 'Here,' he says, pointing with the nib at an area near the bottom of his drawing, 'iss der temporal lobe uff der brain. It hass a very poor supply uff blood. Ven der iss high fever, it needs more oxygen, but can't get. So, some uff it ist dying.' Mum is visibly shaken. 'Ve call zis *medial temporal sclerosis*,' Josef continues, 'und der problem iss zat in zis area iss der control uff der emotions.' He puts his glasses on and grins at me. 'I sink *zat* iss vy Jimmy iss der handful!'

'Will you give me a letter to say I can't box at school?' I ask.

'Vy not?' he says. That's how I get out of a second fight.

So don't worry about it, I think. I'm like I am, and worrying's not going to change anything. What a funny bugger you are, I muse, grinning to myself. Fat Malaika laughs. '*Busi ni mzee, namna huyu!*' She indicates the old man on my side. The bus is old, like him! The *mzee* chuckles. Her laughter is infectious. There's a teeth-rattling grind of gears, and we jerk onto the road. Without warning the twilight is replaced by a cloak of black, penetrated by conical yellow beams from the headlights. The bus-stop's on the outskirts of Kisumu, so it isn't long before the *Land-Rocket*'s in open country. Soon the tar road ends, then we're on bone-shaking dirt and stone.

I'm very tired, even though I slept an hour this afternoon. It's the anxiety about what I'm doing. I yawn. The ancient Bedford bus is heading south, around the eastern edge of the Kavindoro Gulf. The moon comes out and lights up the glass-smooth water. After twenty miles we're heading away from the lake, into the hinterland of Southern Kenya. The road gets even more bumpy.

Fat Malaika's readjusting herself. She pulls a huge arm out from between us, and puts it round me. I don't resist when she pulls me to her. Her well-cushioned chest makes a soft pillow. Somewhere deep inside I hear her heart beating. It's a good heart. '*Lala mtoto*,' she says. Sleep child. I do.

I shift between deep and fitful sleep on the jerky bus with my face propped against a female bosom. We stop to pick up more passengers who get on noisily. I'm too tired to care. I wake and am surprised to see my watch says two hours have slipped by. Mostly I drift off only minutes at a time. There are longer naps, when I dream of being in a storm in my imaginary sea-canoe. Gretchen is with me. I ask her who was hugging her, but she just laughs.

The bus is groaning and grinding to a stop. I open one eye. Nowhere. Nothing. In the moonlight I see palely illuminated, flat, arid country running to the horizon. There's a thin pale line where sky meets earth. I lift my head and rub my eyes. On one side there's an interruption to the flow of the land. A long, low mud building, open on the sides, roofed with grass thatch. There's flickering light coming from it. A fire. I feel Malaika stir.

'*Wapi?*' I ask her when she rubs her eyes. Where?

'*Sijui, katika aw si-mbari Sotik.*' I don't know, but it's near, or not far from, Sotik. If I remember right, that's only forty miles past Kericho, which is forty from Kisumu. I look at my Oris. It's eleven at night. Eighty miles in four hours. Perhaps land snail would be a better name.

'*Ku fanyaje?*' I ask sleepily. To do what? The open-sided hut has more light now. Six points of it. In the still night air I hear the low growl of hurricane-lamps.

'*Chai, mtoto, na makate!*' Tea, child, and bread! '*Njaa?*' Are you hungry? Suddenly I realise I am. Ravenous. The *watu* are getting off the bus. We join them.

The floor is of pounded, swept mud, and there are three long tables of rough planks supported on logs stuck in the ground. The tired passengers are seating themselves on low benches, waiting for the proprietor and his wife to bring food. They expected the bus from Kisumu, and the wood fire is burning with bright yellow flames. There's an arrangement of what looks like old metal ammunition trunks around it. The *mzee*, or old man, in a *kanzu* stokes the fire, and his wife looks into the trunks, muttering.

'*Tiari?*' he asks.

'Nearly ready,' she says.

The wait is forever. It's cold after the heat of day. Finally the *mzee*'s wife pronounces satisfaction. Then *makate*, pronounced mak-ah-teh, is placed on the tables. It's bread rolls, huge ones, in blocks of twelve. It's made of coarsely ground, unrefined wheat. Bread has never tasted as delicious, even without butter or jam. It's hot, yeasty, coarse and chewy, and just what I need. *Chai* is brought in huge teapots, which have been boiling on the fire. It's got everything in, tea, milk, lots of sugar. Hot, stewed, sweet *chai*. Swahili-style. Poured into old baked-beans tins, or *kopos*. Perfect! I drink a big *kopo*ful, and ask for more. There isn't better sustenance anywhere. Malaika is sitting beside me, eating hungrily, slurping her tea and chewing with her mouth open. Just like me and the other diners. Malaika grins.

'*Mu-Africa!*' she laughs. An African! I nod. I am, *I am!*

'*Una jaa?*' Kalebu asks, coming over to check on me. Are you full?

'*Karibu ku zaidi,*' I say through a mouthful of *makate*. I'm nearly satisfied. He pats me on the back and laughs.

'*Wewe ni mSwahili kabisa!*' he says. You are a complete Swahili! He heads back to his bus, still laughing. That's a compliment I value.

368

Forty-two

The journey south continues. We can't see much, because there's no moonlight now, and the headlights point jaundicedly ahead. Kalebu must have the eyes of a *fisi,* Malaika says. Only they can see in the dark. It's witchcraft. *Mganga-Mchawi* things! She talks like Amina. For a while we roar along the edge of a dark plain, then we slow to walking pace. The dirt road from Sotik to Narok is only thirty miles long, but parts of it were washed away in last year's monsoon floods. In the low-lying areas it's gone completely, along with dozens of villages. Elsewhere the surface has been breached in many places by deep gulleys or *dongas.* The PWD, or Public Works Department, are doing their best to repair the road, but it's taking time. Kalebu has told Malaika what to expect.

We jolt and shake as the Land Rocket slows and descends obliquely into a wide washaway, crosses the rocky bottom and struggles up the other side. For a few minutes we're on a road again, then there's another washaway. It's incredible how this ancient bus manages to climb out of the holes. Even a Land Rover would struggle. I'm thinking that as we begin to ascend the far side of a deep gulley. We reach half-way, then the back wheels spin, we slew round and slip backwards. Kalebu reverses and tries again. Same result. Three more times he tries. Then he orders everyone off.

Pushing a bus up an incline of one in five at two in the morning, in total darkness, on the side of a muddy slope, in the company of *watu* of both sexes and all ages, is a unique experience. The *watu* sing as they labour. Not a song, more a rhythm made up of harmony of numbers. It can only ever be like this in the heart of Africa. '*Moja, mbili, tatu!*' One, two, three! At three everyone heaves. Kalebu releases the clutch and floors the accelerator. The exhaust bellows and coughs black smoke, the back wheels spin, spattering us with mud and small stones, and we push. Ever so slowly we inch her upwards. As we relax to draw breath, we hear Kalebu pull up the handbrake. Even so, we lose some of the gain by back-sliding. Like the dean of discipline always accuses me of.

The passengers are a determined lot. No amount of failure dents their enthusiasm. With conviction like this, the bus *has* to move. In slow, painful, steps it does. Bit by bit, we reach a point where, suddenly, on the dozenth attempt, the wheels find purchase, and the monster roars and gains the lip of the gulley. It's back on the road, or *bit* of road. A ragged cheer rises from the exhausted passengers. Kalebu stops. Covered in mud, we clamber on board. Our rest is brief. Fifteen minutes later we're stuck again. Off, on again. Washaways every mile. Mostly Kalebu manages without passenger-power, but there's five pushes in two hours.

I'm exhausted, filthy and itchy. I recognise the itch. Mosquito-bite. I've been eaten alive, outside pushing, or last evening waiting for the bus in Kisumu. It's hard trying to scratch through a layer of caked mud. I try to sleep, but can't. Even fat Malaika is scratching. I feel sorry for her. Of all the passengers, she pushed hardest. I'm sure her enormous breasts are really made of muscle. Now she's exhausted, itchy and restless. Like me. The *dongas* or washaways are less frequent, and shallower. Kalebu treats them with disrespect, roaring and jolting down one side and up the other at full throttle. It's five in the morning, and the eastern horizon is just beginning to suffuse itself with a suggestion of soft light, when we reach a wooden pole with a fading stencilled sign:

YOU AR   LE VING KEN A
OP   OU   NJO ED YOU   ISIT
'KWA ERI'

A hundred yards further are two tall posts with a huge sign between them:

W LCOM   TO TA ZAN A
ENJOY   OU   VIS T

Thank heavens the signs are so clear!

I'm in my home country now. Shortly we trundle into the mud-hut village of Narok. It's taken five hours to do thirty miles from Sotik, where we feasted so hungrily on bread and tea. This is as far as Kalebu and his bus take me. Here he turns left, towards a village a hundred miles to the west.

I'm standing under a gnarled tree with a bus-stop sign nailed on. The horizon is lighting up as the rising sun lips the far side of a jagged, rocky hillock. Kalebu brings my suitcase. '*Ngoja hapa,*' he says to me. Wait here. 'At two hours a bus will come from Ikoma. It will take you there, then you get another to Mwanza.' Two hours is eight am Swahili-time. Three hours to wait. Malaika is continuing her journey. It's her village they're going to. She gives me a very sweaty hug, then clambers back on board. The old bus roars off. It needs a new exhaust. To start with! I'm the only one who got off. I sit on my case to wait. There's a cluster of silent mud huts down the road, and nearby a solitary rooster greets the rose-coloured dawn. It's hauntingly beautiful. The itching's less, but I'm exhausted and sore all over.

I've never fallen asleep sitting up, without even a backrest. I do now. It's a strange sleep, because I'm dimly aware of rocking slowly forward, until I'm about to fall on my face, then rocking back again. But I'm asleep, and even dream for two hours, because it's seven when I sit up straight and look at my watch. I'm stiff and sore, but that's not what's woken me. I look around and see six naked or semi-naked *totos,* aged three to twelve, appraising me. They're laughing and giggling. 'Look,' one says, 'the *Mzungu* is awake!' Hello Rip van Winkle, Gulliver, *whoever!* At least I'm not tied up with tiny ropes!

'*Jambo,*' I say, '*habari*?' Hello, how are you? There's a look of delighted surprise on their faces. They didn't expect me to speak their language. They burst out laughing. This is sport indeed, a young *Mzungu* sitting on a suitcase on the side of the road in the early morning, and he speaks Swahili! Nothing as exciting as this ever happens.

'*Njaa,*' I say, I'm hungry. The biggest *toto* steps forward tentatively. He's wearing a *kanzu,* or loincloth, round his waist, and nothing else. He reminds me painfully of Lutoli, only he's thinner.

'*Njaa?*' he asks.

'*Ndio,*' I say, yes.

'*Gina lako?*' he asks, your name?

'Jimu,' I say, '*Lako?*' Yours?

'Steveni,' he replies, grinning. '*Kuja,* Jimu,' he says, come. He turns and walks in the direction of the huts. I pick up my case and follow Steveni, and the others skip along behind us.

It's seven thirty by my watch, and the sun is already high and dazzling. I feel I've been sleeping forever. I really am like Rip van Winkle, waking to find the world has changed while I slept. It's that

371

over-tired, detached and dreamy state I've known before. When I had the malaria half-way up Kilimanjaro. It's just tiredness, I assure myself. I don't feel cold now, I'm not nauseous and I'm not shivering either. We walk into a large swept-earth compound connecting three mud and thatch huts.

'*Mzungu!*' Steveni announces excitedly to an old woman bent over a fire. It's a large one, of burning logs between three big rocks. Just like Amina cooks. Balanced on the rocks is an enormous blackened *sufuria*, and I know the smell of the bubbling contents. It's *ugali,* or maize-meal porridge. This one's made thin and runny. It's drinking-porridge, or *ugi*. The woman straightens and examines me with one eye. Her other one's missing, and the eyelid's closed over a hollow place where the eye should be. She's old, very old, and as thin as a stick. I have met another *masikini*. She smiles, revealing she has no teeth.

'*Karibu Mzungu!*' she sputters. Welcome *Mzungu*.

'*Mzungu ana njaa,*' Steveni says. The *Mzungu's* hungry.

'*Ana fahamu?*' she asks. Does he understand?

'*Na jua Swahili,*' Steveni affirms, smiling at me. He knows Swahili. It's as if Lutoli is back. I knows it isn't, but Steveni has something about him, like I've known him all my life. What do I know of these things? It's so strange, and comforting at the same time. Maybe Lutoli is never really going to be dead to me.

'*Karibu sana!*' the old lady says, smiling more widely. Welcome-a-lot!

'*Asante!*' I say. She puts a long wooden spoon into the pot, withdraws it and tastes the porridge.

'*Tiari,*' she says. It's ready. Steveni has plucked two lemons from a gnarled little tree. He gives them to her and she cuts them with a knife-blade without a handle. She squeezes the juice into the pot, and stirs. She's got an old tin with sugar. She shakes some into the mix. One of Steveni's friends hands out the *kopos*, and the old lady fills them, using another on a long stick as a ladle.

The *ugi* is hot and sour and sweet. It's the favourite breakfast for children all over East Africa. I drink mine as fast as I can without scorching my mouth. Steveni and his friends, and the old lady, watch in fascination. They don't see *Wazungu* often, and they've probably never seen such a hungry one. I drain my *kopo*, and it's refilled.

After my second helping I feel satisfied. My hunger was extreme. Must be all that bus-pushing last night. The village is coming to life. An old *Mzee* has come out of a hut, and is sitting on a wooden stool. The lady's husband, I presume. He looks a hundred. A young woman

372

with pendulant breasts appears, carrying a naked baby on her hip. *Kukus* scratch at the dry ground. I feel very tired. I glance at my watch. It's nearly eight o'clock, or two-hours. That's when Kalebu said the bus would come from Ikoma. I thank my hosts, and give the old lady a five shilling note from my pocket-money. She's overwhelmed, and claps her hands in gratitude. Even the old man claps. Steveni and the *totos* accompany me back to the bus-stop under the gnarled tree.

In Tanzania eight o'clock means anything from nine to twelve. Time hasn't got much urgency. I talk with Steveni until we run out of things to say. It's so much like talking to Lutoli. Then I can't help myself. The sleepy feeling starts again. There's something else. I'm getting a headache. It's all over my head, a sharp, lancing pain. The type of headache I once described to Mum as two men sword-fighting in my head. The sun's high in the sky, blasting heat at the baked earth. I should be feeling hot, but I'm not. I'm beginning to feel cold. Suddenly I notice my teeth begin to chatter, and I feel shivers running through my body. Oh no, I think, not the malaria again! I drift into a strange sleep. Images come and go. Gretchen, Mum, Becky, Umali. They all seem to be trying to warn me about something, but I can't hear. I've got some kind of strange-shaped helmet on my head, covering my ears. Is it an army helmet, or the machula's bucket, I wonder.

It's almost twelve when Steveni jumps to his feet and shouts that a *busi* is coming. I've nodded off again, and I jolt awake. When I open my eyes it's on a world which has gone blurry and painfully bright. And freezing. My head is exploding. I can hardly stop my lower jaw from quaking and my teeth from chattering. The muscles of my legs and arms are twitching uncontrollably, and my knees are knocking together. I shade my eyes and look down the road. I can see a cloud of dust coming my way, nothing else. I have to close my eyes as the pain shoots through my head.

The bus squeaks to a halt. I don't know or care what kind of bus it is. I manage to ask the driver if he's going to Ikoma, and he says he is. Two other passengers have come out from the village. Unlike me, they don't wait here for hours. I get on and pay my two-shilling fare. Then I collapse into a seat behind the driver. Steveni's waving goodbye. I feel so close to him, so sad to leave.

The bus turns and goes back the way it came. I lick my lips. They're very dry and sore. It must be the dust and the heat, even though I feel so cold.

I fall into a fitful sleep, and dream I'm being chased by the rotting *mzoga,* or corpse, of Mr Valari (senior), who has two ferocious black fisis, with bright blood dripping from their teeth, as assistants. High in a branch of an acacia tree, Gretchen, wearing jeans and a T-shirt, and looking gorgeous, waves cheerily at me. What does it mean? I'm relieved to wake and find I'm only on a bus. We stop at the village of Lambayala, but I'm only dimly aware of it. I'm very ill. The shivering is quaking through my whole body. Even my head rocks as my neck muscles declare independence. My lips are on fire. I lick them and taste salty blood. We continue our journey. I sleep.

The bus stops, and everyone gets off, except me. I'm unable to stand up. The driver comes to look at me. '*Ngonjwa, Mzungu?*' he asks. Are you ill, *Mzungu?*

'*Ndio,*' I manage to say. Yes.

'*Una kwenda wapi?*'

'Mwanza,' I say between shivers. That's where I'm going.

'*Ni mbari,*' he says. It's far.

'*Hapa?*' I ask. Here?

'Ikoma,' he says. He's right. It's another hundred and twenty miles to Mwanza. I look at my watch. It's seven in the evening. I've been sleeping for ages, almost all the way from Narok. We left there at midday, so it's taken seven hours to do a hundred miles. I don't know how I can continue.

'*Busi ko Mwanza,*' he says, pointing. The bus for Mwanza is there. Its engine is running. It's about to leave and I'm going to miss it. The driver sees the panic in my eyes. He jumps out his bus and waves frantically. The other bus has just started to move. He brakes in a cloud of red dust.

'*Mzungu!*' my driver shouts. Next thing, with help from this kind man, I'm seated again, and on the road south once more, towards Manyanya, and finally Mwanza. I realise I haven't given any thought to what I'll do when I get there. Obviously, I'll have to get someone to contact Geita. But what will I say? How will I explain being back in Mwanza? It's difficult thinking about this. My headache's bad enough without the effort. When I think, it gets worse.

This bus is almost empty. I'm so cold, it's like my bones are in ice. My body's too tired to shiver. I feel my lips with my fingers. They're thick, like a big steak. And throbbing. When I grimace the skin cracks open, and warm blood oozes into my mouth. I don't know how, but I fall asleep again. It's thirty-six hours since *Victoria* arrived in Kisumu, and twenty-six since I boarded the first bus. It's still a hundred miles to Mwanza.

Now I'm being buried in a grave, although I'm not dead. The trouble is I can't move, or speak. I'm paralysed, but awake. I can't do anything to let them know I'm not dead. Mum, Becky and Gretchen are there, crying their eyes out. I don't know how I know, because the coffin's nailed down. We're in the little church in Geita one minute, then at Samina. I'm being lowered into a freshly dug grave. It's between Dad and Mrs Williams, even though there's really no space for another grave. My eyes are cameras outside my coffin. I can see everyone. At the back of the burial party are Umali and Amina. They're crying. Odd, Lutoli's with them. He's laughing! Then I see someone else. Behind everyone, shaking a bony finger at me, is the rotting corpse of Mr Valari. As I watch, a scorpion scampers out of his eye socket and down his disintegrating cheek.

I fall into deeper, non-dreaming sleep. It's as if I'm dead. A few times I'm aware of distant voices, of stops and starts, or just extreme cold or pain, but I drift back into soft cottonwool sleep. The hours and miles pass. I dream of Gretchen again. She's very beautiful in white. The boy who hugged her is nowhere to be seen. We pass through the dusty village of Mananya.

The bus reaches Mwanza. I don't know time anymore. I also don't know how I get to the Mwanza Hotel. Next thing I'm in a bed, in a coma. I find out later how I get there. The driver carries me to the hotel. He's the last in a series of good Samaritans I've met on the road. It's early morning, forty-eight hours after *Victoria* docked in Kisumu, thirty-six since I caught the bus in Kisumu, and twenty-four since I should have arrived in Nairobi. I don't realise I'm famous throughout East Africa.

When I don't get off the train from Kisumu yesterday morning, Father O'Sullivan goes back to St Mary's and telephones Geita via the radiophone. Mr Snel answers, and sends for Mum.

'Jimmy's missing,' he says. Mum feels a cold hand seize her heart.

'What do you mean?' she asks him.

'He didn't arrive in Nairobi. Nobody knows where he is!' Mum faints. Mr Snel just catches her in time to prevent her hurting herself. When she comes to, he's taken command of the situation.

'I've sent out messages to everyone,' he says. 'First, to the steamer *Victoria*. Maybe the little bugger's hiding on the boat. She's on her way back to Mwanza, and East African Railways and Harbours are contacting her by radio. I've told the police in Kenya, Uganda *and* Tanzania to look out for him. Maybe he got off the Nairobi train somewhere, and forgot to get back on.' He gives Mum a cup of hot, sweet tea for shock. 'I've also contacted the *East African Standard*. Maybe someone will read about and recognise him.'

Mum and Becky have a day and night of hell. If I'd known I'd cause such distress, I wouldn't have done it.

The radio-phone jangles in the head office. Mr Snel picks up the receiver. It's the manager of the Mwanza Hotel. 'Read the *Standard* this morning,' he says, 'and I've got your missing boy!'

Mum and Mr Snel are driven to Mwanza by Fritz, who complains he can't go as fast as they demand. When they arrive at Mwanza Hotel, it's six hours since I got there. They're let into my room by the manager. I'm there all right, but they can't rouse me. I'm in a high fever. I'm bundled up and taken to Geita, where Josef Weiss is waiting. He confirms the diagnosis they suspected. It's malaria again. And total exhaustion.

I don't know much about the next few days. Then I'm better. They allow me a week to convalesce. At the end of that time, I'm taken by Fritz and Mr Snel himself to Mwanza, and put on a direct flight to Embakazi airport, Nairobi. They're taking no chances. There will be no mistake, no escape, this time. Father O'Sullivan will be waiting on the landing strip.

Forty-three

It's May 1966. I'm fifteen, and the gold-mine is closing. The government in Dar-es-Salaam have taxed it to death. Not satisfied with doubling company tax, they've invented other ways to wring money out of foreign-owned enterprises, and the mine closes in three months.

Things move fast. People are leaving each day, heading home to England, South Africa, Italy, the Seychelles, Germany, and other places. There are very few foreigners left. It's strange, isn't it – all the *Wazungu* who've ever come here leave in the end. Like Vorbeck himself, my great hero, we're finally leaving too. I'd hoped it'd never really happen.

I've been home from St Mary's for a month. I'm never going there again. Only one person I'll miss. Kim. It was a tearful goodbye, though I've given him an address in Cornwall, and he said he'll come and see me. But we're leaving home in three days. Leaving Geita forever, leaving East Africa. I'm heartbroken. So are Becky and Mum. There's even more heartache for me. Antonio says Gretchen has been seeing Arnoldo Bachelli, a swish Italian bachelor who came to Geita last year. Was he the one hugging her in my dream? She and Dieti have been sleeping over at his house. It's too painful to think about. What has he done to her? Dieti won't say when I ask. While I've never even let myself think about her that way, even closed my eyes to protect her nakedness underwater, along comes this interloper, and ruthlessly grabs that which was always only meant for me! Gretchen's eighteen, and Mum and Becky say it's natural she should have a boyfriend, and I'm far too young for her. Don't I know that? There'll be a girl for me one day. This does nothing for me. I hate her now, with all my heart. How can she *do* this to me? I've loved her so long, dreamt about her so many, many times. Is there no justice, was she never able to see the value of pure, unselfish love and devotion? Then there's another feeling. We're leaving, I may never even see her again. Good! I don't want to! But then there's this nagging pain, like a hard painful lump deep in my throat, and under my ribs.

There's more agony. We're leaving Umali and Amina. Their love has always been *certain*, not just hoped for! Tembo too. Poor chap, he's only ever been good to me. Sandy's going to stay with Umali and Amina. Mum's done something awful. She had no choice but to give all our *kukus* to Umali, who removed them to his *shamba*. He doesn't want Gooloogooloo, our infamous *batamzinga,* because Amina is too afraid of him. So Mum donates him to the club. She feels very guilty telling me it took *three strong men* to hold him down and cut his throat. What was the alternative? she asks. The alternative to the *murder* of my friend? If we just left him, the *fisis* and every other wild thing would tear him to pieces, and it'd be a much worse death. Anyway, she says, the people said he made a great curry! Mum and Becky say they didn't eat any. I wonder if Gretchen did. I haven't spoken to her since I heard about Arnoldo Bachelli. Even hid in the grass when I saw her on Top Road. Becky says I'm silly, and she's sure Gretchen and Arnoldo didn't 'do anything'. Gretchen's very upset that I think so. Especially as this is so soon before we go away, and maybe never meet again.

It's our second-last night. I'm lying crying in bed. The silence of the night is shattered by a soul-piercing, unearthly, inhuman scream, and loud, excited hyena giggles. It's coming from up the hill, the direction of Top Road. Becky and I are jolted awake, and, in panic, run to Mum's room, where she collides with us going the other way.

'What is it?' Becky asks, her voice strangled with fear. The screaming has stopped, but the hyenas haven't. They sound very close. They're making yapping, growling and maniacal giggling sounds, all at the same time. There's lots of them out there. Mum calls us to her room and locks the door. Even Sandy's with us. In case they get in to the house. We pull the curtain aside, and try to see where the noise is coming from. The giggling continues, with loud growling sounds too. Suddenly there's an ear-splitting bang. It's a shot from a big rifle, I'd know the sound anywhere. The giggling ceases. There's a blood-curdling scream of a creature in agony. Then silence. We wait a long time. Nothing. Finally we all get into bed together. Even Sandy. It's two in the morning. Someone has dealt with the problem.

When Umali comes to work at seven, for his very last time, he's got terrible news. Did we hear the commotion last night? Yes? Well, a friend of his was coming down to the mine from Compound Hill an hour ago, when he discovered a most terrible thing. Did we notice the racket came from up there? Yes? Well, who do we know lives on the corner of Top Road and Compound Hill, in a hut next to a big flat rock, or *mwamba?*

'Mlozi, the *mchawi,* sorcerer,' I say.

'*Ndio,*' says Umali. 'There isn't much left of him!'

In ten minutes I'm dressed and heading for Top Road. I reach Mlozi's place to find my old *askari* friend, Kaiser. Like me, he's come to see what's happened. He's lost his *askari*-job, and it's the first time I see him out of uniform.

'*Mambo mbaya,*' he says gravely. Bad matters.

'Mlozi?' I ask. He nods, and points at something on the ground. It's a piece of *kanzu,* or loincloth, and I recognise the zigzag black and yellow pattern. It's Mlozi's. It's heavily bloodstained. Lying on the ground next to it is part of a severed human foot. Two toes and a piece of skin. Nothing else, except a foot-wide streak of blood on the rock, going in the direction of the tree-clad hillside.

'*Wari chukua yeye!*' Kaizer says. They took him.

'*Fisi?*' I ask. Hyena?

'*Fisi mingi, sita, labda saba.*' Lots of *fisis,* six, maybe seven.

'Who fired a gun?' I ask him.

'Oh, *Bwana* Higgs, he shot from his window, to frighten them away.' Higgs, Kaizer's brother-in-law, has lost his job as *askari*-boss, but he's being retained to salvage material from the mine. They're demolishing his house last.

'Drunk?' I ask.

'*Lazima,*' he says, of course. 'But he hit one. Did you hear it scream?'

'I did,' I say.

When I get home Umali is waiting. I tell him what I've seen. He shakes his head. 'Everyone knew Mlozi was a mad *mchawi,*' he says, 'but it is horrible to be eaten by a pack of *blurryfucken fisis!*' True, I think. And we always thought Mlozi himself changed into a *fisi* at night! Now *fisis* have eaten him. . . That couldn't have been part of his plan.

I look at my old friend and mentor. Even this terrible thing about Mlozi doesn't change the awful fact we're about to leave Geita forever. There's a deep sadness in Umali. He looks ancient now, a broken little old man. I haven't noticed it quite so much before, although he was always old to me. He's even thinner than before, and his old eyes are misty. His devilish sense of humour has all but abandoned him. He's avoided the subject of us leaving. His irascible, jocular self is no more.

It's like it won't be true we're going if it isn't confirmed by talking. I know how he feels. I'm the same. It's our last day. I don't know how we'll get through it.

I sleep very little that night. Our garden is a dead place now. The *kuku*-run is empty, there's no gentle clucking from the little houses. No *jogoo* will greet the dawn with a raucous '*cock-a-doodle-doo*'. There will never be another '*Gooloo-gooloo-gooloogooloo!*' Even the surrounding bush is saying goodbye. Where is my old friend the *bundi-msitu* bird? How can he *know* we're going? Call to me, spook me, just one more time, I implore. He doesn't. Finally a faraway hyena giggles, some crickets creak, throaty frogs croak from their bushy water-places. The bush can't be completely quiet, no matter how hard it tries. At about three I hear a farewell roar from an old lion. I'm going to miss you, I think miserably, as I try to get to sleep. There's a long journey tomorrow's hateful morning. One day a fellow East African, though from Kenya, will write a song called '*Morning please don't come. . .*' It isn't written yet, but it's what I'm praying.

I'm sitting on my suitcase. All our furniture, except the beds, had been taken away yesterday. They could have left it one more day! Sandy is lying on the floor beside me. Does she know what's happening? Does she know we're going, and she'll never see us again? I look at her. She's very subdued. Of course she knows! At least Umali will look after her. He's always been fond of her.

It's going on for five in the morning. I hear Umali clanging about in the kitchen. Packing up pots and pans for collection by someone. He's just got to keep busy. I know him so well. If he stops, he might fall apart. Bustling about is his only way of dealing with pain and anguish. Mum and Becky have finished stuffing last-minute things into their cases. They're doing final checks in different rooms. Just in case they've forgotten something. There's a bright flash of moving light on the trees down the road. Headlights. Shortly it's in our drive, and there's a crunch of gravel under tyres. A Land Rover hooter shatters the silence. Fritz has arrived. Gretchen is with him. It's time to go.

Amina is controlling her feelings. She isn't crying. She hugs each of us in turn, taking particular time with Becky. They were always close. She hugs me briefly, and gives me a mock-*finya* on the arm, just for old times. I can see she's worried about Umali. He's still dawdling in the kitchen, trying to avoid reality.

'*Kuja, Umali!*' she shouts at last, commanding him to come.

Umali shuffles reluctantly out of the kitchen at the last moment. It's as if clattering about in there was shielding him from the truth. He's standing in front of me. I haven't realised I've grown so much bigger than him. When did it happen? His expression is fixed, as if that way he can control his feelings. His shirt, as always, is torn and full of holes, and his ribs are prominent on his chest. His stick-like arms are reaching out to give me a goodbye hug. I put my arms around him, and it's like caressing a bag of articulated bones. In my arms I'm holding the dearest friend I ever had, more dear even than poor Lutoli, and now I have to let him go, get in the car, and drive away forever. It's Umali who breaks away and pushes me towards the open Land Rover.

I get in beside Gretchen. She told Becky she wants to sit next to me. She wants to 'sort things out' with me. She doesn't want fifteen years of growing up in the bush together to end badly. Becky gets in the other side. Mum climbs in the front passenger seat next to Fritz.

The doors are closed. Umali and Amina are standing together at the bottom of the steps. Amina's crying openly now, intermittently pulling her open hand across her face. Umali looks wooden. There's no expression at all, just a fixed stare. I want to jump out again, give him another, very last, hug, but Fritz has started the engine, and we're beginning to roll down the gravel drive. Suddenly Umali turns and runs around the side of the house, out of sight. I notice Tembo standing at the entrance to the drive. He's holding up a hand in farewell. Probably the most demonstrative thing I've seen him do. My vision is obscured by tears, and the lump in my throat threatens to choke me.

'You know, Mrs Penhaligon,' Gretchen says in a mature and adult voice, 'we children had the best upbringing in the world, here in Geita!' Even in this desperate state, I can't disagree. I wouldn't have wanted to grow up anywhere else. The sun's coming up now, illuminating the familiar bush beyond Compound Hill.

Not very far from here is the little road to Samina, where Dad has rested in his granite grave these ten years, all alone, except for Mrs Williams and Mr Valari (senior). Even nearer is the lonely grave of Fritz's brother, Mrs Williams' driver that fateful morning on the Mwanza road. Lutoli's grave isn't far either. And poor old Mlozi? If he was eaten up by the *fisi*s, which seems certain, what has become of his physical body? Worse than a *mzoga* in its own ground. He'll be *fisi*-droppings soon, like those Lutoli and I collected and threw into Becky and Gretchen's independent country of *Chola*, near our republic of *Kichoncho* on Compound Hill. It's so long ago. Sad for anyone to end that way. Cycle of life, something we should just accept?

Now I think of it, I don't want to take all this with me. There's got to be another life for us somewhere. I'm leaving Geita, but Geita's leaving me too. The place, the people, dead and alive. Even pretty, sweet Gretchen, sitting right next to me, smiling with those sky-blue eyes, is not part of my future. This is the last time I'll see her. She'll be someone else's wife one day. Can it be that unrequited love ever endured so long in one boy's life? I turn my face to the window. I remember something said by a Father at St Mary's. 'The past,' he said, 'is a foreign country!' I know my past will forever be that, a foreign country. Will I come back as a man one day in the far future? If so, what will I find? Will the ghosts of my childhood be waiting here? And if they aren't? If on that future day I stare out from Compound Hill, to Ridgate and Lone Cone, with a great Black *mwewe*-bird circling high above, will I find it impossible to believe anything important ever happened here at all?

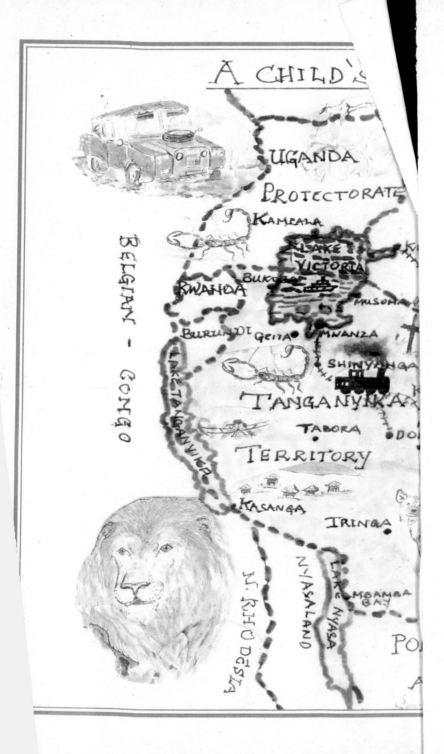

A CHILD'S

UGANDA
PROTECTORATE

KAMPALA

LAKE
VICTORIA

BUKOBA
RWANDA
MUSOMA
BURUNDI   GEITA   MWANZA
SHINYANGA
TANGANYIKA

TABORA   DO

TERRITORY

KASANGA
IRINGA

BELGIAN - CONGO

LAKE TANGANYIKA

N. RHODESIA

NYASALAND

LAKE NYASA

MBAMBA BAY

PO